Quantico Marine
Corps Base

A History of Our Own:
Stafford County, Virginia

Albert Z. Conner Jr.

May all your Stafford memories be happy ones, — Conner

It's a pleasure to share with others what we've known for many years.

Stafford is a community among the finest in the nation.

We work here by fortune; we live here by choice.

Colonial Circuits

(Cover) Stafford Courthouse, the central location or "heart" of Stafford County
(Allison Sisson/Stafford County)

A History of Our Own:
Stafford County, Virginia

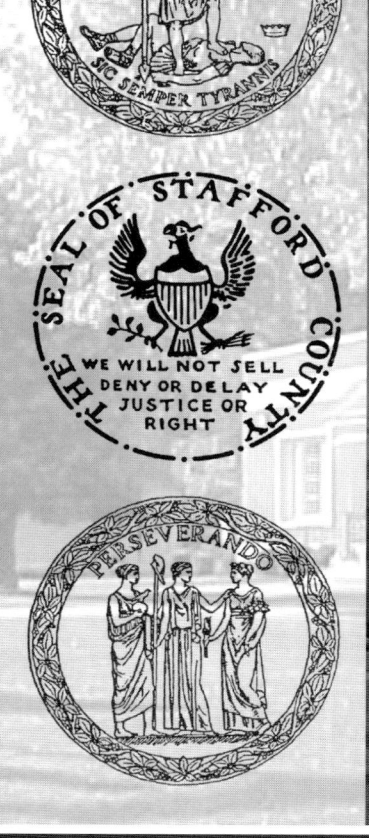

Albert Z. Conner Jr.

THE
DONNING COMPANY
PUBLISHERS

Dedication

This pictorial history is dedicated to the Stafford County Historical Society and others who, motivated by their love for "Old Stafford," have aided in preserving her history.

Copyright 2003 by Albert Z. Conner Jr.

All rights reserved, including the right to reproduce this work in any form whatsoever without permission in writing from the publisher, except for brief passages in connection with a review. For information, please write:

The Donning Company Publishers
184 Business Park Drive, Suite 206
Virginia Beach, Virginia 23462

Steve Mull, General Manager
Barbara Buchanan, Office Manager
Marshall McClure, Design Production Coordinator
Kathleen Sheridan, Editor
Thad Pickett, Graphic Designer
Mary Ellen Wheeler, Proofreader/Editorial Assistant
Cassie Perry, Imaging Artist
Dennis Walton, Project Director
Anne Cordray, Project Research Coordinator
Scott Rule, Director of Marketing
Travis Gallup, Marketing Coordinator

Library of Congress Cataloging-in-Publication Data

Conner, Albert Z., 1943-
    A history of our own: Stafford County, Virginia / Albert Z. Conner Jr.
      p. cm.
    Includes bibliographical references (p.) and index.
    ISBN 1-57864-219-1 (alk. paper)
    1. Stafford County (Va.)-History-Pictorial works. 2. Stafford County (Va.)-History.
    I. Title.

F232.S86C66 2003
975.5'26-dc21

2003055173

Printed in the United States of America

Table of Contents

Foreword

Preface

Introduction

Chapter 1	Prehistoric Visitors and First Americans	**10**
Chapter 2	Liberty and Religious Tolerance	**18**
Chapter 3	Staffordians All	**30**
Chapter 4	Staffordians in War	**72**
Chapter 5	Visitors of Note	**102**
Chapter 6	Birthstones of Freedom	**124**
Chapter 7	Places of the Heart: Stafford's Homes	**130**
Chapter 8	Places of the Spirit: Stafford's Churches	**158**
Chapter 9	Places of the Mind: Stafford's Schools	**176**
Chapter 10	Stafford's Industries and Businesses	**194**
Chapter 11	History Lives in Stafford	**220**

Epilogue

Bibliography

Index

Foreword

Modern Stafford, one of Virginia's and America's fastest-growing counties, is becoming predominantly a place of young and educated families. Currently home to more than 100,000 people, Stafford has 50,000 men and women in the civilian work force and substantial numbers serving in the military. Some 25,000 people come to work every day in Stafford's 1,400 businesses. Children are educated in a first-class school system, and the James Monroe Center of Mary Washington College promotes professional development and lifelong learning. With abundant green spaces, recreational facilities, infrastructure, home sites, places of worship, law enforcement, emergency services and educational opportunities, Stafford has everything we value in suburban or rural American quality of life.

We also have a remarkable history. All "Staffordians," regardless of our time here, can take pride in our county's contributions to our nation, commonwealth and region. As will be made clear in this book, however, Stafford currently lacks a sense of place, community and identity to match its potentials. That gap can only be filled with learning and knowledge. We all wish to establish roots in a community and, in the end, we are all in this together. Therefore, this pictorial history is our Stafford "community family album," documenting our history and describing the lives of many exceptional and ordinary people who have gone before us. More importantly, it traces the ideas that have guided our country's progress and will continue to do so in the future.

A History of Our Own paints a sweeping picture of Stafford's prehistory and nearly 400 years of recorded history. Ideas—especially liberty and religious tolerance—flourished here. People—Native Americans; English Catholics; Puritans, Quakers, and Anglicans; European indentured servants and African indentured servants and slaves; French Huguenots; and Dutch, Scots, Irish, and Germans, and others—made Stafford their homes and visited here. It is amazing that a humble American place such as Stafford has produced so wide a variety of unique and gifted individuals. Our county's material gifts are equally impressive. And all of these stories are told fairly and thoughtfully as seen through the eyes of many objective historians.

We must understand, however, that Stafford was never a land of "gods roaming the earth." Rather, it has always been a place of flawed, flesh-and-blood people with exceptionally individualistic minds and views, a people who put one foot in front of the other on the rocky path and common walks of life. Thus, the history of Stafford should not be viewed as one of mythical perfection measured down to today's world. It is best seen as the story of people's upward progress in the harshest and most brutal circumstances. The story ventures from hacking out a subsistence living on tobacco farms and plantations on the edge of hostile forests and fishing on dangerous waters, to carving out an economy from depleted soils and tapped-out mineral deposits. It moves from ignoring or not responding to cries for social justice and legal equality, to suffering modern war, to rebuilding all that had been devastated and lost. It traces our society from feudalism to oligarchy to representative democracy. Finally, it progresses to making and preserving a place where all people can live together in peace, freedom and opportunity.

As Staffordians ourselves, aware of our past but living in the reality of the twenty-first century, we commend this unique pictorial history to all readers. We do so in the hope that our beloved county's past will truly become its more glorious prologue, and that the history contained in these pages will yield a better world than the one given to us by our ancestors and predecessors. We owe our posterity a clear-eyed view of all that has passed. Our state seal bears two sentiments: *Sic Semper Tyrannis* or "Thus Ever to Tyrants" and *Perseverando* or "By Enduring." Both mottoes speak volumes about Stafford's past.

William J. Howell, Speaker of the Virginia House of Delegates
John H. Chichester, President Pro Tempore of Virginia Senate

Preface

The genesis of this pictorial history occurred at my first Stafford County Historical Society meeting. I was welcomed by a member who remarked, "You know, we have quite a history of our own!" This odd remark about such an ancient place was soon understood. Stafford County, long overshadowed by nearby Fredericksburg despite a history second to none in Virginia or America, has struggled for identity throughout its recorded history.

For many years that made sense, as Fredericksburg was larger and more prosperous. Yet that perception inexplicably continued into the 1930s, when the two became equal-sized, and into the present when Stafford, with more than 105,000 people, dwarfs Fredericksburg, with less than 20,000. Similar conditions exist in other nearby counties having joint histories with Fredericksburg and one other. Each county and the city has its distinctive history, yet Stafford has lagged behind the others in forging identity and recognizing its history. Currently, it alone lacks a museum to inform its residents and visitors of "our own history." Everywhere, it seems, Stafford's attainments and places are attributed to Fredericksburg. This historical "theft," however benign or unintentional, has been aided and abetted by historians who have developed remarkable numbers of ways not to mention the word "Stafford." It remains today largely the place "across the river" and "north of Fredericksburg." Further aid and comfort have come from well-intentioned businesses and governmental organizations seeking quick fixes for that all-important "location, location, location." Identity begins with name recognition. It is hoped this will change, but change depends on wider knowledge and sensitivity than is now evident.

Surprisingly, Stafford's lack of community identity does not stem from a lack of research. Substantial numbers of historical works describe various aspects of Stafford's past. Yet no single comprehensive work has been written including all of what we know at this point—and I must quickly add that, despite incorporating information from previous works and new data, this book is not yet that comprehensive history. More than any previous book, however, *A History of Our Own: Stafford County, Virginia* presents an illustrated overview—using previously published and unpublished images—of Stafford's entire history in one volume. This information deserves to be featured in a first-class museum and archives to provide residents and visitors with the means to discover Stafford's rich history and interesting places. All Staffordians can now share our fascinating history and recognize a substantial stake in preserving it. The stories and images of those who have preceded us and the places they left behind, even at a distance of four centuries, explain their links to us in the great chain of life. Armed with this knowledge, we can all initiate or renew efforts to learn about and preserve Stafford's heritage.

I would add some cautionary and explanatory notes. This is an updated history that provides the latest in our understanding of events and dates in a long and complex story. Errors in detail (I hope they are minimal) are inevitable when dealing with so many facts, many now unverifiable, and diverse sources. Many Stafford dates and facts are but one document or one archaeological discovery away from requiring correction. Continuing work will be needed to refine what we now "know." Names and place spellings vary widely. I hope it will not inconvenience the reader that I have left names and places as they appear in original documents or sources and included alternative renderings. Finally,

I have attributed source authors in the text (with less specificity than I would wish—purely to save space). Wherever possible, I have tried to use a person's or his/her contemporary's own words—these are set in italics—as well as pictures to tell their own story. I hope neither principals, authors, nor contributors have been misrepresented.

This book is aided by tremendous support in our county. I am most grateful to Colonial Circuits Inc. for its corporate sponsorship and the Stafford County Historical Society Board for its endorsement of this project. I especially wish to acknowledge an incalculable debt to current Stafford authors Jerrilynn Eby, Homer D. Musselman, Lee Woolf, and other staff writers (see text and Chapter 11) of the *Free Lance-Star*; former editor Ben Bagwell and other staff writers (see text and Chapter 11) of the *Stafford County Sun*; Ruth Coder Fitzgerald; and, especially, to Jane M. Conner, the beating heart of Stafford's history and my resident expert. All these authors have graciously allowed their materials and conclusions to be used and quoted. My gratitude to other authors is also great: specifically, John Tackett Goolrick; George L. Gordon; Thomas McCarty Moncure Jr.; Molly A. Pynn; the Historical and Archaeological Committee of Citizens to Serve Stafford (CCSS): Dr. H. Stewart Jones, Lisa B. Anderson, Estheleen "Hutch" Blackburn, and Ruth Carlone (also Chairman of CCSS); J. William Mann; Paula Felder; Thena S. Jones; the Oral History Committee of the Stafford County Historical Society: Anita Dodd, Barbara Flack, Barbara Kirby, and Suzanne Rowdon; and William L. Deyo, Historian of the Patawomeck Tribe. Wherever possible, I have quoted these authors' interpretations.

Jerrilynn Eby, Jane M. Conner, Homer D. Musselman, Mary Cary Kendall, Steve Gambaro, and Barbara Kirby provided invaluable draft-review comments and encouragement. I would also like to thank the leaders of the organizations that preserve some of Stafford's greatest historical treasures, namely David Berreth, Director, and Joanna D. Catron, Curator of the Gari Melchers Estate and Memorial Gallery, Mary Washington College; W. Vernon Edenfield of George Washington's Fredericksburg Foundation; and John Hennessy of the Fredericksburg and Spotsylvania National Military Park, headquartered at "Chatham," both for their leading preservation efforts and assistance. Shirley C. Heim provided unique support on the history of Stafford's schools, and Jim Mann of the *Free Lance-Star* provided tremendous imagery support. Keg Good, Stafford County GIS Specialist, provided excellent aerial photographic support. *The Stafford County Sun*, the National Archives, Library of Virginia, Virginia Historical Society, and Nancy Southworth all provided important photographic and archival materials. A host of Stafford's citizens and friends provided specific materials used in the work: Felicia Parlier; Mike and Marty Lyman; Tim and Kristin Baroody; Diane and Herb Harmon; Mary Rust; John Haile Cloe and Peggy Cloe; Mary Cary Kendall; Dorothy Jackson; Nancy Dickinson; Robert Burton; Norman and Lenetta Schools; Walter V. "Pete" Roberts; Don and Ila McCoy; and Rosie and Edgar Morris. I also wish to acknowledge the research and production assistance of Owen L. Conner and Gavin C. Conner, without whom this work could not have been completed. Finally, I would like to thank special photographers Stephen A. Gambaro, Suzanne Carr, Jane M. Conner, Owen L. Conner, and Marshall A. Conner, as well as the corps of talented photographers [see text] of the regional media.

Albert Z. Conner Jr.

Introduction

This pictorial history reveals Stafford's unique story as a luxuriant tapestry flowing through time like the two rivers that border our county. A "flower which blooms unseen," its story is not readily discerned in casual contact. The depth of Stafford's prehistory and history defines it as one of America's oldest and most historic counties.

Few would notice the missing "familiar landmarks" lost to misfortune (especially fires), wars, and indifference, or know that Stafford's primary contributions to the nation were in the form of the ideas that took root here—bold and imaginative conceptions of liberty, individual rights, popular sovereignty, and religious toleration.

Fewer still would recall the fascinating people spawned by this rural Virginia county during its 400-year recorded journey. Although obscured by recent growth, Stafford remains a unique place—if only because President George Washington and George Mason (IV), author of the Virginia Declaration of Rights, spent their formative years here. Its historic residents include Mistress Margaret Brent, seventeenth-century Maryland and Virginia landowner and "America's first woman attorney," and James Hunter, who armed and equipped the American Revolution from his Stafford ironworks. And, despite the county's population not exceeding 10,000 souls until the 1950s, Stafford has contributed an American president, a U.S. Supreme Court justice, two U.S. senators, two members of the U.S. Constitutional Convention, and three members of the Continental Congress and/or U.S. House of Representatives. Further, Stafford has provided many state officials, including governors of Virginia, Maryland, and Kentucky; a Louisiana House speaker; and the present speaker of the Virginia House of Delegates and president pro tempore of the Virginia Senate. Among its natives and residents have been social activists, humanitarians, clergymen, artists, soldiers, businessmen, lawyers, editors, slaves, spies, entertainers, Olympic athletes, and many extraordinary "ordinary people"—merchants, farmers, watermen, railroad men, homemakers, and teachers.

High among Stafford's material gifts to the nation was the Aquia Stone used to create both the White House and U.S. Capitol, our two enduring architectural symbols of freedom. Stafford also proudly co-hosts the Quantico Marine Base, a modern symbol of national resolve. Twenty-first-century Stafford County remains a place of enormous natural beauty and environmental vitality revealed in extensive river coastlines, streams, wetlands, and pastoral spaces.

Our kaleidoscopic trip in Stafford's time machine begins 110 million years ago when prehistoric sea and land creatures flourish. Later, "Paleo-Indians" and Native Americans—including the "lost tribe" of the Potomacs—live here. Stafford emerges from the Jamestown era as the rugged northern frontier jumping-off point for far Virginia territories, and a place of settlers; Indians and Indian fighters; Virginia's first Catholic settlers, the Brents; and "Mary Brent," or Kittamaquad, the Piscataway princess. A new "tribe"—the English—suddenly appears with the seventeenth-century Cavalier infusion, and Masons, Fowkes, Wallers, Fitzhughs,

Peytons and others join the population. An early site of European and African indentured servitude and African slavery, Stafford becomes a measuring stick for Virginia's and America's slow racial progress. Three Colonial towns, Marlborough, Woodstock and Falmouth, spring to life but give way to transportation links, iron mines and forges, flour mills, gold mines, and riverine industries, and only one town survives. In three wars, Stafford suffers military intrusions, especially during the American Civil War with near-biblical destruction. Staffordians fight in all of America's wars, from Colonial Indian skirmishes to modern conflicts. Operational and logistical activities and maneuvers related to the Fredericksburg, Chancellorsville, Wilderness, and Spotsylvania Civil War campaigns to the south take place in Stafford. Civil War destruction retards economic, social, and population growth until after the Second World War—when one-fifth of the county is confiscated for the war effort. A modest business community evolves, and schools and churches emerge as agents and reflections of change and progress.

The time machine comes to a stop in the twenty-first century and assesses what has gone before and what is to come.

Stafford's historical "visitors" form another fascinating list: Capt. John Smith and Pocahontas; America's first Catholic archbishop; the designer of Washington, D.C.; the father of American architecture; and nine U.S. presidents and a British prime minister. The long list also includes author Charles Dickens; Confederate and Union Armies; a Prussian prince and princess; a future Supreme Court justice; Clara Barton; Walt Whitman; Confederate spies, assassins and "Gray Ghost" Col. John Mosby; Gen. Robert E. Lee; aviation pioneers; inventors; historians; industrialists; generals; and film stars. Their stories and many more await discovery.

Twenty-first-century Stafford comprises 217 square miles (approximately 180,000 acres) and 105,000 people. Located about forty miles south of Washington, D.C., and sixty miles north of Richmond, Virginia, Stafford's enormous natural beauty is reflected in fifty miles of Potomac River and Rappahannock River shorelines flowing into the Chesapeake Bay, and vast wetlands stretching from the Widewater area to Aquia, Accokeek and Potomac Creeks. Pastoral farmlands and forested lands—still amounting to some 120,000 acres—speak serenely. Bounded by Prince William County to the north; the Potomac River and King George County to the east; the Rappahannock River to the south (Caroline County, Fredericksburg, and Spotsylvania County); and Culpeper and Fauquier Counties to the southwest and west, Stafford's eastern coastal plain and western piedmont plateau are, despite recent growth, still rural and residential. No heavy industries mar its skyline vistas or assault its environment. Although its back roads are now more heavily traveled, they are still peaceful reminders of former times.

Finally, we discover Stafford is a place where history still lives, and we examine recent stories of county life in which citizens, government, schools, churches, businesses, and private groups preserve our common inheritance.

Chapter One
Prehistoric Visitors and First Americans

Histories focus on man's relatively brief period on earth and ignore the fact that, in geologic time, the scale of man's existence equates only to the width of a thin dime atop the Empire State Building. The earth is 4.5 billion years old, while man's existence is reckoned only at 3 million years, and recorded history currently dates from about 3,000 B.C. (in western Asia).

Prehistoric Visitors

Stafford's first "visitors" consisted of prehistoric creatures. In October 1995, paleontologist and Staffordian Jon Bachman found desktop-sized tracks of a theropod, a flesh-eating dinosaur, in Stafford County. Such dinosaurs were about nine feet long and three feet high at the hips, walking primarily on their hind legs. Another type of dinosaur tracks from a plant-eating ornithopod were found at the same time. With Robert Weems of the U.S. Geological Survey, Bachman had been looking for leaf fossils in central Stafford when he found the 110 million-year-old tracks. (FLS)

Sauroposeidon, a 70-foot herbivore, left its footprint in an ancient stream. (Free Lance-Star)

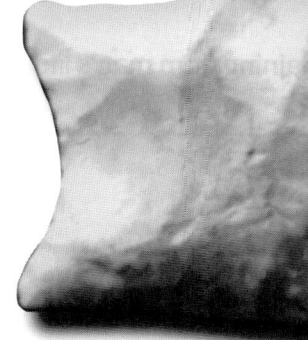

Two years later, evidence of anurans, or amphibian toads or frogs, was found (the only such finding in the world). Weems and Bachman dated the specimens (now in the Smithsonian Institution) to the Cretaceous Period of the Mesozoic era, a period when toothed birds and dinosaurs died out and early mammals developed. From these finds, it is believed this area had freshwater and was similar to today's New Zealand tropical rain forests. Compared with similar dinosaur track finds in Culpeper and Prince William Counties dated at 210 million years and 220 million years old, respectively, Stafford's tracks were relatively "new," but later digs here found thousands of Eocene-era fossils, including 118 species of sharks, rays, fish, reptiles, and birds, plus nine plant types. Two fish specimens, one plant, and one lizard were previously unknown. The Eocene era began 55 million years ago and lasted about 20 million years. Also prominent in the Stafford Eocene discovery were Richard Brezina and Michael Flomer. Weems estimated that the Stafford site had been under fifty to one hundred feet of water and the ocean coastline was west of present U.S. Interstate 95. (Robert Weems and Gary Grimsley; Virginia Division of Mineral Resources—VDMR)

In 2001 Weems and Bachman identified further evidence along the Rappahannock River in Stafford and Spotsylvania Counties. New findings included eight dinosaur species tracks, including a seventy-foot-long plant-eater, Sauroposeidon, the largest yet found in Virginia. Other specimens included prints from Iguanadont, Hypsilophodont, Archaeoornithominus, Priconodon, Eolambia, Irenesauripus, and a prehistoric crocodile. (Cathy Jett) (See Chapter 11)

Man's Earliest Footprints

Recent discoveries reveal humans have been in Virginia for at least 16,000 years B.P. (Before Present) or 14,000 B.C. (Before Christ). The earliest, known as Paleo-Indians, were "hunter-gatherers" who arrived after the Ice Age. They roamed grasslands in small bands, hunting mastodon, bison, elk, deer, and smaller mammals, and gathered edible and medicinal plants using a wide range of percussion-flaked stone tools and throwing weapons to hunt and prepare food. (Virginia Historical Society—VHS; Virginia Department of Historic Resources—VDHR)

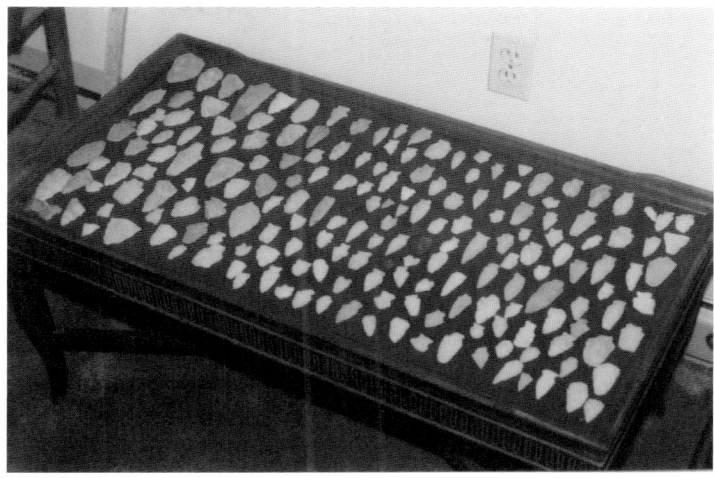

Many Stafford families have a projectile point collection.
(Blaisdell Collection; Myron E. and Mary Lyman)

About 10,000 B.P. (8,000 B.C.) (Archaic Period) there was a warming trend with decreased precipitation, exposing large sections of the continental shelf on which Tidewater Virginia sits. Forests adjusted, providing oak and pine trees. Hunter-gatherers, still classified as Paleo-Indians, developed greater reliance on plants and smaller animals, especially deer, turkey, and turtle. From 8,500–5000 B.P. (6,500–3,000 B.C.), they mastered woodland habitats, refined stone weapons and tools, and continued to form larger "band-level societies" in temporary camps with family units.

Left, clovis point, evidence of Paleo-Indians found in archeological sites
(Virginia Department of Historic Resources)

With populations increasing and climatic changes spreading deciduous forests inland, the Paleo-Indians first moved into Virginia's upland interiors above river fall lines. As more permanent villages were established along streams and rivers, they evolved into "sedentary foragers." Soon groups became tribal units and developed trade with other tribes (5,000 B.P. or 3,000 B.C.–A.D.900). In the late Archaic Period, camps were pushed to the foothills of the Blue Ridge Mountains, and the bands subsisted on varieties of nuts and small game while moving from one camp to another. (VHS; George Washington's Fredericksburg Foundation—GWFF)

Ax ca. 7,000 B.P. or 5,000 B.C.
Virginia Department of Historic Resources

During the Woodland Period (3,200 B.P. or 1,200 B.C.–1600 A.D.), pottery (especially ceramic bowls), bows and arrows, food storage, more elaborate burials, corn and bean agriculture, and more formal societal structures (increased populations) appeared in the tribes. As hamlets and villages grew, the now American Indians or Native Americans increasingly turned to farming and more developed tribal hierarchies and social infrastructures. During the Middle Woodland Period (ca. 2,500 B.P. or 500 B.C.) Virginia's Native Americans developed into tribes and took on many of the cultural traits we now associate with American Indians. (VHS; GWFF)

After 1607 A.D. (Historic Period), contacts with European colonists increasingly affected Indian tribes; new tools, technologies, religions, ideas, clothing, and lifestyles were introduced. Some innovations yielded positive short-term results, but the net effect was a drastically diminished American Indian population and an end to their way of life. Compared with the 50,000 Indians living in Virginia ninety years earlier, by 1700 only a few hundred were present. (VHS; GWFF)

Ax head (Virginia Department of Historic Resources)

Right, Stone knife with antler hilt (Virginia Department of Historic Resources)

Using 1520-period Spanish maps to explore the Chesapeake Bay region, Capt. John Smith made two visits to present-day Stafford. During the first trip, he was wounded by a sting ray-like creature and rendered unconscious. On the second visit, he was guided by Mosco, probably of French-Indian origins, who had lived with the Potomacs at Marlborough Point. Smith's party, believed to have landed near present-day Scott's Island, Brooks Park, and "Chatham," observed a palisaded long house, village, and garden plots that looked "cleaner than our English gardens." Near present-day "Belmont," they encountered hostile Manahoac Indians and were saved by Mosco's suggested woven shields mounted to their boats. Smith also visited Aquia Creek. (VHS; Marion Brooks Robinson—Robinson)

Detail of Capt. John Smith's map of Powhatan Confederacy or Empire and Virginia ca. 1612 (Virginia Historical Society)

Manahoacs and Powhatans (including the Potomacs) were the Indians that had lived in the Stafford area.

Manahoacs (Mahocks or Mannahoacs), a tribal group that originated in the Ohio Valley and were of the Siouan linguistic family, were likely related to the Monacan, Moneton, and Tutelo tribes. Virginia's Manahoacs occupied the east-west territory between the falls of the rivers and the mountains and from the Potomac River in the north to the North Anna River in the south. Subtribes were identified on the headwaters of the Rappahannock. The only Manahoac village known by name was Mahaskohod, located along the Rappahannock River. When Capt. John Smith "discovered" them in 1608, they were at war with the Powhatan Empire and allied with the Monacans and probably the Susquehannas to the north. Manahoacs conceivably numbered 1,500 at that time. In the 1650s they camped on the falls of the James River, and in alliance with other tribes defeated westward incursion by English settlers and their Indian allies (ca. 1654–1656). "Mahocks" were on the James River. In 1700–1723, they united with the Tutelo and Saponi. Per Jefferson (1801), the main division of the Manahoacs was in the western parts of modern Stafford and Spotsylvania Counties. (John W. Swanton—Swanton)

Manahoacs and Powhatans led annual raids against one another, but this hostility ceased under the greater threat of Englishmen. Before that, the Manahoacs (probably inhabiting present-day Hartwood and other areas above the Rappahannock's fall line) were relatively powerful, accepting tribute from southern and western tribes, including the Shackakonies (Spotsylvania); Whonkenties and Tauxitanians (Fauquier); Tegninaties and Hassinungaes (Culpeper); and Ontponies and Stegarakies (Orange). Mahaskahod is believed by some archeologists to have been located in Hartwood as a gathering place for ceremonial hunts. (Helen C. Rountree—Rountree; Lisa S. Anderson in *Foundation Stones of Stafford County*—Foundation Stones)

The Powhatans were a tribe in the Algonquin linguistic group. The term originally referred to one tribal group, but English settlers used it generally to describe the chief, Powhatan (Wahunsonacock or Wahunsenacawh), and his Powhatan Empire. This tribal alliance extended from the Potomac to the divide between the James River and Albemarle Sound, and east-west from Virginia's Eastern Shore to the rivers' fall lines. Powhatan's Empire included modern Stafford and twenty other counties and was described by Smith as having "32 Kingdomes" with 161 villages:

The forme of their Common wealth is a monarchicall governement. One as Emperour ruleth over many kings or governours. Their chiefe ruler is called Powhatan, and taketh his name of the principal place of dwelling called Powhatan. But his proper name is Wahunsonacock. (Swanton; Foundation Stones; Miriam Haynie—Haynie)

The Powhatan Empire's tribal group in current Stafford and King George Counties was the Potomacs (Potawomecks, Patawomeks, etc.). Their main village, "Petomek," was "about 55 miles in a straight line from the Chesapeake Bay on a peninsula in what is now Stafford County, formed by the Potomac River and Potomac Creek." The Powhatans were visited by explorers in the late 1400s and were known to the Spanish. In 1570 Jesuit missionaries in Virginia were murdered by Powhatans near present-day Williamsburg. With Jamestown's establishment in 1607,

Gov. John White's depiction of Indian village and farm areas near the first Virginia settlement (Roanoke Island). They are similar to Smith's descriptions of the Powhatan Empire's Stafford-area villages and farmed areas. (British Museum)

White's depiction of an Indian palisade and village, believed similar to those of the Powhatan Empire in present-day Stafford (British Museum)

Capt. John Smith (Library of Congress)

Woodcut depiction of Pocahontas being lured onto Argall's ship by Japazaws
(Katherine Wetzel/Virginia Historical Society)

inevitable contact between the colonists and Indians occurred. Relations alternated between peaceful and warlike, but during Chief Powhatan's life, an accord was struck. The marriage of his daughter, Pocahontas (Matoaka or Metoaka), to John Rolfe contributed to that peace. However, in 1622 Powhatan's second successor, Opechancanough, led an Indian uprising against the colony, destroying all settlements except Jamestown and continuing warfare until 1636. Another equally devastating uprising took place in 1644, ending in Opechancanough's capture and death. In 1675 Indians initiated raids, resulting in retaliation led by colonists under Nathaniel Bacon, and "Bacon's Rebellion" ensued. The Powhatans, perhaps numbering 9,000 in 1600, gradually were reduced by 1,758 to two tribes, the Pamunkey and Mattaponi. The early 1800s saw Powhatans mixing with Virginia's isolated black and white populations. This led to their essential disappearance. Lost in this mix were the Potomacs, becoming a "lost tribe." (Swanton; *Foundation Stones*; Haynie)

Stafford's Potomacs Meet A New Tribe: The English

When Capt. John Smith explored the Stafford area, he encountered well-developed Indian villages. "Petomek," on the Marlborough Point and Indian Point peninsula, had about 1,000 acres cleared for corn. Smith also encountered nearby Piscataways, Anacostins, and Doegs living on both shores of the Potomac River and its tributaries. Potomacs manned the northern frontier of the Empire against Manahoac incursions. Smith visited Quiyough, or "the place of the gulls" (Aquia Creek), Potomac Creek, and the Rappahannock River. From 1609 to ca. 1620, Virginia colonists established a trading post at Marlborough Point, and the Potomacs, like their Powhatan brothers, soon developed a taste for English tools and weapons, trading food for them. The post was destroyed by Indians. (Jerrilynn Eby—Eby)

With Japazaws, King of the Patowmeke, Smith moved up Aquia Creek, then called "Quiyough," as far as the water depth would allow. With six men, he left the barge. Surrounded by Indians, Smith bribed them to safely guide him to an antimony mine. (Haynie)

Jamestown people accompanied Smith and established Marlborough Point's trading post. Despite civilized pretensions, the English were but little more advanced in organization, behavior, weapons, and equipment than their Powhatan neighbors, and their external relations were not on a higher plane than interactions among Indian tribes. Language barriers were overcome, technologies were compared and traded, but tenuous relations expanded into warfare whenever one side saw clear advantage. A few examples of civil behavior, neighborliness, and assimilation are documented, but the English settlers' internal problems prevented their dealing wisely with the Indians. (Haynie; Eby)

Pocahontas' Story

Shortly after Smith's first explorations at Indian Point, Pocahontas was kidnapped by and allegedly traded to Capt. Samuel Argall for a copper pot. Argall, generally portrayed as a freebooter, played a significant role in ending the Anglo-Powhatan War of 1609–1614. (Library of Virginia's Dictionary of Virginia Biography-DVB LV)

Powhatan's most famous daughter, Metoaka—"Pocahontas" was a nickname meaning "little mischievous one"—must have been exceptional to stand out among the innumerable offspring of one hundred wives. Evidence suggests Pocahontas was indeed special in treatment; she was allowed to hunt and fish with her brothers and to sit at tribal councils. The adventurous twelve-year-old soon made contact with the Jamestown colonists and undoubtedly promoted friendly relations. Some historical doubt exists about the reported incident in which she protected Smith from her father's wrath (as it did not appear until the third edition of Smith's account and he later related similar adventures in other lands). (Robinson)

Far less doubt surrounds Pocahontas' humanitarian efforts in making biweekly Jamestown visits with corn, fish, and game for the settlers during hard winter times. She also welcomed Gov. Lord de la Warre and second-wave Jamestown colonists in 1610. The governor and his family, welcomed as guests by Powhatan and Pocahontas, returned the courtesies. (Haynie)

The most famous event in Pocahontas' brief life took place in Stafford. Her visit to Japazaws, "King of Patowmeke," in 1611 brought her to Indian Point on a trade mission. Powhatan may also have been distancing his daughter from the Jamestown colonists. While Pocahontas was at Indian Point, Capt. Samuel Argall learned of her presence. Seizing an opportunity to force agreements with Powhatan, Argall entangled Japazaws and his wife in a plot to lure the princess aboard the nearby anchored ship and kidnap her. On the promise of a new copper kettle for persuading Pocahontas to board, Japazaws' wife convinced the princess. Once aboard, Pocahontas was seized and spirited off to Jamestown. Ransom notes to Powhatan ambiguously promised his daughter would be "well used" and treated as an honored guest. Powhatan may or may not have refused ransom demands, but his daughter remained by choice at Jamestown. Her hosts, Sir Thomas Dale (chief marshal of

Depiction of the kidnapping of Pocahontas by artist Jean Leon Gerome Ferris ca. 1910
(Virginia Historical Society)

Pocahontas or Metoaka or Matoaka, princess of the Powhatan Empire, 1616, by Simon van de Passe (Virginia Historical Society)

Reconstruction of a Powhatan Empire village near Jamestown, Virginia
(Jane M. Conner)

Right, detail of reconstructed Powhatan Empire dwelling
(Jane M. Conner)

the colony) and Lady Dale, employed Rev. Alexander Whitaker to teach Pocahontas English and Christianity. Both efforts quickly succeeded. John Rolfe, a widower who had helped with Pocahontas' education and conversion, also fell in love with her. Pocahontas joined the Anglican Church in March 1613:

> ...baptized in the presence of the governor and his family as "Rebecca." Wearing the same white dress in which she would later be married, she accepted the faith. On July 13, 1613, in Westminster Abbey, a special service celebrating her conversion was held with King James and Queen Anne in attendance. Pocahontas married John Rolfe in Jamestown on September 11, 1614. A year later, their son, Thomas, was born. "Rebecca" was reportedly a good stepmother to Rolfe's other children and did her best to bridge the cultural gap, becoming wife, mother and household mistress. The Rolfes, in Indian garb, paid a call on Powhatan some six weeks after Thomas' birth at the Chickahominy settlement. They were reportedly quite happy as a family, living somewhat between the two worlds. (Robinson)

Subsequently, Rolfe was sent to England. Pocahontas, now a celebrated person, was welcomed in October 1616 by both aristocracy and commoners. She captivated both groups, and investments soared, further attesting to her charm, but she reportedly longed for her home. One account says she dreamed in September 1617 that she would die before seeing her native land again. Passage was booked and farewells said as she and Rolfe prepared to return to the New World. On November 5 they departed, but Pocahontas died that night. Rolfe took her to Gravesend and buried her at St. George's Church. Her son, Thomas, returned to Virginia in 1634. Proud of his Indian heritage, he learned Algonquin and became a successful planter on the Chickahominy River plantation his father had built, and Pocahontas' bloodlines continued into many Virginia families. (Robinson)

Another representative of English-Powhatan relations was Henry Spelman. The third son of Sir Henry Spelman of Congham, Norfolk, England, arrived in Jamestown in 1609 and was taken by Capt. John Smith to visit Powhatan. Smith reportedly traded Spelman to Powhatan for a town site near present-day Richmond. Powhatan later gave Spelman to the "King of Patowmeke," putting him into the present-day Stafford and King George area. Pocahontas' probable intervention saved the boy from her father's wrath and may have also been the reason she visited the empire's northern reaches. Spelman continued to live with the Indians, learning their languages. Exchanged, he returned to England. Mistreated, he came back to Virginia and acted as interpreter, trading with the tribes along the Potomac River between Potomac Creek to the falls of the river. He was killed by Anacostins. [Haynie] Another Indian princess, Kittamaquad, played a more substantial role in Stafford's history and English-Indian relations. (See Chapter 2)

Peaceful coexistence or assimilation might have solved colonist-Indian relations. In greater numbers than might be suspected, white and black colonists actually joined Indian societies, creating opportunities for an integrated and mutually beneficial society. Such chances passed quickly, however, as English colonial social order dispossessed the Indians of their lands. (James W. Loewen—Loewen)

Relations with the Indian nations became more formalized. In 1662 Virginia presented a silver medallion to "Ye King of Patomeck." Such devices, used as "passports," permitted safe passage for reliable allies to visit English Virginia settlements. Silver passports were issued to chieftains and copper to warriors. This particular specimen was excavated in Caroline County in 1832. Passports or badges for Indians were described in 1663 colony law. (VHS; Warren M. Billings—Billings)

Subsequent Developments

As the Colonial era progressed, Indian culture receded and the tribes ceased playing prominent roles. By 1677 all of Virginia's eastern Indians became "vassals of the English king." Confined to reservations, their populations shriveled and lands were taken. By 1700, a county history relates, "most of the Indians had fled." By 1800 only the Pamunkey and Mattaponi tribes were recognizable in the wider region.

All of Virginia's tribes were officially "Christianized," spoke English, and wore the same clothing as the whites. Increasingly denied their Indian identity and subsequently considered "people of color" in discriminatory actions, they later fell under the "one drop of black blood" rule, confusingly lumped into population data either as blacks or "colored" and stigmatized.

By the 1990s, tribal registers of the eight organized tribes and two reservations contained only 2,500 people, although some 15,280 people of Native American ancestry were believed living in Virginia. (VHS)

According to the 2000 U.S. census, some 417 Native Americans; 464 "White and Native Americans;" 85 "Black and Native Americans" were living in Stafford County. Thanks to sustained efforts to preserve their culture, the various Virginia tribes developed Indian churches and schools, encouraged wear of Indian costumes and regalia, promoted preservation of Indian knowledge, crafts and skills, and revived Indian pageants. Beyond that, a more progressive society has found the capacity for accepting diversity and celebrating the cultures of the various Indian tribes.

The story of Stafford's Potomacs continues, however. (See Chapter 11)

Silver medallion (obverse and reverse)
(Virginia Historical Society)

Chapter Two
Liberty and Religious Tolerance

Stafford's greatest contributions to our national and state heritage may have been its role in developing enduring ideas. The qualification is because no historian can reckon precisely when an idea enters a young person's brain. Analysis of influences, circumstances and opportunities must suffice. Thus bold new conceptions of liberty, individual rights, popular sovereignty, and religious toleration appear to have county roots, as did the perceived need for an effective national government that would work effectively in concert with individual rights.

Initially Virginia's and Stafford's elites were guided by an English conception of "liberty":

... a right to rule, to have one's own way and not to be ruled by the whims or will of others. In this view of life, the world was a harsh place that did not apportion liberty equally. Some men had more than others, and some had none at all—which explains why George Washington and his fellow Virginians saw no essential conflict between being fervent devotees of liberty and owners of slaves. (Thomas Fleming—Fleming)

Virginia personified this view, but what emerged from Stafford, also called liberty," was something quite different. It evolved into a stronger conceptualization of individual rights and popular sovereignty as a basis of governing and the conceptual extension of those rights to all people juxtaposed with constitutional government.

Two of our greatest Americans, Stafford's "two Georges"—Mason (IV) and Washington—played leading roles in formulating these ideas, and both men lived in Stafford in their formative years, lost their fathers at early ages, were reared by strong mothers and other relatives, received their educations here, and grew to prominence in Colonial and Revolutionary America. Although quite different

Crucifix monument, Stafford (Marshall A. Conner)

personally and physically and entirely different in their intellectual approaches to political theory, both were instrumental in founding the American republic.

George Mason (IV) was born in 1725 in the Dogue's Neck area of then Stafford County. That area is now in Fairfax County, but Mason's Stafford roots ran deep. George Mason (I) had settled in Stafford in 1651–1652 at "Accakeek Farm" (Marlborough Point and Brooke Roads). George Masons (I, II, and III) were militia colonels and House of Burgesses members from Stafford. The latter two lived at "Chopawamsic Farm" in northern Stafford (now part of Quantico Marine Base). When George Mason (III) drowned in the Potomac in 1735, his widow, Ann Thomson Mason, managed the estate and raised her children there. George Mason (IV)'s early education combined tutelage by Rev. Alexander Scott of Aquia Church, brief attendance at a Maryland academy, and individual study in uncle John Mercer's "Marlborough" library, one of Virginia's largest. A reluctant public figure, George Mason (IV) of "Gunston Hall" was primarily and rightly renowned for his contributions to American political theory. (Thomas M. Moncure Jr.—Moncure; Eby; VHS)

Assigned in May 1776 to a committee tasked with writing the Virginia Declaration of Rights, George Mason (IV) became the primary author. His original words, in a draft proclaimed on June 12, 1776, reveal his deep thinking and the indisputable impact of his ideas on America's charter documents, the Declaration of Independence (July 4, 1776), the U.S. Constitution (1787), and the Bill of Rights (1791):

...That all Men are by nature equally free and independent and have certain inherent rights...namely the enjoyment of Life and Liberty, with the Means of attaining and possessing Property, and pursuing and obtaining Happiness and Safety.

His Virginia Declaration—published in *the Virginia Gazette* on June 1, 1776; *Pennsylvania Evening Post* on June 6; *Newport Mercury* (Rhode Island) on June 20; and the *Essex Journal* (Connecticut) on July 5—had immediate revolutionary impact throughout the colonies. Mason's declaration later influenced the French Declaration of the Rights of Man and the Citizen (1789).

George Mason (IV), author of the Virginia Declaration of Rights (Virginia Historical Society)

Admired for his intellectual qualities by all the leading men of his day and other "founding fathers," Mason's passion for liberty later clashed with pragmatic Federalist efforts (led by George Washington) to organize a functioning government—one capable of raising revenues, paying its debts, and defending the nation. Mason's greatest concerns were potential tyranny and oppression by future American governments. Though it put him in opposition with his friends Washington and Madison, he fought for inclusion of a bill of rights, similar to the Virginia Declaration of Rights, in the body of the U.S. Constitution. He had also proposed the elimination of slavery, although Mason himself owned slaves. Slavery, he believed, made slaveholders "petty tyrants," inconsistent with liberty. Blocked on both counts, he refused to sign the final Constitution, returned home and, representing Stafford County, fought ratification in Virginia's 1788 convention. Though ratification had already been legally secured when the Virginians convened, the national standing of this group mandated passage. Failure to ratify would have moved the new country to crisis.

Virginia's delegates brilliantly argued the potential pitfalls for the new republic.

Some vivid examples of Mason's Ratification Convention arguments stand out:

Right, bust of George Mason (IV)
(Stephen A Gambaro)

The liberty or misery of millions yet unborn are deeply concerned in our decision. (IX,1162) I wish for such amendments, and such only, as are necessary to secure the dearest rights of the people. (IX,940) To make representation real and actual, the number of Representatives ought to be adequate; they ought to mix with the people, think as they think, feel as they feel, ought to be perfectly amenable to them, and thoroughly acquainted with their interest and condition. (IX,938)

When we come to the Judiciary, we shall be more convinced, that this (Federal) Government will terminate in the annihilation of the State Governments: The question will be, whether a consolidated Government can preserve the freedom, and secure the rights of the people. (IX, 940)

If Congress hath this power without controul, the taxes will be laid by those who have no fellow–feeling or acquaintance with the people. (IX, 940)

We wish only our rights to be secured. We must have such amendments as will secure the liberties and happiness of the people, on a plain simple construction, not on a doubtful ground...But in its present form we can never accede to it. Our duty to God and to our posterity forbids it. (IX, 1162–1163) Is it not probable, that those Gentlemen who will be elected Senators will fix themselves in the federal town, and become citizens of that town more than of our own State? (X, 1292)

George Washington by Rembrandt Peale, ca. 1853
(Washington and Lee University)

The 89–79 vote secured Virginia's ratification. James Madison promised that the "Bill of Rights" would be added as the first ten constitutional amendments and, true to his word, he introduced them in Congress in 1789. They were approved in 1791. Perhaps it was what Mason had waited for; he died at "Gunston Hall" in 1792. (Moncure; Denise McHugh, *Discover George Mason*)

In George Mason (IV), through his education here, Stafford gave the world one of its greatest political thinkers and author of the Virginia Declaration of Rights, with its direct contributions to the Declaration of Independence, U.S. Constitution, Bill of Rights and French Declaration of the Rights of Man. The embodiment of conceptual "liberty," Mason believed America's revolution was intended to produce a different kind of nation, one governed and defended by the people, and constitutionally free from the oppression of any central government. In this way, the United States would become truly unique from any previous nation. When the Federalists moved to institute a strong central government without a bill of rights for the people, Mason and his ally, Patrick Henry, opposed them. By holding their ground, they forced inclusion of the Bill of Rights in the Constitution, ensuring the preeminence of liberty and making America forever different.

George Washington, a Stafford resident and surveyor, later served as America's first president. Born in Westmoreland County ("Wakefield") in 1732, his family moved to Little Hunting Creek or "Mount Vernon" and, after 1738 (to be closer to Stafford's Accokeek Furnace), made their home at "Rappahannock River plantation" or "Ferry Farm"—in present-day Stafford County. George's father, Augustine, was employed with the Principio Company's Accokeek Furnace in Stafford [near Colonial Forge High School]. Augustine took an active management role in the furnace after 1735, and the Washingtons moved to "Ferry Farm" three years later. Augustine Washington died when George was eleven years old.

Washington's Stafford roots were strong and his boyhood home in present-day Stafford (then King George County) has a history of its own. Rappahannock River plantation was one of the three primary residences in Washington's life. The farm's original three tracts, where Washington spent his boyhood years, were part of the 2,000-acre patent (1666) of Col. John Catlett.

Purchased from Anthony Strother's family in 1738, the farm was near "Deep Run," land inherited by Mary Ball Washington, George's mother. When his father died in 1743, George inherited "Ferry Farm," town lots in Fredericksburg, and half of "Deep Run." He commenced his surveying and military careers there and Washington's mother, Mary Ball Washington, continued to live at the plantation until 1772, when she moved to Fredericksburg.

Rappahannock River plantation was the purported scene of the legendary cherry tree and coin- or rock-tossing incidents. Their historical accuracy cannot be proved or disproved.

Detail from Michail Porvus' rendition of Washington's Rappahannock River Plantation or "Ferry Farm" farm house. The farm house was believed to be a one-and-a-half-story structure about twenty-eight feet by forty feet. (Virginia Education Association)

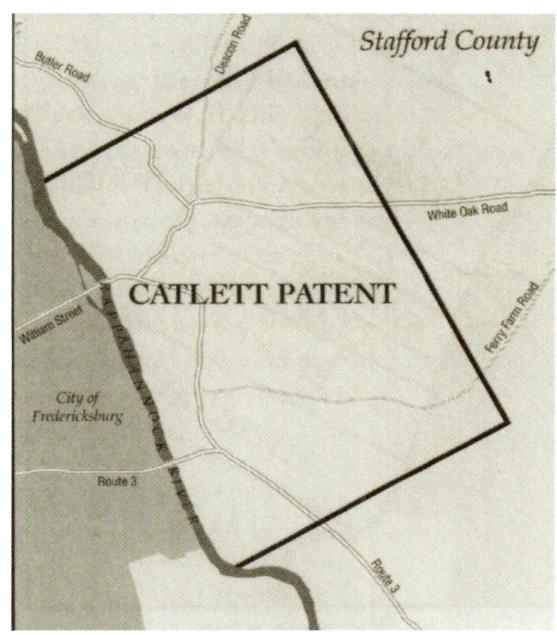
Original 1666 Catlett Patent superimposed over a modern map
(Thena S. Jones/Historic Fredericksburg Foundation Inc.)

Mary Ball Washington, mother of George Washington and Stafford resident from 1738–1772 (Virginia Historical Society)

Stafford County, Virginia

Right, Detail from artist Michail Porvus' depiction of George Washington, surveyor (Virginia Education Association)

Artist Michail Porvus' depiction of the cherry tree incident at "Ferry Farm" (Virginia Education Association)

Michail Porvus' depiction of the coin-tossing incident at "Ferry Farm" (Virginia Education Association)

In 1774 Washington sold the place to Dr. Hugh Mercer (soon a Revolutionary War general). Originally consisting of about 580 acres, its total acreage comprised the waterfront site of the current boyhood home property plus the land housing the current Ferry Farms Shopping Center, North Ferry Farms, Blythedale, Millsbrook and part of Ferry Farms subdivisions of Stafford. A "Home House" farm, its house, kitchen garden, dairy, storehouses, barns, and other outbuildings comprised the "domestic complex," generally identified archeologically. (Paula S. Felder—Felder; U.S. National Park Service—NPS)

As he moved up life's ladder at young ages, George Washington's public career was never far removed from his Stafford youth. He was a surveyor at fifteen, adjutant of the Southern District at twenty, a major at twenty-one, and a lieutenant colonel at twenty-two. From ages twenty-seven to forty-two, Washington served in the House of Burgesses. At thirty-seven, he led Virginia's opposition to British Colonial policies. At forty-two to forty-three, he was a delegate to the First and Second Continental Congresses, and, in June 1775, aged forty-three, he was unanimously named to command the Continental Army. In May 1787 at the age of fifty-five, he led the Virginia delegation to the Constitutional Convention and was unanimously elected presiding officer. After the Constitution was approved and ratified, he became president in 1789 (age fifty-seven) and was reelected in 1792. Refusing to run for a third term, he retired again. Called once again in 1798 to head the armies in a crisis with France, Washington died in 1799 at "Mount Vernon" at age sixty-seven.

Life's experiences had convinced Washington that, as important as Mason's conceptions of liberty were, America needed a national government that could stand practically among and apart from the nations of the world, pay its own way, and defend itself. To this end, some degree of centralization was necessary and the Federalists proposed a structure that divided power producing means to govern. Without Washington's stature behind them, the Federalists would not have carried the day against the anti-Federalists, led by Mason and Henry.

Ironically, Stafford's two Georges, once firm friends, grew distant in their advanced years. George Mason (IV), who believed most in liberty, individual rights and limited government, and

George Washington, who wanted a functional government were both ultimately proved correct in their unreconciled views. While neither man—nor any person—has lived to see the full fruition of their revolution, they set the bar very high for what America could and should be. It is their (and thus Stafford's) most precious legacy and our greatest inheritance.

John Mercer of "Marlborough"
(Virginia Historical Society)

Washington's ideas were gained by long public experience, but the original source of Mason's ideas is less clear. Existing evidence suggests his Stafford uncle, John Mercer of "Marlborough," played a key role. Based on the premise that both George Mason (IV) and John Francis Mercer were both reared and educated by John Mercer, it could not be coincidental that his nephew (representing Virginia) and his son (representing Maryland) were two of only sixteen delegates who refused to sign the completed U.S. Constitution. Rejecting it for lacking a bill of rights and granting too much federal power, they both opposed ratification in their respective Virginia and Maryland conventions.

Both men had been raised by Staffordian John Mercer and educated in his same "Marlborough" library. The former appears more significant than the latter, as Mercer's celebrated 1,800-volume library, second in Virginia only to William Byrd's, contained no known political theory works. It must therefore be assumed that the Mercers' and Mason's ideas were largely formed from readings in history and biography, literature and periodicals, and by association and practical experience. In all of these, John Mercer must have been the major influence in both men's lives. (C. Malcolm Watkins, *Cultural History of Marlborough*—Watkins)

John Mercer, born in Dublin, Ireland, in 1704 and educated at Trinity College, arrived in the New World in 1720. Prior to arriving at Marlborough Town, Mercer was a Maryland trader. Educated but not a wealthy man, he was soon befriended by Stafford's prominent Masons, marrying Catherine Mason in 1725. Rev. Alexander Scott of Overwharton Parish, who would later tutor George Mason (IV), officiated at their wedding at Mrs. Ann Fitzhugh's house. They settled in Marlborough's only standing house, built by Thomas Ballard in 1726. Believing in Marlborough's potential, Mercer purchased additional land and built several larger homes. As he prospered, Mercer (1746) built his plantation house, "Marlborough." Mercer's wife died in 1750;

The neighborhood of John Mercer
(Library of Congress)

Stafford County, Virginia

he later remarried, but his fortunes slid. He led Stafford opposition to the 1765 Stamp Act. Heavily indebted and increasingly confrontational with authority, he died in 1768. (Eby)

John Mercer of "Marlborough" had four sons. The oldest, George Mercer (1733–1784), was a captain in the Virginia Regiment during the French and Indian War and aide-de-camp to Washington at Fort Necessity (wounded). A member of the Fredericksburg Masonic lodge and a Burgess, Mercer became the London agent of the Ohio Company in 1763. His career turned sour in 1765, when he was appointed stamp collector for Virginia. This act, opposed by his family, county, and colony, resulted in his remaining in England for the rest of his life. Mercer's second son, John Fenton Mercer (1735–1756), was killed in the French and Indian War near Fort Edwards. His third son, James, also served in the Virginia Regiment at Fort Loudoun and became a judge (see Chapter 3). His fourth son was John Francis Mercer (see Chapter 3). (The *Rappahannock Patriot*—RP)

Too little of John Mercer's life is known to be absolutely certain, but it appears he helped form the concept of liberty and knowledge in the minds of his sons and nephew. More egalitarian than his contemporaries, Mercer believed in the power of working people. He encouraged his sons to work with their hands and to become competent in doing things, rejecting traditional gentlemanly lifestyles. In 1755, the year John Mercer finally established ownership for Marlborough Town, his professional British soldier brother, Capt. James Mercer, came to Alexandria. Their meeting uncovered pronounced differences between them. John Mercer took his son, James, to meet his uncle and namesake, and the Americans were shocked at the captain's "false pride." Capt. Mercer was equally perplexed with the leveling influences of Colonial life. The captain, who would die at Albany in 1757, was critical of his nephew's being taught a practical trade. On their way to Marlborough, the Mercers visited cousin George Mason (IV), then working on "Gunston Hall." (Watkins)

A revolutionary in his own right, Mercer had believed strongly enough in individual rights to lead in opposing the notorious 1765 Stamp Act. Known to have influenced Patrick Henry in this regard, the seed of liberty—meaning advancement of the individual power and restraint on governmental power—was thus passed from the "Marlborough" plantation to Virginia's two greatest proponents of liberty, Henry and Mason, as well as to his prominent sons.

Birth of Religious Tolerance: Catholic Brents in Anglican Virginia

In 1930 the Catholic Women's Club of Richmond placed a plaque and large bronze crucifix at Aquia Creek. It commemorated the first English Catholic settlers in Virginia, the Brents. Their settlement was honored, as was their solicitation of an edict of religious tolerance from King James II for those in the "Brenton" tract. (It was later incorrectly believed Stafford was the martyrdom site for Jesuit missionaries who came from Florida to Virginia in February 1570 and were massacred.) (Clifford M. Lewis and Albert Loomie)

The story of Stafford's first English settlers, the Catholic Brents, and the beginnings of religious toleration began in southern Maryland in the winter of 1640 when Father Andrew White baptized the Piscataway emperor (or tayac) and his wife. White, an English Catholic Jesuit missionary, had arrived at St. Mary's City, Maryland, in 1634 carrying a gift from King Charles I that demonstrated his mission's importance: a glass-enclosed, silver-tipped relic purportedly a piece of the True Cross. He also worked with the emperor's daughter, Kittamaquad. Far less famous than fellow Indian princess Pocahontas, Kittamaquad had a more lasting influence on early Stafford. The Piscataway tayac's daughter also had a remarkable story. The Piscataways (Conoy, Canawese or Ganbawese) were of Algonquin linguistic stock and an intermediate tribe between the Nanticokes and Powhatans. (Haynie; Edward Steers Jr.; Swanton)

The tayac desired Kittamaquad's education and conversion and placed his seven-year-old daughter in White's care. The "little Empress" was significantly adopted by Mistress Margaret Brent. By 1642 Kittamaquad had learned English and was baptized as "Mary." Romance soon entered her life. Margaret's brother, Giles Brent (I), who had come from England with her on the Elizabeth in 1638, married the Indian princess, then age twelve. They lived alternately on Kent Island and with sister, Margaret, and about 1646 Giles and Kittamaquad settled on the north shore of Aquia Creek. In their house, called "Peace," the Brents were the northernmost English residents in Virginia. When settlers pushed northward to patent land (ca. 1651), "Peace" became their last stop for provisions and information—a "point of departure into the unknown." Giles built another home, called "Retirement," and traded with the Indians, no doubt aided by Mary Brent (I)'s linguistic skills and cultural knowledge. They preserved the peace, maintained their way station, and patented Northern Neck lands. Unfortunately, Kittamaquad or Mary (I) died, leaving their three

Crucifix monument to Stafford's Catholic settlers (Jane M. Conner)

children, Richard, Giles (II) and Mary (II), who by Indian law, inherited her mother's Maryland lands. As he had done when he married Kittamaquad, Giles (I) unsuccessfully laid claim to most of Maryland in his daughter's name. (Haynie)

One account suggests, "Giles' naming of 'Peace' was either wishful or optimistic because life there was far from peaceful." When Lord Baltimore discovered Giles had settled across the river, he ordered Gov. William Stone to issue land patents in the Northern Neck including "that place where Mr. Giles Brent now resides and called by him 'Peace.'" Settlers began arriving at Brent's Point bearing grants with Lord Baltimore's seal; but in 1654, Brent petitioned the Jamestown court for protection from Northern Neck encroachments. Maryland patents in Virginia terminated. Giles' sisters, Margaret and Mary, joined the family enclave, as did their nephew George Brent, who built "Woodstock" and played an important role in Brenton. (Eby)

After French King Louis XIV's 1685 revocation of Henry IV's 1598 Edict of Nantes granting religious toleration to French Protestants, some 300,000 Huguenots left France for Europe and America. The Calvinist Huguenots who came to America were quickly absorbed into Protestant churches. On January 11, 1686, however, George Brent, Richard Foote, Nicholas Hayward, and Robert Bristow obtained a patent on 30,000 acres of Lord Culpeper's land, which became known as Brenton or Brent Town. The boundaries of Brent Town were vague—"between the Courses of the said Two rivers, Rappahannock and Patowmack, backwards at least six miles Distant from the said Main River and from any Land Already seated and inhabited, and upon and Between the Southwest and Northeast Branches of Ocaquan Creek and from thence towards the Mountains"—but apparently were in present Fauquier and Prince William Counties (then Stafford). Brent and his partners, hoping Brenton would develop, petitioned King James II for a "Grant of the Right of Religious Freedom" for those who settled there. Issued on February 10, 1686, it guaranteed Huguenots nonpersecution if they settled at Brenton. Brent, whose motives were naturally suspected, was also allowed to open the tract to Catholics and others. Brenton did not fully come to fruition even into the 1700s and most Huguenots had been assimilated. So the property was subdivided among the original owners' heirs, and Prince William places such as Bristow and Brentsville are vestiges of "this unprofitable venture." Some French refugees did find homes in Stafford; they included such families as Cabel (Cabell), Batie (Patie), Diresubawn, Lebounie, Reineau (Reno), and Traquette (Tackett). (Eby; Kirby)

Mariner's cross, depicting the crucifixion of Christ, on an anchor motif. Recovered from the "Woodstock" Brent house archeological site in Stafford.
(Northern Virginia Chapter of the Archaeological Society of Virginia)

More importantly, the Brents had laid a foundation of religious tolerance that exceeded standards achieved elsewhere in Colonial Virginia and America. They also exceeded the Golden Rule by treating others better than they were treated. With the arrival of English Cavaliers in Virginia, it was merely a matter of time until the establishment of the Anglican church. The Brents then had to exercise their religion illegally and covertly; but their special status—as "unindicted papists"—allowed both the Brents and Stafford's small Catholic community to function, if not flourish. Margaret Brent's vast land holdings included property that would be used in Stafford for many years by Wallers and Cliftons (believed to be Catholics) families. The Brents of "Richland" and "Woodstock" and the Cliftons of "Clifton," tied to the Wallers of "Concord" and later "Richland" and "Clifton," constituted a formidable Catholic community based in Widewater. Later, the Brents united with the Carrolls of Marlborough, Maryland, and their network of family alliances (including those with Protestants) expanded. (Eby)

And it was to Stafford that Father John Carroll, S.J., sailed from England. Born in Upper Marlboro, Maryland, in 1735, John Carroll was the brother of Daniel Carroll II ("The Commissioner"), a signer of the U.S. Constitution, Eleanor Carroll Brent and Anne Carroll Brent. Thus, he was also the brother-in-law of William Brent (III) of "Richland" and Robert Brent of "Woodstock" (1730–1780). Educated in England, Carroll returned by ship to Aquia and "Richland" in June 1774. In 1776, he assisted the Quebec mission of Benjamin Franklin, Samuel Chase and Daniel Carroll of Carrollton enlisting French Canadian support for the Revolution. Father Carroll subsequently preached in Widewater and returned to preach in later years at "Richland." He became the bishop of Baltimore (1790) and first American archbishop.

Archbishop John Carroll (Library of Congress)

Archbishop John Carroll also founded Georgetown College in 1789, and he may well have borrowed from his in-laws' experience; although the college was staffed by Jesuits, it was always conceived to educate members of other faiths. A college history states:

…Members of Congress and Officers of the Army, while stationed in the Capital, sent their boys to Georgetown College as a matter of course. The fact that the school was operated under Roman Catholic auspices did not militate against the true catholicity of its student body. John Carroll in 1789 had seen to that, providing that Georgetown "will be open to students of every religious profession. They, who in this respect, differ from the Superintendent of the Academy, will be at liberty to frequent the places of worship and instruction appointed by their parents; but with respect to their moral conduct, all must be subject to general and uniform discipline. (James S. Ruby)

Stafford's greatest contribution to America may well been in serving as the boyhood homes for two of our country's greatest statesmen, George Washington and George Mason (IV). The formative years of both men were spent in Stafford. (Mason photo; Stephen A. Gambaro & Washington photo; Washington and Lee University)

Virtually all of the colleges created at that time were aligned with specific religious denominations, and only in the nineteenth century did some public institutions become truly nondenominational.

Perhaps it was a coincidence, as Patrick Henry was known to have authored the draft paragraph on religious freedom in George Mason (IV)'s Virginia Declaration of Rights, but that precept may have also been influenced by reflections on Stafford's Brents and Catholic community and the destructive nature of an established church to liberty:

That Religion, or the Duty which we owe to our Creator, and the Manner of discharging it, can be directed only by Reason and Conviction, not by Force or Violence, and therefore that all Men should enjoy the fullest Toleration in the Exercise of Religion, according to the Dictates of Conscience, unpunished and unrestrained by the Magistrate; unless under Colour of Religion, any Man disturb the Peace, the Happiness, or the Safety of Society. And it is the mutual Duty of all to practise Christian Forbearance, Love, and Charity towards each other.

Another interesting connection is that George Mason (IV)'s second marriage in 1780 was to Sarah Brent (1730–1806), a daughter of George Brent of "Woodstock." This marriage, to a member of Stafford's oldest Catholic family, may have further influenced Mason's views on religious toleration by the time of the constitutional convention.

A short distance down Virginia 637 is the woodland entrance to the Brent Cemetery, where many members of that famous Stafford family are interred. (See Chapter 11.) A 1998 updated Virginia historical sign, "First Roman Catholic Settlement in Virginia, E-76," is also at the crucifix site and reads:

The crucifix by sculptor Georg J. Lober was erected in 1930, commemorates the first English Roman Catholic settlement in Virginia. Fleeing political and religious turmoil in Maryland, Giles Brent and his sisters Margaret and Mary established two plantations called Peace and Retirement on the north side of Aquia Creek between 1647 and 1650. Later, they jointly acquired 15,000 acres in Northern Virginia, including the site of present-day Alexandria. Their nephew George Brent, whose plantation Woodstock and family cemetery were located nearby, represented Stafford County in the House of Burgesses in 1688, the only Roman Catholic delegate in the colonial period.

Commemorative plaque honoring the first Catholic settlers in Virginia. (Stephen A. Gambaro)

Chapter Three
Staffordians All

Stafford's population levels since the first U.S. Census in 1790, show several distinct events: steady decline between 1810–1850, reflecting the westward migration; major reduction between 1865–1870, reflecting the departure of African Americans and some ex-Confederates; and significant increases beginning in the 1940s and accelerating in the late 1970s, reflecting Stafford's "suburbanization." Federal census numbers tell the story:

Federal Census	Population	Change
1790	9,588	
1800	9,951	+363
1810	9,830	−121
1820	9,517	−313
1830	9,362	−155
1840	8,454	−908
1850	8,004	−450
1860	8,555	+551
1870	6,420	−2,135
1880	7,211	+791
1890	7,362	+151
1900	8,097	+ 735
1910	8,070	−27
1920	8,104	+34
1930	8,050	−54
1940	9,548	+1,498
1950	11,902	+2,354
1960	16,876	+4,974
1970	24,587	+7,711
1980	40,168	+15,581
1990	61,263	+21,095
2000	92,446	+31,183
July 2002	102,700	+10,254 (estimates*)
July 2003	106,800	+4,100 (projection*)

Brent Cemetery (Jane M. Conner)

(* Weldon Cooper Center of the University of Virginia. In the July 2002 statistics, Stafford is the eighth most populous county of ninety-five Virginia counties.)

Beyond these gross population numbers are individual and collective stories that represent those who lived in the county. Their biographical sketches and, where possible, their images and words are used to illuminate their times.

Colonial Era

Virginia, unlike other colonies, was not established to promote either political or religious freedom. Jamestown (1607) and the previously failed Virginia Company 1585 colonization at Roanoke Island were created for the crown's economic advantage, rewarding investors, and for bold adventurers and venture capitalists to build fortunes. The result was "an unfree society based on servitude for most whites, slavery for most blacks, and the subordination of women." Adding Indian subjugation and/or assimilation into the colony's underclass, a picture of harsh reality emerges. Viewed through this filter, Colonial Virginia's and Stafford's transition through feudalism, oligarchy, indentured servitude, slavery, and romance with illegality become more understandable. (Gwen Litchfield, VHS—Litchfield/VHS)

Seventeenth-century Virginia colonists lived in an oppressive political and social environment, made worse by a religious component focused not on religious freedom but on "saving" purported heathens from the "Armes of the Divell." Highest priority always went to enlarging the king's dominions and rewarding venture participants, and Virginia aided England in securing raw materials in ways similar to other European colonies. Virginia, however, included disproportionate numbers of "nobility and gentry" who lacked rudimentary working and survival skills, resulting in malnutrition and disease. (Billings)

The survivors convinced the Virginia Company that more "working class and servants" would be needed. Despite that need, the established church intruded itself into ordinary people's lives. For example, in 1611 failure to attend twice-daily church assemblies resulted in loss of provisions, and if repeated, to whippings and death. The death penalty was liberally applied for murder; adultery; sodomy; rape; church trespass or robbery; food theft; treason against Colony leaders; mistreating Indians; and selling company supplies, tools, or provisions to those who could resell them. Soldiers deserting or abandoning the colony faced death sentences; those who failed to adhere to oaths merely faced galley-slavery. Fornication, offenses against authority, or embezzlement brought whippings and other public humiliations before church congregations. (Billings)

Early Colonists faced severe trials in dealing with harsh elements, Indians, and each other. Yet Virginia and Stafford emerge as amazing stories of human resilience, and the myths, legends and reality found in American history textbooks explain why Jamestown is omitted in favor of Plymouth Rock as the archetypal U.S. birthplace. Bluntly put, Virginia "ill-served" historians' search

Colonial Jamestown-era reenactment scene
(Jane M. Conner)

Artist's conception of Margaret Brent confronting the Maryland Council in 1648
(Stephen A Gambaro)

for the mythic origins of American culture because it lacked moral intent in its creation. British Virginians took Indian prisoners, forcing them to teach colonists farming. In 1623 they poisoned Chiskiak's Potomac River tribe while offering a toast "symbolizing eternal friendship," and spent their "early days digging random holes in the ground, haplessly looking for gold instead of planting crops," and were "soon starving and digging up putrid Indian corpses to eat or renting themselves out to Indian families as servants." During the "Starving Time" of 1609–1610 alone, the small colony suffered 350 deaths. (James W. Loewen—Loewen; T. H. Breen; DVB [LV])

From this dreadful beginning, Virginia and America glacially emerge; but Stafford's early story is remarkable considering just how much happened here— Capt. John Smith's explorations; Indian trading; Pocahontas' kidnapping; and the Brents and Kittamaquad establishing Stafford's first permanent English settlement, Virginia's first English Catholic settlement, and opening settlement to people of all faiths. Then English Cavaliers arrived. Dislodged by their support of Charles I against Cromwell, they immigrated in substantial numbers, as did French Huguenots and a few English Puritans. Col. Giles Brent (I) and his Piscataway princess developed reasonably friendly relations with the Indians and new arrivals. His sister, Margaret Brent, already famous as the first female attorney and one of the largest landowners of Maryland, came to live here and acquired vast Virginia acreage. Their nephew, George Brent, joined them from England (1660–1663). All these events took place before Stafford County was formally established—detached from Westmoreland County—in 1664. At that point and for some time to come, Stafford extended north to the falls of the Potomac River and west to the Blue Ridge Mountains—"according to some sources, the act by the British Crown establishing Stafford County included the Ohio Valley within its boundaries." In any case, for more than seventy years Stafford would constitute Virginia's northern frontier. (Homer D. Musselman—Musselman)

Margaret Brent, arguably the most remarkable person in a remarkable clan, was born in 1601 in Gloucestershire. The seventh child of Sir Richard Brent (1573–1652) and Lady Elizabeth Willoughby de Broke landed in 1638 at St. Mary's City. No common immigrant, she came with four maidservants, five male servants, and two letters from Cecil Calvert, Lord Baltimore, granting all the lands she could manage. By any measure, she could manage quite a bit: administering her own and sister Mary's affairs; as executrix for deceased Gov. Leonard Calvert; and representing the legal interests of her brother, Giles (I). She appeared before Provincial Court at least 124 times between 1642 and 1650. Her own estate was "Sisters Freehold," and she managed "Trinity," "St. Gabriel," and "Fort Kent." Probably the largest landowner and most influential person in the Maryland colony, she shocked the Maryland Council in 1648 by confronting them with legal requests and demanding the vote (actually two votes) on the council. Rebuffed by the council (and by Calvert from England), Margaret shifted her interests and residence to Virginia. After many successful ventures, she died in Stafford County in 1671. Among her land holdings were the original site of Alexandria, which she had owned since 1654 (the town would be named for another Staffordian, John Alexander); and the future site of Fredericksburg (1658), which she saw as a potential town. Although not confirmed, she was probably buried in the Brent Family Cemetery or at "Peace" plantation in Stafford—gravestones there were destroyed and pilfered during the Civil War and other periods. Although her gravesite may be unknown, her fame was lasting. Supreme Court associate justice Ruth Bader Ginsburg remarked (1993):

> Awards were made in the name of Margaret Brent, a great lady of the mid-1600s, celebrated as first woman lawyer in America. Her position as a woman, yet possessor of power, so confused her contemporaries that she was sometimes named in court records, not as Mistress Margaret Brent, but as Gentleman Margaret Brent. (Brent Genealogy; DVB [LV])

Between 1642 and 1675, "distressed Cavaliers" and indentured servants immigrated to Virginia and Stafford primarily from the south of England. Gov. Sir William Berkeley grew Virginia from 8,000 to 40,000 inhabitants in thirty years. He established social and legal systems that would shape immigration patterns for generations. Berkeley actively recruited Royalist elites who had sided with Charles I and Charles II and fled to Europe. He brought those destined to become the so-called "first families of Virginia" (FFV)—forgetting Indians, Roanoke Islanders, Spanish, Jamestowners, black and white servants, and Catholic Marylanders. Nevertheless, Cavalier impact in what became Stafford County (which they named for Staffordshire, where some had aided Charles II and resided) was substantial. The Masons arrived in 1651/1652. Especially after Charles II's Restoration in 1660, "younger sons" of Britain's ruling elites—deprived of inheritances by primogeniture—came and, amazingly, replicated the same British social order, a hierarchy of aristocrats, gentry, yeomanry, and servants. Virginia Cavaliers came mainly from the English counties of Kent, Gloucester, Northampton, Somerset, London, Yorkshire, Surrey, Devon, Berkshire, Hampshire, Shropshire, Bedfordshire, Dorsetshire, Middlesex, Norfolk, Suffolk, Sussex, Warwickshire, Wiltshire, Buckinghamshire,

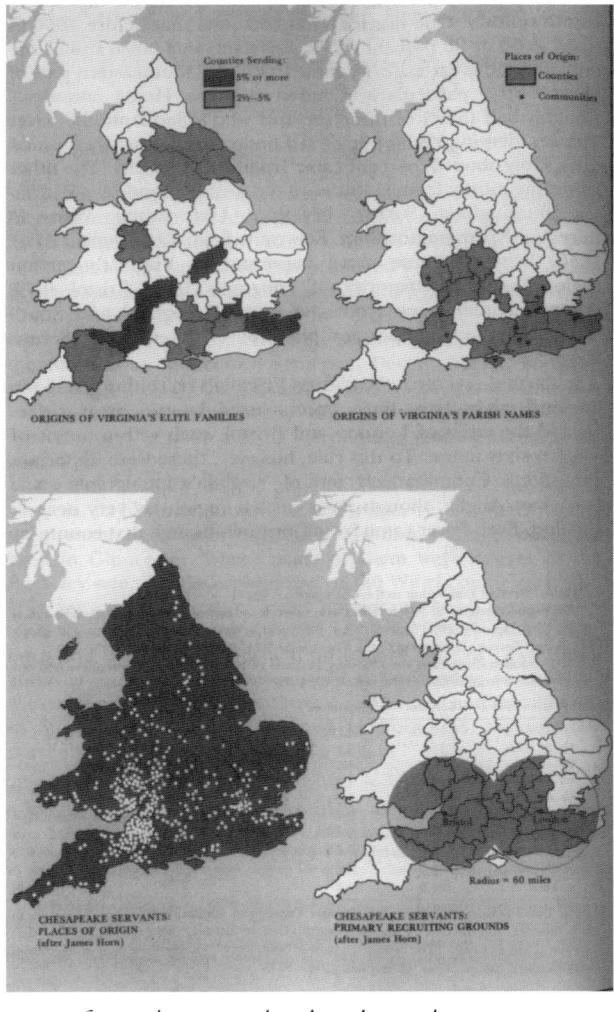

Map of Southern England and Cavalier Folkways to Virginia (David Hackett Fischer)

Essex, Leicestershire, Lincolnshire, Staffordshire, Worcestershire, Cambridgeshire, Cheshire, Cornwall, Cumberland, Derbyshire, Hertfordshire, Huntingdonshire, Lancashire, Rutland, Westmoreland, and the Channel Islands. An estimated 82,000 people immigrated to Virginia from 1607 to 1699, some of them to Stafford. (David Hackett Fischer—Fischer)

Less historical ink describes the Virginia immigration of "humble people of low rank"—ranking below the aristocracy and gentry, but above the vagrants and paupers remaining in England—but their impact, especially in settling the frontier "back country," was crucial. Most came as servants, mainly indentured servants, and half of those sailing from Bristol between 1654 and 1678 came to Virginia. About 75 percent were indentured, mostly agrarian tenants. They were predominantly (4–6:1) male and youngsters. Before 1650, 80 percent to 90 percent of the servants had come from London and southeastern counties. Afterward, they mostly came from the "south of England" places from which aristocracy and gentry had immigrated. (Fischer)

English ties to Virginia and Stafford were quite direct. The names given to the Virginia places directly related to native English places: Of twenty-five Virginia counties extant in 1703, eight had royalist names; eight had southern and western English names (including Stafford); and four had northern names. Only two had American Indian names. (Fischer)

"Stafford" was suggested by George Mason (I) and Gerrard Fowke, forever linking it to the mother country. Pretentious names given to modest Colonial farms and plantations, such as "Boscobel" and George Mason's (IV) "Gunston Hall" (now in Fairfax County), derived from Staffordshire. (John Tackett Goolrick—J. T. Goolrick; Eby)

One historian writes, "The Potomac shores of Stafford became somewhat crowded in the later half of the 1600s" as immigrants arrived and Indian relations worsened. George Brent, nephew of Giles (I) and Margaret, joined the Aquia Creek contingent. Immigrating directly from England, he built "Woodstock" plantation on the low ridge overlooking Aquia Creek. Brent's plantation, on which he would be buried, survived until about 1725. In 1670 "George Brent of Oquia Creeke, Gent.," was identified as an attorney representing a Londoner's Northern Neck interests. In 1679 Brent became Stafford's surveyor. By 1683 he was a law partner of William Fitzhugh, a leading Protestant. In 1677 Brent had married Elizabeth Greene of Bermuda; they had three sons and two daughters before Elizabeth died in childbirth (1686). A year and a day later, he married Mary Sewell Chandler, a widow with two sons and three daughters, and she and George Brent would have at least one son and three daughters before she too died in childbirth (1694). (Eby; DVB [LV])

About 1671 a fort was authorized for Stafford's defense with Capt. Peter Knight in command. In 1675 a militia force led by Col. George Mason (I) and Giles Brent (II) (half-Indian, his actions were sometimes confused with those of George Brent, who most likely did not participate) crossed the Potomac to avenge an Englishman's murder by Maryland-side Indians. This was a part of a chain of events known as "Bacon's Rebellion," dubbed the first popular revolt against British authority in the Colonies. It also ended Sir William Berkeley's career (he had severely punished the rebels). Verdicts on the rebellion's "rights and wrongs" vary—the Indian picture is even more muddled—but it is clear that the militia, styled "mounted rangers" in companies of twenty horsemen, were established in Stafford by 1682. (Fischer; Eby; DVB [LV])

Giles Brent (II), representing a darker side of the generally positive union between his English father and Indian mother, was born about 1652, reportedly dwelling in "two worlds." His father and cousin had established themselves in respectable society, but he lived a frontier existence and learned the Indian language until his father's death (1672). Giles inherited the estate, becoming a planter, militia captain, and (in 1674) Stafford's tobacco tax collector. Primarily, his Virginia fame arises from Bacon's Rebellion. In July 1675, Capt. Brent served in Col. George Mason (I)'s party, which pursued an Indian contingent into Maryland and killed several in retaliation for the Indians' killing some Virginians. Despite confusion over Giles' and his cousin, George's, roles, Giles Brent (II) definitely joined forces loyal to Nathaniel Bacon to battle Pamunkeys and other tribes. Referred to as "Colonel" Brent, he collaborated with Bacon until the rebel leader turned his forces

Left, King James II tuppence piece, pierced for a pendant, found at "Woodstock" archeological site in Stafford
(Northern Virginia Chapter of the Archaeological Society of Virginia)

against Gov. Berkeley (1676) and laid siege to Jamestown. Brent then turned against Bacon and gathered approximately 1,000 men to confront Bacon's forces. When the men learned Bacon had burned Jamestown, they deserted. Brent's part then ended (saving him from execution). His final conflicts were domestic—his fiery temperament resulted in his threatening family members. In 1679 Brent's wife made an unprecedented petition to governor and council for protection and "separate maintenance." The council found against Brent, who then moved to Middlesex County, where he died in September 1679. He had converted, as he was on the registry and buried in the Anglican cemetery there. (DVB [LV])

George Brent and William Fitzhugh had provisioned the Potomac garrison in 1681, and in 1684 Brent led "an expedition to defend the inhabitants of Rappahannock River settlements from attacks by the Seneca." From 1686 to 1688 Brent was acting attorney general for the Virginia Colony. In 1688 "unindicted papist" Brent was elected from Stafford to the House of Burgesses. Likely in deference to his family's pioneer status, as he refused to take an anti-Catholic oath of supremacy, Brent took his seat and participated fully, the only known Catholic to serve. (DVB [LV])

The established Anglican church in Virginia required the Brents, "pre-FFVs" though they were, to exercise their religion covertly. Those of conscience were at special disadvantage:

> (when) Virginia became a royal colony, an ideal of Anglican conformity began to be more actively pursued. In 1632 the Assembly enacted seventeen laws which required "uniformity throughout this colony, both in substance and circumstance to the canons and constitutions of the Church of England."

Repression of the other faiths (Puritans, Quakers, and Presbyterians) followed. Even where practicing their faiths was overlooked, they had to tithe to the state church. (DVB [LV]; Fischer)

For the Brents, repression was fast catching up. Events in England in 1688 ended his promising public career, as "the glorious Revolution unleashed anti-Catholic feelings in the Colonies, and as the most prominent Catholic in Virginia, he suffered the consequences." Rumors spread in March 1689 that Brent was conspiring with Maryland Catholics and Indians to kill Protestants, and some Virginia leaders ordered him to take refuge at William Fitzhugh's house. In February 1690, Brent must have complicated matters when he sheltered a fleeing Franciscan priest from Maryland at "Woodstock." Although he had proposed to turn the Brenton tract into a refuge for Huguenots, English Catholics and others, anti-Catholicism took its toll. He never again held public office and, despite Stafford's leaders efforts to shield him, he lost his law practice. Nevertheless, George Brent continued serving the Northern Neck proprietors as ranger general in charge of defense (1690), and three years later he and Fitzhugh became the proprietors' joint agents. They favored each other and their friends with large tracts of land, enriching themselves but retarding settlement. In this way, Brent acquired a great deal of land and "owned more than 15,000 acres in Virginia plus land in Maryland and England at the time of his death" (1700). (DVB [LV]; Fischer)

By 1724/1725 Virginia's Anglican Church fully dominated the Colony. Overwharton Parish, which included Stafford, reported three churches serving 650 families, "full attendance at church," and an average of eighty to one hundred communicants. Later in the eighteenth century, Virginia saw "disestablishment" and an increase of Presbyterians, Baptists and Methodists. But for six generations, the Anglican Church in Virginia had shaped the culture of the Colony and was intertwined with the Colony's government. (Fischer)

The early 1700s were prosperous for Stafford. Agricultural production was bountiful; gold mines and ironworks were working; and Falmouth developed into a thriving port. This prosperity would be relatively brief because after the Revolution and into the 1800s, population eroded. With soil overworked by tobacco, and mineral deposits depleted, industries struggled, leading to a natural westward shift to new lands and opportunities. (Moncure)

Not all Staffordians lived bucolic lives, however. John Rowzee Peyton (1754–1799) of "Stony Hill" (near Aquia Towne Center) is an example. Per John Lewis Peyton's *The Adventures of My Grandfather*, John Rowzee Peyton's life from 1768 to 1774 included a trip to Jamaica and romance with future wife, Anne Howe (from Occoquan), and a return trip to Stafford, including being taken hostage by pirates off New Orleans and marched in shackles to a Sante Fe prison. He returned home through an Indian fight in the Appalachians at Point Pleasant, then married Anne (1777); they lived at "Stony Hill." (Eby)

Stafford (established in 1664) became a geographic revolving doorway connecting Northern Virginia with the somewhat overlapping areas of the Northern Neck, Middle Neck, Central Virginia, Tidewater, and Piedmont. Astride both the Potomac and Rappahannock Rivers, it was tied to those historic waters and Chesapeake Bay. Stafford also served as the gateway between eastern Virginia and Fauquier, Prince William, Fairfax, and Loudoun Counties directly to the west. Closely tied historically to King George and Spotsylvania Counties (both established in 1721), Caroline County (1727), Prince William County (1731), Fairfax County (1742), and Fauquier County (1759), Stafford was also closely linked to the history of Fredericksburg (1728). (Eby)

Exemplary of state Revolutionary era political figures was William Brent (1732– ca. 1782). The son of William Brent and Jane Brent was born in Stafford. He married (ca. 1754) Eleanor Carroll of Maryland, the sister of Father John Carroll. Despite such strong Catholic roots, William converted to Anglicanism. This move, ironically coupled with continued adherence by Catholic family members, ensured him a successful public life and his children's potential to marry into wider—Maryland and Virginia, Catholic and Protestant—society. Such marriages, alliances really, were concluded by the Brents with Amblers, Carrolls, Hills, Lees, Fitzhughs, and Sewells. William and Eleanor's middle son, Richard Brent, later served in the U.S. Congress. William Brent inherited thousands of acres of land in King George, Prince William, Stafford, and Westmoreland Counties as well as in Maryland and the ill-defined "West." A successful horse breeder, he acquired cash and slaves from his stallions' famous services. His first public office was Stafford justice of the peace (1757). Brent joined other justices resigning in protest to the 1765 Stamp Act; his resignation was ignored and he continued in office until his death some seventeen years later. In 1774 he was elected to the Stafford committee enforcing nonimportation associations enacted by the Virginia Revolutionary Conventions and Continental Congress. Brent was elected one of two delegates from Stafford to the 1776 Virginia Revolutionary Convention, which approved independence, Mason's Virginia Declaration of Rights, and the first Virginia constitution. Brent's "elegant brick" home, "Richland," was burned by a raiding party from HMS *Roebuck*, which landed in Stafford on July 23, 1776—an exclamation point on the patriots' Philadelphia pledge in the Declaration of Independence. Brent rebuilt his home and served in the House of Delegates, representing Stafford in the fall of 1776. He returned in 1778, and in 1780 was elected to the Virginia Senate, representing Stafford, King George and Westmoreland Counties. Brent died in office before April 1782, and was buried on his estate. He did not live to see the end of the Revolution. (DVB [LV])

The *Rappahannock Patriot* alludes to further Revolutionary War destruction in Stafford, including at "Marlborough". It adds the full quotation of the story of "Richland's" burning in Purdie's *Virginia Gazette* (August 2, 1776):

Lord Dunmore with his motley band of pirates and renegadoes have burnt the elegant brick house of William Brent, esq., at the mouth of Aquia Creek, in Stafford County, as also two other houses lower down the Potomac river, both the property of widow ladies. The author describes an 1834 widow's pension application from Mary Posey, stating her husband, George Thornton of Stafford, was a militia officer "at the bombardment of Marlboro, the seat of Judge (James) Mercer…"

The Colonial Afro-Virginian Experience

By at least 1619, Africans were first brought into the Virginia Colony. Ironically, the word on the first Afro-Virginians (and Stafford's Indians) came from John Rolfe, Pocahontas' husband:

About the last of August (1619) came in a dutch man of warre that sold us twenty Negars and Iapazous King of Patawomeck, came to James towne, to desire two ships come trade in his River, for a more plentifull yeere of Corne had not beene in along time, yet very contagious, and by the trechery of one Poule, in a manner turned heathen, wee were very jealous the Salvages would surprise us. (Billings)

It is now known some Africans were present in Virginia by at least March 1619. (VHS)

The earliest black Virginians also tended to be indentured servants, freed after seven years' service in the New World. Chattel slavery evolved later. (Ruth Coder Fitzgerald—Fitzgerald)

"A colonial society is imperfect because it lacks some of the essential attributes of a matured social organism," stiffly relates one historian. Virginia simply needed workers (in short supply in seventeenth-century England) and "Englishmen devised two solutions to the problem: indentured servitude and chattel slavery." Successful cultivation of tobacco further necessitated a larger, cheaper labor force. (Billings)

In yet another naked exercise of feudalism, hereditary slavery became legal in the 1670s. An estimated 2 million Africans would be transported to British colonies by the Revolution. By the late 1600s, they were being brought into the sparsely settled middle Rappahannock Valley. In common with white yeoman settlers and white indentured servants, slaves initially and primarily filled roles as agricultural workers. In fact, white indentured servants outnumbered African slaves throughout seventeenth-century America. (Fleming; Fitzgerald)

Another account adds:

Historians argue whether Europeans enslaved Africans because of inherent prejudice against the color black or whether the fact that Africans enslaved one another gave rise to a degraded view of them. In either case, the establishment of the tobacco plantation system as the economic mainstay of Virginia and the reality that slave labor produced tobacco most economically transformed an inconsistent prejudice into a rigid system of perpetual racial bondage. Beginning in the 1660s, Virginia codified slavery laws that were copied throughout the later British colonies. (Litchfield/VHS)

Falmouth emerged in the 1700s as an important trade center and port (if only through its relation to Fredericksburg), from which a variety of agricultural products, mainly tobacco and flour, were shipped to England. African slaves landed in Falmouth (Falmouth Beach) and slave auctions were held. (Eby; Fitzgerald)

All aspects of Stafford life had African-American dimensions. Slaves unloaded and loaded supplies. Colonial Staffordians gathered at taverns on public highways and at public buildings such as magistrates' offices, where slaves were bought, sold, and bartered. Eventually, free blacks and slave artisans such as blacksmiths, coopers, cobblers, and draymen became integral to the economy. Slaves worked on farms and docks; in iron industries, mines, quarries, mills, mercantile businesses, construction enterprises; and as domestic servants. On the Rappahannock and Potomac, African Americans worked as commercial fishermen and ship/boat crewmen. (Fitzgerald)

Irony came fairly early. John Mercer of "Marlborough," though an early advocate of individual rights and guardian of George Mason (IV), future author of Virginia's Declaration of Rights, was also a slaveholder. Mercer's land-poor indebtedness stretched his resources and he increasingly turned to cheap "Negro slave" labor. Between 1731 and 1750, Mercer purchased eighty-nine "Negroes," most listed by name in his ledger. Forty-six died and twenty-five were born, leaving a net total of sixty-six slaves in 1750. There was no indication of Mercer's mistreatment, and his slaves did not revolt. His references to them by name, children's names, and birth dates, and journal notations of slave births suggest a paternalistic attitude. Motivated perhaps by self-interest, slave medical care was also reflected: "To Cash, pd Doctor Lynn for delivering Deborah." (Watkins)

Afro-Staffordians were enslaved on large and modest plantations such as William Fitzhugh's "Chatham" and the Washington home at "Ferry Farm." Other slaves worked on smaller farms as field workers or servants. In larger industrial and agricultural enterprises, slaves were either directly owned or were hired from their owners. In the 1770s the average landless laborer annually earned thirty pounds. Indentured servants (white or black) and slaves (all black) fell at the bottom of a colonial social order, dominated by propertied white men of the Anglican Church. Indentured servants could earn freedom or serve out their period of servitude and then move on to town trades or to the back–country frontier to live. African-American slaves and their owners were increasingly trapped in the slave system. Slaves, of course, were last to reap the benefits of expanding New World wealth— American Colonists enjoyed the highest per-capita income in the civilized world, though the wealth was disproportionately distributed (e.g., 10 percent of Southerners owned 75 percent of the region's wealth).

Again, Virginia's elites were guided by the English conception of "liberty." By 1776, the year of the Declaration of Independence, one in six Americans was black, and 99 percent of America's blacks were slaves, distributed mostly in the South but also heavily in New York and New Jersey. (Fleming; Fitzgerald)

Stafford's American Revolutionary Symbolism in White and Black

The Revolution brought the first substantial changes in Stafford's whites' and blacks' lives. James Hunter's ironworks, east of Falmouth, was Stafford's major industrial enterprise and one of Virginia's and America's early major industrial plants. In the Revolution, it produced weapons and implements for the Continental Army and Navy. The complex contained a blast furnace and forge; slitting, hammer, merchant, wire, plating, grist, saw, and steel mills; naileries and tanyards; carpenter, cooper, smith, and wheelwright shops; coal houses; stables; storage buildings; and quarters. Hunter and his ironworks were credited with significant contributions to the cause of American independence. (Lymans) Yet in 1783, Hunter paid taxes on some 260 slaves—the pragmatic Scotsman did everything possible to increase production for the Revolution, including using slave labor. (Eby) Thus, while Hunter's slaves ultimately helped win the war for independence, its victory eluded and excluded them for two more centuries.

Representative of Stafford's revolutionary symbolism was John De Baptist. A free black from the island of St. Kitts and nearby Spotsylvania County, he was one of as many as ten Afro-Virginians who served on the *Dragon*, launched October 1777 to patrol the Rappahannock and Chesapeake. From the late war years until his death in 1804, DeBaptist operated a Falmouth ferry. His later "Publick Claim" sought recompense for eight days of transporting French troops across the Rappahannock at Falmouth in May 1783. (Lymans)

Irony persisted. James Hunter, a slave owner, had sacrificed everything in the cause of independence. Never adequately compensated for his efforts, he died in weakened financial condition. Hunter's grave marker, either by design or accident, is a fence-enclosed tree. Free black DeBaptist, owner of considerable property when he died, was able to afford a finer tombstone. Regardless, they lie buried close to one another

Wall gun produced at Hunter's Iron Works. Hunter, an undoubted patriot and major contributor to the success of the American Revolution, was aided by 260 slaves.
(Mike and Marty Lyman and Springfield, MA, Armory)

Hunter (above) and DeBaptist (left) gravesites, Union Cemetery, Falmouth
(Jane M. Conner)

Stafford County, Virginia

Basil (or Bazil) Gordon
(Virginia Historical Society)

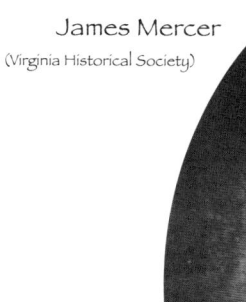

James Mercer
(Virginia Historical Society)

in Falmouth's Union Church Cemetery, where both have been honored by Revolutionary heritage groups. (Lymans; Fitzgerald)

Federal-era Staffordian Basil (or Bazil) Gordon exemplified financial and economic success in the newly independent country. Born in 1768, the Scotsman was one of America's earliest millionaires and "a merchant without peer." Gordon also was highly successful in acquiring real estate. Settling with his brother, Samuel Gordon, in 1783 Falmouth, he added shipping and warehousing to his lucrative businesses. Basil Gordon married Annie Campbell Knox. His Falmouth home on River Road still stands, as does one of his warehouses on Cambridge Street. (Eby)

James Mercer was born at "Marlborough" in Stafford in February 1735/1736. Schooled at home and the College of William and Mary, he was a captain in the French and Indian War, commanding at Winchester's Fort Loudoun. Mercer served in the House of Burgesses from 1762 to 1776 and was a member of the Virginia Conventions in 1774, 1775, and 1776. He was a member of the Committee of Public Safety. Although he was John Mercer's third son (George Mercer, the oldest, remained in England and John Fenton Mercer had been killed by Indians in 1756), James inherited his father's estate, "Marlborough." He served in the first Virginia Constitutional Convention (1776) and in the Continental Congress (1779 and 1780). From 1779 to 1789 he was a judge in the General Court of Virginia. Trustee and president of Fredericksburg Academy from 1786 to 1790, he was a judge in the first Virginia Court of Appeals from 1789 until his death in Richmond on October 31, 1793. Also a prominent Masonic leader, Mercer was buried in St. John's Church Cemetery in Richmond. (*Dictionary of the American Congress 1774–1961* [DAC]

Richard Brent, of Stafford's earliest settler family, was born about 1757 at "Richland" in Widewater. A prominent Federal-era political figure, his father, William Brent, had converted to the Anglican faith, but Richard's faith, if any, was unknown. An intellectual and orator, he inherited his father's King George property in 1782 and acquired land in Stafford and Prince William Counties, allowing him to represent both in the House of Delegates in 1788 (Stafford) and in 1793 and 1794 (Prince William), respectively. In 1795, Richard Brent defeated Federalist Richard Bland Lee for a seat in the U.S. House of Representatives. Representing the district including Fairfax, Loudoun and Prince William, Brent, a Jeffersonian Republican, opposed the Jay Treaty appropriation and a Federalist bill raising a provisional army during the diplomatic crisis with France. Brent, who felt those acts granted too much presidential power, also voted against the Alien and Sedition Acts in 1798. He either ran for a third term and was defeated or declined to run in 1799 but was a Jefferson presidential elector in 1800. Brent returned to the House of Delegates in 1800 and 1801. From 1803 to 1808 he managed his plantations—by 1810 he possessed sixty-five slaves. In 1808 he had been elected to the Virginia Senate from Fairfax and Prince William, and in 1809 the General Assembly elected him to the U.S. Senate. He assisted President Madison by helping persuade Gov. James Monroe to accept the position of Secretary of State. Brent voted in support of the Madison administration through the War of 1812, including military appropriations and national bank chartering. With the Senate evenly divided on war with Great Britain and knowing Brent would support the administration, the British ambassador conspired to get Brent drunk so that he could not participate in the vote. The trick failed: drunk or sober, Brent seldom missed a roll call. On 17 June 1812 he voted to declare war (passed 19–13). Brent died in office in Washington on December 30, 1814, shortly after (December 8) voting for the bank chartering bill. He was buried at "Richland." (DAC ; DVB [LV])

Slavery after the Revolution

When the first Federal Census took place in 1790, Stafford's population of 9,588 included 5,465 whites and 4,123 people of color. With the creation of the nation's capital in the District of Columbia, slaves and free blacks worked alongside white artisans on Stafford's Government Island, where they quarried and moved the Aquia sandstone needed for the White House, center section of the U.S. Capitol, and other buildings. America's two greatest symbols of freedom were thus ironically built with slave labor, white working-class men, and European immigrants.

Taxable property in 1812 Stafford included those owning more than sixteen slaves: John T. Brooke of "Mill Vale" (twenty); Daniel C. Brent of "Richland" (forty-seven); John Cooke of "Marlborough"/"West Farm" (fifty-three); Travers Daniel Sr. of "Crow's Nest" (nineteen); Travers Daniel Jr. (deceased—twenty-one); Moses Kendall (twenty-three); John Moncure of "Somerset" (sixteen); Mrs. Mary Seddon of "Snowden" (nineteen); and Bailey Washington of "Tusculum" (nineteen). Owners of ten to fifteen slaves included the Alexander, Downman, Ficklen, Fitzhugh, Mountjoy, Morton, Mason, Peyton, Reddish, Suttle, Stern, Voss, and Waller families. A total of 1,121 slaves netted $493.24 in tax revenues to Stafford County. (Eby)

Stafford's large slave population, especially large numbers of slaves working in the stone quarries and larger plantations, caused local concerns. Staffordians recalled an 1805 slave rebellion here. In January, slaves of William Fitzhugh refused to return to work after Christmas holiday. They overpowered an overseer and severely whipped him; he escaped (aided by a slave) and returned with help to suppress the rebellion. One slave leader was killed while trying to escape; another fell through the ice and drowned in the Rappahannock. Other slaves involved in the revolt were imprisoned. (Fitzgerald)

By 1810 Stafford County had a black population of about 4,200 slaves and 350 free blacks compared with 5,400 whites. In purely financial terms, the slaves were valuable commodities, and constituted most of the tangible wealth in agrarian, "land-poor" Stafford. During the 1800s, slaves could generally be sold for ready money, so they were valued as investments as well as workers.

Although the famous 1831 Nat Turner slave rebellion took place in Southampton County 120 miles south of Stafford, rumors of "servile insurrection" terrorized the state and county thereafter. Virginia laws changed so that Afro-Virginians, whether slave or free, were treated more repressively.

A Staffordian wrote about slave prices in 1839:

"Negroes are selling higher at this time than I have ever seen them. Best man ($)1450 to 1550. Best field Girls ($)1300 to 1350." (Eby; Fitzgerald; Barbara Kirby—Kirby)

Peter Vivian Daniel (Virginia Historical Society)

Antebellum Period

Stage coaches were replaced by boat transportation between Washington and Aquia Creek, and work began on the railroad link from Richmond (see Chapter 10). Staffordians, white and black alike, faced another new world, this one in their own back yard.

Peter Vivian Daniel, Stafford's only U.S. Supreme Court justice, was born at "Crow's Nest" in April 1784. Daniel—a Staffordian of independent mind regardless of consequences or ramifications—was "the personification of Jeffersonian Republicanism, agrarianism, and strict constructionism in a rapidly changing antebellum America." Most of his eighteen years on the Court saw him dissenting from majority opinions. Daniel had attended the College of New Jersey (now Princeton University) and read law in Richmond with Edmund Randolph (marrying Lucy Randolph). Of the planter class, Daniel addressed matters of honor with duels, including an 1808 affair of honor with Capt. John Seddon of Stafford. Seddon "received his antagonist's ball in the right side, languished till about 8 o'clock on Monday morning, and died." Daniel, admitted to the bar in 1808, was elected in 1809 to the House of Delegates representing Stafford. Three years later he was elevated to the Privy Council, where he served for twenty-three years, mostly as lieutenant governor. While practicing in Richmond, Daniel became a Jacksonian Democrat. In 1836 Andrew Jackson appointed him to the U.S. District Court for Eastern Virginia. In 1841 Daniel's friend, President Martin Van Buren, appointed him to the U.S. Supreme Court. Although Whig senators opposed him, he was confirmed March 2–3, 1841:

...selected more for his political loyalty than his legal ability or judicial stature, Daniel joined the Court in December 1841 unswervingly opposed to banks, corporations, and economic consolidation of any sort, an extreme defender of states' rights, limited government, and the institution of slavery, and consumed with a hatred for anything northern.

Daniel wrote the majority opinion in *West River Bridge v. Dix* (1849) and joined the majority in the Dred Scott decision (1857) on the Fugitive Slave Act. "Highly principled but markedly out of step with the legal and constitutional developments of his day, Daniel's carefully articulated but extreme opinions left little mark on constitutional law." He died in May 1860 and was interred in Richmond's Hollywood Cemetery, thus spared our greatest national trial and the destruction of his native county. (E. Lee Shepard; Eby)

Moncure Daniel Conway, a Staffordian from a slaveholding family, emerged in the antebellum period as one of the county's most remarkable historic figures. Naturally, most of his relatives supported the South's "peculiar institution," but Conway, educated in Pennsylvania's Dickinson College and Boston's Harvard Divinity School, was exposed to a wider world. His abolitionism divided his family, church and community, but he held strongly to his views. Conway recognized antebellum Virginia's white oligarchy was tied to established social strata: the poorest groups were immigrant yeomen, poor mountain whites, and rural paupers. This last group, with no sympathy for slaves, were slave catchers and overseers whom Conway caustically painted as "serfs of the soil...employed in doing nothing " except producing "innumerable brats and squalid children."

Another historian holds they were no more than white slaves. Conway characterized them as bumpkin voters, duped into putting rich, smooth-talking slaveholders into office only to be ignored till the next election. Conway also disclosed Falmouth's infamous Capt. Pickett, slave whipper of choice. Masters, unwilling or unable to beat their slaves, engaged Pickett's services and vilified Conway:

Moncure Daniel Conway (Norman and Lenetta Schools)

(his) family disowned him during the Civil War, congregations sent him packing for his feverish anti-slavery sermons, and he traveled constantly, following causes to far-flung cities, from Boston to Cincinnati to Paris. By the end of his life, in 1907, he had stood up for women's rights, world peace, and other humanitarian causes. But he is best remembered for his fierce attacks on slavery. It was a Southern institution he learned from the inside out—in his own family home in southern Stafford County. (Moncure Daniel Conway—M. D. Conway; Ervin L. Jordan Jr.—Jordan; and Judith H. Jones, FLS—J. H. Jones/FLS)

Antebellum-Period Slavery

Sully Watson, originally a Moncure family slave at "Windsor Forest" in northern Stafford, was described as light-skinned with green or blue eyes. Born there in 1780, Watson managed to buy his freedom and lived as a free man in Stafford until 1834, when he moved to Ohio and Wisconsin. Working as a whitewasher and bricklayer, Watson purchased property in Milwaukee. When he died in 1862 at the age of eighty-two, he left an estate worth $5,000. His oldest son, William Watson, was subsequently a leader in Milwaukee's black community, and his great-granddaughter, Mabel Raimey, was Wisconsin's first black female attorney. (Eby)

By 1850, reflecting difficult economic times, Stafford's population had decreased to 3,360 slaves, 165 free blacks and 4,418 whites. Concerns over runaway slaves became a priority. Some 280,000 Virginia slaves were sold to the lower South between 1830 and 1860. (Jordan)

A nationally known test case of the 1850 Fugitive Slave Law involved Stafford slave Anthony Burns, who escaped by ship in February 1854, and was arrested in Boston on May 24, 1854. Born on Stafford's Suttle estate in 1834 (or 1829), "Tony" Burns had defied local laws by learning (assisted by local white children) to read and write. His master, Charles F. Suttle, had trusted Burns, thus facilitating his escape from Richmond. Stowing away on a north-bound ship, he escaped to Boston, where slavery had been abolished, but adherence to the Fugitive Slave Act mandated runaway slaves could be recaptured and returned. This law faced its first challenge when Boston police captured Burns. Abolitionists met at Faneuil Hall and, led by a minister, Thomas Wentworth Higginson, "protested" Burns' incarceration, accidentally killing a law officer. At trial (Burns' attorney was Richard Henry Dana Jr.), it was decided he would be returned to Virginia. Some 2,000 guards escorted Burns to a waiting ship, and 50,000 outraged Bostonians rallied in the streets. After returning to slavery, Burns was sold to a North Carolina slave dealer. A group of Bostonians, prominently abolitionist Leonard A. Grimes, raised $676 of the $1,300 "asking

Anthony Burns (Library of Congress)

price" for Burns. Bank cashier Charles C. Barry loaned Grimes the remainder of the money. Other accounts say he was purchased by a black church, but Barry's two checks, dated February 22, 1855, are in the Massachusetts Historical Society. Anthony Burns was "resold" to Boston and set free. After attending Oberlin College, he became a minister in St. Catherines, Ontario, Canada. Burns died in 1862 and was buried there. (M. D. Conway; Massachusetts Historical Society; Lee Woolf, FLS—L. Woolf/FLS.)

The Burns Case solidified many abolitionist beliefs, including Moncure Daniel Conway's. Conway had known Burns in Stafford and his views soon caused him to leave to become a leading national spokesman for emancipation. Conway's writings shed unique light on slavery and its harmful effects on blacks and whites alike. Obviously, he had learned these things from his Stafford experiences. Conway's insider knowledge of the slaveholder society was devastating as he could not easily be dismissed by Southerners. Threatened by "tar and feathers" and a lynching on brief trips home, he was unmolested when he returned with Union troops to free his family slaves. A friend of Ralph Waldo Emerson and Walt Whitman and a noted author (more than seventy works), he had discussions with President Lincoln. Ironically, recognition of his picture by Federal troops saved his Falmouth home (Chapter 4). (M. D. Conway)

Hannah Coalter of "Chatham"
(National Park Service)

In October 1856, John W. D. Ford was cited by the sheriff of Stafford County for "permitting slaves under his control to go at large."
(Nancy Southworth)

Slavery, which irrevocably divided some Stafford families and churches, also brought out humane acts by others. In 1857 Mrs. Hannah Coalter of "Chatham" attempted in her will to free ninety-two of her slaves. Their manumission was to take place in January 1858 but was blocked successfully in the Virginia courts by J. Horace Lacy, a Coalter relation who bought the plantation.

Right, J. Horace Lacy of "Chatham," one of Stafford's largest slaveholders (National Park Service)

Alexander Gardner photograph of "Lacy House" ("Chatham"), December 1862 (Library of Congress)

P. M. TABB & SON,
Negro Hirers and General Agents.

The subscribers have been engaged for the last thirty years in

HIRING OUT NEGROES, RENTING OUT HOUSES
AND THE COLLECTION OF CLAIMS OF EVERY DESCRIPTION,

And can, with confidence, offer their services to all persons having business in their line. They also attend to the

SALES OF REAL ESTATE AND NEGROES,

Publicly and privately, and upon sales made through their agency, whether public or private, only one commission will be charged, that being the usual commission charged by all of the auctioneers.

Their office rooms being large, negroes sent to them for hire will not suffer by exposure to the weather, as many do, during the hiring season, who are sent to our city for hire, and who are not thus provided with good and sufficient shelter. They have also provided ample accommodations for negroes at night, until they are hired out.

In cases of sickness, they see that every attention is paid, employing their own family physician, except when some other is preferred by the owner.

For their responsibility, and for the manner and promptness with which they attend to business entrusted to them, they refer to the citizens of Richmond generally, but more particularly to the following gentlemen, who are now amongst the number of their patrons:

Judge George H. Lee, Court of Appeals.
Judge John Robertson, Richmond.
Judge John A. Meredith, "
Joseph Mayo, Mayor, "
Hon. John B. Tucker, "
Hon. P. H. Aylett, "
Col. John Rutherford, "
Col. Samuel T. Bayly, "
John M. Patton, Jr. Esq. "
Nathaniel H. Tyler, Esq. "
B. R. Wellford, Esq. "
Dr. L. S. Joynes, "
Drs. R. H. and R. G. Cabell, "
R. T. Daniel, Esq. "
Hon. Wilson Lee, Portsmouth.
Wm. H. Wilson, Esq. "

Rev. Wm. Norwood, Alexandria.
Gen. Wm. B. Taliaferro, Gloucester County.
W. T. Taliaferro, Esq. "
Dr. H. W. Tabb, Matthews "
Messrs. Ailworth & Allen, Accomac "
Thomas Parramore, Esq. "
Dr. George T. Yerby, Northampton "
H. S. Neale, Esq. "
W. P. Conway, Esq. Fredericksburg.
John C. Moncure, Esq. "
Wm. K. Gordon, Esq. "
John M. Conway, Esq. Stafford County.
Henry R. Conway, Esq. "
John Moncure, Esq. "
John C. Rutherford, Esq. Goochland County.

OFFICE IN THE OLD POST OFFICE, UNDER EXCHANGE HOTEL,
RICHMOND, VA.

OCTOBER 1860.
P. M. TABB, Sen'r.
JOHN P. TABB.

"Hiring Out Negroes" was a profitable enterprise in 1860 Richmond. A number of Stafford residents and relatives were listed among this firm's patrons. (Nancy Southworth)

Anna Maria Sarah Goldsborough Fitzhugh as a young woman (Virginia Historical Society)

John Brown's 1859 Harpers Ferry raid renewed old fears of slave insurrection, and Virginia militia companies were rapidly formed. Prewar business as usual continued in Stafford, where slaves now worked as domestic and plantation/farm workers; Captain Pickett continued to whip errant slaves; and the "underground railway" was run by whites and free blacks, reportedly including the DeBaptist, or now DeBaptiste, family.

A remarkable Stafford figure during and after the Civil War was Mrs. William Henry Fitzhugh, Anna Maria Sarah Goldsborough Fitzhugh. A daughter of Maryland Gov. Charles Goldsborough, she was Fitzhugh's wife (1814) and widow (1830). Childless, Anna Maria took an active interest in supporting the Lee family and other relatives and friends. Robert E. Lee respected her opinions: from at least the 1840s, he wrote to her on serious subjects. During the Civil War, she managed her vast holdings from "Ravensworth" in Fairfax, allowing the family of Robert E. Lee to "refugee" there from Alexandria. She also allowed the Whitings to occupy her Stafford property, "Richland," during the war. After the war, she made "Richland" available to the family of Sydney Smith Lee. Robert Carter Lee described her:

> ...a very smart woman, Anna Maria Sarah Goldsborough Fitzhugh had never had much faith in Confederate currency. Before the war began she transferred most of her considerable funds to Baltimore banks. Unlike so many Southerners who lost their property when they were unable to pay taxes on it, she had retained all of hers, including Richland. When she insisted that we move to that plantation forty miles south of Washington in Stafford County, we gladly accepted. (Ardyce Kinsley—Kinsley)

Particularly solicitous of Gen. Fitzhugh Lee, her godson and namesake, she bequeathed "Richland" to him when she died in April 1874. Anna Maria was buried at "Ravensworth," but in 1957 her remains were moved to Fairfax County's Pohick Church.

Anna Maria Sarah Goldsborough Fitzhugh shortly before her death
(Virginia Historical Society)

Civil War and Reconstruction for Afro-Staffordians

Although no major battles had taken place in Stafford, the area suffered terribly from Confederate occupation in 1861–1862 and from the Union's 1862–1863 winter occupation by some 150,000 troops. The latter occupation, from Hartwood to the King George boundary, resulted in further changes for Stafford's white and black populations. Those slaves who wished could free themselves and move north to greater safety. In spring 1862, Moncure Conway returned and removed thirty-one of his family's slaves to freedom in Yellow Springs, Ohio, where descendants live today. (Fitzgerald; J. H. Jones/FLS)

A Stafford slave named "Dabney" provided detailed information on Confederate forces across the river and acted as a guide for Union troops. One of Dabney's Fredericksburg agents reportedly signaled unit dispositions and strengths using an ingenious system of coded clothing on clotheslines. As Stafford contained the main grouping of the Army of the Potomac, it soon became a rallying place for runaway slaves. Some were shepherded north, and some took paying jobs serving Union officers and units. Others found their way into Union ranks, as did approximately 180,000 other black soldiers. (Fitzgerald)

When hostilities ceased, many of Stafford's African Americans went north to Washington, D.C., and beyond. Seeking better job opportunities and a better life, this black exodus from Stafford has been traced to communities along what is now U.S. Route 1 in Maryland, Pennsylvania, and farther north. Some of these emigrants would later return to Stafford, either permanently or to visit families. Stafford's postwar black population decreased by 60 percent as they "voted with their feet" on the Old South. Those who stayed began new lives, schools and churches in an atmosphere of emancipation but with neither legal nor social equality. Working in many of the same occupations as before and during the war, they now experienced not only greater freedom but also uncertainty. With some opportunity to acquire wealth and property through their efforts, they began to gain their own farms and businesses. Some worked full or part time for their old owners. Well-meaning but heavy-handed actions by the Freedman's

Dabney by Edwin Forbes
(Edwin Forbes/William Forrest Dawson)

Bureau and harsh Federal Reconstruction policies caused a white Southern backlash, and the need for national reconciliation between 1880 and 1920 came at the direct expense of black progress. Virginia's Readjuster Party allied black Republicans, poor mountain whites, and smaller factions under former Confederate general and railroad magnate, William Mahone. This coalition advanced black voting rights to some extent and was merged into the Virginia Republican Party at the end of the nineteenth century. Stafford, judging by the gubernatorial election of 1889, did not support the Readjusters and "Mahoneism." To most Virginians of that time, the Republican Party was a reminder of the war and Lincoln, and the re-creation of the Democratic Party under Thomas Staples Martin and later Harry F. Byrd was assured. This coincided with repression of black suffrage and civil rights. (Thomas Morris—Morris; David W. Blight)

A letter from the "Virginia Manual Labor School of the Negro Reformatory Association of Virginia" to the clerk of Stafford County addressing the case of "the boy, Clarence Parker" and his admission to the school
(Barbara Kirby)

Right, Staffordian "Uncle Jim" Rowser of Falmouth, by Gari Melchers, 1918
(Belmont/Mary Washington College)

Stafford's nascent black community was strengthened by the county's many black churches. Initially meeting in homes and "brush arbors," churches raised funds and buildings. Early black Baptist churches included Mount Olive, Bethlehem Primitive, Oak Grove, Shiloh, Mount Hope, Little Shiloh, Little Forest, Macedonia, Locust Grove, Mount Zion, Howard Grove, and Union Belle. Schools also began in the 1870s in the Aquia and Rock Hill districts. By 1883 there were eight one-room Stafford schools for African Americans. Early teachers included Dishmans and Cunninghams, Annie Morton, Albert Ray, Jason Grant, Addie Poole, and Henry Harrison Poole.

The Twentieth Century Begins in Black and White

Like Virginia as a whole, turn-of-the-(twentieth)-century Stafford continued post-Reconstruction era disenfranchisement of black voters. The Virginia Constitutional Convention of 1901–02 recorded:

Mr. (Carter) Glass:...the article of suffrage which the Convention will to-day adopt does not necessarily deprive a single white man of the ballot, but will inevitably cut from the existing electorate four-fifths of the negro voters. (Applause)...

Mr. Pedigo: Will it not be done by fraud and discrimination?

Mr. Glass: By fraud, no; by discrimination, yes... Discrimination! Why, that is precisely what we propose; that, exactly, is what this Constitution was elected for—to discriminate to the very extremity of permissible action under the limitations of the Federal Constitution, with a view to the elimination of every negro voter who can be gotten rid of, legally, without materially impairing the numerical strength of the white electorate.
(Morris and A. E. Dick Howard)

Gari Melchers, a self-portrait, 1896
(Belmont/Mary Washington College)

Under the 1902 Constitution and similar enactments, advances for Afro-Virginians marked time through periods of segregation and white "massive resistance" until the early 1960s (six to ten years after the *Brown v. Topeka* Supreme Court decision), when schools and public accommodations were slowly opened to all. These events took place during the Civil War centennial, at last bringing to life Lincoln's Gettysburg promises of government of and by the people, and "a new birth of freedom." Still operating under the flawed "separate-but-equal" mandate of *Plessy v. Ferguson*, H. H. Poole became the supervisor of black schools in Stafford and King George, serving from 1930 to 1953. Black students in high school commuted or boarded at the Fredericksburg Normal and Industrial Institute in Mayfield (Fredericksburg) after the establishment of that school in 1905. The pattern persisted long afterward in which area black students were required to commute long hours from home to a segregated school. This was part of a general pattern of living requiring long travel to find stores that treated blacks with fairness and respect. Life at this survival/subsistence level was the common black experience in twentieth-century Stafford and other rural Virginia counties. (Frank White Jr.—White Jr.)

Gari Melchers (1860–1932), photographed about 1930
(Belmont/Mary Washington College)

Other black elementary schools operating during the 1930s, '40s and '50s were located in White Oak, Widewater, Brooke, Falmouth, Leeland, Hartwood, Concord, and Berea. Those students attending high school were bused to Walker-Grant in Fredericksburg. (White Jr.)

Two Stafford artists, one white and one black, preserved African-American life in Stafford during the 1920s–1930s: Gari Melchers of "Belmont" (whose Falmouth home included a studio, now a museum) painted local black citizens; and Palmer C. Hayden (Peyton Cole Hedgeman) preserved his Widewater roots, promoting black culture in his work. (See below.)

Stafford County, Virginia

Staffordians Who Made Their Marks Elsewhere

John Francis Mercer was born at "Marlborough" in May 1759. Educated at home and at the College of William and Mary (he graduated in 1775), Mercer practiced law in Williamsburg. In the Revolution he was a lieutenant in the 3rd Virginia Regiment, probably fought at Harlem Heights, and was wounded at Brandywine. In 1777 he was promoted to captain, was at Valley Forge, and (1778–1779) was an aide-de-camp to Gen. Charles Lee. After briefly returning to "Marlborough," Mercer raised and equipped a cavalry troop at his own expense. They joined Gen. Robert Lawson's brigade and fought at Guilford Courthouse before joining Lafayette. At some point, Mercer was promoted to lieutenant colonel and fought his final battles at Greenspring and Gloucester Point in 1781. A Virginia delegate to the Continental Congress from 1782 to 1785, Mercer moved to Anne Arundel County, Maryland, and represented Maryland at the Annapolis Convention of 1787 and Maryland Constitutional Ratification Convention in 1788. Mercer served in the state legislature in 1788, 1789, 1791, and 1792. He was elected as a Democrat to the Second U.S. Congress (replacing William Pinckney) and was reelected for the Third Congress (1792–1794). In 1800 and from 1803 to 1806 Mercer served again in the Maryland Legislature. He was Governor of Maryland from 1801 to 1803.

Mercer retired to his home, "Cedar Park," in West River, Maryland. He died in Philadelphia on August 30, 1821, and was buried in St. Peter's Church there. His remains were later returned to "Cedar Park." (DAC; RP)

The *Foundation Stones* add John Francis Mercer had married Sophia Sprigg of Maryland in 1785, then moved to Anne Arundel County and "Cedar Park." Like his cousin, George Mason (IV), he was one of sixteen delegates who refused to sign the U.S. Constitution. James Madison wrote of him, "Mr. Mercer expressed his dislike of the whole plan, and his opinion is that it never could succeed." Indeed, he had attended none of the June or July sessions in Philadelphia and was present only from August 6 to 17, 1787. Because the document centralized government power, John Francis Mercer and Luther Martin, both Maryland anti-Federalists and anti-nationalists, joined Mason in strongly opposing ratification in their states. Their efforts failed. Ironically, Mercer would swear allegiance in Congress to that Constitution and ally with Federalists opposing war with England during Jefferson's administration (DAC; Barbara Pratt Willis—Willis)

Stevens Thomson Mason, born at "Chappawamsic," Stafford County, on December 29, 1760, was educated at home and William and Mary. He later studied law and practiced in Dumfries. Mason

John Francis Mercer (Virginia Historical Society)

served in the Revolution as an aide-de-camp to George Washington at Yorktown. After the war, he served in the Virginia House of Delegates in 1783 and 1794 and in the Virginia Senate (1787–1790). At some point, a brigadier general in the Virginia Militia, Mason served in the Virginia Constitutional Convention of 1788. When James Monroe resigned, Mason was elected as a Democrat to fill the vacancy in the U.S. Senate. Reelected in 1797 and 1803, he served in the Senate from 1794 until his death in Philadelphia on May 10, 1803. He was buried at "Raspberry Plain" in Loudoun. His son, Armistead Thomson Mason, also a U.S. Senator (1816–1817), was killed in a duel with his brother-in-law, John Mason McCarty, at Bladensburg, Maryland, in 1819. (DAC)

John Moncure Daniel was born in Stafford's "Crow's Nest" in 1825. His maternal grandfather was Thomas Stone, a Maryland signer of the Declaration of Independence, and his uncle was Justice Peter Vivian Daniel of the U.S. Supreme Court (Stone's daughters, Margaret and Mildred, married Stafford Daniel brothers and were thus related to Moncures, Ashbys, Tolsons, Conways, Nelsons, and Wallaces. Stafford's nineteenth-century notable Dr. Hawkins Stone (namesake of the road and commercial complex), was also a Thomas Stone descendant. In his early twenties, John Moncure Daniel became editor in chief and later owner of the *Richmond Examiner*. A staunch supporter of Democrats and fierce assailant of Whigs, Daniel became known for his acerbic wit and caustic style and as a literary supporter of Edgar Allan Poe. Duels, an occupational hazard for Southern editors, involved Daniel at least nine times. In 1852 his paper strongly supported the presidential candidacy of Franklin Pierce, for which Daniel was appointed charge d'affaires to the Kingdom of Sardinia. Old enemies in America and Daniel's acid tongue and pen soon explosively combined: his diplomatic service ruptured when a private letter—stating Sardinian women were uglier, the men had fewer ideas than in America, and that the whole place stank of garlic—was published in Richmond, Boston, New York, and Turin. Daniel's diplomatic effectiveness thus impaired, he did manage to hang on until Lincoln's election and South Carolina's secession. He returned to the *Examiner*, urging Virginia's prompt secession and dubbing Lincoln an "Orang-Outang," but Daniel soon became a Confederate government critic. He did foresee the brutality to come and recommended immediate conscription of every available Southern white man. To his credit, unlike many contemporaries, Daniel joined the Army on General Floyd's staff in western Virginia. Later, he served on A. P. Hill's staff in the

John Moncure Daniel (Virginia Historical Society)

Seven Days' battles (June 25–July 1, 1862) and was wounded by a musket round. Medically discharged with his "red badge of courage," he resumed editorial duties. Defying government wishes, Daniel reported Richmond's April 1863 bread riot (blaming the rioters). Daniel and his editor, E. A. Pollard, opposed President Jefferson Davis while continuing to criticize everything Lincoln did or said—even the Gettysburg Address. His attacks on Davis brought yet another duel, this time with Confederate treasurer E. C. Elmore. Daniel, forced to fire left-handed due to his war wound, missed and Elmore hit him in the leg. Tuberculosis compounded his health problems, but Daniel managed to oppose Confederate black soldier conscription in November 1864. At the beginning of 1865, while the Confederate Congress approved black conscription, Daniel's thoughts turned to Stafford, where he dreamt of rebuilding "Crow's Nest." He also advocated Robert E. Lee's command of all Confederate forces—though he had earlier criticized him as "Evacuating Lee." Believing rumors of a Southern victory, Daniel died on March 30, 1865. (Peter Bridges, *Pen of Fire*; L. Woolf/FLS; Kirby)

John Conway Moncure
(Virginia Military Institute Archives)

John Conway Moncure, born in Stafford in January 1827, matriculated into VMI from Falmouth and rose to cadet first captain, the highest-ranking cadet (the next Staffordian to earn that rank was Matthew S. Thompson in the VMI Class of 2002). After graduating (1847), Moncure became a lawyer and married Fannie Dulany Tomlin (1850); they had eight children. From 1851 to 1860 he was Stafford's commonwealth's attorney, warden of Aquia Church, and a member of the VMI Board of Visitors (the first from Stafford). After brief war service as an enlisted cavalryman, Moncure was commissioned a captain. As a captain and major, he served on the staff of Maj. Gen. Camille Armand Jules Marie Prince de Polignac, who commanded a brigade and a division in the West. They participated in battle at Mansfield, Sabine Crossroads and Pleasant Hill (April 1864); and the Red River Campaign before being sent to France (March 17, 1865) to seek intervention by Napoleon III (they arrived too late). After the war, Moncure practiced law in Shreveport, Louisiana (1865–1880). He remained in Louisiana, where he was elected state treasurer in 1874 (unable to serve due to Reconstruction). Thrice elected a member of the Louisiana Legislature (twice elected speaker), Moncure also served as a judge in the Superior Court of Louisiana and the Louisiana Circuit Court of Appeals. Judge Moncure, the oldest of fourteen children, showed concern for siblings and families even at a distance of 2,000 miles. He purchased a portion of Stafford's "Glencairne" on which he built a modest home called "Mont Anna," giving it to his sister's (Anna Jane) husband's parents, the Hulls. Moncure died tragically in Shreveport in December 1916 as a result of gas stove burns. Despite his advanced age of eighty-nine, Moncure reputedly was in good health (he hadn't retired until 1914) and was noted for his bearing. After his death, Moncure's court was adjourned in his honor. (VMI Archives)

James Vass Brooke, born in Falmouth on October 10, 1824, was the son of merchant William Brooke and Scottish native Jane Morrison Brooke. Named for his mother's half-brother, Falmouth merchant James Vass, first owner of "Moncure Conway House," Brooke's education was in private schools, and in 1841 he read law with Stafford's R. C. L. Moncure while keeping accounts for Fredericksburg merchants. The following year he moved to Warrenton, where he read law with Samuel Chilton. Admitted to the bar in 1843, Brooke began a fifty-five-year legal career and a political career that included city offices and mayor of Warrenton, and representative of Fauquier County in the Virginia Secession Convention. In the war, he commanded an artillery battery (Company "A"[1]) in the 12th Virginia Light Artillery Battalion in the lower Shenandoah Valley, and despite a disabling ankle injury, fought through the battles of Chancellorsville (May 1863) and Gettysburg (July 1863). Medically discharged, he went home and was elected to three wartime sessions of the House of Delegates. After the war, he built a substantial legal practice and served again in the House of Delegates and in the Virginia Senate. Brooke died on October 9, 1898. (DVB [LV])

James Vass Brooke (Virginia Historical Society)

Samuel Selden Brooke was born at "Mill Vale" in Brooke on November 10, 1841. Educated in Washington, D.C., and Ashland, Brooke entered VMI with the Class of 1861, leaving after one year. When the war began, he was a student at the University of Virginia. On April 21, 1861, he enlisted in "The Stafford Guards," later Company "I," 30th Virginia Infantry. On 12 May 1861, Brooke was commissioned as "Second Lieutenant of Light Infantry in the 45th Regiment of the 5th Brigade and Second Division of the Virginia Militia" (The 45th remained a Stafford County militia regiment under Lt. Col. J. M. Holmes.) His company transferred to the 47th Virginia Infantry as Company "I"(3) in September 1861. Assigned to the Department of Fredericksburg on picket and defensive duties in French's Brigade in the Aquia District, Brooke was reelected in April 1862 and present for duty through February 1862. Despite sick leaves in March, May through June, and September through October 1862, Brooke fought in the Seven Days' battles and 2nd Manassas. He probably

Samuel Selden Brooke (Virginia Military Institute Archives)

Kate Waller Barrett, about 1876
(Mary Cary Kendall)

"Clifton" (Mary Cary Kendall)

missed the 1862 Maryland Campaign but may have returned for Fredericksburg and Chancellorsville. He probably fought at Gettysburg. In August 1863 in camp near Orange Courthouse, Brooke wrote to his sister:

> We heard yesterday that the Yankees had returned to the other side of the Rappahanock. What their next move will be I don't know. Some seem to think that they will go to the Peninsulas or somewhere on the southside of the James River but I do not think so. I think they will always keep an army between us & Washington & their army is now to weak to be divided…

Brooke fought in the Bristow and Mine Run Campaigns, followed by the Overland Campaign (May 1864) and 2nd Cold Harbor. His regiment served in the Petersburg Siege, but in November 1864 Brooke was detailed to Camp Lee, Richmond, on recruiting duty. Returning to the 47th by December 1864, he fought his final battle at Sayler's Creek (April 6, 1865), surrendering at Appomattox. Brooke was paroled on April 30 at Ashland and took the amnesty oath at the provost marshal's office in Fredericksburg on June 8, 1865. Returning home, he attempted to build a lumber business, but it failed and he became a Stafford farmer. In April 1872 Brooke married Betty (also Bettie) Lewis Young of Fredericksburg; they had four children. (VMI Archives)

Unsuccessful at farming, Brooke studied law in Fredericksburg, practicing and editing the *Fredericksburg News* and *Virginia Star* (ca. 1881–1882). After a trip to South America, he moved to newly chartered Roanoke in 1882. He formed the Leader Printing Company, and after September 1882 reported, edited and published the *Roanoke Leader*, an important documentary source for city history. In fall 1886 Brooke was appointed the clerk of County Court (later the City Court and the Corporation Court) and served for the next thirty-one years. He also organized the Roanoke Light Infantry in 1889 and served as captain. Later a lieutenant colonel in the Virginia National Guard, Brooke was a leading citizen of Roanoke, president of the Board of Trade (Chamber of Commerce) and a vestryman in St. John's Episcopal Church. He died at home in January 1918 and was buried in the old City Cemetery. (VMI Archives)

The Brookes made something of a family tradition putting "Mill Vale" into debt. His grandfather, John Taliaferro Brooke, had auctioned it off in 1825, and his father, Samuel Selden Brooke Sr., raised $3,147.16 to buy it back. He, too, struggled to keep the place, and when he died in 1870, Samuel Selden Brooke Jr. and sister, Louisa, inherited "Mill Vale" and its debts; they traded parcels in 1871 and Samuel ended up with the house. (Eby)

Dr. Kate Waller Barrett was born at "Clifton" in Widewater on January 24, 1857/1858. Katherine Harwood Waller's family engaged in farming and fishing. At age nineteen, she married Robert Barrett, rector of Aquia Church. A few years later they moved to Richmond, where her husband's church was located in a poor section. There Kate was exposed to the worst of urban society. A parent herself—she raised six children—she found time to take nursing classes and developed an interest in medicine. She also developed a social reform perspective from interacting with young mothers of similar age who lacked her opportunities and family support. While living in Georgia in the 1890s, Barrett earned a medical degree. She soon opened a home for unwed mothers, an unpopular but vitally needed social remedy, and later became general superintendent of the National Florence Crittenden Mission. Focusing on unwed mothers, abused women and family services, the Mission established seventy-eight homes in the United States and abroad.

The Barrett family, 1896. Shortly after the death of Rev. Robert South Barrett, Kate Waller Barrett and her children were photographed together. (Mary Cary Kendall)

At the end of the First World War, she was one of ten women appointed by President Woodrow Wilson to attend the Versailles Conference, making her the first woman to cross the Atlantic in a battleship. In 1924 at about age sixty-seven, she attended the Democratic National Convention in New York to second a "favorite son" presidential nomination of Carter Glass:

Dr. Kate Waller Barrett, 1920s (Mary Cary Kendall)

…when it came time for her to address the convention near the end of a tiring afternoon, she cast aside her notes and, according to one account, "poured out ideas and her message in a brief, spirited and extemporaneous speech which obviously came direct from the heart"…Her remarks "roused the jaded delegates like an electric current," according to the account, And when she finished, "they rose in a great ovation, forcing her to return and bow her acknowledgments again and again." The moment was so powerful, in fact, that a delegate from New Jersey stepped to the microphone and in a spontaneous gesture nominated the speaker—Dr. Kate Waller Barrett of Stafford County—for the office of vice president.

Barrett's life and career, by any measure, had been remarkable. In addition to her Crittenden Mission work, she became a tireless worker for women's and children's causes: charter member of the League of Women Voters; four-time president of the National Council of Women; and chairwoman of the National Congress

Dr. Kate Waller Barrett's grave, Aquia Episcopal Churchyard (Lee Woolf/Free Lance-Star)

of Mothers and Parent-Teachers Associations. A supporter of America's servicemen and veterans, in 1922 she was the president of the American Legion Auxiliary, which she had helped create. The first woman member of the board of visitors of the College of William and Mary, she was also deeply concerned with environmental issues, history and preservation. Barrett helped restore the Custis-Lee Mansion and establish Shenandoah National Park. She was also state regent for the Virginia Daughters of the American Revolution. Dr. Kate Waller Barrett died on February 23, 1925, at sixty-eight years of age. The first woman in Virginia history for whom the flags of the state were ordered to half-staff was buried in Stafford's Aquia Church Cemetery. In 2003 Dr. Kate Waller Barrett Elementary opened in her native Stafford—the first Stafford historical figure to be so honored. She was previously honored with a building at the College of William Mary, a library branch in Alexandria, and an elementary school in Arlington. (L. Woolf/FLS; DVB [LV])

Born Peyton Cole Hedgeman on January 15, 1890, in Stafford's Widewater section, Palmer C. Hayden's father, James, was a professional hunter and guide there. His family was active in Oak Grove Baptist Church, and he and his sisters attended the segregated schools of his day. Artistically gifted by age four, inspired by his older brother and encouraged by his mother, Hayden moved north to Washington, D.C., in 1906. Working as a circus roustabout, he painted pictures of the performers. Hoping to study art, but with little opportunity and impoverished, he joined the U.S. Army in 1912. Hayden served with the famed "Buffalo Soldiers" on duty with the 24th U.S. Infantry in the Philippines, and with the 10th U.S. Cavalry at West Point after 1916. He studied art in New York by correspondence, and after 1916, full time. From 1920 to 1924 he worked as a letter carrier and maintenance man. Hayden, a member of the famed "Harlem Renaissance," achieved fame as he depicted other blacks as builders of America. Acquiring financial resources through painting sales, he studied in the United States and Europe and led an eventful life. His works have a primitive or folk quality mixed with rich expressions of traditional values and feelings of community. A few of his paintings, such as a moving depiction of a Widewater baptism, portray Stafford themes. Most, however, portray urban life in Harlem. Most of Hayden's paintings are in the collection of the Museum of African-American Art, Los Angeles. They are among the first in America to portray black historical and cultural themes. Dr. Allan M. Gordon of the museum adds:

Palmer C. Hayden (Peyton Cole Hedgeman) (Widewater Association)

...the themes and subjects that Hayden gradually evolved into painting were a declaration of the importance of the unheroic, ordinary aspects of the black experience. His choice of the mundane—often flavored by nostalgic, archaic memories of his own—connects him directly to the common people admired by Langston Hughes—the folk "who have their nip of gin on Saturday nights and do not particularly care whether they are like white folks or anybody else."

Baptism, 1958,
by Palmer Hayden (Stafford County)

As far as is known, Hayden never returned to his Stafford roots. But through his paintings, especially *Baptizing Day* (ca.1945–1946), he never really left home. He died on February 18, 1973, at the age of eighty-three.

Representative Reconstruction and Twentieth-Century Staffordians

Sydney Smith Lee was the brother of Gen. Robert E. Lee and the father of Fitzhugh Lee and six other children. Born in Camden, New Jersey, in 1802, he served in the U.S. Navy from 1820 until April 1861, resigning as a commander to enter the service of Virginia and Confederacy. In the Mexican War, Lee had commanded a steamer at Veracruz and the flagship of Commodore Perry, the USS Mississippi, when Japan was opened in 1850 for relations with the United States. Lee also was commandant of the U.S. Naval Academy, and commanded the Philadelphia Navy Yard. He was chief of the Bureau of Coast Survey at the outbreak of the Civil War, during which he served in the upper echelons of the Confederate Navy. After the war, owing to the continued benevolence of Anna Maria Fitzhugh, he and his family moved to "Richland" in Stafford. Sydney Smith Lee died there on July 22, 1869.

Sydney Smith Lee (Virginia Historical Society)

One of Stafford's most remarkable residents, the only governor of Virginia from the county, was Gen. Fitzhugh Lee. Born in Fairfax County in 1835, he was named for Mrs. Fitzhugh, his godmother. The son of Sydney Smith Lee (1802–1869) and nephew of Gen. Robert E. Lee (1807–1870), his mother was the former Anna Maria "Nannie" Mason, granddaughter of George Mason (IV). After schooling in Virginia and Maryland, "Fitz" Lee entered West Point in 1852. Despite poor disciplinary and academic records, he graduated (forty-fifth of forty-nine). First assigned to drilling cavalry recruits at Carlisle Barracks and then to the 2nd U.S. Cavalry on frontier duty, in spring 1858 he wrote his godmother:

> I go out on a scout next month and then I have to come down to what is called the rough service of the horse (fighting) the Indians. They have been very bad this season, killing the citizens and drawing off horses, etc.

Wounded in a May 1859 Commanche fight in Texas, Lee was shot by an arrow in his lungs and bled from the mouth during a two hundred-mile journey on a mule litter. He recovered within three months. On a January 1860 patrol, Lee personally wrestled with and shot one of the raiding Indians, and later proudly paraded into camp with the Indian's shield, weapons and headdress. After extended leave at home, he was assigned as a West Point cavalry instructor. Generally acknowledged as the most popular officer there, Lee and America struggled over the sectional crisis and he resigned in May 1861. (James L. Nichols—Nichols)

Fitzhugh Lee, Confederate major general (Virginia Historical Society)

Initially a first lieutenant on Gen. R. S. Ewell's staff, Lee was appointed lieutenant colonel, 1st Virginia Cavalry, in August 1861. "Little Fitz" Lee's ability as a cavalryman and his courage were evident as he frequently led charges himself. Promoted to Colonel, 1st Virginia Cavalry (April 1862), Lee commanded it on Stuart's first ride around McClellan and in the Seven Days' battles. By July 1862, Lee was a brigadier general. He raided towards Bowling Green, Port Royal, Moss Neck Creek, and Massaponax, enveloping a Federal raiding force, then fought at 2nd Manassas; South Mountain and Sharpsburg in Maryland; and at Kelly's Ford (December 1862). From September to November 1862, he was absent after receiving a mule kick. (Nichols)

At Hartwood Church in February 1863, Lee led the Confederate cavalry forces in the largest cavalry skirmish in Stafford:

> R. E. Lee decided to pierce Hooker's lines for information, so Stuart sent Fitz Lee on February 24 to do the job. Fitz crossed the Rappahannock with 400 selected men at Kelly's Ford. The next day, he "drove the enemy's pickets near Hartwood Church, and attacked his reserve and main body. Routed them, and pursued them within five miles of Falmouth to their infantry lines." He captured five officers and 145 men. The cavalry party recrossed the river on the 26th with their prisoners, having lost fourteen men. (Musselman)

During the Hartwood fight, Lee sent a taunting message to former schoolmate, General W. W. Averell (who retaliated by attacking Lee's brigade at Kelly's Ford in March 1863). Lee next fought at Chancellorsville, after which, ill from rheumatism, he missed the famous cavalry battle at Brandy Station. Returned to duty by June 1863, he participated in the Gettysburg Campaign, leading his brigade in the large cavalry engagement on the third day. Exhausted, in a driving rain they conducted a successful rear guard action protecting the army's retreat from Pennsylvania. Lee then commanded a cavalry division and was promoted to major general (to rank from August 1863). In December 1863, he led his division against his old nemesis, W. W. Averell, in the Shenandoah Valley. When Lee suffered a bad case of "frozen feet" in January 1864, a surgeon considered amputation. Lee's greatest moment came at Spotsylvania when his division assisted First Corps' seizure of the critical crossroads prior to Grant's arrival. In August 1864 Lee was confined to bed with a fever; but he returned to duty to participate in 3rd Winchester. Wounded in the left thigh, he recuperated in a hospital, but his wound became infected. In March 1865 he rejoined his troops and succeeded Gen. Wade Hampton in command of the "remnants of the Cavalry Corps," holding on until Appomattox. Actually, he fought his way out at Appomattox but surrendered on April 11. He went first to Farmville, then Richmond and on to Mrs. Fitzhugh's Stafford property, "Richland." (Nichols)

Initially "unreconstructed," Lee slowly became interested in Stafford farming, writing in February 1866:

This unsuccessful attempt at revolution has left us all in a bad way, but I am in hopes that all our sacrifices have not been in vain. I am down here on the Potomac having like Cincinattus turned my "sword into a ploughshare" but find it dull work...

In September 1866, his uncle, Gen. R. E. Lee, ever mindful of family ties, wrote:

I am glad you are about establishing yourself in Stafford. It is a county in which the Lees were once well known...I have always heard that Richland was a beautiful & productive farm & I hope will make you a pleasant home.

Writing in October 1867, from "Richland, Garrisonville P.O., Stafford Co., Virginia," Fitz freely expressed his feelings to an old friend:

...Here am I busy ploughing and mowing, reaping and sowing as Iverson used to sing about at Carlisle, perfectly contented. I don't care a damn to vote—am glad I have sinned beyond forgiveness, love the radicals about as much as I do Mr. Johnson—and in the language of the "Old Rebel," "am glad I fit agin it, only wish I'd won and aint gwine to ax no parding for anything I've done"—I am living...on the Potomac River some 40 miles below Washington and about four above Aquia Cr. and am going to make

Right, Ellen Bernard Fowle Lee
(Virginia Historical Society)

Fitzhugh Lee as a Stafford farmer
(Virginia Historical Society)

Maj. Gen. Fitzhugh Lee and staff, Cuba
(Virginia Historical Society)

a model farmer. I just wish you could see Squire Lee of Stafford as he rides through the growing corn, his broad brim hat and long coat tails oscillating against the golden grain. I work four Negro men, one half Negro and half white, one Dutchman, one woman and two boys (black), have four horses, 1 lame, 1 blind, 1 thickminded and one with only one eye. Still, unreconstructed as I am, I raise more corn than I ever got from the Quartermaster...

Focused on local matters, he joined the Potomac Agricultural Club. Especially after his father's death in 1869, Lee managed "Richland" exclusively. The farm increased in size to 1,175 acres (600 acres under cultivation) with 15 miles of fencing, 35 buildings and nearly 100 people employed. In the late 1860s and early '70s, he and his brothers became cash-strapped and had to sell off small land parcels. Economic trials didn't deter his search for a wife, however. After a number of failed courtships and flirtations, in October 1869 he met Ellen ("Nellie") Bernard Fowle of Alexandria. She was half his age when they married in April 1870. They would have seven children, of which five lived to adulthood. Anna Maria Fitzhugh bequeathed "Richland" to Fitzhugh (as he now wished to be known) Lee; her will was probated on April 21, 1874. (Kinsley; Eby)

As president of the Association of the Army of Northern Virginia, he participated in the debates over R. E. Lee's and Longstreet's Gettysburg actions. After losing a half-hearted 1879 House of Delegates campaign to Falmouth's Duff Green, he became more serious politically. The Fitzhugh Lees were involved in an 1884 church picnic at Clifton Chapel on the Widewater Road. Lee remained at "Richland," apparently quite contentedly, until he was elected Virginia's governor in 1885. He defeated popular

John S. Wise in an exceptionally civil election—Lee won by 16,000 votes. He served as governor until 1890, using the state militia (including black troops for the first time) to preserve order in Warwick and Tazewell Counties, and at Petersburg. The R. E. Lee Camp Confederate Veterans Home in Richmond was established, and repayment of war debts to England was resolved. Lee often represented the South in patriotic venues aiding sectional reconciliation. After leaving office, Lee was briefly in business in Rockbridge County's rising town of Glasgow. In 1892 he took on another new Virginia town, Chicago. Despite great popularity, Lee was defeated in 1893 for the U.S. Senate by Thomas Staples Martin, organizer of the Democratic coalition. Although Martin's election spurred direct, popular election of senators, it left Lee unemployed. President Cleveland appointed him Federal revenue collector, and in 1894 his book on his uncle Robert was published in New York. Appointed consul-general in Cuba, Lee finally sold "Richland." He served in Cuba from 1896 to 1898, doing everything possible to avoid war with Spain. (Nichols; Kinsley)

Ranking from May 4, 1898, Lee was appointed a major general of volunteers and participated in the Spanish-American War. Given his "Yankee" uniform, he debated "wearing it or shooting it" and wondered how Gen. Jubal Early might respond. At war's end, however, Lee wrote a revealing farewell to his successful VIIth Corps troops:

It is gratifying to review the career and remember the harmony which existed among the forty thousand soldiers who answered the roll calls… Whether it was the "Volunteers" who afterwards…broke ranks and resumed the duties of American citizenship, or the "Regulars," whose standards are still flying and who are now the advance sentinels of American progress and civilization, the soldiers of the North and South took the sunshine and storm of camp together and marched side by side, under one flag, in one cause, for our country.

U.S. Army Maj. Gen. Fitzhugh Lee
(Virginia Historical Society)

Remaining in Cuba, he served as governor of the Havana Department. Retired as brigadier general, USA, in 1901, Lee spoke throughout the country and state on Civil War topics and politics. While traveling by train, he had a stroke (a doctor traveling with him administered strychnine) and was taken to a hospital in Washington, D.C., where

Stafford County, Virginia

he lingered until dying of apoplexy on April, 28, 1905, at the age of seventy. Buried in Richmond's Hollywood Cemetery, Lee had led Southern forces in the only real land engagement to fully take place in Stafford, his adopted home, during the war. He lived here after the war and because of his name and service became a strong symbol of national reunification—one of only two men who served as major generals in both the Confederate and U.S. Armies. (Nichols; Kinsley; Musselman)

John Bowie Gray, born at "Travellers' Rest" in southeast Stafford in May 1846, was educated at Fredericksburg Academy and attended the University of North Carolina before he was notified of his state cadetship to VMI. After a delay—excused by Maj. John Seddon of "Snowden" (brother of Confederate War Secretary James A. Seddon)—Gray entered VMI in September 1863. His mother was involved in spying operations in Stafford. During the battle of New Market, where he switched places with another cadet who was later killed, Gray was a private in Company "D," VMI Cadet Battalion. Gray related a gallows–humor anecdote of the cadets who, lying behind a stone wall as shot and shell roared overhead, amused themselves by throwing stones at frightened comrades. He remained with the cadet corps in the Richmond trenches. After the war, Gray finished ninth of eleven graduates (181 were later declared honorary graduates) in an original class of 295. Later a farmer and stock raiser at "Travellers' Rest," he married Mary Hunter of Alexandria (1870); they had four children. Gray produced "Pure-bred Jersey and Short Horn Cattle…Pure Cotswold Sheep…and Registered Poland China Swine," which he shipped to Germany, Cuba, and "all the Southern states."

John Bowie Gray
(Virginia Military Institute Archives)

His wife died in 1920, and Gray died at home on October 8, 1930. After his death, "Travellers' Rest"— built, unfortunately, on a sand foundation—deteriorated and collapsed. His brother, Robert, a veteran of the 9th Virginia Cavalry who owned adjacent "Eastwood," used the bricks from "Traveller's Rest" to construct a wing of his home, which still stands. The only remaining evidence of "Travellers' Rest" are some trees and the family burial lot, including the grave of John Bowie Gray. (VMI Archives)

His gravestone spoke for the entire county (34th Psalm):

Many are the Afflictions of the righteous: but the Lord delivereth him out of them all.

Other former Confederates suffered in postwar Stafford. Rev. Jaquelin M. Meredith of Aquia Church and Rectory P.O. in Widewater wrote to a niece in January 1914:

Now the War is over 49 years, and still we are here. My wife has suffered much with rheumatic feet for 3 years. I have rheumatism since 1868—contracted in Wartime, yet I still feed 2 horses, 2 cows, 12 turkeys and 100 hens and roosters...(Mary Cary Kendall—Kendall)

Daniel Murray Lee, grandson of Gen. "Light Horse Harry" Lee and Gen. John Mason; great-grandson of George Mason (IV); nephew of General R. E. Lee; son of Commodore Sydney Smith Lee; and brother of Gen. Fitzhugh Lee, was born in July 1844. Educated in Washington, D.C., and at VMI with the Class of 1864, he left in April 1861 with Maj. T. J. Jackson to serve as drillmaster at Camp Lee, Richmond. After service with Whiting's Brigade at 1st Manassas, he joined the Confederate Navy in July 1861, appointed as acting midshipman. Lee served on the CS receiving ship United States in Norfolk; the CSS Jamestown in the Hampton Roads Naval Battle; and with the Drewry's Bluff Naval Battery (both 1862). From 1862 to 1863, he served on the CS Ram Richmond on the James River. Promoted to midshipman, from 1863 to 1864 he served on another "ironclad," the CSS Chicora, in Charleston Harbor. In 1864, assigned to the school ship Patrick Henry on the James River, he was promoted to passed midshipman. From 1864 to 1865, Lee served on the CS Cruiser Chickamauga, then as officer-in-charge of the naval battery on Mechanicsville Road, near Cold Harbor (ca. February 1865). This battery, under Admiral Tucker's Naval Brigade, left with the army in its retreat towards Appomattox. At Sayler's Creek, the naval command was captured, but Lee eluded escaped, joining brother Fitzhugh Lee's cavalry staff as a voluntary aide-de-camp. He surrendered with Lee's staff. (VMI Archives)

After the war, the Lees settled in Stafford. Daniel Murray Lee served in the merchant marine from June 1865 until 1872, and in 1875 married Nannie Ficklen of "Belmont," described as "a young lady of remarkable beauty and attractive loveliness in nature and manners"; they had six children. Later Lee owned "Highland Home" in Stafford, a 135-acre stock farm producing Guernsey cattle and Berkshire hogs. The main house, built around 1880, was an impressive Victorian structure. At that time, Lee also received a part of "Arkendale," one of the Lee tracts (part of the original Brent tracts as well). Some 1,779 acres were divided among four Lee brothers (Daniel Murray Lee, John Mason Lee ("Westwood"), Henry Lee, and Smith Lee), and Daniel received 535 acres and a fish house, the portion known as "The Anchorage." In 1909, he authored *The Last Fight of the Confederate States Navy*. Lee died at "Highland Home" on Dec 17, 1916, in his seventy-third year.

John Wesley Knight
(Washington Post/Walter V. Roberts)

A boyhood D.C. school friend recalled: "He has no equal for Devilment, Bravery and dash. " (VMI Archives; Kendall)

Representative of Stafford's river men was Capt. J. W. Knight. Providing unique insights into his life, he and his seventy years on the Potomac River were profiled in December 1933:

Not an old salt, but a river captain who has sailed the Potomac for 70 years, John Wesley Knight refuses to lose sight, even for a day, of the waters on which he has spent his life. Capt. Knight will be 87 years old next Thursday. High time for him to be spending his days by the fireside, his young folks think. But each morning finds this white-haired seaman down at Coal Landing. He owns an old fisherman's store here which has served Stafford County rivermen for more than half a century. From its worn, stone steps, he can look far across Acquia Creek to the spot where all that remains of The Five Sisters, his old sailing vessel, is moored.

"They don't make ships like her any more," this weather-beaten captain mourns. "The Potomac used to be full of them, but now there's not a long boat left on the river."

Capt. Knight began his river career as a young boy. Although born on a Stafford farm only a mile inland, plowing fields held no charm for him. He spent his days on the banks of the river, finally stowing on as cook on the old sailing schooner, Ipsawasson, which ran lumber from Stafford to Alexandria. "There were no commission merchants in those days," Capt. Knight smiles. The captain sold the wood himself. "We shipped 30 to 40 cords. I've seen as many as 2,000 cords stacked for us here at Coal Landing."

After three years as cook, Knight shipped as a hand on a long boat, running from Colonial Beach to Washington. Before he was twenty-seven, he had become a captain. A strapping, skillful sailor, his services were much in demand among Potomac ship owners. He captained twelve of the hardiest sailing ships on the river, among them the May Leaves, for Richard Lacey of Fairfax County, and Barney Seagull's Mill Boy.

Sailing men themselves tell you that few knew the whims and vagaries of the Potomac like Capt. Knight. "The river's an open book to Knight," they say. But all that this genial old captain will reply is a drawled, "Guess I've run on enough shoals to make a good captain out of me!"

Although Knight, to use his own words, has been in a heap of hard places," he has yet to fail to bring his ship in safely. With his sails reefed and double reefed, Knight has weathered storms lasting 36 hours in which he didn't tack in to shore. "You know some folks think the Potomac doesn't get rough in a storm," he says. "But I just tell them they ought to get out on it then. One night I was anchored out in the middle of the river opposite Powell's Creek. A nor'wester blew up all of a sudden, carrying both masts and sails away. I had to speed the rest of the night holding aloft an oar with a lantern tied to it."...Strangers many times have asked Capt. Knight why he has never gone to sea. Although the lure of the deep has called many of his mates, Knight has steadfastly refused to leave the Potomac. Looking down the stream, a bit dim of vision but sturdy yet, this amazing 87-year-old, who still tends his fisherman's store unaided, merely remarks simply: "I guess the river's in my bones." (Washington Post)

The twentieth century brought two extraordinary men to Stafford—Gari Melchers and John Lee Pratt.

Artist Gari Melchers, born in Detroit, Michigan, in 1860, was world-famous when he came to Stafford. At age seventeen, he had studied in Dusseldorf and Paris and established studios in Holland, France, and Germany. Rising to prominence as a painter of realistic subjects and portraits, Melchers became an academician of the National Academy of Design and a member of the American Academy of Arts and Letters. He also chaired the Smithsonian Commission to create a National Gallery of Art and served on the Virginia Arts Commission, which investigated creation of the Virginia Museum of Fine Arts. Melchers purchased "Belmont" in 1916 and established a studio on the grounds in the early 1920s. Designed by Detroit architect John Donaldson and built by Fredericksburg architect Philip Stern, the studio was completed in 1924. At least one Stafford mason, George Payne of Falmouth, worked on the building. The studio now houses a gallery where rotating shows of Melchers' and others' works are shown to the public. His paintings are maintained at "Belmont" and occasionally loaned to shows and to a U.S. State Department program that temporarily places them in U.S. embassies. In 1942, Melchers' widow, Corinne, deeded the property to Virginia; it is administered by Mary Washington College, interpreted as both Melchers' residence and an art museum. Melchers' Stafford-focused paintings depict places (see Chapter 7) now but a memory, and Staffordians live on in his art.

Gari Melchers on his porch at "Belmont," 1929
(Belmont/Mary Washington College)

John Lee Pratt, one of Stafford's most successful residents and preservationists, was born in 1879 in "Aspen Grove" on the Stafford-King George boundary. The son of a Confederate 9th Virginia Cavalry trooper, Pratt was raised on the Passapatanzy farm, reportedly working year-round except for Easter and July 4th fishing holidays. Educated at Locust Dale Academy (Orange), Randolph-Macon College in Ashland, and graduating in civil engineering from the University of Virginia in 1905, he briefly taught school before going to work for the Delaware explosives and munitions firm of E. I. duPont de Nemours and Company (1906–1919). After World War I, during which he served in several special assignments, the DuPont

Young Woman Sewing, painted by Gari Melchers in 1919, depicts his wife, Corinne, as she looked shortly after coming to Stafford.
(Belmont/Mary Washington College)

John Lee Pratt (National Park Service)

Stafford County, Virginia

John Culley, a Brooke farmer, about 1910-1915 (Dorothy Jackson)

While he passed a farm near Garrisonville in about 1925, Staffordian artist Gari Melchers noticed Annie DeShields. *A Native of Virginia*, shown here, was the result of several humorous sittings in which she first showed up in her "Sunday best" dress and then insisted on ironing her working clothes between sittings.
(Belmont/Mary Washington College)

executive assisted the fledgling General Motors. He rose to GM director by 1923 and was vice president from 1922 until his retirement in 1937. A multimillionaire industrialist, Pratt was one of America's wealthiest men. In 1931 he purchased "Chatham" in Stafford. During World War II, Pratt served as one of the famed "dollar-a-year men," assisting U.S. government wartime projects. As a point of honor, during the war Mr. and Mrs. Pratt lived in one of "Chatham's" outbuildings to conserve energy. A philanthropist, Pratt donated large sums to cultural and academic causes and gave large tracts of land to the NPS, Stafford County and Fredericksburg. Two parks, named for St. Clair Brooks and Pratt, were donated to Stafford County. He gave "Chatham" to the nation, and it is now the headquarters of the Fredericksburg and Spotsylvania National Battlefield Park, NPS, and an important historic site in its own right. (Ralph Happel—Happel; John Goolrick)

John Goolrick provides some additional perspectives:

As the elderly man in the tan fedora and faded blue suit walked across Fredericksburg's Chatham Bridge during a light rain, a young man stopped his car and offered him a ride. The older man stopped and said politely, "Thank you, son, but I don't have far to go." The young driver pulled away, not realizing that the gentleman for whom he had shown such concern could have had any car he wished from the vast General Motors... He was John Lee Pratt, one of the richest men in America.

Pratt helped develop Freon as a refrigerant for General Motors infant Frigidaire division; coordinated World War II lend-lease assistance to Great Britain; sold, at little or no profit, the local farms he had purchased to young people who promised to farm the land; and shunned publicity when his estimated $300 million fortune (equivalent to $1 billion in today's terms) guaranteed him notoriety and fame. His brother, Dr. Frank Pratt, founded the Pratt Clinic, serving Fredericksburg and Stafford. Goolrick concludes:

I recall sitting with John Lee Pratt in one of the rooms in the magnificently appointed Chatham Manor and asking him to what he attributed his great success in life.

He reflected on the question a minute and said, "I don't really know. I always enjoyed hard work, but much of what happened to me came through the good fortune of meeting the right people...if I had any advice to give young people it would be to always persevere, always believe you can get things done if you keep trying."

Twentieth-Century Stafford Farmers

On August 31, 1999, Hunter W. Greenlaw, a Stafford farmer for more than sixty years, died at age 81. Scheduled for recognition at the Ruritan Club a month later, Greenlaw was remembered thoughtfully:

...His farm land, spread over the eastern part of the county on State Route 3, has been a landmark for decades. He was a farmer, maybe even a "southern planter" as his friend, John Gray, describes him. Gray was the agricultural agent in Stafford for nine years while Greenlaw scaled back his own physical labor in the fields he'd worked and managed most of his life. Even Greenlaw had to make some concessions to age and infirmity, "To the end of his life, if you gave him a seed, he'd just have to plant it," Gray said.

Gray explained that Greenlaw was innovative, always laying out test plots and testing his soil to prevent worn-out fields. He also was one of the first farmers in the area to use chemicals to enhance crop production.

Mary Lou Greenlaw says that her husband's scientific interests were satisfied by other aspects of farm life, too. "If his father hadn't died, he might have studied medicine," she recalled. "He always did his own veterinary work in all kinds of weather and at any time during the night."

Greenlaw was fifteen (ca. 1933) when his father died suddenly, leaving the boy in charge of Albion Farm with its 370 acres. Some of the land was wooded, but most of it was laid out in neat fields. His father's tractor was ready for a final ride to the junkyard, so young Hunter plowed fields using horses. But the pressures of managing his family's farm didn't cause him to lose sight of other things. He was named salutatorian when he graduated from Falmouth High School, and by all accounts he could negotiate a basketball court in fine form, too.

After high school, Greenlaw toiled at farm chores all day long and buried his nose in farm journals and account books at night. He put out record yields at Albion Farm in 1938 and won the Star Farmer Award, a coveted national honor from the Future Farmers of America, given to the young man then known as "America's Number One Farmer."

Hunter Greenlaw (Judith Jones/Free Lance-Star)

Stafford County, Virginia

Artist's rendition of "Sherwood Forest" by Jerrilynn Eby

…As Greenlaw's skill in farming developed, he expanded his enterprise to include a registered herd of Hereford cattle, numbering 400 head in peak years. His midlife and later years were busy with a long list of associations and business clubs. The list included the Ruritans, but he also was a leader in the Virginia Hereford Association, the founder and director of the Virginia Agri-Business Council, and the president of the Virginia Soybean Association, just to name a few.

As Greenlaw's health deteriorated, Ralph Sutton and Charles Henderson farmed his land and kept up his state-of-the-art interest in agriculture. Sutton says that Greenlaw was renowned for his hard-working ways. "He was a very determined person…Some people can recall driving on (Route) 3 at two o'clock in the morning, and the lights of his tractor would still be going."

Hunter Greenlaw died while driving his tractor around the garden. Mary Lou Greenlaw said that to the end of his life, he lived it just as he wished. "And the last check he wrote in his checkbook was a donation. That is just typical of him."

Greenlaw's reflections on the award he had won in 1938 speak volumes on him and Stafford's other farmers over the past 400 years: "I felt that the powers that be put their trust into me. I felt I should try better than ever to live up to that…" (J. H. Jones/FLS)

Hunter Greenlaw had purchased "Albion" in 1942 from N. S. Greenlaw, who had bought the place in 1907 but never lived there. It was one of the Colonial "ancestor homes" of Stafford. Nearby "Sherwood Forest" was also purchased by Hunter and Mary Lou Greenlaw in 1961 but later (1987) sold to a developer, a disturbing but understandable trend in Stafford's farming community. That should not detract from the recognition of the efforts of Stafford's farmers through centuries of adversity. (Eby)

Curtis Dickinson, age twelve, winner of 1946 Sears 4-H Prize for his China Poland sow
(Nancy Dickinson)

Recent Years

In the early 1960s, 300 years after its establishment as a county, Stafford began to truly open to the wider world. Interstate 95 was completed, providing a new access to and from the county and new patterns of living and commuting. Perhaps reflecting this expansion of horizons, during this period Stafford was also noteworthy in the struggle for civil rights. As Stafford progressed into the 1970s, it was clear that the status quo could not be maintained indefinitely. By the 1980s and 1990s it was clear that old days and ways had been replaced.

Stafford came to national attention in other ways: 1996 Olympic gold medalists Jeff Rouse (later Stafford tourism director) and Mark Lenzi; and Miss Virginia, Staffordian Michelle Kang.

In the period from 1990 to 2000 alone, Stafford added 30,000 people to its population—equivalent to one and one-half Fredericksburgs. In 2002 Stafford was determined to be the ninth fastest-growing county in America among counties with more than 10,000 population.

Common to all such social and economic changes, the results yielded mixed blessings. As one observer expressed it in 1993: "A traditionally agrarian County is yielding to all the benefits and detriments of American suburbia." This account added:

The history of Stafford demonstrates the amazing resiliency of both the land and its people. Staffordians have shown that there are no hardships that cannot be overcome. It should be our privilege to preserve the struggles and triumphs of Stafford for our posterity. (Moncure)

Curtis Dickinson with farm horses at "Breezy Knoll Farm" (Nancy Dickinson)

Jeff Rouse and Mark Lenzi, Stafford Olympians (Stafford County)

Gerry, Edwin, and Wayne Young, part of a family that had operated "Blysdale Farm" for forty-five years. Their farm, surrounded by Ferry Farms, Briarwood and Town & County subdivisions, was headed for development in 1988. (Nancy Dickinson; Norm Shafer/Free Lance-Star)

Chapter Four
Staffordians in War

Monument to Stafford's Veterans, courthouse
(Jane M. Conner)

Revolutionary War officer's tent (reenactment) (Jane M. Conner)

Colonial Indian Wars and Bacon's Rebellion

At least forty-five officers and one noncommissioned officer from Stafford served in Colonial wars. The actual number is much higher because enlisted men were not adequately counted. Units generally consisted of mounted ranger companies with about twenty horsemen per company. The Stafford Rangers were created in this period. (Musselman [*Stafford County, Virginia: Veterans and Cemeteries*])

French and Indian War

Some 109 Staffordians served in the French and Indian War. Of these, sixty-four names are known. The war in Virginia mainly spread from north to south along the Appalachians. (Musselman; Watkins)

The Revolutionary War

Stafford's American Revolution cohort consisted of sixty-six men in the Continental Army and 489 whose approved Revolutionary War Public Service Claims are on file in the Virginia State Library. Perhaps as many as 1,000 Staffordians were involved in the Revolution at one time or another. (Musselman)

Through April 2000, evidence has been found of Stafford burials of eighteen "Revolutionary Soldiers and Patriots" (who served or supported independence): David Briggs, Travers Daniel Jr., Frances Daniel, John DeBaptist, John Hedges, Gerald Hooe, Elias Hore, James Hunter Sr., Arthur Morson, George Norman, Thomas Norman, William Phillips, Wily Roy, Joseph Sanford, William Stark, Hawkins Stone, John Wallace, and William Waller Sr. (Lymans)

It is unknown whether black Staffordians were among the army combatants in the Revolution; however, given the numbers of serving white Staffordians and the county's north-south communications position, it is likely that some served. Black soldiers fought in both the Continental Army and in British service on promise of freedom for service. By 1779 an estimated 15 percent of the Continental Army and an unknown portion of the Navy (such as John DeBaptist) were African Americans. This participation is credited with convincing some Northerners that slavery was a poor policy. (Fleming)

Representative of Colonial and Revolutionary era Staffordians were the Wallaces of "Ellerslie" (located on the south side of Virginia 652 and 654). Their story begins with indentured servitude of Scotsman Michael Wallace to Dr. Gustavus Brown of Maryland. Michael studied medicine with Dr. Brown during his indenture, but interrupted his studies to elope with Brown's daughter. Brown didn't press the issue and the Wallaces settled in Falmouth, where he established a medical practice covering Stafford and surrounding counties. In 1748 he purchased Waugh tract land and built "Ellerslie," named for an ancestral Scottish estate. The Wallaces rebuilt their house in 1754 after it was partially burned (the second dwelling apparently used part of the original as some burnt timbers are evident). The story continues:

Ellerslie's most famous resident was Dr. Michael Wallace's son, Lt. Col. Gustavus Brown Wallace (1751–1802). After attending school in Fredericksburg, he began studying law in 1774. His studies were interrupted by the death of his aunt in Scotland necessitating a trip abroad in 1775. That same year he returned to Virginia and enlisted in the Continental Army as a captain. In the fall of 1777 he was promoted to major and served under Col. Daniel Morgan. Major Wallace spent the terrible winter with his men at Valley Forge. He was transferred from the 3rd to the 25th Virginia Regiment and finally to the 2nd Virginia Regiment. During the late 1770s he was captured by the British at Charleston. At the request of Gov. Thomas Nelson, Lord Cornwallis released him on parole so that he could return to Virginia. There he was to make arrangements for officers of the Virginia line to pay the debts they incurred at Charleston. After the Revolution, Wallace was given 7,000 acres of land in Virginia for his services during the war. He was also given an additional 960 acres for special services.

In 1802 Colonel Wallace made a business trip to Scotland. On the return voyage, he contracted typhus. Reaching Potomac Creek, the ship's captain put Wallace off the boat, fortunately on property belonging to his cousin, Mrs. Travers Daniel of "Crow's Nest." Servants found Colonel Wallace and notified Mrs. Daniel. She sent a cart for him and had him taken to a Fredericksburg doctor. Several days later, he died and was buried at the Masonic Cemetery in Fredericksburg. He died unmarried. (Eby)

The War of 1812

Musselman identified 153 Staffordians, almost all in the 45th Virginia Militia Regiment, who served in the War of 1812. Subsequent research by the Lymans indicates that as many as 1,000 Staffordians participated in the War of 1812. That war left Stafford untouched except for the burning of Potomac Church in the Brooke area. Eby relates:

Southern states soldiers of the line and artillery ca. 1782 by H. Charles McBarron
(U.S. Army)

Grave of Lt. Col. Gustavus Brown Wallace of "Ellerslie," Masonic Cemetery, Fredericksburg
(Albert Z. Conner)

On August 1, 1814, William Brent Jr., Daniel Carroll Brent, John Cooke, John Moncure, Hancock Eustace, and Rowzee Peyton wrote to the governor asking him to return the Stafford militia to the county immediately as they believed a British invasion was imminent. The militia had been sent to Mattox Bridge in Westmoreland (County) and only thirty men were stationed on Hope Run, four and one-half miles from the mouth of the creek. The men's concern was well-founded, as Potomac Church was burned by British soldiers on their way to Washington…

Recent (2002) research sheds additional light on Staffordians in the War of 1812. In June to July 1813, Lt. Col. Peyton's 45th Militia Regiment was activated in Stafford and deployed for local defense of Potomac River sectors. A small regular army unit of thirteen men was also assigned to Aquia during the fall of 1813. Captain Edrington's Company of Stafford was called up and stationed in the Norfolk area (January to April 1814). Stafford militia units were activated in July 1814. A battalion of militia from Spotsylvania under Lt. Col. Stapleton Crutchfield (ancestor of the Civil War artillery officer) was stationed in the Fredericksburg area, and some of his men were believed to have been posted on the Stafford side of the Rappahannock. In July 1814 Colonel Peyton took about two-thirds of the 45th Militia Regiment (less thirty men left at Aquia) to reinforce in Westmoreland County, where the British had landed about 1,500 men and occupied Montross. They were also deployed to Mattox Bridge in Westmoreland. In August 1814, the 45th returned to Stafford for mustering out. From August to December 1814, a number of units from surrounding counties occupied positions in Stafford, including Belle Plain. The Lymans have identified 887 men who served in the 45th Militia Regiment. (Lymans)

The Lymans and Musselman have identified twenty-eight War of 1812 veterans' burial sites in Stafford: Charles Bussell, Berryman Cox, George Curtis, John C. Edrington, Jonathan Finnel, William C. Fitzhugh, Thomas Fristoe, Barnett Fritter, Joshua Kendall, William Kendall, Isaac Limberick, Edwin C. Moncure, John Moncure Jr., John Moncure Sr., Edward Norman, Matthew Norman, Thomas Norman, Alexander O'Bryhim, Thomas Roberson, William W. Robertson, Archibald Rollow, Lawrence Sanford, John Starke, Barnett Stewart, William Scandrett Stone, Jonas Sullivan, Benjamin T. Sullivan, and Thomas Wallace.

The Mexican War

Two Staffordians have been identified by Musselman to have served in the Mexican War.

The Civil War

Virginians were citizen-soldiers by long tradition. For example, the Virginia Militia in 1840 had consisted of more than 111,000 men compared with a U.S. Regular Army of more than 8,000. These numbers were maintained in the antebellum period. One historian describes Hartwood's contribution:

Militias, as state-level military organizations, were mustered by counties and even small communities like Hartwood. They included all male citizens of a certain age (usually 18 and above). Yearly or sometimes twice annually, musters were held to drill and otherwise train and organize members…In 1851, the Hartwood Company held musters in April and October, with attendance or absence marked by an "X" or "O." (Kelly O'Grady, *Hartwood's Venerable Ledger: Rare 1851 Militia Roll...*"—O'Grady)

Stafford's strong militia tradition was reinvigorated by the 1800 Gabriel Prosser slave revolt in Caroline County, the 1805 slave unrest at "Chatham," and the Nat Turner Rebellion. George M. Cooke stated slaves were acting impudently and were in a "high spirit of rebellion" when he wrote to the governor (September 13, 1831) of the:

…defenseless conditions of the white population and the danger to which they are exposed. The militia are without arms in every county of my brigade comprising the counties of Fauquier, Prince William, Stafford and King George, in all which there is an over grown slave population. (Fitzgerald)

The 1851 Hartwood militia company of Capt. George Wellford Cropp was part of the 45th Regiment of Virginia Militia. Verbatim family names (some misspelled) listed on the Hartwood Company's 1851 muster roll included Cropp and Alexander, Armstrong, Anderson, Benson, Bridges, Bradshaw, Burton, Beach, Ballard, Brown, Bloxham, Bowling, Brooks, Bettis, Butler, Curtis, Conyers, Courtney, Dunnington, Dodd, Dye, Duerson, Ellignton, Ennis, French, Graves, Garner, Groves, Grinnam, Harding, Humphrey, Harris, Heflin, Herndon, Hickerson, Helm, Jackson, Jacobs, Jones, Johnson, Kellogg, Limbrick, Latham, Lunsford, Lane, Littrell, Leach, Monroe, Mills, Nash, Porch, Patton, Patterson, Powell, Rodgers, Rose, Roberson, Smith, Swetnam, Scooler, Stephens, Timberlake, Timmons, and Tompins. Many Stafford and Hartwood families would serve in the Civil War in the 47th and 30th Virginia Infantry Regiments and 9th Virginia Cavalry as well as the Stafford Light Artillery and Fredericksburg Artillery. (O'Grady)

John Brown's 1859 raid electrified Southside and Tidewater (including Stafford), where slave populations were largest. In 1860 Stafford's population was 57 percent white and 43 percent black (39 percent of the total population were slaves). Stafford raised a number of companies for Virginia's Confederate contingents–1,000 Staffordians "joined the colors." Confederate forces, including units raised here, occupied the county in 1861—1862 as part of a "Mount Vernon-Rappahannock Defense Line." The first engagement by the U.S. Navy with shore-based Confederate batteries took place at Aquia Landing, which soon became a major logistical and transportation base. The entire Union Army of the Potomac wintered here in the critical 1862–1863 time frame. (Musselman)

Civil War fights in Stafford were limited to the Aquia Landing naval fight in 1861 and cavalry skirmishes at Hartwood Church, along with smaller skirmishes. But the county itself played critical roles in Union military infrastructure (logistics, transportation, intelligence, and command and control and communications) in all of the battles to the south. Union forces fought the Fredericksburg and Chancellorsville battles from Stafford, and only the narrowest interpretation of these battles would fail to recognize the county's roles in fire support, maneuver areas, medical support, resupply and engineering. Stafford willingly provided the "infernal mud" that bogged down Federal forces at key junctures in those fights and crucially hindered pontoon bridging movement before 1st Fredericksburg. Wartime spying and communications took place as the first of the Confederate Signal Corps and Secret Service's "Secret Lines" crossed into Maryland from Aquia and Potomac Creeks. Belle Plain in White Oak emerged as the next great Union logistical center, used extensively in the 1864 Overland Campaign until it was replaced by City Point on the James River. Stafford may have been the first jurisdiction in the country to suffer the devastation of a modern war—from which it did not recover until the 1940s. (Musselman)

Artist's rendition of Civil War cavalryman, ordnance officer, and wagon trains by H. Charles McBarron. Such scenes were common between Aquia Landing and Belle Plain during the Fredericksburg, Chancellorsville and Spotsylvania battles from 1862 to 1864.

(U.S. Army)

Aquia Landing

Maj. Thomas Hoomes Williamson of the VMI faculty and Lt. Hunter H. Lewis of the Virginia Navy surveyed, designed and constructed defenses for Aquia Landing. Artillery batteries, some manned by volunteers from the "Stafford Guards," protected access points to Aquia Landing and its vital rail facilities. Stafford and Aquia Landing became strategic objectives as Federal control of the port and railroad would provide transportation access and resupply all the way to Fredericksburg and Richmond. The 1861–1862 Potomac defense line, under the command of Daniel Ruggles and later Theophilus H. Holmes, would naturally be compromised as well. This soon brought on a naval engagement that was one of the first significant actions of the war:

On May 14, 1861, the USS *Mount Vernon* steamed into Aquia Creek, where Lt. J. Glendy Sproston discovered a Confederate four-gun battery aimed at his ship. While Sproston watched, some trees that partially shielded the battery were cut down. About fifty men, some in uniform and some carrying muskets, were in and about the battery. No shots were fired. Ironically, the ship that carried Sproston into Aquia Creek to discover the battery was one of four steamers of the Potomac Steamship Company that had carried passengers from Aquia Creek to Washington before it was seized by the U.S. Government in April. The *Fredericksburg Recorder* expressed disappointment that there had not been an engagement. Stafford County offered to supply "six foot farms for forty thousand Yankees."

Several efforts were made to determine the extent of Confederate occupation and defenses, creating an atmosphere of overreaction as the Union was not yet in position to invade. Naval action was another matter, however. On May 29, 1861, two Federal steamers fired a total of fourteen shells at the artillery defenses on the south shore of Aquia Creek. Ruggles rushed the 2nd Tennessee Regiment (700 men) up the rail line from Fredericksburg. On May 31, 1861, Cmdr. James Harmon Ward of the Potomac Flotilla arrived ready for action. A two- to three-hour fight, beginning about 10 A.M., commenced. The USS *Thomas Freeborn*—USS *Anacostia* and USS *Resolute* were held back, lacking rifled guns—bombarded the Confederate shore battery. The Union vessels withdrew when their long-range ammunition was expended. A second Confederate battery, established on a more commanding height, then made a difference as Federal ships could not elevate their guns sufficiently to engage it. (Musselman [*Stafford County in the Civil War*])

The engagement set off a torrent of recriminations about Ruggles' actions. Although Commander Ward reported that the Rebel guns were not a threat to the Potomac River channel, he returned the next day with *Anacostia, Reliance, Pawnee,* and *Freeborn* and the latter two engaged shore batteries at 11:30 A.M. The Southerners, believing the Federal ships were using the end of the wharf to sight on the battery, burned a building, resulting in loss of the whole wharf (a loss of $11,200 to the R,F&P and small gain for the Southern cause). The Confederates had employed at least eight guns in the fight, but the Federal gunners drove most away from their positions. The fight ended at 4:30 P.M. on June 1, 1861. Although casualties were light, *Freeborn* and *Pawnee* had

The June 22, 1861, edition of *Harper's Weekly* featured this depiction of the engagement at Aquia Creek, from a sketch by Lieutenant Cash during the action. (Don and Ila McCoy)

On October 5, 1861, *Harper's Weekly* contained this sketch by "Lieutenant Osbon" of the "Rebel Steamer *Page*, now lying at Acquia Creek"....An article related that the *Page* had been constructed seven years earlier by Thomas Collyer and had avoided destruction by its speed and shallow draft of four feet.

(Don and Ila McCoy)

sustained hits from the shore batteries. Nearly 600 rounds had been fired. No future engagements would take place there, but the Union kept the Potomac Flotilla patrolling off Brent's Point, and occasionally shots were exchanged from shore and/or ship. (Musselman) (See Chapter 10.)

Col. Thomas Conway Waller, a citizen-soldier with brief prewar militia experience, was typical of men who entered the ranks at relatively low levels, learned by experience, and gained in responsibility during the war. Born at "Grafton" in Stafford in December 1832, Waller was a prewar slaveholder and militia officer (1860). On April 21, 1861, he entered the 9th Virginia Cavalry as captain, Company "A" (the Stafford Rangers). In October 1862, he was promoted to major of his regiment. Lieutenant colonel of the 9th (September 16, 1864, but ranking from May 1864), on January 6, 1865, he became its colonel. Wounded at Brandy Station on October 11, 1863, he was paroled at Ashland on April 25, 1865. (Robert K. Krick—Krick)

Waller's company served in the Stafford sector of the 1861–1862 Confederate defenses until the U.S. occupation of Fredericksburg on April 19, 1862. They fought in Stuart's first ride around McClellan, the Seven Days battles, Stuart's Hanover Court House to Fredericksburg expedition, 2nd Manassas, and Sharpsburg. After his promotion to major, Waller fought at Mountville, Leeds' Ferry, Fredericksburg, and the Dumfries-Fairfax Station cavalry raid.

One of his best moments came in December 1862 just prior

A crude form of mine warfare came early in the war in Stafford. On July 7, 1861, Captain Budd of the *Resolute* discovered this "infernal machine designed by the Confederates" lying in wait for *Pawnee* and the Potomac Flotilla. The contraption combined watertight 80-gallon oil casks as buoy and twenty fathoms of three-and-a-half-inch rope with cork buoys along every two feet of rope. These held explosive canisters six feet under water. Fuses in gutta-percha tubes completed the mine array. (Mary Rust)

to Fredericksburg when he led a midnight riverine raid across the icy Rappahannock River from Layton's Ferry to Leedstown. They captured forty-nine Union troopers (8th Pennsylvania Cavalry) with their horses and equipment, earning praise from Generals Stuart and R. E. Lee. In 1863, still as regimental major, Waller fought at Rappahannock Bridge, Kelly's Ford, Welford's Ford, and Beverly Ford between April 14–15; then participated in countering Federal General Stoneman's cavalry raid. On June 9, 1863, he fought with the 9th at Brandy Station in the largest cavalry clash of the war. In June they fought at Middleburg and Hanover, Pennsylvania, before fighting at Gettysburg in July 1863. Waller and the 9th returned to Virginia, next fighting in the Bristow Campaign (he was wounded at Brandy Station on October 11 leading his regiment). He apparently returned in time for the 9th's next major engagement at the Wilderness and seems to have acted as lieutenant colonel. Major Waller fought at Spotsylvania, North Anna, Haw's Shop (all May 1864), and 2nd Cold Harbor. During the Petersburg Siege, Waller rose to lieutenant colonel and colonel. He commanded the 9th after October 1864 till war's end.

Waller's would-be nation lost its "Second American Revolution," and he returned to a largely destroyed county. His family's homes and farms seem to have survived, and he lived for another thirty years. After the war, he lived primarily near Garrisonville. In 1868, he married Sallie Medora Wickliffe (1837–1921). Waller died on either December 23 or 28, 1895, at "Wayside," which he had built, and was buried there. "Wayside" later fell into disrepair and was burned down by vandals on July 4, 1983. "Grafton" is also gone. Anne E. Moncure Elementary School and businesses fill their space. (Krick; Eby)

Col. Thomas Conway Waller, 9th Virginia Cavalry, the highest-ranking antebellum Staffordian (Felicia Parlier)

Col. Thomas Waller (right) with (from left) his wife, Sallie Medora Wickliffe Waller; their oldest son, Thomas Jackson Waller (1869–1948); and his wife, Alice Page Nelson Waller (1865–1957). The family is at "Richland."
(Felicia Parlier)

Gravestone of Col. Thomas Conway Waller
(Owen L. Conner)

Representative of Stafford's Confederate infantrymen, Sgt. John William Watson was born in the Brooke area about 1831 and was in Company "I," 47th Virginia Infantry. He had married Falmouth girl Margaret Garner in 1854; they had three children. Enlisting in 1861, he was a corporal by July/August. Present on all muster rolls through December 1862. Watson was wounded (right thigh) at Gettysburg on July 1, 1863. Admitted to Richmond's Chimborazo Hospital that month, he had survived the Peninsula Campaign; Cedar Mountain and 2nd Manassas; Harpers Ferry and Sharpsburg (both September 1862); Fredericksburg; and Chancellorsville. Watson returned for the Mine Run Campaign, where he developed a fatal illness. Pneumonia sent him to a Lynchburg hospital, where he died on May 3, 1864; he was buried there. (Musselman; FLS)

What sets Watson apart from his comrades is the preservation of his wartime letters, now in the Virginia Historical Society. A dedicated and considerate parent and husband, he was something of a literary man despite a lack of formal education. Like most farmboys of his generation, he wrote like he spoke and spelled like it sounded, thus preserving the "sounds" of the war in addition to the facts. After one month's service, Watson wrote:

Aprel the 11, 1862
My Dear Wife

I take this oportunity to write you a few lines to let you know where I am at this time and how I am. we are in Fredericksburg at this time… I am well at presant except a cold. we had marching orders tuesday morning at seven oclock we march that day through the rain and mud from the camp down to town and through falmouth down to hopewell and staid there untill the next day about ten oclock and then march back to the camp through the mud rain and hail and when we got there we could have no fire to cook any thing that night and next morning came to town and we dont know what we went for yet have you herd of any yankees near by lately when you were in town. I would have give any thing to come down to have seen you but I could not get… I am verry much obliged to you for the butter and eggs and bread you sent me. they made me thinck of home…give all my respects to all my frends if I have any but keep the largest portion for your self and my little babys…

Ironically, he instructed Margaret to burn all of his letters. His letter following the Maryland Campaign provides a unique common soldier's view of a major campaign:

September 1862
Dear Wife

I take this oportunity to write you a few lines to let you know how I am geting along. I am a little better than I was when I wrote before but I am march nearly to death. We march from mearland back to Virginia and by martainburg down to harpers ferry and had a battle there on the 14 September and on monday the 15 they surrendered. We took 13 thousand prisoners and about 45 peaces of cannon and twelve hundred horses and others stores and goods of all kinds and on tuesday we sent them home on parol of oner we left then on tuesday morning and march about five miles and back to harpers ferry that eavning and staid til next morning and went back to mearland and had a battle over there and then came back to Virginia again and had a verry hard battle near Sheaperd ville and then we march in about two miles of martainburg and camped... we sertainly have seen a hard time since we left Richmond and as for towns and villegs we past thrue I cant recerlect how many nor the names of them. I would be verry glad to know the names of them all... I understand the yankes have left Stafford county. I hope and trust they have not ingered you all much. I have herd they did not do much damage there and I hope it may be so...

Watson's letters showed increasing anxiety, homesickness, fatalism, and melancholy about the war and his comrades:

October the 5, 1862
Dear wife

I this eavning ingage my self a few moments in writeing you a few words to pas the time away in thinking of the. I shall go crasy if I cant get a letter from you soon and hear how every thing is...I heard from Farther he said all was well but that wont satisfy me until I get a letter from you. Send me wird what for a crop farther has and if you have any sweet potatoes and if you have any keep some for me for if I cant get home no other way. I will runaway and come home soon as I get a good chance. I hate mity bad to runaway but I want to see you all so bad that I think I shall try that trick if I cant hear from you soon. I am all ways thinking about you all how did James Henry get along with the yankes and Abram Bloxham and send me wird what the yankes have taken from all the nabours. I heard that they had taken uncle William Payne house and I heard that cousin Mary Groves was dead and miss Sally Rockafellow. We are all well at presant. Send me word if the children talk about me much or not and if willy

The Wallers' small family graveyard is nestled between a Texaco quick-stop station and a Jiffy Lube, a sad ending somehow typical of Stafford County's history between 1865 and present. (Owen L. Conner)

Sgt. John William Watson, 47th Virginia Infantry
(Tim Baroody)

Stafford County, Virginia - 81 -

can talk yet. O I would be so glad to see him... I was at preaching this eavning. we have meating every sunday when we are in camp we are encamped in about one and half miles of bungers hill and twelve from winchester we cam here saturday a week a goe last night. I expect you have ben hard up for money but I could not send you any I have not had no way to send it you must excuse me for writing to you with a pensyl for ink pen and paper are hard to get here.

After the battle of Fredericksburg, Watson was actually moved to write some poetry. Less than memorable from a literary perspective, the last two verses shed light on his Southern pride and stolid determination:

Mayers (Meagher's) famous Irish brigade,
The Northern bost and pride,
Twas met with southern lead and steel.

Surviving the battle of Chancellorsville, Watson next participated in the Pennsylvania Campaign. He wrote to Margaret on June 29, 1863, from Franklin County there:

My Dear Wife

I sit my self down with grief and troubles to write you a few lines to let you known where I am and how I am. I am well as could be expected after such a long and werrisome march that we have taken from 1 mile below Fredericksburg up through the vally of Virginia and crosed the potomac river at Shepherd town and marched thrugh maryland and into pensylvania. we got there friday 26 of June about 2oclock and marched again on Saturday and camped near the mountain about harrisonburg (sic) the capital of pensylvania. I dont know whither weare going there or not it is impossible for us to know where we are going until we get there. we rested Sunday but are redy to march this morning. but we are here waiting for further orders. I read a letter from Stafford County yesterday from mrs Lucy Boller to her brother Lewis Payne. She says he would not know the place whene he got in sight of it. and says the place is cut down and burned up so that it is a desolate looking place...you must write me as soon as you get this and let me hear from you and Mother and farther and all the familys around. and let me (know the) harm the yankees have done in Stafford...we are now in enimy cuntry we know not what will befall us for some of our solders have done mity bad since they have ben here but orders was read out last eavning prohibiting any private property being taken only by quarter masters...

Wounded in the thigh at Gettysburg, he wrote Margaret from Winchester on July 8, 1863:

I have just goten here this eavning and had my wound drest. I got wounded last wednesday and started from getersburg on Saturday and traveled day and night for 4 days and 3 night. I suffer a great deal riding in a wagon but I stood it out & my wound is not daingerous I hope it is a flesh wound in my right thy... my dear I recived your kind and affectionate letter on thursday July 2, 1863 and was happy to hear from you and my little children and also all my relations and friends...

After recuperating in a Richmond hospital, Watson rejoined his regiment on November 16, 1863, and fought in his final engagement in the Mine Run Campaign. He went into winter camp in the Shenandoah Valley in the winter of 1863—1864 and contracted his final illness in the spring of 1864. From January 1864, his letters were almost exclusively concerns for his wife, family and friends in Stafford. Swept up in the army's 1864 religious revival, he wrote increasingly of God and his faith. He admonished his family and friends to lead faithful lives so that they might all be in heaven together. His faith in his country's cause had been tested in the carnage of the battlefield and the ill-discipline of camp—including executions of three men from his brigade—but he remained "steadfast to the last." He rests with his comrades in a Lynchburg cemetery far from the Stafford scenes, family and friends he loved so well. (VHS; Tim Baroody)

The Civil War Homefront in Stafford

Many American communities suffered losses in the war. Stafford's destruction and dislocation reminded one historian, Thomas M. Moncure Jr., of biblical times, as suggested in Psalm 74:23:

Forget not the voice of thine enemies: the tumult of those that rise up against thee increaseth continually.

Not all of Stafford's Civil War stories deal with men-in-arms. One of Stafford's casualties during Union occupation was the courthouse and its records. A July 1, 1891, story in the *Fredericksburg Star* told a fascinating tale of lost history in which E. M. Young, a probate clerk in Silver City, New Mexico, had come by "a rare relic of colonial days" — the Stafford County seal from the period of King George II (ruled 1728–1760). Young was visiting his father in Fredericksburg and the story continues that the seal had been taken from the courthouse in March 1862 by the troops of General Dan Sickles, who had crossed over from Liverpool Point. Federal Capt. William H. Hugo and Company "C," 70th New York Volunteers, led the advance capturing the courthouse. The seal, described as being round in shape (one and one-half inch in diameter) and made of iron, and weighing about a pound, was taken. It depicted an enthroned king, flanked by female figures on either side, representing "Justice" and "Right." Beneath them was the description "We will not sell, deny or delay justice or right." Over the king's head was the inscription: "Geo. II R." Around the seal were the words "The Seal of the Stafford Court in Virginia." An old English Bible, also taken from the courthouse, was dropped and lost in Aquia Creek. Sadly the article ends, "Probably Mr. Young will restore this ancient relic to the county court of Stafford, where it will no doubt be zealously preserved and greatly appreciated." If Young returned the seal, it was lost. Most likely it was not returned and remains, like so many Stafford relics at best, in private or public collections.

An interesting court document reveals community intentions assisting Confederate soldiers' families. The Stafford County Court on May 15, 1861, ordered a committee of three "judicious Citizens of the county" from each Magisterial district "whose duty it shall be to ascertain and supply the pressing wants of families of such citizens of said County as have enlisted in the service of the Country during the present war & who have left their family needy and dependent." Citizens named were: (District No. 1) William Pollock, Wm. H. Hasbrough, and Walker P. Conway; (District No. 2) John C. Shelton, G. W. Wallace, and Thos J. Skinker; (District No. 3) C. A. Tackett, Wm. T. Patton, and James Tolson; and (District No. 4) William E. Moncure, Saml. S. Brooke, and Albert Clift. Families of soldiers were amended: they included the wives of John DeShazo, R. T. Brown, B. Brooks, George Dye, Wallace Heflin, George Lightner, John Suthard, George Payne, William Buxton, Murray West, William A. Jett, Newton Turner and Henry Pollard. (Kirby)

"Moncure Conway House," at right. To the left is the "Basil Gordon House."
(Belmont/Mary Washington College)

Phillips House ruins, February 1863
(National Park Service)

Another interesting wartime incident occurred at Moncure Conway's former Stafford home:

It had been long since tidings concerning my relatives in Virginia had reached me. A small parcel containing an old china cup and saucer and silver spoon had been sent me from Washington at the request of a Union soldier who had saved them from the wreck of things in Conway House, Falmouth. These relics are connected with a curious incident. When the Union army under General McDowell entered Falmouth they found the village deserted by the whites. My father was in Fredericksburg, and my two brothers far away in the Confederate ranks. The house was left empty and locked up, the house servants remaining in their abode in the back yard. Yet as the Union soldiers were filing past a shot was fired from a window of Conway House, or from a corner of its yard, and a soldier wounded. It was never known who fired the shot; our negroes assured me that the house was locked and watched. The Union soldiers, alarmed and enraged, battered down the doors, and, finding no one, began vengeance on the furniture. It happened, however, that in my mother's bedroom was hung a portrait of myself, and this caught the eye of a youth who had known me in Washington. He cried to his furious comrades to stop. The servants were called in, and were much relieved when they found that it was to speak of my portrait. Old Eliza cried, "It's mars' Monc the preacher, as good abolitionist as any of you!" It was some consolation to me that, though long regarded as the black sheep of the family, my portrait saved Conway House from destruction, for that was contemplated. (M. D. Conway)

Other homes did not fare as well. At the outbreak of the war, "Snowden" and "Chatham" were both assessed at $10,000, the two most valuable homes in Stafford. Union troops sailing up the Rappahannock River mistook "Snowden" to be the home of owner John's brother, James A. Seddon, Confederate secretary of war. From the river, the ships opened fire on the house and the Seddons had only moments to get out. Taking shelter in the laundry building, they watched their home burn to the foundation. "Phillips House," a short distance behind the "Lacy House" or "Chatham" and General Burnside's headquarters during the first Fredericksburg battle, was accidentally burned in February 1863 when a camp stove tipped over in the attic. (Eby)

Andrew J. Russell photograph of Phillips House ruins after February 1863. Lacy House ("Chatham") and Fredericksburg are visible in the distance. (Medford MA Historical Society)

Hosting the headquarters of Federal generals saved some of Stafford's largest houses. "Carlton" (across U.S. 17 from "Belmont"), according to family history, was used in December 1862 as headquarters by Rutherford B. Hayes, colonel of the 23rd Ohio Infantry and later president of the United States.

"Ingleside," west of "Belmont," hosted a Federal artillery position on its grounds and provided the green sprigs favored by the Irish Brigade during Fredericksburg. According to Charles Siegel of the Rappahannock Valley Civil War Roundtable, Gen. Joseph Hooker used several Stafford homes as headquarters, including "Clearview" in Falmouth in 1862 (an artillery position was also located on the grounds and, per Eby, General Burnside "camped there"). Siegel continues that "Chatham" served as headquarters to Generals McDowell, Burnside, and Sumner at various points and as a general hospital and artillery emplacement. Also, "Abraham Lincoln visited here and reviewed troops in the fields to the rear of the house." Despite universal reverence for George Washington—Federal troops stood at silent attention with caps off passing "Mount Vernon" and Southern troops resented Union allusions to Washington—"Ferry Farm" was not spared during the war. Artillery and engineering positions and a pontoon bridge across the Rappahannock were established on the property. At "Rumford," Mrs. Pollock, fifty-two years of age, was forced

Artist's rendition of "Carlton" by Jerrilynn Eby

to cook meals for twenty to thirty Union soldiers daily. The Pollocks had given thirty-two horses, twelve mules, eleven four-horse wagons, and other equipment to the Second Corps Artillery, Army of Northern Virginia. Likewise, "Sherwood Forest" and "Eastwood" were used as hospitals and bivouac sites for two Pennsylvania regiments.

General Burnside may have used "Little Whim" (Virginia 218) as a headquarters, but it is confirmed that the home was used by Gen. Marsena Patrick, provost marshal of the Army of the Potomac.

At least five Union generals were headquartered at "Bell-Aire" (Virginia 626/Leeland Road, one mile from Route 607). (Also see Chapter 8.)

During the winter of 1862–1863, a series of cavalry skirmishes and engagements took place in Stafford County. These running fights resulted from the strategic pause following the battle of Fredericksburg, during which the Union Army of the Potomac occupied a large area of Stafford in the winter of 1862–1863. The main body of the army was positioned from the current intersection of Interstate 95 and U.S. 17 to the Stafford-King George Line. To the west on the Warrenton Road, infantry outpost lines were established as far as Berea Church, and cavalry outposts as far as Hartwood Church. Many of the Confederates involved in the fighting at Hartwood Church were prominent members in the Army of Northern Virginia's cavalry corps.

Andrew J. Russell photograph of "General Whipple's headquarters, Falmouth" on April 5, 1863 (Library of Congress)

Andrew J. Russell photograph of Union thirty-two-pounder battery in position in Stafford. The vulnerability of Fredericksburg to the Union guns north of the Rappahannock is easily seen here. (Library of Congress)

The Union cavalry had established an outpost in and around the Hartwood Church along the Warrenton Road. Further west, they established videttes (mounted sentry[ies] guarding an approach route). Even during this period of relative inactivity, both sides used their cavalry to gain information and tactical advantage. Confederate scouting parties had been active making reconnaissance raids into Union positions; one of these took place on February 6, 1863. Federal cavalry Gen. William W. Averell complained:

There are scattered over the country between the right flank of the army and the railroad many young rebels, who assemble, mount, and form scouting parties at the shortest notice. Upon the approach of any superior force they are suddenly transformed into idle, loitering citizens, without arms, and professing great ignorance of the country.

Scouting parties destroyed Union communications lines, threatened cavalry picket lines and outposts, and attacked Yankee targets of opportunity. They conducted guerrilla operations in the county. Tactical intelligence, under the purview of the cavalry arm, was provided by a spy network in place in western Stafford (spying had also been active in Widewater and White Oak sections) providing information on Federal troop movements and activities. (Musselman)

Hartwood Church had become a shelter for men, horses, grain, and rations, and a source for firewood, and its position near the Warrenton Road mandated its outpost use. In his raid toward Hartwood Church, Brig. Gen. Fitzhugh Lee commanded the 1st, 2nd and 3rd Virginia Cavalry Regiments, a combined force of about 400 troopers. Although Union General Hooker had created extensive cavalry covering forces and infantry defense lines from Dumfries down to the Rappahannock at Falmouth and west to Berea and Hartwood, the terrain in western Stafford favored Confederate cavalry actions. Union troop complained of the "full sympathy " given by "every inhabitant " of the county. A Pennsylvania cavalry officer added:

Women and children as well as men took a patriotic pride in giving information as to our movements, and vied with each other in schemes and ruses by which to discover and convey to the enemy facts which we strove to conceal.

Hartwood Presbyterian Church, site of Fitz Lee's 1863 cavalry raid (Stafford County)

Fitz Lee's Cavalry Brigade was best exemplified by Col. Thomas T. Munford's 2nd Virginia Cavalry. The 2nd had been at Fredericksburg in December 1862, then had made the Christmas raid on Dumfries and Fairfax Station. In January 1863, the regiment was on picket duty along the Rappahannock and in winter camp. Their routine had been interrupted only by a review parade, normally a happy break from the unending drudgery of cavalry operations and a chance for the troopers to show off in front of appreciative generals, staffs and, most importantly, local females. In this case, the regiment had been compelled to ride some fifteen cold and wet miles from their camp to perform in the review. Rain reduced visibility to fifty yards, no doubt discouraging all local females from attending. Afterward, the Rebel troopers rode through more mud and rain fifteen miles back to their camp's limited forage and comforts. (Musselman; Official Reports—O.R.)

In February 1863, the regiment braved snow and cold as they moved forward on a raid, first to Waller's Tavern and occupying a picket line along the Rappahannock. On the 11th they had fought a combination of snow, hail, and rain. Probably because of the harsh conditions, Colonel Munford himself led the 2nd's raid on Hartwood Church. Fitz Lee took his command from Stevensburg, Culpeper County, on February 24, 1863. They crossed the Rappahannock at Kelly's Ford and moved along the Warrenton Road from Morrisville (eighteen miles from Falmouth) to Hartwood through a daunting fifteen inches of snowfall. On the 25th around 9:30 A.M., Fitz Lee divided his force and ordered their approach march to Hartwood Church. (Musselman; O.R.)

Unfortunately, Averell's Union cavalry were changing the guard at Hartwood Church at noon when the Confederates struck. Apparently mistaking Lee's blue overcoat-clad troopers for fellow Federals, they were surprised and trapped in file formations, unable to maneuver in the mud and snow. Fitz Lee's troopers rounded up prisoners and horses and moved toward Falmouth. En route, the Confederates scattered the 16th Pennsylvania and 4th New York Cavalry Regiments, which had reinforced the Hartwood outpost. The 3rd Virginia foiled at least one counterattacking Federal force by charging on Fitz Lee's order. A Northern observer wryly added: "considering the (poor) conditions of the roads, (the Federals) made very good time to the rear." By 7 P.M. on the 25th, Fitz Lee's cavalry finally encountered Union infantry defenses near Berea Baptist Church and withdrew in good order toward Morrisville. The successful raid cost the Rebels fourteen casualties, while capturing 125–150 Yankee cavalrymen, their horses, and much-needed equipment. Lee praised Colonel Munford and Maj. Cary Breckinridge for their gallantry. (Musselman; OR)

While the Hartwood engagement was a tactical success for Fitz Lee's brigade, it had little effect on the situation. New York infantryman Emmet Irwin wrote:

Lt. Hugh Adie Jr., Stafford cavalryman
(Mary Cary Kendall)

We have about 16 hours clear weather and then 3 stormy. Everything is quiet I believe in the army with a few exceptions. Our cavalry picketts were drove in last Wednesday, some of them came in our camp as hard (as) they jump. The rebel cavalry followed them as far as the infantry picketts then wheeled about and off again.

Lt. Hugh Adie Jr. was representative of the cavalrymen who fought throughout the entire Civil War. Six feet one inch tall (half a foot taller than the average soldier of both American armies), he had a dark complexion, dark hair, and eyes so dark that they seemed "black" to casual observers. Born in February 1838 in Delaware, Adie enlisted on April 21, 1861, as a sergeant in Company "A," 9th Virginia Cavalry, the Stafford Rangers. He served continually until September 9, 1862, when he was taken prisoner near Poolesville, Maryland, by the 8th Illinois Cavalry, and shipped to Washington, D.C. After brief confinement, he was paroled and exchanged on September 27, 1862, at Aiken's Landing, on the James River. Adie returned to duty by November 1862, and on December 18, 1862, he was promoted to lieutenant. He served in that capacity until 1864, when he was detailed to the provost marshal's duty. After the war, he again lived in Stafford, where he died (at "Woodford") on March 30, 1918, at the age of 80. He was buried in the cemetery of the Aquia Episcopal Church. (Krick)

Lt. Hugh Adie's shotgun, now in the White Oak Civil War Museum (Free Lance-Star)

Closer examination of his record reveals Adie had been enlisted by then Capt. Thomas Conway Waller and his horse was valued at $150. He later received $50 bounty for extending his enlistment. On June 9, 1863, he was promoted to first lieutenant. "Soldiering on" into 1864, he acted as company commander several times and was on detached service as well. On December 19, 1864, he was furloughed. Hugh Adie Jr. probably fought in most of his regiment's battles, including: the U.S. occupation of Fredericksburg; Stuart's First Ride Around McClellan; the Seven Days' battles; Stuart's Hanover Court House to Fredericksburg Expedition; and 2nd Manassas. As a prisoner from September 9–November 1862, Adie missed battles at Sharpsburg and Mountville. He probably returned in time for the fights at Leeds Ferry; Fredericksburg; the Dumfries and Fairfax Station Raid; Rappahannock Bridge and Fords; countering Stoneman's Raid; Brandy Station; Middleburg; Hanover and Gettysburg, Pennsylvania; Bristow Campaign; Mine Run Campaign; the Wilderness, Spotsylvania Court House, North Anna, and Haw's Shop (all May 1864); Cold Harbor; the Petersburg Siege (including Jones' Farm on September 30, 1864, and Vaughan Road on October 2, 1864); and Appomattox.

When Adie returned to the farm, his weapons and equipment were stolen. He later served as sheriff of Stafford County. By his death, Hugh Adie had seen America reunify during the Spanish-American War, and U.S. troops were fighting in France. The old soldier perhaps laughed as fools called it the "war to end war." He had not lived long enough to see Stafford recover economically from its Civil War wounds. Recently, Hugh Adie's shotgun reappeared for sale at a Bealeton gun show. A South Carolina dealer sold it to D. P. Newton of the White Oak Civil War Museum, and the weapon was returned to Stafford. The shotgun Adie carried in the war can now be seen as a "piece of history" in the museum. (National Archives—NA; FLS)

There was an African-American component of Stafford's Civil War Confederate contingent as well. Cornelius Lucas was a slave before the war and served as cook and servant to Capt. John Gray Pollock of the Fredericksburg Artillery. After the war, Rev. Cornelius S. Lucas led the Little Shiloh Baptist Church and was the moderator of the Howard Grove Baptist Church near Berea. In 1876 he ran unsuccessfully for the city council in Fredericksburg. He also ran a grocery store on Douglas Street and a coffeehouse on William Street in Fredericksburg. Before his death in 1927, Lucas received a Virginia state pension and a citation from the Fredericksburg chapter of the United Daughters of the Confederacy for his wartime Confederate service. (Musselman; Fitzgerald)

The 1910 census was the first to identify surviving veterans, thus allowing a reasonable accounting of Confederate survivors and their wartime units. Of those alive in 1910:

248 47th Virginia Infantry
201 9th Virginia Cavalry
148 30th Virginia Infantry
115 Stafford Light Artillery
43 Fredericksburg Artillery

Other Stafford Confederate veterans had served in the 4th, 6th, 15th, 23rd, and 24th Virginia Cavalry Regiments; the 7th, 13th, 17th, 55th, 62nd (Mounted) Virginia Infantry Regiments; 9th Virginia Infantry Battalion; 25th Virginia Militia Battalion; 43rd Virginia Cavalry Battalion (Mosby's Command); and VMI Cadet Battalion. Confederate veterans also served in 2nd Maryland Infantry; 5th Texas Infantry; 15th Louisiana Infantry; 16th Mississippi Infantry; Purcell Light Artillery (Va.); Staunton Light Artillery (Va.); Terry's Texas Rangers; staffs; C. S. Navy; and unknown units. Also included were men who had worked for the Confederate Congress and government and in state and county governments during the war. (Musselman)

Perhaps reflecting a societal sea change, veterans of Union units were also among the 1910 Stafford veterans. Their units included the 9th Pennsylvania Cavalry; 10th West Virginia Infantry; 16th New York Cavalry; 51st Pennsylvania Infantry; 56th Pennsylvania Volunteers; 98th Pennsylvania Infantry; 118th Pennsylvania Volunteers; staffs; and unknown units. (Musselman)

Spanish-American War

In the Spanish-American War, Stafford again provided her sons to serve on foreign fields, this time fighting for a reunited nation. Musselman has identified seven Staffordians who fought in the Spanish-American War. Luther Lancaster died on the USS *Maine*.

World War I

Musselman identified 329 men and women who served in the First World War. During that war, the Quantico Marine Base was established, beginning a long relationship with Stafford County. The Quantico Marine Corps Reservation now occupies approximately fifty-one square miles of the northern portion of Stafford County and constitutes about 18 percent of the county's land area. The joint history between the county and the base has developed into a warm friendship and pride in mutually shared experiences.

Illustrative of Stafford's World War I soldiers was Pvt. William Weedon Cloe. A compilation of his father's letters and military experiences by historian John Haile Cloe permits direct comparison with Stafford Civil War soldier letters.

"Weedon" Cloe was born on June 12, 1898, in Shacklet, Stafford County. His grandfather had served in Company "A" (Stafford Rangers) of the 9th Virginia Cavalry in the Civil War. His father was a farmer who served on the county school board for 33 years while holding a local mail delivery contract. The Cloes were farmers in a poor, agricultural community; they lived modestly, and opportunities to view the outside world were rare. Weedon Cloe spent his youth on the farm and received a typical seventh-grade education. As he came of age, Europe was embroiled in the "Great War" (1914). On April 6, 1917, the day the United States declared war, he enlisted (age eighteen) in the 1st Virginia Infantry Regiment, Virginia National Guard. Three days later, Weedon wrote to his mother:

Pvt. William Weedon Cloe, 116th U.S. Infantry
(John Haile Cloe)

I am now a member of Richmond Grays "1" Va. Inf. I am now in a drug store writing this. Would have written before but didn't finish exam until this morning. I went through every drill they have. We have two drills a day. You need not get uneasy if you don't hear from me real often…I stayed at the (Grays) Armory last night and we are fixed up pretty good. Have lots better eating than I expected when I came and the Officers are all seem to be fairly good men. I get 15 dollars a month, board and clothes. now as soon as we go in Federal service will get 30 each month, but of course don't know how soon that will be, but will try send you money every month. Now don't worry about me because I am looking out for No.1.
Your Loving Son
W. W. Cloe
PS I sent a few dollars you can have. Will sent my picture as soon as I have it taken.

Mustered into Federal service in Richmond between July and August 1917, his unit was shipped to Camp McClellan, Alabama, in September 1917, becoming the 116th U.S. Infantry, 29th "Blue-Gray" Infantry Division. Company "B," Cloe's unit, trained until May 1918 when they left for France. Homesick, on October 5, 1917, he wrote to his family:

What is the matter that I haven't heard from you? We were transferred this morning. I am now in B Company. It is no longer any Richmond Grays company for A and C divided their men between B and M companies. I am glad that they put me in B for that is from Richmond and I know right many boys in it…

They departed from Hoboken, New Jersey, and crossed the Atlantic safely. Weedon wrote snippets of letters to relieve home-front anxiety. Like so many Americans, he witnessed foreign devastation, expressing gratitude that America and his home were spared. On June 28 he wrote to his mother:

Co B 116 U.S. Inf
AEF, June 28,
1918

I reached here all safe and sound. We were on the waters thirteen days and never got sick on the whole way over. That is not like some. I was a little sick one evening but was chiefly cause of something I ate…Well, I can't tell you much of this place as I haven't been here long enough but something I was surprised to see the condition so many little children look to be. There are not any young men I have seen at all that haven't got a uniform on, and lots of old men are also carrying the rifle. When I look at the little pitiful children I don't blame anybody for going to do what they possibly can. The women are doing all the men's work such as loading wagons, etc. This is a right large city but there are not any street cars. Everything rides bicycles. We will only be in this place a short time. I have sure seen some (of) this world in the last month. Everything I have seen over here reminds me of the pictures I have seen of the old colonial days. Everything looks like it is a hundred years behind times. We have several persons in this company that can speak French and one was talking to four little children that came up close to our shelter and I asked him what they said and he told me that they asked him where there father was and said the Germans had killed him. Now who wouldn't be willing to go and help whip the heathens so that women and children that have brothers and husbands at the front can come back with peace that will last. Of course it is hard for you all over in the states but I pray that it won't be like it is over here. Now it may not be so bad all over France like it is here as I have seen only small portions of it yet…When you write let me know where Ainsley (his brother was in the 6th Infantry Division) is and how you are all getting along. You ought to be proud to have two men in the Army. I know I would be if I were you…

After additional training in France, the 29th moved (August 8) into a defensive sector, Haute Alsace, near the Swiss Border. They were attacked by the Germans, and when withdrawn from the line on August 29, 1918, they had suffered 744 casualties. Like his Confederate grandfather, although not in the main action, he had now "seen the elephant":

Co B 116 U.S Inf
APO 765, American EF
Aug 30, 1918
My Dear Mother

Well I haven't written to you for over a week and I guess you have begun to wonder what is the matter with me. Well I have been in the front line trenches for some time and you know any one there doesn't have much time to write. We came out yesterday eve to clean up a little but are now just a little way back and I guess I will go back there tonight but don't expect to stay long. This company was real lucky had few casualties. I never saw but very few Germans. But I got to shoot at one anyway. I feel fine and just as happy as a lark and I hope I will see a Hun fall from the shot of my rifle before I leave this sector. You must not be uneasy just because I am close to the Boches as they are not too dangerous as anyone would think...No Mans land is lonesome looking when there is nothing going on. But there is enough to keep most anyone awake most of the time. I will have enough to tell when I get back to keep me talking for the rest of my life. I doubt if they will let me tell much as I have written you or not so I will just have to wait and tell you when the war is over.

The 29th was placed in reserve near Verdun in late September 1918 until the St. Mihiel Offensive commenced. Pershing committed the 29th and 33rd U.S. Divisions and two French divisions on October 8 to seize the Meuse Heights above that river. The 29th seized its objectives by October 9 and 10. During the period of twenty-three days in the Meuse-Argonne, the 29th had suffered 1,053 killed and 4,514 wounded. His October 19, 1918, letter reveals (by omission) he now truly understood the horrors of war:

Dear Mother,

Just a few lines to let you know I am safe and all OK. I have received several letters from you lately and all of them came in so good and am so glad to hear that you all are getting along so nicely. I haven't heard anything from Ainsley for so long that I have begun to think that he has forgotten me. But I hope he has written to you every chance he gets. We have been driving the Germans now for some time and will write and tell you more about it as soon as I get more chance. Certainly have had some experiences in the fighting line and I thank God that he has carried me through. You must give my love to all and tell them I am doing what they expect me to and that is my best. Will write again when I can.

George Wilson, Brooke resident, about 1918 in France (Dorothy Jackson)

Safely behind the lines on October 31, 1918, Weedon was able to take stock of his experiences—equal parts joy, humility, sorrow, pride, and survivor's guilt—more reflectively. Hospitalized in Revigne, near Bar-Le-Duc, on November 3, 1918, he had bronchial pneumonia. The war ended eight days later with him still in hospital (where he remained until January 1919). Returning to his company he found that much had changed; the boredom of waiting to return home was palpable. After another illness (mumps) and hospitalization, Cloe finally went home. He mustered out at Camp Lee in May 1919 and returned home. (Cloe)

In 1923 Cloe married his sweetheart, Elizabeth; they honeymooned in New York. Their home, "Laurel Hill," initially lacked electricity and running water. Cloe remedied those situations by installing a gas carbide generating light system and a gasoline-powered pump. He connected a battery-powered telephone line to his parents' home. Weedon Cloe became a substantial member of his community. He was a member of Aquia Episcopal Church (a vestryman), the Masons, the Ruritan Club, and the American Legion, and served on the county Board of Supervisors, representing Aquia District. Cloe would be tested once more at the beginning of the Second World War. He died on January 8, 1947, aged 48, shortly after surgery for a brain tumor. (Cloe)

World War II

War came unexpectedly to all Americans on December 7, 1941. It came to Stafford in October 1942, when the Marine Corps Base at Quantico required expansion of its training facilities and maneuver areas. On October 6, 1942, the U.S. Government formally notified those living in the northernmost one-fifth of Stafford that their lands were to be confiscated within two weeks and to vacate their properties. Some of those families had sent sons to fight in the Civil War, endured Union occupation, and sent sons to Cuba in 1898 and France in 1917–1918. Now they were being dispossessed, including William Weedon Cloe. On October 8, the *Washington Post* featured an article titled "The War Comes Home to Farmers in Nearby Virginia." That article described Cloe as "solid and substantial" and quoted him:

I went through the last war, volunteered as a matter of fact the day after the war was declared (it was the same day), and if they need my farm to get through this war, then they can have it...I'm classified 3-A now and if they need me for this one, I'm ready. (Cloe)

Falmouth boys in the First World War: Burton, Fritter, Boutchyard brothers, and Gallahan (Robert Burton)

Cloe may not have spoken for all of his neighbors, but the effect of their sacrifice was the same. They gave up their homes for their country. The farm, about 160 acres in 1942, now lies mostly under Lunga Reservoir. Another Cloe home, "Laurel Spring," which had been purchased by William S. Cloe from the Burroughs family in 1863, had burned in 1942 prior to the Quantico expansion. "Laurel View," associated with the Stark and Cloe families, was built about 1840. It was taken over by Union troops at one point during the Civil War, and:

Artist's depiction of "Laurel View" by Jerrilynn Eby

> In 1923 William Weedon Cloe purchased the property from the Starke heirs. He and his wife effected many repairs, replaced dilapidated outbuildings, and improved and modernized the house. They opened a dairy that later became a Grade A Retail Permit operation. Some of the modernizations included the installation of running water (courtesy of a gasoline-powered pump), a carbide gas lighting system, and a battery-operated telephone system carried on the barbed wire fence between and the adjoining farm. (Eby)

Some of northern Stafford's oldest home sites were lost during the 1942 Quantico Base expansion. These "lost estates" included "Chopawamsic Farm," "Dipple," "Clermont," "Somerset," "Rectory," "Chelsea," "Providence," and "Bloomington." (Eby)

"Stafford Springs," "Locust Grove," "Marble Hill," "Mount Olive," "Spring Dale," and "Springfield," six churches and many smaller farms were also lost. A number were historically significant. "Chopawamsic Farm" and "Dipple" had been associated with the youth of George Mason (IV).

Artist's depiction of "Bloomington" by Jerrilynn Eby

George Mason (II) had lived at "Chopawamsic Farm" after 1709; the property ran from current Boswell's Corner on the west to "Clermont" in the east. The main house, constructed using local sandstone, was inherited by George Mason (III), who lived with his family on Aquia Creek until his accidental drowning. Mason's widow then moved her family (including George Mason (IV) to "Chopawamsic Farm." It was left by George Mason (IV) in his 1785 will to his wife (for her lifetime) and then to his son. Sold to William H. Fitzhugh in 1850, remnants are along George Mason Road. Another lost home, associated with Aquia Church, was "Dipple," a glebe farm (i.e., owned by the parish). Rev. Alexander Scott also tutored George Mason (IV). Scott, born in Dipple Parish in Scotland, purchased the property in 1724. Owing to a diversion of the Chopawamsic Creek to build an airfield, much of "Dipple" was submerged. "St. Mary's" was believed to be a part of "Dipple." "Clermont" was acquired by Rev. John Moncure, a Scottish immigrant, in 1727. He built a house that passed to John Moncure II in 1786 and to John Moncure III in 1796. "Clermont" remained in the Moncure family until about 1886 when it was sold to a Philadelphian named George

"Somerset" was a part of "Clermont" at first.
(Felicia Parlier)

Middleton. In 1920 it was purchased by Frank Hill. The house burned in 1940 and was rebuilt in 1941 only to be confiscated in 1942.

"Somerset" was originally part of "Clermont." It apparently remained in the Moncure family until it was confiscated in 1942. The "Rectory," associated with Rev. Jaquelin Marshall Meredith, was owned by Moncures at the time of the 1942 expansion. "Chelsea," built in 1819, is another Widewater home associated with John Moncure and George V. Moncure; it was also included in the Quantico expansion. "Providence," adjoining "Bloomington," was associated with the Wallers and Fords and, after the Civil War, with Rev. Jaquelin Meredith. Also lost was "Stafford Springs," once a Stafford resort and Confederate spy center. It was associated with the Blackburn, Fitzhugh, Dickinson, Cannon, Brawner, and King families prior to 1942. "Locust Grove," home to the Gaines and Alexander families, was located near Bellfair Mills overlooking Stafford Run. (Eby)

Little is known of some other homes lost in Quantico's expansion: "Marble Hill" was on the north bank of Beaverdam Run; "Mount Olive," an 1859 farm owned by Hannah Stone's heirs; "Spring Dale," named for the numerous springs on it, was owned by the Downmans and Tolsons until the expansion; and "Springfield." Even less is known about "Stafford Store," now in Lunga Reservoir, and "Traveler's Rest" (not to be confused with the southern Stafford place). The churches lost in 1942 were: Bellehaven Missionary Baptist Church; Church of the United Brethren in Christ; Massadonia Baptist Church; Mount Zion Baptist Church; Providence Church; and Stafford Store Baptist Church. Missouri Mills, a Stafford mill that had operated for 150 years, and Belfair Mills, which operated until the original establishment of the Quantico Base in 1917, were in the area. Other mills on the current base were Stone's Mill, Tolson's Mills (two), Master's Mill (Wigginton Mill), Purcell's Mill, and Dr. Wheat's Mill. (Eby; John Janney Johnson—Johnson)

Stafford provided troops for war against the Axis Powers of Germany, Japan, and Italy. For example, William Weedon Cloe's oldest son, of the same name, served in the Army engineers. The Cloes received $8,500 compensation for their farm and moved farther south in Stafford. Weedon Cloe took a job with the Richmond, Fredericksburg, and Potomac Railroad as station manager. He joined the Virginia Reserve Militia (see below). War heroes came in all shapes, sizes, genders, and ages. (Cloe)

The Stafford Home Front

The Stafford home front contributed to the war effort with bond drives, victory gardens and recycling campaigns. Representative of the spirit of the home front was Miss Edmo Corbin Lee, daughter of Civil War veteran Daniel Murray Lee. Born at "Westwood," she had taken over the running of "Highland Home" after her father's death. As a child she had contributed her pennies for construction of a Confederate memorial in Fredericksburg. "Miss Edmo" was also the first woman to serve on the Stafford County School Board. During the Second World War, she "traveled throughout the country in her green 1938 Chevrolet convertible to help monitor rationing for the Office of Price Administration. In 1956 she sold "Highland Home" (now a subdivision). A nephew, remarking on her long and remarkable life at one hundred years, said somewhat prematurely: "This woman is a Victorian and she ought to have gone to the Virginia Military Institute like so many men in the family did." In 1979, she turned one hundred years of age. (FLS)

World War II also brought to reality the concept of a nation at war. A local company of the Virginia Reserve Militia (VRM) was formed to guard vital transportation nodes in the county. On May 18, 1942, Brig. Gen. S. Gardner Waller, Virginia's Adjutant General, announced the mission of the VRM:

To furnish immediate local protection against saboteurs and raiding parties, destroying them or serving as a holding force, pending the arrival of better equipped troops.

In the parlance of 2003, they were a tangible force in homeland security. In the world of 1942 they were a practical recognition that German saboteurs were capable of infiltrating and disrupting the American war industries and economic system—a month after the VRM was created, German sabotage agents infiltrated at Long Island, New York, with plans to operate along the U.S. East Coast. Each county or city was to form one company, commanded by a

VRM "Minute Man" poses for photo. Three officers and forty-three men were needed for unit status.
(Richmond News Leader)

captain and two lieutenants, with fifty enlisted men. Companies consisted of two platoons of four squads each. Each squad, led by a corporal, was organized by locality. Each VRM member had to own an automobile capable of transporting an entire squad at one time, and the company was required to organize transportation so that squads arrived at their posts together. Each member also had to own a telephone and his own rifle or shotgun with ammunition. The Adjutant General's Office cautioned that each man should be a reliable communicator and source of intelligence as well, adding: *"The great value of the Virginia Reserve Militia lies in the ability to strike raiders, particularly parachutists, before the enemy has had the opportunity to organize for attack."* VRM membership required U.S. citizenship "of unquestionable loyalty; ages sixteen to thirty-five years (parental consent for those under eighteen); physical fitness; and required weapon, ammunition, telephone, and automobile (capable of transporting five passengers at forty miles per hour). "Minute Men" wore a forest-green, fatigue-type jump suit, floppy fatigue hat of the period, and low-quarter shoes. The large letters "VRM" were sewn over the right breast in line with the left upper pocket. The uniform, which cost $3.95 for the coverall and 95 cents for the hat, would add the appropriate rank or chevrons for officers and noncommissioned officers. A far cry from the stuff of glory and a clear break from earlier days, the uniforms were at least functional. (Moncure; *Richmond News-Leader*)

The Stafford VRM "Minute Men" Company mustered at Falmouth High School on October 17, 1942. Selected captain was Daniel M. Chichester; his lieutenants were Frank Moncure and Herbert L. Thornton. First sergeant was Clem Goodman, and Norman Brown was a sergeant. As there was no VRM officer to administer oaths, Justice of the Peace Fisher swore them in as special police. Four posts were outlined in Falmouth. Falmouth Boy Scouts were used as messengers. The local newspaper soon reported "Minute Men Unit Ready in Stafford" with forty-six men and three officers on the initial roster. In addition to Chichester, Moncure, and Thornton, the following family names were listed (some may be misspelled): Armstrong; Bayliss; Beagle; Beckham; Bolton; Brickert; Bridwell; Brooks; Brown; Catlett; Cleverley; DeShazo; DeShields; Flack; Goodman; Gordon; Green; Haleman; Harris; Heflin; Jett; Lunsford; MacGregor; Massie; McDaniel; Miller; Huntington; Monroe; Musante; Patton; Pearson; Snellings;

Stone; Sullivan; Thomas; Tulloss; Walker; Wirman; Wyne; and Young. They were "Stafford Company No. 90, Virginia Reserve Militia (Minute Men)." Others soon joined, and full strength of sixty three officers and men was achieved. Captain Chichester sent a committee to confer with the Board of Supervisors to see about helping with the $4.90 cost for each enlisted man's uniform. Company headquarters was established at "Four Gables" on U.S. 1 four miles north of Falmouth. Sergeants were soon designated and, not surprisingly, the name of W. Weedon Cloe of Stafford appeared, as did Norman B. Brown of Falmouth. As further insight into Weedon Cloe's character, he was forty-four years old (thus exceeded the maximum VRM age) when he joined the VRM shortly after his home had been confiscated. Corporals were John W. Patton (Berea); H. A. Flack (Roseville); William N. Cleverley (Falmouth); B .J. Musante Jr. (Falmouth); Charles E. Walker (Falmouth); James E. DeShazo (Route 2, Fredericksburg); E. Dallas Wyne (Falmouth); J. Lewis Monroe (Garrisonville); Andrew Truslow (Stafford); and J. Churchill Gordon Jr. (Stafford). New family names appearing on the roster of privates during the company's service were: Biglin; Bradshaw; Castle; Cox; Decatur; Dillon; Duncan; Homes; Karz/Kurz; Knight; Lockhart; Lowrey; Perkinson; Price; Solomon; Steward/Stewart; Timmons; Vaughn/Vaughan; Wine; and Woodwar. By December 1942, William Cleverley was added as staff sergeant; Robert Bridwell of Garrisonville was a sergeant; and Alaric R. MacGregor of Stafford and Leonard C. Haleman of Falmouth were added to the corporals. (Moncure)

The company received Training Memorandum No. 1, detailing possible chemical warfare agents they might be exposed to, their identification, and treatment. The company's posts were at "critical points," and two to three men were assigned to each. Highway bridges along U.S. Route 1 over Aquia Creek, Austin Run, Accokeek Creek, and Potomac Creek were specified in addition to the Falmouth Bridge over the Rappahannock. Railroad bridges of the RF&P. over Aquia Creek, Accokeek Creek and Potomac Creek were also listed as critical points in Stafford. Orders reflect that men were mustered out when ordered to active service in the U.S. Armed Forces. (Moncure)

Other Wars and Conflicts

Staffordians participated in the Korean War, Vietnam War, Cold War, and Expeditionary Conflicts in Grenada and Panama. They also served in the Gulf War. Unfortunately, no numbers or lists are currently available.

The War on Terrorism

America's latest war came crashing into every home in the worst direct assault by foreigners on this country since the War of 1812. Staffordians were working in the Pentagon on September 11, 2001, when the largest act of international terrorism ever perpetrated on American soil crashed three commercial airliners into occupied buildings there and at the World Trade Center's twin towers in New York. Representative is Louise Kurtz, a Staffordian who suffered 70 percent burns, including her fingers and parts of her ears. Other Staffordians were also direct witnesses to the horrific assault on the Pentagon.

2000 Census—Still a Place of Veterans

An estimated 13.75 percent of Stafford's residents are veterans, compared with a statewide average of 11.11 percent. The county placed twelfth in percentage of veterans in its population. Ten counties and independent cities had varied levels of 13 percent (i.e., from 13.01–13.92 percent). Among the counties and cities in Stafford's region, only King George County (13.87 percent) was listed among the top twenty-five Virginia jurisdictions. None of the larger Northern Virginia jurisdictions were in the highest 25 percent (although Fairfax and Prince William Counties had higher raw numbers of 96,389 and 34,639, respectively).

1. Willie C. Harris served in the Inter-war U.S. Army in the Engineers. Earlier, in the 1920s, he had served with the 10th U.S. Cavalry in Arizona and Texas. (Dorothy Jackson)

2. Sylvester Hamn, U.S. Army Medical Corps or Medical Service Corps, about 1943 (Dorothy Jackson)

3. Pfc. Carl B. Dickinson; bride, Dorothy Dickinson; and Tech 5 Ernest Stone, June 1943, Morrison Field, Florida. Carl B. Dickinson, U.S. Army Air Corps, 1944 (Nancy Dickinson)

4. Pvt. Reginald Montague, U.S. Army [original negative reversed] (Dorothy Jackson)

5. Leonard Johnson, U.S. Army, wounded in Korea (Dorothy Jackson)

6. Seaman Robert Burton, U.S. Navy, 1949 (Robert Burton)

7. Pvt. Clinton Johnson, U.S. Army (Dorothy Jackson)

8. Samuel Jackson, U.S. Air Force, Korea era (Dorothy Jackson)

9. Louis Massie, U.S. Army, Korea era (Dorothy Jackson)

Stafford veterans of the Inter-war period—World War II, Korea and the early Cold War

Stafford County, Virginia

Chapter Five
Visitors of Note

Stafford's long list of visits by important historical figures is impressive. Some were welcome and some were not, but all played roles in the county's story.

Early Visitors

Early visitors Capt. John Smith, Pocahontas, and Capt. Samuel Argall were discussed in Chapter 1, and Archbishop John Carroll in Chapter 2.

General Count Donatien de Rochambeau and French troops transited Stafford in mid-September 1781. In fact, French Army troops of Rochambeau twice used Falmouth ford. Gen. George Washington, in New York, planned use of the 5,000-man French expeditionary force. When he became aware the French fleet was headed for the Chesapeake from the West Indies, he directed his forces to the Virginia Peninsula. Washington wrote to Rochambeau and his Continental troops on the march south:

From (Georgetown) a rout must be pursued to Fredericksburg, that will avoid an inconvenient ferry over Occoquan, and Rappahannock river at the Town of Fredericksburg. The latter may, I believe, be forded at Falmouth…

After the Yorktown victory in October 1781, Washington and his French allies moved north through Falmouth. A French engineer sketched the ford at Falmouth. It is estimated that 4,000 French troops and 2,500 Continentals crossed at the ford. (Erik F. Nelson)

In July 1785, John Marshall visited Stafford's "Richland" to aid his sister-in-law, Elizabeth Jacquelin Ambler, who had married Col. William Brent in March 1785. Brent was the son of William (1733–1782) and Eleanor Carroll Brent and had been an aide-de-camp to General Alexander, a lieutenant colonel of the 1st Virginia Regiment and colonel of the 2nd Virginia Regiment during the Revolution. He had died in June 15, 1785. On July 10, 1785,

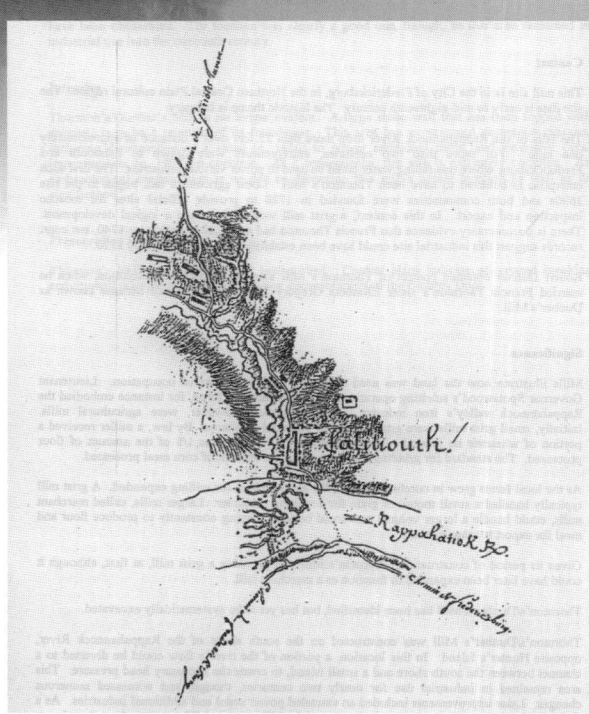

1782 map of Falmouth and its associated ford in Map of Eleventh Camp at Falmouth
(Library of Virginia)

General Count Donatien de Rochambeau, ally of Washington (Granger Collection)

Chief Justice John Marshall, U.S. Supreme Court
(Frick Art Reference Library)

Elizabeth Ambler Brent wrote:

> ...widowed, wretched and forlorn—a month since I was the happiest of wives...The 15th of June, a day never to be forgotten, my adored husband was snatched from my arms. The melancholy news soon reached my father and with his wonted tenderness he dispatched his carriage with my darling Brother (John) Marshall to bring me to my old apartment where now I sit miserable, oh how miserable.

Elizabeth Ambler Brent later married Col. Edward Carrington of Cumberland. At the time of his visit to Stafford, John Marshall was a Richmond lawyer and serving his first term in the Virginia General Assembly. John Marshall also had other ties to the region. (Brent's descendants [C. H. Brent] and Kendall)

Pierre L'Enfant, designer of Washington, D.C., and Benjamin Henry Latrobe, President Jefferson's architect of the Capitol, both visited Stafford. L'Enfant traveled down the Potomac in October and selected the Brent Quarry and its Aquia Stone pursuant to July 1791 capital city plans with President Washington to use sandstone for the Capitol and Presidential Mansion. In December the United States took title of what is now Government Island. Benjamin Henry Latrobe visited Stafford in 1806 to assess potential yields of Aquia Stone for additional construction. His notebook captured the visit and he sketched the Robertson home site on Austin Run (see Chapter 11). Jefferson's Architect of the Capitol concluded that no "fine" stone could be found, although in the future, such as in the 1820s, Aquia Stone was quarried to create the Capitol's east front columns.

Maj. Pierre Charles L'Enfant, designer of Washington, D.C. (National Archives)

Benjamin Henry Latrobe, "father of American architecture" (White House Historical Association)

President Martin Van Buren (Funk & Wagnalls)

Stafford County, Virginia

Charles Dickens (Civil War Times Illustrated)

Symbolic of the many Civil War visitors to Stafford are the names, units, dates, and initials carved on the Aquia Stone quoins of Aquia Church. Shown here are inscriptions from Confederates and Union soldiers as well as later locals. Note 5th Texas. (Lou Carcero)

According to Paul Wilstach's 1920 work, *Potomac Landings*:

There is a tradition that Martin Van Buren came in great style to "Richland" in his coach behind four white horses and liveried footmen to pay court to its mistress, a member of the Fitzhugh family, but that unsympathetic lady declined his hand.

This sounds suspiciously similar to the account of George Washington's unsuccessful courting of Mildred Strother of "Albion." Nevertheless, the story cannot be discounted, and Van Buren must be considered a visitor to Stafford. Renowned as a "dandy" and political "fox," such an event probably took place during his vice presidency and powerful role in the Jacksonian party. His known friendship with Peter Vivian Daniel of "Crow's Nest" may also have been a factor.

Charles Dickens, the famed English author, passed through Stafford going to Richmond and returned the same way in March 1842.

Civil War Visitors

President Abraham Lincoln and his secretary of war visited Union troops in Stafford, and Lincoln later visited Stafford County again. He had taken office in March 1861 shortly before the Confederacy was formed. Lincoln, whose main policy had been preservation of the Union, later expanded the goals of the war to include an end to slavery. He struggled doggedly to form a volunteer army to fight the Confederacy on its own ground and find a general or combination of generals who could deliver victory. Those goals were not achieved by either of Lincoln's Stafford visits (May 1862 and April 1863). Landing by boat at Aquia Creek, his party moved by military railway baggage car to Falmouth. There he visited Gen. Irvin McDowell at "Chatham" or "Lacy House." During this trip, Lincoln observed the tall Potomac Creek railroad bridge erected by Gen. Herman Haupt. Amazed, he said:

Texas Confederates of Wigfall's Brigade in Stafford or Prince William County camp. This brigade consisted of the 1st, 4th and 5th Texas (the latter scratched on Aquia Church quoin). (Lossing)

President Abraham Lincoln
(Library of Congress)

Secretary of War Edwin M. Stanton
(Library of Congress)

...it is the most remarkable structure that human eyes ever rested upon...This man Haupt has built a bridge across Potomac Creek about 400 feet long and nearly 100 feet high, over which loaded trains are running every hour, and, upon my word, gentlemen, there is nothing in it but beanpoles and cornstalks.
War Secretary Edwin McMasters Stanton, who accompanied the president's first trip, was agitated while crossing Haupt's rickety bridge. (See Chapter 10.) The troop review, involving some 70,000, took place near the current Grafton Village subdivision. One witness wrote:

Grand Review of the Army of the Potomac during President Lincoln's visit to Stafford (Century magazine)

The Army of the Potomac abandoning its winter camp "near Falmouth" (Century magazine)

Clara Barton (Library of Congress)

Mr. Lincoln on horseback is not a model of beauty such as an artist would select. A more awkward specimen of humanity I cannot well imagine.

Walt Whitman (Lossing)

More specifically, it was in the Boscobel section, east of the current intersection of Virginia Routes 608 and 607, that Lincoln reviewed Union troops. He also reviewed troops on the Deacon farm "Grafton" (not to be confused with the Waller home in northern Stafford). Union IIIrd Corps encampments were nearby. (Deacon farm is now the site of the Grafton Elementary School.) The review was highlighted by a frightened mule train's response when artillery saluted the president; the witness recorded: "how the panic stricken mules did whee-haw and the army wagons rattle-bank that day over the Stafford plains." (Musselman; Eby; FLS)

President Lincoln came to Stafford again after the winter of 1862–1863, visiting the revamped Army of the Potomac, then under Gen. Joseph Hooker. Hooker would prove a disappointment, but his reform and training of the army, carried out completely on Stafford's territory, improved performance at Chancellorsville in May 1863 and laid the foundations for victory at Gettysburg (July 1863) and frequently thereafter. (Musselman; Eby; FLS)

Two famous Americans visited Civil War Stafford as medical volunteers. Clara Barton, later founder of the American Red Cross, came to "Chatham" on December 8, 1862. She wrote her cousin from "Camp near Falmouth, Va." on December 12 at 2 A.M.:

Artist Edwin Forbes depicted Walt Whitman, company aid man, as third in line for chow in a Stafford camp scene. (Edwin Forbes/William Forrest Dawson)

Stafford County, Virginia

Rutherford B. Hayes
(New York Historical Society)

Oliver Wendell Holmes Jr.
(U.S. Army Military History Institute)

Five minutes time with you; and God only knows what those five minutes might be worth to the maybe-doomed thousands sleeping around me. It is the night before a battle. The enemy, Fredericksburg, and its mighty entrenchments lie before us, the river between—at tomorrow's dawn our troops will essay to cross, and the guns of the enemy will sweep those frail bridges at every breath. The moon is shining through the soft haze with a brightness almost prophetic. For the last half hour I have stood alone in the awful stillness of its glimmering light gazing upon the strange sad scene around me striving to say "Thy will Oh God be done."

Barton, born in Massachusetts in 1821, had worked as a schoolteacher and founded several prewar "free schools." A Patent Office clerk when hostilities commenced, she sought to distribute food and medical supplies to Union troops. Later, she assisted the wounded on both sides of the conflict. Her front-line efforts, organized and effective, rightly earned her the title "Angel of the Battlefield." Armed only with a disciplined mind, able assistants, donated and purchased resources, and her father's Masonic pin (to gain access to the influential and powerful on both sides), Miss Barton achieved remarkable results. She visited Stafford twice during the war for a duration of two weeks. At "Chatham" in December 1862, she treated at least 1,200 wounded, filling the twelve available rooms with as many soldiers as possible, then filling floors, closets, and pantries. Forced to also use outside grounds, she had fires built and brick outbuildings torn down to provide heated bricks wrapped in blankets to comfort the exposed, wounded men. At war's end she organized a Washington office to account for the missing and dead Union soldiers (that office has recently been rediscovered, complete with artifacts of Barton's tenure there). (Donald C. Pfanz—Pfanz; Happel)

Poet Walt Whitman came to "Chatham" on December 21 in search of a wounded brother. The battle situation, then a week old, had not significantly improved, causing his remark, "the house is quite crowded everything impromptu, no system, all bad enough, but I have no doubt the best that can be done; all the wounds pretty bad, some frightful, the men in their old clothes, unclean and bloody." As Whitman picked his way through the building, he stopped to write letters for wounded men or to talk to the wounded of both sides. (Pfanz; Happel)

Two men destined to occupy future high places in American government accompanied the Union occupying forces in Stafford. "Carlton" (across U.S. 17 from "Belmont") was reportedly used in December 1862 as a headquarters by then Col. Rutherford B. Hayes, 23rd Ohio Infantry, and later president of the United States. Oliver Wendell Holmes Jr., later associate justice of the U.S. Supreme Court, was a captain in the 20th Massachusetts Infantry. Following graduation from Harvard, he was commissioned. Holmes was wounded at Ball's Bluff (October 1861); after recovering, he returned to his regiment (March 1862), fighting in the Peninsula Campaign and at Antietam, where he again was wounded (neck). After recuperation, Holmes rejoined his regiment in Falmouth—he and another man had walked from Warrenton in November, transiting Stafford. Contracting dysentery in early December, he was in a hospital tent during the battle. After the battle, Holmes was on provost duty in Falmouth in January 1863. He and other officers of the 20th lodged at Mrs. Dunbar's house on Prince (now Carter) Street. When Duff Green, a neighbor, was arrested for allegedly signaling the enemy, Holmes presided and released him (perhaps an error as the Greens, with three sons in the Confederate army, were certainly suspect). Holmes and his regiment remained in Falmouth until the Chancellorsville battles, where he was wounded for the fourth and final time. By the time he recovered in January 1864, his 20th Massachusetts Regiment had been mustered out, and Holmes was discharged. (T. Jones; *Foundation Stones*)

Prince Felix Salm-Salm of Prussia (Free Lance-Star)

Princess Agnes of Prussia (Free Lance-star)

Prussian royalty was among wartime visitors to Stafford. In conjunction with their honeymoon, newlyweds Princess Agnes and Prince Felix Salm-Salm also celebrated their mutual December 25 birthdays in a Union Army camp near Aquia Creek. Thus beginning an adventurous life together, in the next eight years they followed the Union Army to Tennessee, Alabama, and Georgia, then almost rescued the ill-fated Emperor Maxmillian in Mexico. Their love story ended on a Franco-Prussian War battlefield. Prince Felix, born in 1828 in Westphalia, Prussia, was an aide-de-camp to Union Gen. Louis Blenker. He had married Agnes, a Canadian, in Quebec in August 1862. On their mutual birthdays they awoke

Belle Boyd (Time-Life)

Frank Stringfellow (Virginia Historical Society)

to a serenade by German troops and celebrated all that day. They had already visited the White House and President Lincoln. The prince died at Gravelotte on August 18, 1870, while with the Prussian Grenadier Guards. Agnes mourned greatly, but soon married an Englishman. The marriage soon ended, and she moved to Switzerland. She returned once again to the United States for a visit in 1899. Agnes died in December 1912 in Karlsruhe, Germany. (Barbara Crookshanks; FLS)

Among the more shadowy figures to visit Stafford were Confederate spies, scouts, and mappers. During the battle of Fredericksburg in December 1862, famed Confederate spy Belle Boyd tried to cross the Rappahannock at Falmouth. Though disguised as a man, she was soon caught and detained at a guard house established at an old grist mill near Falls Run (off Warrenton Road, now U.S. 17). The equally famed Confederate scout Frank Stringfellow was known to have taken refuge in Aquia Episcopal Church during a thunderstorm. The context of his scouting mission has been lost, but a "ghost story" tells of Stringfellow's presence. There also appears to be a Stafford component in what has been called the "Come Retribution" hypothesis—in the fall of 1864, facing an increasingly desperate situation, the Confederacy was considering a wide range of "secret service" activities to complement the strategies devised by Jefferson Davis, Judah P. Benjamin, Robert E. Lee, and others. These actions were all intended to bring about a favorable outcome to the long and brutal war. Known plans included attacks on the Union leadership (including bombing the White House and/or Capitol) and kidnapping Abraham Lincoln with an aim of holding him hostage for a negotiated peace settlement.

Little direct evidence of this period in our Civil War history remains. An exception is a map, accomplished with high command-driven urgency at a time when Stafford County had seemingly lost its military significance to the Army of Northern Virginia (then defending Richmond and Petersburg against Grant's relentless offensives). Despite the fact the mappers had completed a two-part map of Stafford in 1863 (now in the Virginia Historical Society), an urgent new project was ordered. On August 21, 1864, Confederate topographic engineer Lt. B. Lewis Blackford was ordered by the adjutant and Inspector General's Office to cease activities in North Carolina and report to Capt. Albert H. Campbell in Richmond. On September 2, Campbell ordered him to "proceed as soon as possible with your party to resume the survey of Stafford County…After completing Stafford, secure as much as possible of the county of Prince William, and Fauquier as far north as the Orange and Alexandria Railroad." Despite sickness and other difficulties, Blackford's party (fifteen men or 20 percent of the topographic work force) worked through September and October. Perhaps significantly, Blackford personally surveyed Stafford's Potomac River coastline, the "Secret Line" to Maryland. On October 25, Campbell ordered Blackford, after completing Stafford, to move with his party to King William to map the main roads into Caroline County. Campbell added that Maj. Gen. Jeremy Gilmer, chief of engineers, was *still anxious about Stafford.* On October 31 (the ordered date of completion and that marked on the map), the Topographic Department sent a last, urgent message: *"On completing your map of Stafford, report with it, in person, to this Headquarters."* Blackford subsequently mapped King William, Caroline, King George, and Hanover Counties until February 21, 1865, when he rejoined the Army of Northern Virginia. At the end of the war he was mapping in the Danville area, the "Last Capital of the Confederacy," and the planned destination for Lee's army. (This "Gilmer" or "Come Retribution" Map has been reproduced by the Stafford County Historical Society and can be purchased at the White Oak Museum, Stafford Court Clerk's Office, and Brooke Post Office. It is a detailed snapshot of 1864 Stafford.) (William A. Tidwell, James O. Hall and David. W. Gaddy—Tidwell, et al.)

Detail from 1864 Gilmer or "Come Retribution" Map
(U.S. Military Academy Archives)

Two interesting notations on the Stafford "Gilmer Map" relate to the extensive Secret Service activity that took place during the Civil War in the Union Army's rear area. In the upper left (northwest) corner of the map, written outside the boundary of the county are the neatly printed words "Stafford Springs." The only reason for such a notation would be to find easy access to an obscure place. The *Foundation Stones* describe "Stafford Springs" as an early-eighteenth-century farm, health resort, inn, and stagecoach stop on the road to Centreville and Manassas and the roads to Brentsville and Bristow; and add:

> During the Civil War, the business of the farm changed from entertainment for those seeking pleasure to the gravity of war, as Stafford Springs became the headquarters of Confederate spy operations. Its desolate location close to the Prince William County line, with few roads in that part of the county, allowed Confederates access to the neighboring county and woods and undergrowth into which to fade when they had completed their assignments.

In May 1864 Confederates returned to Belle Plain awaiting shipment to prisoner-of-war camps such as Point Lookout, Maryland, and Johnson's Island, Ohio. (Lossing)

Col. John S. Mosby (Library of Congress)

On the other (southeast) end of the county is a notation for "Traveller's Rest," home of the Gray family implicated by Union provost marshal Marsena Patrick for spying activities. "Snowden" and "Hollywood," connected with the Morsons and Seddons, both of whom were related to the Confederate war secretary, were similarly distinctively noted.

Mosby's Rangers, most storied of Confederate irregular forces, also visited Stafford. The "Gray Ghost," Col. John Singleton Mosby, led a May 1864 raid into Stafford. The raid is recounted:

…Mosby…led the remaining Rangers to interdict the Federal supply lines between Fredericksburg and Aquia Creek, a major supply depot for the Union army. Shortly after midnight on May 12, (1864,) the raiders found a wagon train about half way between Belle Plain and Fredericksburg. Mosby sent Charles Grogan, Company D, with half the raiders to the rear of the convoy. Grogan was told to stop the tenth wagon from the rear and tell the driver to pull off because the train had taken the wrong road. The partisans believed that when one wagon turned off, the others would follow. After Grogan turned the wagons off the road, Ben Palmer and about a dozen men were sent to halt the remaining wagons. Before the Richmond native could reach the lead wagon, it had stopped. The train leader had realized the last few wagons were missing and halted to what had happened. Mosby had instructed Palmer to try to stop the train with as little commotion as possible to avoid alerting the nearby Federal camps. As the young raider's group rode to the head of the column, they were met by the train commander. When the officer was informed that the train had been captured by Mosby, he drew his pistol and fired. Some of the drivers, realizing that this could be their only chance to avoid capture, joined in the fight. The Rangers quickly subdued the wagoneers and gathered their weapons, while some of the Confederates began unhitching the horses and mules. Other raiders went through the wagons—which turned out to be ambulances carrying wounded from the bloody fighting in the Wilderness—searching the injured soldiers for valuables, and gathering the ambulatory wounded. A few of the injured veterans hid their pocket books and timepieces in the straw that covered the wagon beds. When the partisans departed with the horses, mules and prisoners, one Federal remembered, "Our position was rather absurd, wounded men, unable to walk, in ambulances stuck in the mud, without horses or drivers." Alerted by the noise of the attack, the nearby cavalry camps sent detachments to assist the wagons. When they arrived at the scene, they found the raiders had departed with 25 prisoners and 60 horses and mules. A detachment of 300 cavalry pursued the partisans, but failed to overtake them. The raid had been so successful and easy that as soon as he delivered his prisoners in Fauquier County, Mosby gathered additional men, including Marshall Crawford, John Edmonds, and Charlie Hall, and returned to repeat the raid. Arriving in the vicinity of the first attack the

Rangers found their earlier activities had resulted in increased security on the supply route. On May 17, the raiders encountered a Federal detachment from Falmouth under the command of a Captain Nicholls, about four miles from Belle Plain. In the ensuing skirmish, the Union patrol guide, a man identified only as Davis, was wounded in the head. The Federal reports allege that the raiders were dressed in Union uniforms. The Rangers returned safely to Fauquier County on May 19.

Mosby's men, specifically Companies "C," "E," "F," and "G," under Lt. Col. Chapman, would return to Stafford on their way to and from the Northern Neck, where they remained from December 1864 until the final days of the war. This controversial deployment of half of Mosby's command outside his normal operating area has been directly linked to the "Come Retribution" hypothesis. During one of the last actions of the war, Mosby's men were encountered (and captured) escorting Lt. Thomas Harney of the Torpedo Bureau (Secret Service), reportedly intending to place a bomb in the White House. (Hugh C. Keen and Horace Mewborn; Tidwell et al.)

There are other tantalizing stories of scouts and spies in Stafford. John Tackett Goolrick wrote:

…The famed underground telegraph of the Confederacy ran from Washington down the eastern shore of Maryland, across the Potomac to Aquia or Potomac Creek, or to the point most convenient , and through Stafford to Fredericksburg, and onward to Richmond. The Federals, even when they had a hundred thousand or more men camped in the county, had never been able to stop this "telegraph," and they knew it was because of the loyalty of Stafford people…This twilight zone of the war had always been thick with spies, and many homes had harbored Confederate spies, while many watched diligently to discover Federal spies.

A number of spying and scouting incidents occurred in Stafford, and parts of a known communications line ran from Brooke Station to "Camp Clifton" (Clifton Chapel) to Evansport (Quantico) to Manassas. Confederate and Union scouting parties clashed at Wiggenton's Mill in February 1863, and "an extensive spy network existed in Stafford that reported on troop movements along the Potomac, Rappahannock, and Warrenton Road."

Pvt. (later Lt.) Eustace Conway Moncure, 9th Virginia Cavalry, relates a scouting mission of his in May–June 1864. The account demonstrates the extended range of the cavalry scouts in collecting information:

General Hampton told me to return at once and go to Fredericksburg to ascertain if any reinforcements had marched in that direction or if there were any approaching…the next morning I left for Fredericksburg up the Potomac river to Widewater and saw Mr. Williams, who was stationed in that neighborhood to watch the Potomac and report the movements of troops by transports down the river. He informed me of the passage of DeCesnola's troops the week before and that since then no troops had passed by land or sea…I spent a whole day in Stafford, and returned, passing Fredericksburg, and took the old stage road to Bowling Green… At this point my services as a scout ended.(Musselman; Krick)

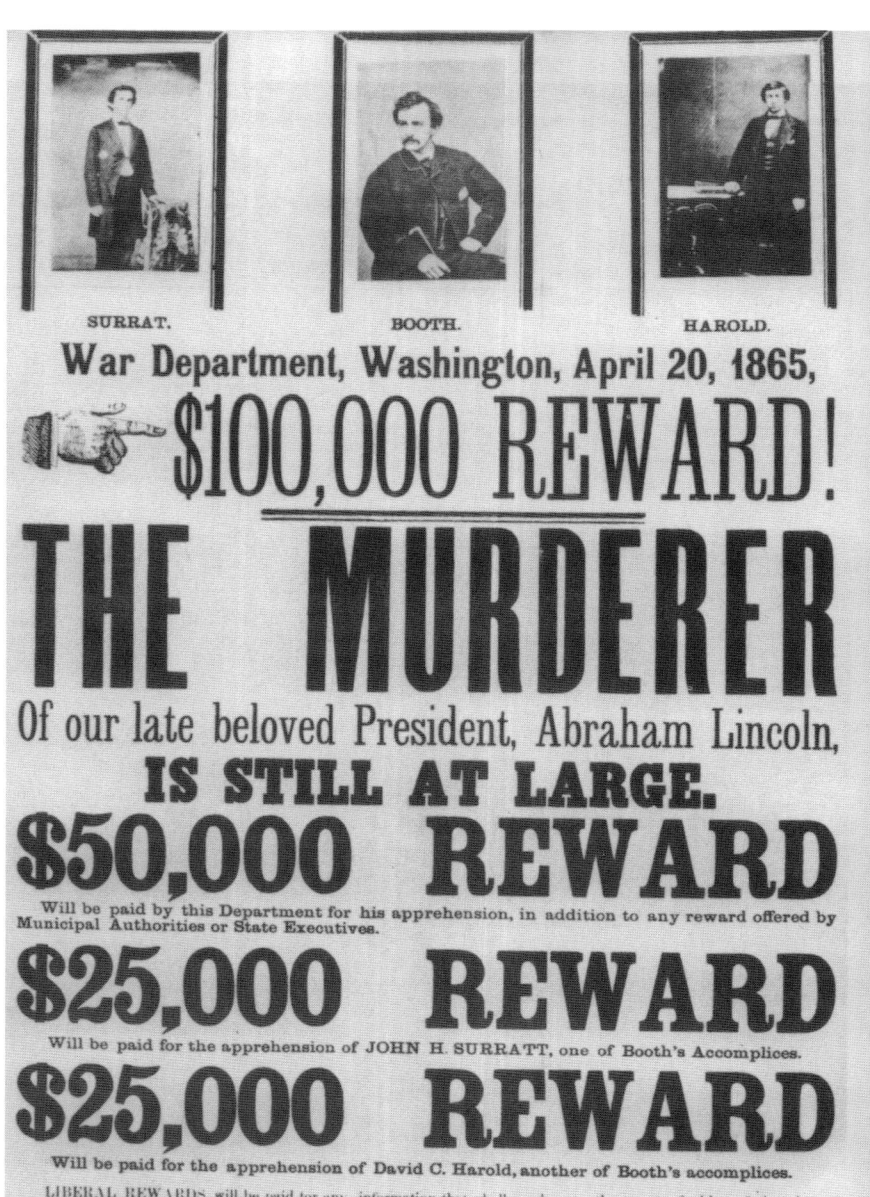

John Wilkes Booth and David Herold appeared together on the same rewards poster published by Union authorities.

(Library of Congress)

Even a facetious use of the term "visitors" does not adequately fit two who passed through Stafford: President Lincoln's assassins. If the planned kidnapping of President Abraham Lincoln had taken place in 1865, John Wilkes Booth and the other conspirators might have all come through Stafford. Instead, Booth shot Lincoln, and he and David Herold escaped into southern Maryland via the "Secret Lines" of the Confederate Secret Service. After eleven days of hiding from pursuing Union troops and U.S. Secret Service detectives, Booth was killed and Herold captured in the Garrett farm in Caroline County. Booth's body and prisoner Herold were transported by wagon and horseback, respectively, through Caroline and Stafford Counties to Belle Plain, where they boarded the steamer *John S. Ide* for the trip up the Potomac River to Washington. White Oak families tell of people receiving word that Booth's body was coming through and watching the roads for the procession. After the trip upriver to the Washington Navy Yard, Booth's body and prisoner Herold were transferred to the ironclad *Montauk*. Herold joined four other suspected conspirators, and an autopsy was conducted on Booth's body. Later, U.S. Detective Bureau agents pretended to dispose of the body, which was buried under the floor of the Old Penitentiary. Herold was later tried and executed.

Some 150,000 Union soldiers qualify as Stafford's most unwanted guests at the time, occupying the county: after the spring 1862 seizure of Fredericksburg; the late fall of 1862 prior to the battle of Fredericksburg (December 1862); the winter of 1862–1863; and in the spring of 1864. Like soldiers in all wars, they found little to like in a place where they were forced to spend a hard winter—one Wisconsin officer likened Stafford's occupation to a Union "Valley Forge."

Troops of the Union 110th Pennsylvania Infantry formed for inspection in their Stafford camp. "Camp near Falmouth" appeared on many letters. (Library of Congress)

Stafford camp of Union Pennsylvania Infantry (Western Reserve Historical Society)

Provost marshal tent in Union Stafford camp (Western Reserve Historical Society)

Stafford camp of Union 12th New York Infantry (Western Reserve Historical Society)

Drum Corps, 61st New York Infantry, Falmouth, March 1863 (Library of Congress)

Union Army Post Office, Falmouth
(Library of Congress)

The "Mud March," the low point of Union operations in Stafford, depicted by Edwin Forbes (Library of Congress)

(Left to right) Union Army Cmdrs. Irwin McDowell, Ambrose Burnside, and Joseph Hooker were among many Federal generals headquartered in Stafford during the war. (Library of Congress)

Col. Paul Joseph Revere, grandson of Paul Revere of Revolutionary War fame, assumed command of the 20th Massachusetts Regiment at Falmouth in May 1863. He led the 20th until his mortal wounding at Gettysburg the following July.
(Norman and Lenetta Schools; 1906 regimental history/George Bruce)

A History of Our Own

Their letters are revealing and insightful—a 1st Pennsylvania Artilleryman writes in a German "accent":

May 15th, 1862
Virginia Staford Co.
Camp Near Falmouth

Dear Cousan, As i have a fue lasur (leisure) moments to write to let you no that i am well at presant and hope that these fue lines will find you and all the rest the same. i wrote to you onse before but did not resieve a answswer so i came to the conclosion to write again. whe have had some pirty heard times sinse i wrote to you last. whe left Camp pierpont one the 10th of March and whe have been marching from one plase to another sinse whe left there and whe had some bad weather reigning the half of the time. there are about 20 of our men in the hospitle and sick report it was very unhealthy all spring but thank god i had no raisin to complain yet fore i in very good health ever sinse i left home. whe are now nere the raihanoe (Rappahannock) about one mile from fredricksburg. there are a great many weomen and children here but the men are most all gone and ther is not much of a union feeling amung them. they do not like the yankey very much. they would tare down the stars and strips if they would dare but i think that the rebles are almost plaid out…

Even less charitable, more racist, and more informative, was a letter written by Union soldier "T.O.M." of the 95th New York Volunteers and published in a New York newspaper:

AQUIA CREEK, VA, May 21 (1862).

I stole away from my squad last Sunday, after working an hour, and went to take a stroll through the country. I find that the poorer class of people around here are as rank abolitionists as ever (Horace) Greeley or (William Cullen) Bryant were. They state that the niggers injure white labor. The large slaveholders all had slaves; and when they had more work than slaves could do they hired the free niggers of the neighborhood in preference to whites—as they worked cheaper, and answered their purpose just as well. A poor white man could only get twenty-five cents per day and board. In fact, from the account that one man gave me, the poor whites are treated as bad as the negroes by the rich planters of the country. The people, taking them altogether, as a class, are the most ignorant I have ever known. One of them—a man who is said to own a thousand acres of land—argued on me, the other day, that South Carolina was a part of Virginia State. The women, young and old, smoke or chew snuff. The most of them are dirty and slip-shod—although I have seen some exceptions, but "like angel's visits, few and far between." The rich people are morose and unsocial. They charge exorbitant prices for the butter, milk, and eggs that the soldiers buy from them. They would show their teeth if they dared; but that time has passed, and it is only in their dark and ominous glances that you can read the hatred they dare not express in words. I met one man, whose name is Butler. He is a poor man, and, of course, is a Unionist. The accounts he gave me of the atrocities committed by the rebel soldiers (in the period of April 1861–April 1862) are dreadful. How General Holmes allowed such deeds to be committed are beyond my comprehension. He has told me that the North Carolina troops, who were stationed here last fall and winter, met a young married woman in the woods near Aquia Village and outraged her person. Her name was Gallatroin. She was found next morning dead where they had left her; and yet the men who committed this barbarous act were never punished for it. The same fellows also went to a free negro's house and violated the persons of his wife and daughter, and shot him dead on the spot because he tried to prevent them. Another man has told me that they could not enter a house without trying to violate the females, or else grossly insulting them before they left. They also burned or scuttled all the boats belonging to the poor fishermen, before they left, and were going to put to the torch to the mill, and thus leave the people to starve, when the news arrived of our approach and prevented them from doing it. The principal town in Stafford County is Stafford Court House. It is composed of a store, a court–house, and three or four private residences. There was a Dr. G.I. Conway who lived there. He was employed by the rebel authorities to hunt up the people of Union sentiments and report them. Two Northern men who had settled there and bought land from the planters were the first informed on. These men's names were Maury. A party of Arkansas soldiers went to their houses in the night–time, dragged them from their beds, and after treating them to a ride on a rail, gave them their choice to either join the Confederate Army or else be shot on the spot. Of course they joined. They were sent away to Louisiana, and the man that sold their land to them had the unparalleled impudence to try and sell it again. There are a good many soldiers, who have deserted from the enemy, or else pretend they have deserted, living in their own homes. I, for my own part, consider them spies, and think that the officers ought to look sharper after them. (William B. Styple, *Writing and Fighting the Civil War*)

Like their Confederate counterparts, Union occupiers foraged and pillaged the county for food and wood and left their graffiti on walls of churches, including the sandstone trim of Aquia Church

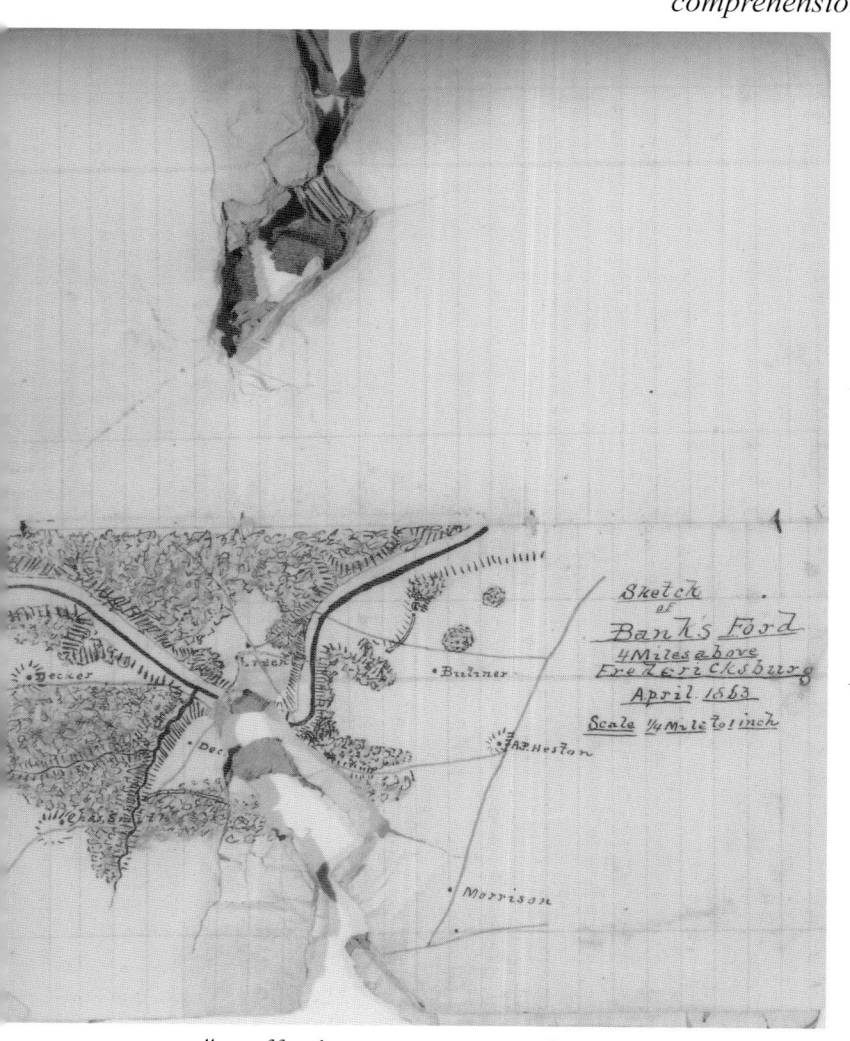

Not all Stafford area visitation was happy, even for Confederates. Capt. James Boswell, "Stonewall" Jackson's chief engineer, was felled in the same volley in which his general was wounded at Chancellorsville. The bullet coursed through his notebook and a map of Banks Ford on the Stafford side of the Rappahannock, site of the Celebrate Virginia complex. (Museum of the Confederacy)

and homes. Federal depredations were not limited to Staffordians who were alive. A wartime letter from Margaret Waller Ford complained that Union soldiers camped on her farm and raided the ancient Brent Cemetery on the "Woodstock" property, carrying off headstones to use for camp fireplaces.

One unintended benefit of Stafford's 150,000 unwanted Yankee guests was their leaving behind substantial supplies when they departed in May and June of 1863. For example, the 15th Virginia Cavalry's regimental quartermaster found abandoned supplies of hard-tack, overcoats, and camp implements that proved useful to neglected Southern troops. No doubt Staffordians also picked over the camp remains of the occupying forces. (Eby; John Fortier)

The Union Balloon Corps was a part of the Federal army in Stafford. During both the Confederate and Union occupations, the Union Army employed reconnaissance balloons in order to acquire information on Confederate troop movements and activities.

In June 1863 a Pennsylvania soldier mentioned reconnaissance balloons in use on the Rappahannock at Banks Ford (ironically the site of Celebrate Virginia's planned gondola line):

Thaddeus Lowe, reconnaissance balloon pioneer (U.S. Army)

Reconnaissance balloon equipment on "Falmouth Heights," drawn by Edwin Forbes. Half-concealed is the balloon, and visible in the foreground are the mobile hydrogen-gas generators. (Library of Congress)

Lowe's mobile gas generators (Lossing)

On December 8, 1861, Union Col. William F. Small, 26th Pennsylvania Volunteers, made a balloon reconnaissance sketch detailing Southern camps from Stafford's Chopawamsic Creek to Prince William's Occoquan Bay. (National Archives)

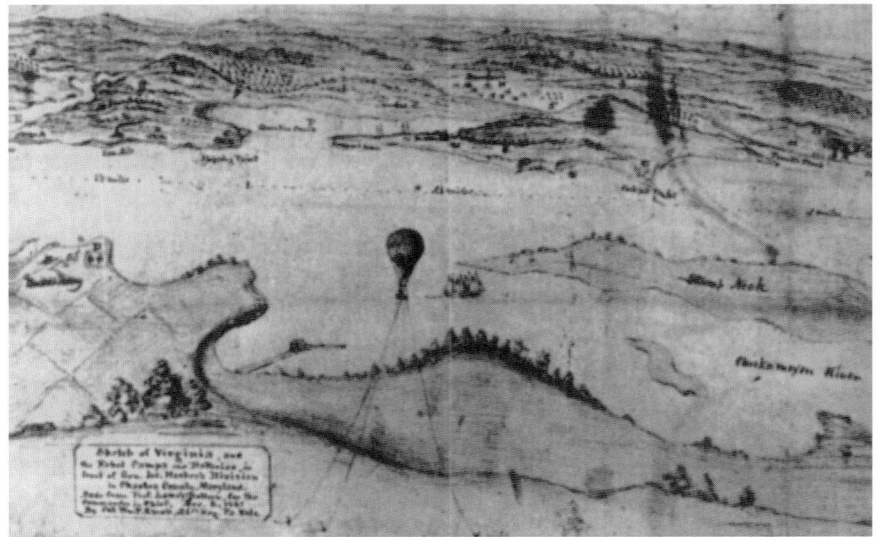

Stafford County, Virginia

Grover Cleveland (Clarence Hornung)

Benjamin Harrison (New York Historical Society)

...This morning the rebs throwed shels at our balloon but did not hit it. They were on one side of the river and we were (on) the other and then the picket commenced fireing, and we returned the fire and silenced them.

A balloon reconnaissance history adds:

...sometime later one of the assistant aeronauts reported to his chief that "Lieutenant Libby took the balloon in tow along the (Rappahannock) River bank." On another occasion James Allen and an engineer officer took observations over a course of two miles from a balloon towed from its position at Banks Ford.

This was reported in a letter to Brig. Gen. G. K. Warren on June 11, 1863 (seven days before the Pennsylvanian's letter above). Balloon Corps Information had kept General Sedgwick aware of the actions at Chancellorsville to the west in the May 1863 battle there. Reconnaissance balloons also operated from a field north of the "Phillips House" (Northside Drive, one-quarter mile off Virginia 218, east of "Little Whim"). (F. Stansbury Haydon)

Several late-nineteenth- and early-twentieth-century U.S. presidents visited Widewater to enjoy its natural beauty and opportunities for hunting and fishing:

While Clifton was most noted for the huge seine fishery..., the property may also have been one of the first duck hunting establishments in the United States. It was extremely well-known for its excellent hunting and the ducks came there in the thousands. Presidents Cleveland and Harrison came regularly to hunt as did many other people. Theodore Roosevelt also came once or twice but not as frequently as Cleveland and Harrison. (Eby)

On February 13, 1896, President Cleveland wrote to Mrs. Waller, "I desire to acknowledge your thoughtfulness and kindness to me on my duck hunting expedition and also the courtesy of Mr. Waller in giving me the opportunity to shoot from his blind at his ducks. The apples you sent to Mrs. Cleveland were greatly enjoyed and she joins me in "returning thanks." He forwarded photographs of "the President and his wife." Cleveland's Widewater adventure was chronicled in the *American Field: The Sportsman's Journal* on March 28, 1896. (Kendall)

Near the December 1861 balloon reconnaissance site, the Widewater flight experiments of Samuel Pierpont Langley took place at the turn of the twentieth century. As one writer expressed it, "Kitty Hawk gets the glory, but credit Stafford County with an assist." A 1966 article adds more detail—although it annoyingly reports the flights took place at "Tidewater," Virginia. Langley, an aviation pioneer and astronomer, indeed conducted his flight experiments off Stafford's Widewater Potomac River banks. A self-educated genius born in 1834, he had worked at the Harvard Observatory in 1865, as a U.S. Naval Academy mathematics professor, as director of Pittsburgh's Allegheny Observatory, and as a professor at Western Reserve University. Langley had been experimenting with flying machines since the 1880s before his appointment as third secretary of the Smithsonian Institution (1887).

On May 6, 1896, he launched a pilotless airplane from a houseboat off Chopawamsic Island, which belongs to Stafford County. The flight, the first mechanically propelled flight by heavier-than-air machines—which Langley called "aerodromes"—covered 3,000 feet, followed by another that traversed 4,200 feet. Some of Langley's 1896 work with "Aerodrome No. 5" was documented and photographed by Alexander Graham Bell. Based on available information, it does not appear that Bell actually visited Stafford, although that is a possibility. He reportedly exited a train at Quantico and made his way to the Potomac from there. Of Langley's work, Bell wrote:

Theodore Roosevelt (Library of Congress)

Professor Samuel Pierpont Langley (Smithsonian Institution)

> *Under the impulse of its engines alone, it advanced against the wind, and while drifting little and slowly ascending, it described a curve of about 100 metres in diameter and having been driven its course for abut a minute and a half at a height in the air which I estimate at 81 feet...*

William McKinley reportedly hunted on Brent's Point at the hunting lodge that is now "Cedar Lodge." (Bettmann Archive)

Stafford County, Virginia

May 1896 Langley Experiment (Smithsonian)

October 1903 Langley Experiment
(Smithsonian; Belmont/Mary Washington College)

Modern view of the Potomac spot where Langley's experiments took place, Widewater
(Owen L. Conner)

The plane landed in the Potomac River, having achieved a top speed of twenty-five miles per hour.

In October 1903, with pilot Charles M. Manly aboard, Langley attempted two trials off Widewater from a houseboat with a full-sized, piloted airplane. These experiments ended in crashes. He tried again off Arsenal Point, where the water was narrower, on December 8, 1903. Those also ended in failure. His experiments had cost $73,000: $50,000 from the Ordnance Board and $23,000 from the Smithsonian. These remarkable events were immediately eclipsed by the December 17, 1903, Wright Brothers' experimental flight at Kill Devil Hills, near Kitty Hawk, North Carolina much shorter flights but with all-important successful landings. Wilbur Wright later wrote that Langley's stature as a scientist had convinced them that manned flight was possible. Langley, who died in 1906, was rightly honored as one of America's aviation pioneers, and the first aircraft carrier and an air force base in Hampton/Newport News were named for him. He also inspired future aviators, including Gen. "Billy" Mitchell. Aviation pioneer Glenn Curtiss continued Langley's work and successfully flew a modified version of an aerodrome on June 2, 1914. (Joseph Curl, *Prince William Journal*; Charles B. van Pelt, *American History Illustrated*)

In addition to presidential visits, Widewater, known as a "wealthy man's hunting paradise," attracted sportsmen, especially between 1917–1941:

Widewater in the years between the world wars remained largely undeveloped, and everyday life was still characterized by farming and fishing...By this time, however, the large former estates of the Brents, Fitzhughs, and Lees had been permanently divided. Though older families such as the Lees and Moncures retained ownership of some smaller parcels, much of the property was now owned by newcomers seeking peaceful country life in Stafford County and by hunting and fishing clubs catering to northern sportsmen. Many underground freshwater springs in Aquia Creek stimulated the growth of underwater plants and kept the creek relatively free of ice in winter. As a result, this area became known as a "wealthy man's hunting paradise" and attracted visitors from Baltimore, Philadelphia, and New York. During this period, the New York Yacht Club maintained a station at Simms Point (west of Brent's Point). (JRIA)

World War II's "Organizer of Victory," General of the Army George C. Marshall, was one of many distinguished guests of John Lee Pratt at "Chatham." George Washington and Abraham Lincoln, and probably Robert E. Lee, were earlier guests in the Stafford house. Ironically, the two men with whom Marshall has been most frequently compared are Washington and Lee. Lee definitely visited "Richland" in Widewater. On May 28, 1869, he wrote his wife from Fredericksburg that "If I can accomplish it, I will go to "Richland" tomorrow, Saturday, and spend Sunday." Lee's son and namesake confirmed the visit:

Gen. Robert E. Lee in 1869
(Dementi Studio Collection, Richmond, VA)

Widewater duck hunters, 1890s
(Felicia Parlier)

From Fredericksburg he went to "Richland," on the Potomac, near Aquia Creek, where his brother (Sydney) Smith (Lee) was then living. This meeting was a great pleasure for them both, for two brothers were never more devoted. This was the last time they saw one another alive, as Smith died two months afterwards.

According to tradition, General Lee also met Kate Waller (later Dr. Kate Waller Barrett) when she was a youngster. It may have been during this visit as the Wallers lived next door at "Clifton," although the story relates that Lee, taken by Kate's gift of a flower, was at "Richland" when he cut a button from his uniform as a gift. Some Confederate veterans, lacking civilian clothing, did wear their uniforms (with cloth-covered buttons) from 1865. But it is unlikely that any were doing so in 1869, especially Robert E. Lee. (Happel; Kendall)

General of the Army George Catlett Marshall
(U.S. Army)

Douglas Southall Freeman (Richmond News Leader)

Prime Minister David Lloyd George (Funk & Wagnalls)

Other visitors to Stafford included the famous industrialist Henry Ford and his wife, who also visited "Chatham" in 1932, and Dr. Douglas Southall Freeman, editor of the *Richmond News-Leader* and one of the most famous Southern historians, who was a guest speaker at Aquia Episcopal Church's bicentennial celebration in 1951.

David Lloyd George, who had ruled UK finances and munitions in World War I and as prime minister had seen the end of the war and was a leading figure in the Versailles Treaty, visited "Belmont" in 1923. A Civil War enthusiast, he also visited several key historical sites in the area. Calvin Coolidge, a Vermonter, visited "Belmont" as vice president (1921–1923) prior to assuming the presidency after the death of Warren Harding in 1923. He was President of the United States until 1929. (Belmont/MWC) Even these Hollywood stars somehow found their way to Stafford:

Hollywood discovered Widewater in the late fifties when limousines bearing Sophia Loren and Cary Grant and flat bed trucks hauling lighting equipment converged on the Arkendale train crossing to film a critical scene in the film *Houseboat*. The film would have you believe that a southbound train and a houseboat being trucked east attempt to occupy the same space—the Arkendale railroad crossing—at the same time and that the laws of physics prevail. Widewater locals were hired to simultaneously throw boards up in the air in order to simulate the results of the "impact." In real life, the "houseboat," just a facade then, is now the landlocked home of a Beach family. Tinseltown came back for more in the early sixties, filming *A Kiss to the President*, (sic) with Fred MacMurray, in the same general area but a little north on (Virginia Route 658. (Mark Miller)

Calvin Coolidge (Funk & Wagnalls)

A History of Our Own

Cary Grant and Sophia Loren with "House Boat" cast (UCLA)

Fred MacMurray in "Kisses For My President" (UCLA)

Stafford's most important "visitor" wasn't a person at all. On June 12, 1993, the rededication of the Stafford County Courthouse featured an unusual and rare appearance of George Mason (IV)'s draft manuscript of the Virginia Declaration of Rights, as adopted in convention in 1776. Because of its fragile condition and historical importance, the Declaration has seldom been removed from Virginia State Archives. On display at the same time was the clerk's copy of the first Virginia Constitution. Among the most important documents in American history, the Virginia Constitution laid out the forms and procedures of an independent Virginia government. The Declaration of Rights, which directly influenced the Declaration of Independence, U.S. Constitution, and Bill of Rights, was Stafford's most honored guest that day or any day.

Chapter Six
Birthstones of Freedom

Government Island from the air
(Lou Cordero)

Government Island quarry site
(Barbara Kirby)

Derived primarily from **A Brief History of Government Island** *by Jane Henderson Conner in "(Aquia Quarry on Government Island)", the final report of the Government Island Committee, January 30, 2002, and an in-progress book.*

Nestled close to Aquia Creek's shore near Aquia Harbour Yacht Basin is a small island. Appearing as an extension of land, its western shore is actually joined to the mainland by a marshy bog. Few recreational boaters passing the inconspicuous island are aware that this unpretentious place, currently known as Government Island, once played a vital and lasting role in the architectural history of America's greatest public buildings. This elemental piece of Americana, also once called Brent's Island and Wiggington's Island, is a national historical treasure.

Beginning in Colonial times, sandstone was quarried to make tombstones, steppingstones, mantels, and architectural trim for buildings. On a larger scale, it was used to build bridges and foundations. Its most important use, however, was in constructing our nation's two most important historical structures, the White House and the U.S. Capitol.

The stone that comprises much of the island is an arkose sandstone that, though strong, can be carved freely. Virginia's early settlers referred to it as "freestone" or "Aquia Stone." The freestone was not limited to the island but appeared in outcroppings in other county sites along Aquia Creek and the Rappahannock River. American-Indian artifacts found on the flat southeastern portion of Government Island date from A.D. 500 to 1600. The island first appeared

Aquia Stone trim, Aquia Church. Built near Government Island, the church is an excellent example of how brick and stone were combined. All eight corners are trimmed in stone quoins, and the keystones around windows and doorways are of stone.
(Lou Cordero)

U.S. Capitol, 1846
(Library of Congress)

in written documents in 1678 in a land patent (which failed completion) from King Charles II. In 1694 the island was deeded to George Brent, nephew of Giles Brent (I), the first settler of Stafford. Brent opened the quarry on the "twelve-acre tract" where freestone was so plentiful. Its rocky cliffs then rose substantially higher than their current twenty- to forty-foot height.

The quarry supplied stone for basements and foundations throughout Colonial and Revolutionary Virginia. Through the mid-1700s, most Virginia houses were made of wood. Plantation owners used brick, and some chose to accent their buildings with Aquia Stone.

White House, 1846
(Library of Congress)

Like Aquia Church, Christ Church in Alexandria and George Mason (IV)'s "Gunston Hall" also combined brick and Aquia Stone. George Washington, who had also spent his boyhood in Stafford, was familiar with the operation on Brent's Island. Pohick Church, in Fairfax County, was trimmed in freestone. Entries in Washington's diary from 1774 and 1786 mention sending men to the quarry to obtain stone for steps for "Mount Vernon" (they are no longer present).

In June 1791, President Washington and Maj. Pierre L'Enfant planned a new capital city on the banks of the Potomac. Freestone was selected for the nation's Capitol and Presidential Mansion. In October, L'Enfant searched along the Potomac for freestone,

Christ Church, Alexandria, ca. 1897
(From stereo-image, Library of Congress)

visiting several quarries. He decided on the island's quarry, which was still operated nearly a century later by a Brent, Daniel Carroll Brent. In December 1791, the United States took title of the island for $6,000, or 1,800 pounds in Virginia currency. Another small quarry on Aquia Creek was rented from John Gibson of Dumfries.

At this point, Government Island entered its most significant period. The human stories and processes associated with the quarries and Washington, D.C., construction sites form a compelling narrative. It is a story of great political figures, skilled designers and architects, immigrant artisans, and free and slave laborers. Using techniques for extraction, transport, setting, and carving the stones that were little changed from ancient or medieval times, this band of American workers created the buildings that would ultimately become the symbolic centerpieces of American democracy and symbols of hope to a world of despots and tyrants.

A *Virginia Herald* advertisement, printed in Fredericksburg and dated December 22, 1794, stated:

Wanted to Hire, for the next year, to work on the freestone quarries, lately occupied by the Public, on Aquia Creek, sixty strong, active Negro men, for whom good wages will be given. They shall be well used and well fed.
Daniel C. Brent
John Cooke
Stafford Co.

Right, Daniel Carroll Brent of "Richland" (Virginia Historical Society)

126 · A History of Our Own

George Mason (IV)'s "Gunston Hall," in Fairfax County (Gunston Hall)

Common labor, provided mostly by slaves hired from their Virginia masters, was not hard to obtain, as residents were eager to have their slaves' "wages" paid to them. However, skilled workers and stonecutters were more difficult to find, so they were enticed from northern states and Europe with offers of free travel, including passage for their wives. Many, perhaps most, of the stonemasons came from Scotland.

Here irony reemerges. The two greatest symbols of freedom and liberty yet devised by man's hand were constructed by slaves, freedmen, and immigrants—none of whom would immediately benefit from the results.

It was the hardest of work: laborers toiled from sunrise to sunset, receiving seventy-five cents per day. The skilled mechanics initially worked from 6 a.m. to 6 p.m. (later reduced to ten hours/day); their daily pay ranged between $1.25 and $1.75, with the exception of the foreman of the stonecutters who received the highest daily wage of $3.75. Besides money, each man received one pound of pork or a pound and a half of beef, along with one pound of flour or bread per day. Quarters were set up on the island and on Gibson's land. Crumbled foundation stones visible on the island today provide mute witness to the island's quarters buildings.

The tools used to quarry the stone were pickaxes, mauls, and wedges. Planned cuts were probably marked with chalk lines, then chipped to a depth of eight to sixteen inches. Wedges were next inserted, and the blocks usually broke away cleanly. Chip marks, still evident on the island cliffs, silently document these two hundred-year-old quarrying techniques.

Quarry cuts into the rock cliffs are readily discernible.
(Lou Cordero)

Stafford County, Virginia

These enormous Aquia Stone columns once graced the U.S. Capitol building. They are now located in the U.S. National Arboretum.
(Lewis Williams/National Arboretum)

Once freestone blocks were created, they were removed using crude derricks or cranes and pulleys. The blocks were extremely heavy—one cubic foot of Aquia Stone weighs 120 pounds—and were placed on wooden sleds to be pulled by oxen down to the wharf. Placed first on flat-bottom boats, they were next transferred to masted ships at Coal Landing and sent south along Aquia Creek for approximately four miles, then north for forty miles along the Potomac River. Symbolically, although a simple matter of maritime necessity, the riverine route took the stones past the properties of George Mason (IV)'s "Gunston Hall" and George Washington's "Mount Vernon." Once the stone reached Washington at one of several off-loading sites, the freestone was removed and hauled to the building sites of either the Capitol or Presidential Mansion.

Concerns surfaced that the quarry would not yield enough stone to complete the Presidential Mansion, which was to be made entirely of stone. In a burst of creative management, the commissioners ordered that a ration of a half-pint of whiskey be issued to each man at the quarries, hoping that this would somehow increase production. They also requested twenty-five more able-bodied male negro slaves. Both of these measures failed to increase production. The commissioners, directly responsible for building the new capital city, then decided that the walls of the Presidential Mansion would consist of brick faced with freestone. The White House and the first section of the Capitol were completed in 1800. The quarry was later reopened whenever substantial amounts of stone were needed. For example, in the 1820s, Aquia Stone was quarried to create the impressive columns on the Capitol's east front. These enormous blocks were cut and sent north to be carved at the construction site.

The boundary marker stones for the District of Columbia were also made of Aquia sandstone. Set a mile apart, most are still present.
(Washington, D.C., Public Library)

The list of buildings known or believed to include Aquia sandstone is impressive by any measure: The White House; Christ Church, Alexandria; "The Octagon," Washington; U.S. Capitol; Aquia Episcopal Church, Stafford County's "Gunston Hall"; Pohick Episcopal Church, Fairfax County; "Mount Vernon" (steps, removed); Cape Henry Lighthouse; "Mount Airy," Richmond County; Fortress Monroe; "Thomas Nelson House," Yorktown; Treasury Building; and Old Patent Office

After the Civil War, Virginia took possession of lands that were deemed abandoned. These included the island, for all documentation of U.S. government ownership was lost or destroyed when Union soldiers looted the Stafford County Courthouse. Amazingly, it was only in the early 1960s that the true ownership of the island was unearthed.

In 1963 the Government Services Administration sold the island for $6,345. The island changed ownership several times. By the late 1970s, it was in the hands of Aquia Harbour Inc., which divided the island into lots for projected development. After reading about the island's history, their lawyer, a Richmond attorney, took possession of the land for ten dollars and services rendered. He held the island for twelve years, putting it on the market for $250,000–$400,000. Aware of its rich historic value and desiring to preserve such a site for future generations, the Stafford County Board of Supervisors purchased the island for $200,000 in August 1998.

(Also see Chapter 11: preservation; Government Island Committee Study; WHHA Christmas Ornament; Congressional Resolution; Special Congressional Session in New York; and Nixon Presidential Library ceremony.)

With paint removed for a recent renovation of the White House, the natural color of the Aquia Stone is revealed.
(Jack Boucher/HABS/Stafford County)

Aquia Stone was used in the Yorktown, Virginia, house of Gov. Thomas Nelson, signer of the Declaration of Independence. (Jane M. Conner)

Chapter Seven
Places of the Heart: Stafford's Homes

"Belmont" at twilight, west facade
(Belmont/Mary Washington College)

Part of 1751 map of Virginia by Joshua Fry and Peter Jefferson
(Library of Congress and George Washington's Fredericksburg Foundation)

Derived primarily from Jerrilynn Eby's 1997 work, They Called Stafford Home, *and the 1992 Historic Resources Survey, authored by consulting firms, Traceries, PMA Consulting Services, and Preservation Technologies, and commissioned by the Stafford County Planning Department and the Virginia Department of Historic Resources.*

Georgian Margaret Mitchell struck resonant cords in 1930s Stafford hearts when she wrote of an antebellum civilization "gone with the wind." Even then, Stafford was a place filled with as many memories as standing structures. Yet, aside from its churches, which survived civil war because of their capacity to shelter soldiers, horses, and supplies, surprising numbers of Stafford's home sites have survived.

There is a seminal spirit behind those structures, captured best in Larry Evans' moving description of Sally Lou Fitzhugh of "Poplar Grove," a descendant of Stafford's earliest families:

There is no way one can verbalize the meaning, the importance of that land. It is certainly something that no dollar can assess. Sally Fitzhugh senses the meaning; she knows what it is just as well as she knows herself, but she doesn't try to analyze it. She touches on that complex meaning when she talks about the family graveyard which sits beneath an evergreen, and where most of the members of her family have been buried since 1861. Southern character has its roots in that brooding land, and Southerners as perceptive as Sally Fitzhugh have been taught humility by that land. They have been taught that there is something larger than themselves. Many of the whites and blacks who have lived with that land of the South seem to share that humility…Sally Fitzhugh, sitting in a chair next to the Singer sewing machine she has used for many years to make clothes for her family, is staring out the window toward the rolling green hills of the farm. Without turning her gaze from that land, she tells me, "My idea of heaven isn't walking on golden streets and eatin' bread and honey. I can't imagine nothing more boring. I hope that heaven is just like this farm and I will be able to roam around it as I please." (Evans/FLS; Eby)

Ancestor Homes of Stafford

The Historic Resources Survey (HRS) states that there are eleven buildings or visible ruins of homes from Stafford's early Colonial period (1649-1789):

"Stanstead," "Concord," "Barnes House," "Cedar Hill Farm," "Albion," "The Fleurry's," "Hampstead," "Chatham," "Chapel Green," "Hickory Hill," and "Smith-Forbes House."

To these should be added "Vowles Tavern" and "Eagle Tavern" ("Temperance Inn"). The latter is described in the Falmouth section of this chapter. (Eby)

"Stanstead" farm, now on the site of Servicetown Truck Stop and surrounding area on U.S. Route 17, was part of four grants to James Innes, Robert Carter's agent, in 1703 or 1704. Totaling 2,331 acres, Falmouth was later built on part of this property. Robert Carter's son, Charles, inherited the property in 1732; after 1746 it belonged to James Hunter, owner of the famed ironworks. It appears on a 1751 map of Virginia. Hunter used the land to sustain his workers and slaves, and it produced income to support his other enterprises, especially his unselfish support of the Revolution. He willed the land to his brother, Adam, who also lived in the plantation house. The original mansion apparently burned sometime around 1784; several houses replaced it. In 1804, it passed to the Ennivers. Union troops camped on the farm in 1862–1863, and Federal General French was headquartered in the farmhouse. There was also a Stanstead stone quarry with a darker gray stone than Aquia Stone. Little survived the Civil War. (HRS; Eby)

"Concord," one of Stafford's oldest standing buildings, was built by the Waller family, who occupied home sites on the south bank of Aquia Creek. An earlier house was built on the creek. The present house, standing by at least 1730, was contemporary with the Washington Rappahannock Plantation House at "Ferry Farm." It was purchased in the 1850s by the MacGregors, who continued to live in it during the war. House and farm were picked clean in March 1863 by foraging Union artillerymen (properly receipted for $3,628 in wood alone). Twentieth-century MacGregors unsuccessfully claimed restitution. The house is being restored by the family. (HRS; Eby)

"Concord" in the 1930s or 1940s (Felicia Parlier)

"Concord" is one of Stafford's oldest standing buildings. (Historic Resources Survey)

"Barnes House," built around 1780, is a fixture in Falmouth. (Stafford County)

"Albion" dates from the early eighteenth century. (Historic Resources Survey)

"The Fleurry's," believed to have been constructed in 1769, was moved to Aquia Episcopal Church. (Jane M. Conner)

The "Barnes House," a Falmouth fixture below "Belmont" on Washington Street, was built around 1780. The early history of the house is unknown, but Joseph Ficklen of Belmont purchased it before 1850 and sold it to Harrison Barnes, who lived there with his sisters. It is a hipped-roof, Early American Colonial style design. When the last of the sisters died in 1890, the house was willed to former Barnes' slaves, Annie Duncan and Daniel Lucas. They lived there in "life tenancy," and Lucas delivered mail. The Barnes House was used as a school for black children (until neighborhood complaints terminated operation). The building, now pathetically propped up, looks as if it may spill over onto Washington Street. (HRS; Eby)

"Cedar Hill Farm" (along with Concord, The Fleurry's, Albion, and Chapel Green) is described in the Historic Resources Survey as a "vernacular expression of architecture" of the Early Colonial Period. It consists of two parts: "a small one-room plan house with a larger two-story, side-passage plan house appended to it. The oldest portion has a steeply pitched roof with porches on both end elevations that have been converted into enclosed spaces."

"Albion" is one of the houses along the Rappahannock River in southeast Stafford. Part of four counties during its lifetime and joining Stafford in 1777, the present house dates from the early eighteenth century (Eby). HRS says it "consists of sections from different building campaigns." The oldest section is a one-and-a-half-story frame structure with a brick end chimney. A larger two-story, three-bay building was added in the mid-nineteenth century. It has been owned by the Greenlaws since the beginning of the twentieth century. "George Washington is said to have courted Mildred Strother of Albion." (Eby)

"The Fleurry's," described as "our latest loss to the developers in Stafford County," was displaced by the Aquia Towne Center Shopping Center. Saved and moved to nearby Aquia Episcopal Church, "The Fleurry's" now houses church offices, giving it purpose into the twenty-first century. However, the loss of its trees, shrubs, and rolling green spaces is rightly mourned. The eighteenth-century house once was on a tract that extended from "Woodstock" to the current site of Anne E. Moncure Elementary School. Variously owned by "Greens, Suttles, Fleurrys, and Moncures," the house was believed to have been constructed in 1769 with nineteenth-century additions. (Eby; HRS)

"Hampstead" was part of Robert Carter's extensive land holdings acquired in the 1720s. The property was purchased in 1771 by James Garrard (1749–1822), who built a fine brick house. At some point, the brick was covered with weatherboarding and the house survived well into the twentieth century. James, the son of Col. William Garrard (ca. 1715–ca. 1786) of Stafford, moved to Kentucky and became the second governor of that state. After 1814, "Hampstead" was owned by the Rose, Skinker, and Briggs families. (Eby) HRS rates it now as a ruin. A family cemetery remains. The ruins are located on Virginia Route 616 (Poplar Road) next to "Poplar Grove" farm.

"Chapel Green" was built by a cousin of Mary Ball Washington. (Historic Resources Survey)

"Chapel Green" is located on the east side of Virginia Route 602, one-half mile south of Virginia Route 218 (White Oak Road). Little is known of its early history, except it was built about 1723 by Col. William Ball, a first cousin of Mary Ball Washington. Restored in the 1970s, the three-bedroom house has six fireplaces. The Balls lived there until 1919.

"Hickory Hill" is described as "beautifully situated on a hill surrounded by large weeping willow trees." At one point it was surrounded by "hickory trees, hence the name." Described as a three-story, hipped-roof structure of five rooms with a hall and a three-tiered staircase, its early history is unknown. The Turner family lived there during the Civil War; later, it was purchased by the Stevens family.

"Smith-Forbes House." Not described in Eby, HRS says it was designed, like the "Barnes House," in Early American Colonial style. *The Foundation Stones* relates that in the 1970s the house was a candidate for demolition and parking lot conversion on Prince Street in Falmouth. Associated with the Forbes family, Murray Forbes purchased the house for his sister, Delia, who married George Smith, a Scottish mill owner in Dumfries. Delia Forbes Smith was the great-grandmother of Mrs. Butler Franklin of "Fall Hill." The house was saved when Richard and Barbara Westebbe purchased it and moved it to "Holly Farm."

"Chatham" or "Lacy House" was one of the great Virginia plantations and had many famous visitors.
(Historic Resources Survey)

Brevet Maj. Churchill Jones of "Chatham" (National Park Service)

William Fitzhugh of "Chatham"
(National Park Service)

"Chatham" deserves (and has received) a history of its own. Southeast of Falmouth, it is the greatest of Stafford's Colonial-era homes and a true national treasure. John Smith gazed on the site in summer 1608. Later part of the Catlett Grant, it was sold to William Fitzhugh, whose ancestor of the same name had arrived in Virginia and Stafford in 1670s. Fitzhugh built the Georgian-style mansion home before the Revolution (constructed between 1768 to 1771) and named it in honor of William Pitt, earl of Chatham. It became one of the great Virginia plantations and was self-sufficient due to slave labor and horse-racing profits. George Washington visited during Fitzhugh's ownership. The next owners were Brevet Maj. Churchill Jones, a Revolutionary War veteran, followed by his brother, William Jones, a Tory during the Revolution. Jones transferred the home to the Coalters and, through marriage, it belonged to J. Horace Lacy before the Civil War. During the war, Abraham Lincoln, Clara Barton, Walt Whitman, and a host of Union generals—notably McDowell, King, Burnside, Sumner, and Gibbon—occupied "Chatham." After the war, the home went through a series of owners—Watsons, Joneses, Mays, Baileys, Howards, Sullivans, Devores, and from 1931 to 1975 John Lee Pratt. Henry Ford and Gen. George C. Marshall were among the distinguished modern Americans who visited "Chatham" during Pratt's tenure. Thanks to John Lee Pratt and the National Park Service, it has been preserved for posterity. (Happel)

"Vowles Tavern," or "Ordinary," was built about 1785 by Henry Vowles (1725–ca.1803). A fine two-story frame building designed to serve Falmouth visitors, it used glazed bricks, and workers fashioned the letters "HV" in the brickwork of one of the massive chimneys. One of five licensed taverns in Falmouth by 1792, it survived into the twentieth century. Threatened by expansion of a parking area for a nearby auto dealer, it was saved by the Westebbe family in 1976, dismantled, and reassembled near Holly Corner. The reassembled structure is now a private home.

Archeological sites: "Marlborough," "Crow's Nest" and "Woodstock"

A *Foundation Stones* article relates:

Citing a lack of towns and resulting inability to attract skilled craftsmen, the House of Burgesses passed an act requiring each county to establish a public port. The town of Marlborough was created shortly thereafter in 1691 as both the seat of government and port of entry for Stafford County. The new town was surveyed on land owned by Giles Brent (II). A courthouse and a few other buildings, including a tavern, actually were constructed. Local landowners, inconvenienced by this change, sought redress from the Burgesses. The act was suspended, sounding Marlborough's death knell. In 1715 the courthouse burned. The next courthouse was at Stoneman's Landing, where it remained until 1783. (The next move was to the site of the current courthouse.) John Mercer occupied the last house in Marlborough about 1726; he was the father of John Francis and James Mercer, and uncle and guardian of George Mason (IV). (Moncure)

It was to Marlborough Point that John Smith had come in 1608, where he met the Potomac Indians and a trading post was established. Following the tribe's departure, "white settlement flourished." A 1680 act established Aquia, Marlborough, and nearby Dumfries as early Virginia towns. Acts of 1691 and 1705 established Marlborough as a port town and population center. Brent's land, held in a lifelong lease by Malachi Peale, was on some maps as "Peale's Point." (Later maps used "New Marlborough," presumably distinguishing it from Lower Marlborough and Upper Marlborough in Maryland.) William Buckland drew up the plans for Marlborough, and court was moved there from private residences used after the earlier court (ca. 1690) had burned. Capt. George Mason (II), "high sheriff of Stafford," suggested the need for a jail. On February 11, 1692, twenty-seven lots were granted to 125 applicants (Waugh, Alexander, Andrews, Ballard, Beach, Brent, Cave, Maddox, Withers, and Mountjoy). A Potomac Creek ferry was established, and two taverns were licensed in 1691 and 1693. Marlborough's name was bestowed in 1706 to honor John Churchill, Duke of Marlborough (ancestor of Prime Minister

Capt. John Smith came to Marlborough Point in 1608. (Stafford County)

Winston Churchill), who had won a great victory at Blenheim in 1704. Rescinding the Port Act in 1710 undermined the town, but it also appears that Marlborough suffered the familiar Virginia malady of too many "gentlemen" and not enough craftsmen or artisans. (Eby)

A 1968 work traces Marlborough's development with the rise and fall of seventeenth-century tobacco fortunes. William Fitzhugh, "a wealthy planter and distinguished leader in the colony," wrote to his London agent: "We have now resolved a cessation of making Tob(acc)o next year…We are also going to make Towns, if you can meet with any tradesmen that will come and live at the town, they may have privileges and immunitys." Stafford's development of towns is also chronicled:

> Under the act of 1680 a town was to be built at "Peace Point"…where Giles Brent (I) had settled nearly forty years before, but there is no evidence that even so much as a survey was made there."

The Act for Ports of 1691 placed the town on Potomac Neck between Accokeek and Potomac Creeks on Brent property, leased for life by Capt. Malachi Peale. The town's cost would be 13,000 pounds of tobacco, paid to Giles Brent (II)'s guardian, Francis Hammersley. Two acres were laid out for the courthouse, and fifty acres were surveyed for the twenty-seven town lots. Of the housing, "brick houses certainly were not the rule. In remote Stafford County, shortly before the port town was built, the houses of even well-placed individuals were sometimes extremely primitive." George Mason (II) (licensed 1691) and George Andrews (1693) ran Marlborough's taverns. Andrews also maintained the Potomac Creek ferry. (Watkins)

After Mercer's death, his executor and son, James, sought to sell his library—noting that 1,200 volumes were available and that another 400 were missing, apparently loaned to friends. Eventually, everything else was also sold off by James and John Francis Mercer. Finally, the plantation itself was sold about 1806 to Staffordian John Cooke (connected with freestone quarries' slave rentals). Cooke insured a one-story brick dwelling, covered with wood, measuring 108 feet 8 inches long by 28 1/2 feet wide with a full-length portico and cellar under about half of the house. After Cooke's death (he did not live in the house; it was occupied by John W. Bronaugh) in 1819, the Marlborough property continued its process of decline and disintegration. (Watkins)

Marlborough was brought back to life only through archeology. In the 1950s, Dr. Oscar H. Darter of Mary Washington College, who had made critical early investigations, influenced the Smithsonian Institution to expand archeological work at Marlborough. Under Frank M. Setzler, a curator of anthropology, and C. Malcolm Watkins, a curator of cultural history, the work proceeded until a comprehensive report was issued in 1968. As the Smithsonian, specifically T. D. Stewart, had been involved in the 1938–1940 excavations of the Patawomeck Indian village, they had a knowledge base with which to begin. The archeologists began with the partially visible stone-and-brick wall system of the plantation and town and the building ("Structure B") believed to be Mercer's plantation house, through which Virginia Route 621 ran.

Farther up Potomac Creek from Marlborough, past Indian Point, was "Crow's Nest:"

In 1662 Rawleigh Travers received a patent for 3,650 acres on Potomac Creek. This land had originally been granted to Col. Gerard Fowke. By 1723 the plantation had been reduced to 3,525 acres. It remains a beautiful piece of property, a peninsula extending into the Potomac River, bounded on the north by Accakeek Creek and on the south by Potomac Creek. A high ridge runs parallel to Potomac Creek, and it was upon this ridge that a magnificent brick house called Crow's Nest was built late in the eighteenth century. Peter Daniel (1706–1777) moved to Stafford County from Middlesex as a young man and married Sarah Travers (1717–1788) of Crow's Nest, daughter of Rawleigh Travers of Stafford. Peter Daniel became one of Stafford's leading citizens, serving as senior presiding justice of the county and a member of the Committee of Safety. Long an advocate for freedom from England, he was the first to sign a protest against the Stamp Act. Peter and Sarah had three children, Hannah Ball Daniel (1737–1829), Travers Daniel (1741–1824), and Elizabeth Travers Daniel, who died an infant. Like his father, Travers was prominent in county affairs and was the official county surveyor from 1763 to 1794. Travers was also a justice for Stafford County and succeeded his father as presiding justice. He married Frances Moncure, daughter of the Rev. Mr. John Moncure of Clermont, by whom he had eleven children. "Crow's Nest" was originally the home of the Travers family and was named after *The Crow*, a black sailing vessel owned by the family. While most planters made use of the services of commercial shipping companies to haul their tobacco, some did own their own ships. "Crow's Nest" and *The Crow* came to the Daniel family through the marriage of Peter Daniel and Sarah Travers. By having their own ship, the Daniels could transport tobacco and necessary supplies as well as the finest wines and manufactured goods from Europe.

"Crow's Nest" was one of the largest and finest area plantations and a self-sufficient village. Future Supreme Court Justice Peter Vivian Daniel (1784–1860) and diplomat and Civil War editor John Moncure Daniel were born there. Maintained through the Civil War, it suffered intrusion and depredation like all of Stafford's larger and strategically placed homes, and declined afterward. The home site and nearby family cemetery lay in ruin. (Eby)

The Town of Woodstock began in August 1734 when the House of Burgesses decided to close the Marlborough tobacco warehouse and open a new one at the Brent's "Woodstock" property. Consistent with the population shift from Marlborough to Aquia Creek, a town built up around the warehouse. In 1772 the House of Burgesses assigned Thomas Ludwell Lee, Thomas Blackburne, Henry Lee, John Fitzhugh, Samuel Selden, and William Alexander to determine the cause (rain and floodwater) and extent (more than 18,000 pounds of tobacco) of damage. A town was formally ordered built on fifty acres of George Brent's land in 1792 (the adjoining plantation had been at least 1,700 acres by 1776). The plantation had eighty-one slaves performing the day-to-day labor in 1792. The town trustees were Travers Daniel Jr., Bailey Washington, John Cooke, Daniel Carroll Brent, John Rowzee Peyton, Valentine Peyton, John Murray, Robert Brent, Thomas Mountjoy, Elijah Threlkeld, and Nathaniel Fox. Mosquitoes, endemic malaria, and wet flats doomed the future success of the town, however, and all but the Brent plantation faded into memory. "Woodstock" and the nearby Brent family cemetery suffered further during the Civil War. The "Stony Hill" property of the Peytons and Moncures that was destroyed during the Civil War adjoined the "Woodstock" property to the south. (Eby)

Falmouth

Named after the British seaport town in Cornwall, Falmouth was intended from the beginning as a trade center for Stafford from which agricultural goods, particularly tobacco, could be shipped to England and other goods could be received. The land for the town was built on fifty acres belonging to William Todd. The House of Burgesses' appointed trustees to govern Falmouth were Robert Carter (president), Nicholas Smith, John Fitzhugh, Charles Carter, Henry Fitzhugh, John Warner, and William Thornton. By 1773 the trustees were an elected body, and the president became an elected mayor. (Eby)

The traditional view of Falmouth is:

> Although a small town, Falmouth was one of the most important business centers in Virginia during the eighteenth and early nineteenth centuries. Business here began to grow as those in Marlborough faded. The town, however, had been a prosperous business center prior to its incorporation in 1727 (also dated to 1728). A tobacco warehouse was built at Falmouth in 1730, and ships carried not only tobacco but also grain and cotton raised to the west of the town. An influx of Scotsmen to Stafford during the first half of the eighteenth century contributed to Falmouth's early success. The Scots were merchants who took over most of the businesses, bringing about widespread prosperity to the area. Basil Gordon, Samuel Gordon, Arthur Morson, James Vass, John O'Bannon, and John Green, most either Scottish or with Scottish ties, were successful businessmen. (Eby)

James Vass, first resident of "Moncure Conway House" (Norman and Lenetta Schools)

The oldest of Stafford's surviving "towns" has struggled to affirm its identity, particularly with regard to its neighbor, Fredericksburg. Illustrative of this view:

> Fredericksburg and Falmouth were both established in 1728. Both had tobacco inspection stations and both fronted on the Rappahannock River. In just over thirty years, however, Fredericksburg had expanded its boundaries to accommodate a growing population, while Falmouth had not yet fully developed its initial town site. In 1781 the Virginia Assembly granted Fredericksburg the status of an independent town. In 1879, despite the devastating impact of the Civil War, Fredericksburg still had a large enough population to be designated as an independent city. Nearly three centuries after it was established, Falmouth remains unincorporated.

Mrs. James Vass
(Norman and Lenetta Schools/ Ms. Elizabeth Olmstead/Vass Descendants)

In short, Fredericksburg prospered because its wharf facilities could accommodate seagoing vessels; Falmouth's primary use was as a north-south river ford, providing access to Fredericksburg. Flat-bed boats from Falmouth, rather than seagoing ships, moved supplies to and from Fredericksburg docks for transshipment. Falmouth also suffered in river depth (as did Fredericksburg to a lesser extent) from silt and sand erosion due to up-river tree cutting related to the Spotswood iron furnace and farming. Fredericksburg also established bulkheads to block silt and to narrow and speed the current. Falmouth did not. This view adds:

> Geology argues against seagoing vessels ever having been able to reach Falmouth. Virginia's fall line is the transition between rocky outcroppings of the Piedmont Plateau and the less resistant sands of the Coastal Plain. The Rappahannock River at Falmouth is extremely rocky and shallow, even before the depositions of silt and sand are considered. Popular accounts that describe Falmouth as a bustling port where ships tied up to local docks are not supported by documentary or physical evidence. (Erik F. Nelson—hereafter Nelson)

The twenty-two-foot drop over one mile in the Rappahannock's falls provided power for Falmouth's burgeoning industries. (Jane M. Conner)

Clearly, particularly in light of what are believed to be dock remnants off present Falmouth Beach and other industrial raceways, dams, etc., further research and evaluation of Falmouth's contributions are needed. In particular, Eby relates that a massive old wharf, last exposed in the flood of 1942 and now covered with sand, sat perpendicular to the Gordon and Vass (Conway) Houses on River Road.

Yet, despite its economic struggles, Falmouth has engendered a high level of loyalty and nostalgia among its natives. Typical is a 1992 *Foundation Stones* account, already a memory, by the indomitable Pina Brooks Swift:

> *Being a native of Falmouth in Stafford County has always made me proud. Most of the area residents use Fredericksburg as their mailing address. When I moved back to the county in*

1977, the postmaster and I had lengthy discussion about my using Falmouth as my mailing address. It was not easy to convince him that I physically did not live in Fredericksburg and had every intention of using Falmouth. I did and still do…Times were simpler then, in Falmouth and in the nation. Mass communications did not play an important role in people's lives. The gathering place and source of news for the people of Stafford was Mr. N. N. Berry's Store. Mr. Berry was county treasurer and folks came to the treasurer's office in the back of his store to pay their taxes and keep up to date on events in Stafford and beyond. And when the news was bad or someone needed help, the people of Falmouth were willing to give of themselves. When President (Woodrow) Wilson had pneumonia, his doctors said he had to have chicken soup made from freshly killed chickens. My mother would kill and dress the chickens in the morning and then take them, packed in ice, to the Falmouth Post Office where postmistress, Miss Edie (Edith) Payne, would prepare them for the mail truck to take them to Washington and then the White House. Can you imagine that happening today?

Pina Brooks Swift of Falmouth
(Stephen A. Gambaro)

Falmouth's homes and other significant buildings are described by Eby. ("Barnes House" has previously been described. Union Church is described in Chapter 8. "Moncure Conway House" is described in Chapter 11.)

"Customs House" (Jane M. Conner)

The surveyor's house or "Customs House" is a small, one-and-a-half-story brick building constructed about 1790 (*Foundation Stones* says 1750–1760). Probably first used by Falmouth's trustees, it was later used to collect customs on outgoing goods. After 1786, it may have also have collected for incoming goods. It was a magistrate's building, town office, council meeting house, and polling place. Too small for those purposes, the building was preserved and belongs to the county. It was briefly used as a small museum.

Stafford County, Virginia

The "Cotton Warehouse," built around 1780, was once used as an early Masonic lodge. (Jane M. Conner)

Another old Falmouth building is the "Cotton Warehouse" at 201 Cambridge Street. This two-story frame building, constructed about 1780, has been used as a warehouse, probably by Basil Gordon; an early Masonic lodge; a residence for the Green and Brooks families; and currently as an office for Simpson and Associates Real Estate.

The "Counting House" at 103 Gordon Street, constructed about 1800, has a farm stone foundation with a steep roof common to older Falmouth buildings.

The old one-room log schoolhouse, known locally as "Master Hobby's School," sits on the fringe of Union Church Cemetery. The building has more questions than answers historically. It is fashioned of logs and brick. Its association with John Hobby or his pupil, George Washington, cannot presently be confirmed or denied, but it is a building of antiquity and deserves preservation and care. As to John Hobby, research by the Lymans has revealed that he was a resident of Falmouth by 1736. Parson Weems' stories are the source of Hobby's serving as Washington's schoolmaster. If he did teach Washington, it would have been in the most basic forms of writing and reading. Hobby was also known to be the sexton of the Brunswick Parish Church (believed to have been situated on the rise behind the Union Church), which the Washington family may have attended. The one-room school building, protected in a larger shelter for a number of years, was moved to its present location in 1930. It was renovated by local preservationist Edward Donn and now belongs to the Stafford County Historical Society.

Log schoolhouse, known locally as "Master Hobby's School" (Jane M. Conner)

"Shelton Cottage" which dates from 1770, is representative of colonial working men's cottages. (Jane M. Conner)

"Shelton Cottage," now located on the regional parks and recreation grounds on River Road, dates from 1770 and is representative of colonial working men's cottages. Actually, it was on the high end of such places as it has six fireplaces and is well constructed. Successfully moved several hundred yards east of its original location by a team assembled by Dr. E. Boyd Graves and Col. Richard Leu, the parks and recreation staff maintains the building, and maintenance collections have been taken up several times.

"Belmont," at 224 Washington Street in Falmouth, is certainly one of the greatest of Stafford's historical treasures. The earliest part of the existing structure dates from about 1790. Successive owners—Richards, Voss, Knox—passed the buildings and land to one another, adding and detracting as they went. Joseph Burwell Ficklen, a flour mill operator from Culpeper, purchased the property in 1824 when it was first identified as "Belmont." Ficklen was married twice, to Ellen McGhee (died 1845) and Ann Eliza Fitzhugh, and the house remained in that family for the next ninety-two years. In 1916 "Belmont" was purchased by artist Gari and Corrine Melchers. Gari Melchers lived and painted there (his studio was built in 1924 and refurbished in the past few years) until his death sixteen years later. When his wife died, the property was deeded to the Commonwealth of Virginia. Mary Washington College administers it as the artist's final home and as an art gallery. Open to the public, it also contains a Stafford County Visitors' Center and gift shop. It

"Belmont" is one of Stafford's greatest historical treasures.
(Dan Fitzpatrick; Belmont/Mary Washington College)

Photograph shows house, studio, and gardens at "Belmont."
(Dan Fitzpatrick; Belmont/Mary Washington College)

Interior view of Gari Melchers' studio, "Belmont" (Belmont/Mary Washington College)

Photo shows exterior view of Gari Melchers' studio at "Belmont."
(Belmont/Mary Washington College)

Melchers' studio is shown through an exterior window at "Belmont."
(Belmont/Mary Washington College)

is both a Registered National Historic Landmark and a Registered Virginia Historic Landmark. (Belmont/MWC)

The area immediately west of Belmont is a hill mass variously called "Richard's Hill," "Ingleside," and "Pill Hill" (humorously referring to a number of doctors' residences there).

Overlooking Falmouth and the Rappahannock is "Carlton," a Georgian-style structure apparently built by John Short, a Falmouth merchant, between 1785 and 1794. The Shorts owned the property until 1837, when John O'Bannon purchased it. O'Bannon, a slaveholder, rented out his slaves. His daughters lived there afterward. The house fell into disrepair and was purchased in 1941 by Dr. and Mrs. E. Boyd Graves, prominent local preservationists.

Another of Falmouth's prominent houses is "Clearview," built as a plantation house about 1740. Its owners included the Dodd, Dixon, and Lawson families. The current house was apparently built about 1786 by Andrew Buchanan, a Revolutionary War veteran. When Buchanan died (before 1805), the home passed through a number of owners, including William James (ca. 1814), Alexander Walker (ca. 1822), John C. Scott, and the Wallace family. The home's most recent owners are Mr. and Mrs. William P. Sale.

"Carlton," built between 1785 and 1794, overlooks Falmouth and the Rappahannock River. (Historic Resources Survey)

This current version of "Clearview" was built around 1786 by a Revolutionary War veteran. (Historic Resources Survey)

"Gordon Green Terrace" was on land purchased by Scotsman Samuel Gordon (1759–1843; brother of Basil Gordon), who built the brick portion about 1784 and terraced the land down to the site of present U.S. Route 1. The house subsequently passed through ownership of the Green, Jones, Humphrey, and Wheeler families. Samuel Gordon's son (of the same name) was an owner of "Kenmore" in Fredericksburg. It is now owned by Irma Clifton.

"Basil Gordon House," at 303 King's Highway or River Road, was built by Gordon, one of America's first millionaires, who lived in the house, which was apparently larger at some point. It was damaged by flood, most recently in 1996. One of its renovators was William Lynn. (See Chapter 4.)

"Temperance Inn," once a warehouse, was converted to a stage inn and tavern around 1835. (Stafford County)

"Temperance Hotel" or "Temperance Tavern," at 121 Washington Street in Falmouth, was built as a warehouse about 1813–1815 by William Brooke Jr. and was converted about 1835–1840 to a stage inn and tavern. In 1844 Walker P. Conway (father of Moncure Daniel Conway) and John W. Slaughter purchased the building. It was occupied by Union troops during the Civil War. The name "Falls Temperance House" appears in an 1884 deed. In 1886 John Brown purchased the building; the Brown family owned it until 1966. The building was recently renovated over ten years by Jack and Gail Edlund. It was also called "Old Eagle Tavern." (Belmont/MWC)

Stafford County, Virginia

"West Cambridge Inn" has had several names and uses over the years.
(Stafford County Historical Society)

Another preserved Falmouth business place, "West Cambridge Inn," at 111 West Cambridge Street, was built about 1820. Originally, it had a general store on the first floor. The upper floor rooms were heated by a fireplace. It has had various uses through the years and has been known as "The Eating House," "Thompson House," and the "Ellis Apartment Building." Most recently, it was a restaurant.

"Lightner's Store," at 104 Cambridge Street, was built as a warehouse in the 1700's and was used by local businessmen Basil Gordon and Duff Green. In 1878 it was purchased by the Lightner family, who converted the first floor to a combination country store, lunch room, and ice cream parlor. The family lived on the second floor. In 1993 Mark and Wendy Osborn purchased the building and renovated it.

A more recent addition to Falmouth's historical landscape on Carter Street is the "Howell Log House." Originally built in the Shenandoah Valley in the late eighteenth century, it was purchased by Delegate and Mrs. William J. Howell, disassembled completely, and transported and reconstructed on its present site. The two-story log structure serves as a law office for Speaker Howell. He and his wife, Cecelia "Cessie" Howell, frequently use it for a variety of historical preservation activities.

This series of images shows the changes to and continuity in Falmouth through the past 140 years:

"Lightner's Store," built as a warehouse in the 1700's, was renovated in 1993.
(Stafford County Historical Society)

"Howell Log House," built in the late eighteenth century, serves as a law office for State Delegate William J. Howell. (Jane M. Corner)

A History of Our Own

Falmouth, 1901 (Barry Fitzgerald; John Hailstock)

Falmouth Civil War sketch
(Free Lance-Star)

Falmouth, Fourth of July, 1907
(Stafford County Historical Society)

Falmouth House, no longer standing, as shown on a postcard. Visible to the left is Lightner's Store.
(Stafford County Historical Society)

Stafford County, Virginia

Early Spring Landscape, painted by Gari Melchers about 1918
(Belmont/Mary Washington College)

Thanks to the fortuitous presence of artist Gari Melchers of "Belmont," a visual record of the Falmouth area during the period 1916–1930 has been preserved.

In Old Virginia, painted by Gari Melchers about 1918
(Belmont/Mary Washington College)

Stafford Heights, painted by Gari Melchers about 1920
(Belmont/Mary Washington College)

Gari Melchers painted *From My Window* in 1920. (Belmont/Mary Washington College)

Grape Arbor, No. 2, was painted by Gari Melchers in 1930.
(Belmont/Mary Washington College)

A History of Our Own

In 1969, Falmouth was registered at the state and national levels as a historic district. In May 2003 it celebrated its 275th anniversary. A Christmas ornament honoring Falmouth's 275th year was introduced by the Stafford County Historical Society.

Falmouth Area Homes

North of Falmouth along U.S. Route 1 is "Glencairne." This home has been present since at least 1804 in some form and has been owned by Carters, Seddons, Finnalls, Langfits, Moncures, and Chichesters. Most construction took place from 1825 to 1882 during the ownership of Judge R. C. L. Moncure, later a chief justice of the Virginia Supreme Court. The house was completely restored in 1957. The original property extended over a wider area and included the space now occupied by Dogwood Air Park, Falmouth Elementary School, and Drew Middle School. Nearby "Mont Anna," built for in-laws by Judge John Conway Moncure after the Civil War, was once part of "Glencairne." (Eby) ("Ellerslie" is discussed in Chapter 4.)

"Glencairne," once owned by the chief justice of the Virginia Supreme Court, was completely restored in 1857.
(Historic Resources Survey)

Stafford County, Virginia

Widewater

(Widewater's and Chopawamsic Creek's historic homes that were lost to the 1942 Quantico Expansion are discussed in Chapter 4.)

"Richland" is one of Stafford's most historic places. It, too, is worthy of a history of its own. Associated with all Stafford's oldest families, its story begins with the Brents, Stafford's first English settlers, in an April 18, 1654, deed as conveyed by Giles Brent (I) to his sister Mary Brent of "Peace": *...the dividend called Rich Land, situated northerly from Peace, containing 1,040 acres.*

"Richland" was created by Stafford's first English settlers in 1654 and is associated with all of Stafford's oldest families. (Jane M. Conner)

The Brents operated a mill on the "Richland" site from the 1600s to 1900. Giles Brent (II) lived there. His son, William (I), born there in 1677, returned to England to claim the inheritance of his great-grandfather, Sir Richard Brent, lord of Stoke and Admington (1573–1652). He married in England in 1709 and died that same year. His widow, Sarah, came to Stafford in 1717 with her son, William (II) (born 1710), to claim his inheritance. She soon met and married (May 1717) Rev. Alexander Scott of "Dipple," rector of Overwharton Parish. Her son (William Brent (II), the only surviving heir of Giles Brent (I), became a Stafford justice of the peace in 1731. William Brent (III) married Eleanor Carroll of Maryland and was prominent in Revolutionary and Federal America. His brother-in-law, Father John Carroll, S.J., came to Aquia from England in June 1774, preached from "Richland" (to which he frequently returned), moved to Rock Creek and became the first American prelate and also founder of Georgetown University. William Brent (III) was elected one of two delegates from Stafford to the 1776 Virginia Revolutionary Convention, which approved independence, the Virginia Declaration of Rights, and the first Virginia Constitution. Brent's "elegant brick" home at "Richland" was burned by a raiding party from HMS *Roebuck*, which landed in Stafford on July 23, 1776. Brent rebuilt his home and served in the House of Delegates, representing Stafford in the fall of 1776. He returned in 1778, and in 1780 was elected to the Virginia Senate. There, representing Stafford, King George, and Westmoreland Counties, Brent died in office sometime before April 1782 and was buried on his estate. William Brent (III)'s son, Daniel Carroll Brent, married

Anne Fenton Lee, daughter of Thomas Ludwell Lee of "Bellevue" and "Berry Hill" in Stafford, in 1782. Daniel Carroll Brent served in the House of Delegates and was a founder of Phi Beta Kappa honor society. His son, William Brent (IV), born at "Richland" in 1783, sold "Richland" and 1,906 acres to Maj. William H. Fitzhugh in 1821. While in the Fitzhugh family, "Richland" became a refuge first for the Whiting family during the Civil War, then a postwar home for Sydney Smith Lee's family. After his father's death, Gen. Fitzhugh Lee managed "Richland," inherited from his godmother, Mrs. William H. Fitzhugh, in 1874. Lee lived there until his successful gubernatorial campaign. In 1893 he sold the place to Edward Pyke, Esq. of Southport, England, as a wedding gift for son, Alfred J. Pyke, and Mary Cary Waller of "Clifton." The Pykes built a private chapel in 1902 where Mass could again be celebrated; it was believed to be the first such celebration since the days of Archbishop Carroll. "Richland" commands a spectacular view of the Potomac River and was a witness to Professor Langley's aviation experiments. The home passed to Mrs. Donald John Kendall (the former Nita Pyke) and her daughter, Mary Cary Kendall, who ends a historical sketch of the home with: "After hundreds of years, peace, joy, contentment, and the unfailing loving care of God continue to be found at Richland, Widewater, Virginia." (Kendall; *Foundation Stones*)

"Clifton" in Widewater was best known for the huge seine fishery and duck hunting there by U.S. Presidents Grover Cleveland, Benjamin Harrison, and Theodore Roosevelt. Located next to "Richland," it once probably belonged to Margaret Brent and was later associated with the Clifton and Waller families. During the Civil War, mistaking it for the Aquia Creek facilities, Union gunboats fired on the house from the Potomac River. The shelling endangered the life of future humanitarian Kate Waller (Barrett), then an infant, and her family (see Chapter 3). "Clifton" was burned in a 1945 Christmas Day fire; a replacement, "Clifton Lodge," was built in the 1960s. (Eby; Kendall) (Also see Chapters 8, 10 and 11.)

"West Farm" was another Widewater home site. Just north of "Clifton," it was probably another part of the Margaret Brent or Brent family grants and was probably built by Col. John Cooke (1755–1819), a prominent Staffordian. It had passed into his daughter, Elizabeth's, hands by 1766. Primarily known for its trans-Potomac ferry to the Kennedy property in southern Maryland, an earlier John Cooke's (died 1733) family had intertwined with the Travers, Doniphans, Masons, and Brents. Col. John Cooke had married Mary Thomson Mason, leading to his acquiring "Marlborough" from the Mercers and to his Aquia Quarry partnership with Daniel Carroll Brent (1760–1815). Withers Waller of "Clifton" bought the "West Farm" from Cooke's estate in 1825. (Eby)

Another Widewater house now gone, "Bloomington" was struck by lightning and destroyed by fire in the 1970s. It was associated with the Adies, Wallers, Fords, and Moncures. "Arkendale," once part of the tract of "Richland," came into the possession of the Lee family "well before the Civil War." Eventually, it would be subdivided among four of the sons of Sydney Smith Lee: Daniel M., John M., Smith, and Henry. "The Anchorage" was the part belonging to Daniel M. Lee, who later lived at "Highland Home" in southern Stafford. Nannie Mason Lee owned "Westwood" (inheriting it from her father, John Mason Lee), on the east side of Virginia 658 and north of the Arkendale Crossing. "Myrtle Grove" was another Widewater site, associated with Edringtons and Moncures, two of whom later opened a store on the property. Another eighteenth-century Widewater home was "Palace Green," owned by the Carters. A Norman family property, "Edge Hill," was adjacent to "Rock Ramore." (Eby; Kendall)

Aquia

("The Fleurry's," "Stony Hill," and "Concord" have been discussed earlier in this chapter.)

One of Stafford's places described as a bit of a mystery was "Hope Grant," "Hope Land," "Hope Line," or "Hope Spring." It was a seventeenth-century grant including "the mouth of Hope Creek (Willow Landing) and running westward to Jackson's Branch, northward on Jackson's Branch to Austin Run, eastward to Aquia Creek, and back to Hope Creek. It may have evolved from the 1654 Hubbert Tract sold to Solomon Day and Daniel Matheny. In 1780 Alexander and Eliza Doyle sold the Day portion of the property to William Hewitt for 25,000 pounds of tobacco. (Eby)

In the 1960s, "Spring Hill," which had been steadily falling into disrepair since the Civil War, had all but rotted away. The farm had been established in the mid-seventeenth century by the Wallers. Its family cemetery was bulldozed in the 1980s for the Vestavia Woods subdivision off Courthouse Road (Virginia Route 630). (Eby)

"Wayside," a Waller farm, was taken over by commercial ventures. (Felicia Parlier)

Garrisonville and Roseville

The historic farms that dotted the current Virginia Route 610, Garrisonville Road, in northern Stafford are mute testimony to the shifting economy of the county. Pastoral places have given way to commercial and residential spaces in an endless assault on historic homes and Civil War camp sites. Perhaps unavoidable and since much damage has already been done, it is probably the best use of these "places of the heart" to demonstrate that loss is truly irreversible.

"Patterson's Place," a frontier farm of the Ralls family in the 1730s, was most recently occupied by Bon Food, Frank's Hardware and Crafts, both now gone, and Rosner Motors. Union soldiers camped there when the Pattersons owned it. (Eby)

"Wayside" was a Waller farm, as was "Grafton" (not to be confused with the southern Stafford place). They were gradually taken over by commercial sites on Virginia Route 610, Garrisonville Road, and Anne E. Moncure Elementary School. The family cemetery rests between a Jiffy Lube and a Texaco quick-stop gas station (see Chapter 4).

"Tusculum" and "Windsor Forest" were two places on the north side of Garrisonville Road, past where Aquia Creek crosses the road. "Tusculum" was a Peyton farm. The Washingtons, by marriage, were also owners. "Windsor Forest" was a home of the Washingtons and Moncures (north of Virginia 610). While Bailey Washington Jr. (1753–1814) owned it, George Washington visited the house. The farm was used as a Union camp as well. Another "Windsor Forest" was on the south side of Virginia 610. A subdivision of the same name is nearby. (Eby; Kirby)

"Grafton" was gradually taken over by commercial sites. (Felicia Parlier)

Waller family and servants at "Wayside," 1900s (Felicia Parlier)

On site of the former Stafford Home and Garden and a residential subdivision was "Woodford," associated with the Eustace and Adie families. Hugh Adie Jr., a descendant of a family that had come to Stafford from England by 1742, purchased this property in 1882 (see Chapter 4). He had served in the 9th Virginia Cavalry in the Civil War and was county sheriff from 1875 to 1889. His father lived at "Woodford" until about 1871. Unexplained is the 1864 "Gilmer Map" Stafford notation of the "H. Adie" home shown on what is now Shelton Shop Road, south of Garrisonville Road.

In the 1700s "Hartwood" or "Irvine House" was the plantation of Arthur Morson, a Scotsman who was a Falmouth merchant and a Stafford justice of the peace.
(Historic Resources Survey)

Hartwood

(See previous discussion of "Hampstead" Farm.)

"Hartwood" was the plantation of Arthur Morson (1734 or 1735–1798), a Scotsman who was a Falmouth merchant and trustee and a Stafford justice of the peace. Acquired in the 1750s, his family lived there until the 1840s, when it was purchased by the Irvines. Morson had donated land for what became Hartwood Yellow Chapel before 1777. After Morson's death in 1798, his son, (another Falmouth merchant) Alexander Morson, of "Hollywood" (1759–1822) inherited the property. The place passed to John and Hugh Morson after 1822. They retained it until it was sold to John and William Irvine in 1848. Located on the south side of Warrenton Road and Marsh Road (both now U.S. Route 17), the house stood on 3,677 acres in 1827. William Irvine and his wife, who apparently built the present house, were successful local business people. In 1850 the plantation had 125 slaves and 5,000 acres (scattered on several working farms). From October 1862 to May 1863, the Irvines were occupied by the 3rd Pennsylvania Cavalry. Their son, John William Irvine, of the 9th Virginia Cavalry was taken prisoner there on November 27, 1862. Per Eby, he was home on furlough seeking a replacement horse when, dressed in civilian clothing, he was taken by Federal troops and held at Hartwood Church, awaiting execution as a spy. Family intercession failed, but a last-minute letter from Gen. Robert E. Lee resulted in a commuted sentence. Eby adds, "He was released and allowed to return to his unit."

Actually, the story is a little more complicated. Irvine's execution was set for December 21, 1862, but Lee's assertion that he was merely seeking a replacement horse carried the day. Irvine was exchanged from Old Capitol Prison—which handled spies and untrustworthy citizens—on May 13, 1863, the same day as W. W. Gordon discussed below. Irvine returned to the 9th but was taken prisoner again, this time on June 30, 1863, at Hanover. He was exchanged again on April 30, 1864, from Point Lookout, Maryland, prison camp. Irvine appeared on the 9th's final official muster in October 1864. The patterns of this story suggest he was involved in scouting or spying in his old neighborhood. (Krick)

"Hartwood" was occupied and used on two occasions by Fitzhugh Lee's and Wade Hampton's troops, and the barn was used as a hospital for Union troops during the Overland Campaign in spring 1864. The property fell into disrepair in the twentieth century. It was rescued by Charles Hudson in 1975 and restored following emergency repairs on the termite-infested building with steel beams and jacks. (Eby)

"Poplar Grove" was briefly occupied by Stafford's Quaker community. By 1830 the Quakers had moved to Ohio, leaving the original stone house. The farm was subsequently owned by the Curtis and French families and is now owned by Sally Lou Fitzhugh. The original house was replaced about 1900, and after it burned in a 1934 fire, a frame farmhouse was constructed on the same site. (Eby)

"Rosedale," associated with the Gordon and Montague families and near the old Concord School, was located on the north side of Mountain View Road (Virginia Route 627), east of the Rock Hill Church Road (Virginia Route 644) intersection. The Gordons lived there from 1813 until after the Civil War, when a Gordon daughter, Celestine, married Dr. Thadeus Claybrook Montague, former Confederate surgeon and later (1881–1887) a Stafford supervisor. Eby recounts a story that Celestine's brother, William Wallace Gordon, a member of the 9th Virginia Cavalry from Stafford, was captured at Hartwood Church on April 10, 1863. The story states he participated in the skirmish there. However, that is unlikely as the Hartwood fight took place the preceding February and the

These structures on Poplar Grove were built in 1900 and replaced the original stone house. They burned in 1934. (Sally Lou Fitzhugh)

9th Virginia Cavalry was not involved. More likely, similar to the Irvine story above, he was either on a scouting mission relating to the approaching Chancellorsville Campaign or was absent without leave. The fact that he was sent to Old Capitol Prison further suggests he was spying. Gordon was exchanged on May 13, 1863 (the same day as Irvine above), but did not rejoin his unit and was listed as absent without leave (an occupational hazard of scouts) until an October 1864 muster. (Eby; Krick)

Other Stafford Places

In the southeast corner of the county, "Snowden" is one of Stafford's most interesting stories. Linked with "Hollywood," both trace to a 1670 grant to John and George Mott. The Motts sold the land to the Thorntons; William Thornton divided the property between his sons, Maj. Francis Thornton and Rowland Thornton. Francis' property became "Hollywood"; Rowland's became "Snowden." The property descended through the Thorntons, and when cousins William Alexander and Sarah Bruce Casson married, the two properties were once again united. Their daughter, Ann, married Falmouth merchant Alexander Morson (1759–1831),

"Eastwood" was built between 1829 and 1831 by John Gray of "Traveller's Rest" as a gift for his son, Atchinson, and bride, Catherine Willis, a descendant of George Washington. When Atchinson died, Catherine married Prince Achilles Murat, a nephew of Napoleon. The couple continued to visit "Eastwood." The last Gray family owner was Stafford Judge Robert Gray. When "Traveller's Rest" collapsed, its bricks were incorporated into "Eastwood," which was later owned by Thomas M. (Jr.) and Margaret C. Moncure and then George and Monecia Taylor.

(Jane M. Conner)

who also acquired "Hollywood." Eby believes there were earlier homes at "Snowden," but the first one documented in an insurance policy was in 1796. This building was destroyed and replaced by a building that was afterward enlarged by several owners. The most significant activity took place during the ownership of John Seddon, who purchased "Snowden" in 1849. He had increased its size and value until in 1857 it was valued at $10,000—the same as "Chatham."

During the war, "Snowden" was unfortunately mistaken by Union gunboats on the Rappahannock for the home of James Seddon, John's brother and Confederate secretary of war. The house was shelled, set ablaze, and destroyed. The land and a few buildings passed from John Seddon's estate in 1882 with 397 1/2 acres going to William A. Little. Subsequently, in the 1940s a new house was built, but plans to preserve the property were lost to a legal settlement. The house at "Hollywood" was destroyed by fire in 1889.

During the Civil War, reconnaissance balloons operated from a field east of "Little Whim." (Historic Resources Survey)

While "Places of the Heart" suggests an idyllic past of plantation and farm homes, other photographs capture a harsher reality. This August 1940 photo of "Charlie Washington's Cabin" in Stafford demonstrates how little had changed in the poverty-laden county for some since the Civil War. (Felicia Parlier)

Stafford County, Virginia

Chapter Eight
Places of the Spirit: Stafford's Churches

Stafford's churches have a remarkable history. Thanks to *Foundation Stones, They Called Stafford Home*, and church histories, it is possible to highlight some of their unique stories. In addition to providing spiritual comfort and religious sustenance to their people, Stafford's churches are historical entities in their own right and part of the county's overall history. (Churches are discussed roughly in order of establishment. Those still in existence are noted with *.)

Stafford's Earliest Churches

Prior to Stafford's creation in 1664 and at least since Westmoreland County had been formed in 1653, the northernmost Anglican Church (Church of England) parish was Potomac Parish. It included the Potomac region from Machodoc Creek (near Dahlgren Naval Surface Weapons Center) to the falls of the Potomac. When established, Stafford coincided with Potomac Parish until reorganized into an "Upper Parish" and "Lower Parish." Upper Parish in time became known as Stafford Parish and after 1702, Overwharton Parish. Lower Parish was named Chotank Parish and then St. Paul's Parish. In 1777, when the Stafford boundaries were redefined, the portions in St. Paul's Parish were added to King George County.

Aquia Episcopal Church, winter
(Jane M. Conner)

Potomac Anglican Church, no longer in existence, was the first major church in Stafford and Overwharton Parish. Believed built in the mid-1600s of brick and covered with a hipped roof, it was located in the modern Brooke area. Alexander Scott, minister of Overwharton Parish for more than twenty-eight years, was known to have preached at both Potomac and Aquia Churches. Bricks and stones from Potomac Church may have been used in constructing the Potomac Creek railroad bridge during the Civil War. Eby describes the site:

Traveling from Fredericksburg to Brooke along State Route 608, one crosses a lovely little creek. On the right-hand side of the road upon a hill once stood Potomac Church, one of the oldest Episcopal churches in the United States. This beautiful house of worship was built on a portion of the ancient Samuel Mathews tract. Thomas Wilkinson bought the parcel from Mathews in 1662, but it is unknown if Wilkinson sold the property to the vestry or if he donated it as a building site.

Potomac was one of the largest Colonial churches in Virginia. Built of brick, the building measured 60 feet by 80 feet. Similarities with the later Aquia Church included arched windows and the texts of the Law, Lord's Prayer, and Nicene Creed painted upon the walls.

The organization of this church was closely tied to the organization of the county. The church was built possibly as early as 1664 and was a part of St. Paul's Parish. Until the building of Aquia Church in 1751, Potomac Church was the principal place of worship in the area, but the date of its construction is unknown. Few records survive to provide information about Potomac Church. John Waugh was probably the first rector there. John Mercer of Marlborough recorded that his infant daughter, Elizabeth Mason Mercer, was baptized there on Easter Sunday, April 12, 1730.

Apparently, Potomac Church was abandoned sometime around 1804. On August 1, 1814, William Brent Jr., Daniel Carroll Brent, John Cooke, John Moncure, Hancock Eustace, and Rowzee Peyton wrote to the governor asking him to return the Stafford militia to the county immediately, as they believed a British invasion was imminent. The militia had been sent to Mattox Bridge in Westmoreland (County) and only thirty men were stationed on Hope Run, four and one-half miles from the mouth of the creek. The men's concern was well-founded, as Potomac Church was burned by British soldiers on their way to Washington… (Eby)

Until it burned down in 1748 or 1750, Muddy Creek Church was, with the early Hartwood "Yellow Chapel" and a church near the site of Union Church in Falmouth, part of the Anglican Brunswick Parish. Located ten miles east of Falmouth and west of Muddy Creek, 200 feet north of Kings Highway (Virginia Route 3), it was reportedly a small frame building built between 1700 and 1745. (Eby)

Interior view of Aquia Church, showing its three-tiered pulpit (Stafford County)

Aquia Episcopal Church, spring (Jane M. Conner)

Aquia Episcopal Church *, built between 1751 and 1757, was probably the third church built on the present site (the oldest may have dated to 1667). Certainly the oldest active church in Stafford, the site has been a local fixture and landmark for so long that it can be truthfully said that Stafford County developed "around" Aquia Church. Its Greek cross shape and two-story configuration, three-tiered pulpit, altar and memorial tablets, and well-maintained interior make it one of the best surviving examples of Colonial church architecture in Virginia and America. Its Aquia sandstone trim, including quoins, door trim, and other features, links it to the White House and U.S. Capitol. Aquia Church, associated with most of Stafford's early Anglican settlers and last vestige of the "established" church, was also once a place of tax collecting and mandatory tithes. The church bears the genteel graffiti of Civil War soldiers, and its cemetery is the final resting place of many significant Staffordians. Located at the intersection of the entrance to Aquia Harbour subdivision (Washington Drive, an extension of Virginia Route 610, and U.S. Route 1), the church is one of Stafford's most impressive and enduring landmarks. The communion service of the church has been buried three times—during the Revolution, War of 1812, and Civil War—to prevent vandalism.

Union Church, Falmouth
(Mike and Marty Lyman)

Union Church, showing missing portions (Mike and Marty Lyman)

(Moncure and Molly A. Pynn; see also Clifton Chapel below.) In 2001, Aquia Episcopal Church celebrated its 250th anniversary with lectures and church tours by docents in Colonial costume. Lectures featured Stafford's Jerrilynn Eby and Dr. Carl L. Lounsbury of Colonial Williamsburg.

Presbyterians appeared in Stafford early. J. William Mann states the minutes of that church's synod in Philadelphia on September 19, 1719, reported a congregation located at Patomeke, Virginia, which Mann locates on Potomac Creek. Members of that faith were later among the worshipers at Union Church in Falmouth.

Although its facade still stands on Falmouth's Carter Street, Union Church no longer exists. The church land was specified in Falmouth's charter in 1728. Almost certainly, this related to an Anglican church of Brunswick Parish, which included (ca. 1792–1796) the Muddy Creek Church and Hartwood "Yellow Chapel." The original Anglican church, built about 1750, survived until it burned in 1818. The existing structure, the third church on the same lot, was built in the early nineteenth century (1820–1840 by another estimate). Episcopalians (arguable use, although they were included in the May 1868 deed), Presbyterians, Methodists, and Baptists used the church on a rotating basis, hence its name. Union Church was used as a Federal military hospital during the Civil War battles in the area (later compensated $800 for damages). The rest of the church was destroyed in a heavy rainstorm in 1950. The adjacent cemetery's oldest standing and identified tombstone is 1738.

Eby relates: "On November 22, 1766, a group of Baptists from the Baptist Church at Broad Run, Fauquier County, established Chopawamsic Baptist Church. Robert and Keziah Million were among the early dissenters in Overwharton (Parish) and their names appear as subscribers to the Covenant of Chopawamsic Baptist Church. The Fristoe family was long associated with Chopawamsic Creek and, later, with the Baptist church there. On April 4, 1770 William Fristoe was ordained at Chopawamsic Baptist Church and was elected to serve as minister." The church survived until the 1942 Quantico expansion.

Hartwood (Old-School) Baptist Church (existed in 1776) and its cemetery once occupied the less than one-acre tract on Shackelford's Well Road in Hartwood. Now only the cemetery remains, fortunately cleaned up, repaired, and rededicated by Citizens to Serve Stafford in 1990. According to Dr. H. Stewart Jones, the church descended from Potomac Baptist Church and was destroyed by Union soldiers during the war. Local history, she relates, recalls the cemetery continued in use until 1900 and the last person buried there was a former slave or daughter of a slave, "Aunt" Puss King. The most notable communicant was Col. James Garrard, a Revolutionary War veteran and member of the state legislature, who moved to Kentucky, where he served in the legislature and was governor (1796–1804). (*Foundation Stones*)

White Oak Primitive Baptist Church, established in 1789, is on the Virginia Landmarks Register and the National Register of Historic Places. (Stafford County)

White Oak Primitive Baptist Church *, established in 1789

as White Oak Church of Christ, was "...declared independent of all others believing and holding forth the doctrine of election and the final perseverance of the saints to which covenant we all agree this 31st of October..." The term "primitive" was introduced into the church's name to reflect belief in the original doctrines of Christ and the Apostles. John Moncure gave the trustees of the church "the meeting house and 1 acre of land attached thereto" in 1835. White Oak Primitive Baptist Church still meets twice monthly with business meetings following the services, a constant practice since 1789. (Eby) White Oak Church is on the Virginia Landmarks Register and the National Register of Historic Places.

Rock Hill Baptist Church was founded in 1812 when "there was unrest among the people..."
(Jane M. Conner)

Rock Hill Baptist Church * was founded in 1812. A church history informs:

> At sometime prior to 1811...there was unrest among the people, especially those who felt the need to have a central place to worship and to share their knowledge and love of Jesus. Rock Hill Baptist Church had its beginning when two men from Chopawamsic (near Quantico (Marine Base) and two from Hartwood (Old-School Baptist Church) met to organize the church. During the period of the War of 1812, many were persecuted for their beliefs. Through their faith in God, they preserved and adopted the Church Constitution on January 12, 1812.

Rock Hill Baptist also helped Shiloh (Old-Site) Baptist Church ("on the road to Stafford Store"; see below). Rock Hill Baptist is located at the intersection of Rock Hill Church Road (Virginia Route 644) and Van Horn Lane (Virginia Route 671). The current church building is the second one constructed on that site. (Ruth Eustace and Carolyn Spence)

Mount Olive Baptist Church
(Jane M. Conner)

Mount Olive Baptist Church *, founded in May 1818, is the oldest of Stafford's many black churches. Originating as a "slab arbor," it grew to a temporary shelter, and later a building was

Stafford County, Virginia

Hartwood Presbyterian Church, on the Virginia Landmarks Register and the National Register of Historic Places, added a museum in 2003.
(Stafford County)

Hartwood Presbyterian Church
(Historic Resources Survey)

raised across from the current church site (395 Mount Olive Road). The current building was constructed between 1957 and 1963, when it celebrated in a procession of members from the old church to the new one. In 2003, the church celebrated its 185th anniversary. The first pastor was Rev. Horace Crutcher, and the original five members were Calvin Strother, Peter Nelson, Ben Clark, Jim Hill, and Susan Nelson. The church history says "they hewed out the wilderness and drew up a highway for coming generations to have a path to follow." (Roxana Parker; Fitzgerald)

Hartwood Presbyterian Church * was originally an Anglican "chapel of ease" called Yellow Chapel. The chapel fell into disuse and was sold with the Morson estate, "Hartwood," to the Irvine family. William Irvine was a Presbyterian who had left Ireland in 1803. On July 22, 1825, the Winchester Presbytery organized a new congregation in Hartwood. The new church met in the Yellow Chapel until about 1858 when the red brick church now present was built at a cost of $2,000 (most of the work, including firing the bricks, was accomplished by members) and named Hartwood Presbyterian Church. During the Civil War, the building survived as a shelter for horses and men. Federal troops used it as a cavalry outpost (burning all interior boards). A cavalry skirmish took place near there in February 1863. After the war, Hartwood's congregation raised the money to rebuild despite widespread poverty. Using contributions from one dollar to ten dollars, the church rebuilt between 1868 and 1872. In 1872, the Irvine family deeded the church and one acre of land. In 1950 some expansion took place. In 2000 the Hartwood Presbyterian Church celebrated its 175th anniversary. The church, located on Hartwood Church Road, a small connector between Hartwood Road (Virginia Route 612) and U.S. Route 17, is on the Virginia Landmarks Register and the National Register of Historic Places. In 2003 the church added a museum. (H. Stewart Jones; Eby)

Berea Baptist Church, founded in 1852, today uses walls from the original structure. (Stafford County)

Berea Baptist Church * was founded in 1852 apparently in a bequest of Miss Sarah Daniel and a land donation by Miss Piny Latham. During the Civil War, Berea was occupied by Union troops and witnessed the abortive Union "Mud March." It was an outpost site at various points, included in the Federal defensive perimeter, probably as a base for infantry pickets. In that action, the Union cavalry outpost at Hartwood Church was driven east to Berea Church. The current church building uses walls from the original 1852 structure. Located at the intersection of Berea Church Road and Fleet Road, near U.S. Route 17 and the Geico complex, for many years Berea Church was a center of activity for the Berea community. (Ella B. Settle)

Clifton Chapel *, located on Clifton Chapel Lane, off Widewater Road (Virginia Route 611), is a part of Aquia Episcopal Church. The chapel was originally built (by at least the 1850s) on two acres of land given from the "Clifton" estate by Withers Waller and Anne Eliza Stribling Waller. Like other older Stafford churches, it was a "chapel of convenience." During the Civil War, it was part of "Camp Clifton," the 1861–1862 camp of the 47th Virginia Infantry, which included Stafford troops. A well-defined place yet remote from view, the chapel probably also played a role in the Confederate communications and intelligence line known to run from Brooke Station to Evansport (Quantico), Dumfries, and Manassas. The Fitzhugh Lees, living at "Richland" after the war, aided earlier restoration efforts. The chapel fell into disrepair, especially after the 1950s; it was recently renovated (see Chapter 11). Clifton Primitive Evangelical Church * also meets in the chapel.

Andrew Methodist Church
(Jane M. Conner)

The original Andrew Methodist Episcopal Church * was built by 1854 on Andrew Chapel Road (Virginia Route 629) near the current church. The original church cemetery is at the older site, which was damaged during the Civil War. The congregation continued to meet in the old building until 1904. At that point, the church split, with one group meeting there until the 1950s and the other, led by their preacher C. L. Potter, establishing the present site on Brooke Road (Virginia Route 608) near the Brooke Railroad Station.

Antioch United Methodist Church *, established in April 1856, is located on Kellogg Mill Road (Virginia Route 651) near Poplar Road (Virginia Route 616). According to Samuel F. Simpson, the church land was donated by Mr. and Mrs. James Armstrong Jr., and the congregation and meetings may well have predated the church building, perhaps as early as 1822. (Eby states that cemetery graves date to 1822, although the earliest date recorded

Antioch United Methodist Church
(Jane M. Conner)

by Homer Musselman is 1897.) The original building was destroyed by fire about 1865. Some mystery exists as to the origin of the fire. The Federal army was naturally suspected; however, Simpson adds that when Berea and Hartwood Churches received compensation for Union wartime depredations under the War Claims Act of 1915, Antioch was not included. Services were conducted in local homes and in the open until a new church building could be constructed around 1891 (used until 1960, when the current building was constructed). The current building is on land deeded April 7, 1856.

Ebenezer United Methodist Church, which celebrated its one hundredth anniversary in 1956, moved from this location in 1991. (Stafford County)

Ebenezer United Methodist Church * was also built in 1856 on land donated by James Holms. Originally, the church was located at the intersection of Ebenezer Church Road (Virginia Route 696) and Onville Road (Virginia Route 641). According to Frances S. Cloe and Jerrilynn Eby, the original brick building was conceived by Baltimore architect Thomas Towson, who owned a stone quarry between Garrisonville Road (Virginia Route 610) and Courthouse Road (Virginia Route 630), and used bricks manufactured on-site. This building replaced an earlier log structure that was used until construction was complete. Ebenezer was also inhabited by Union troops during the Civil War and its "floors were burned, windows were broken, and walls were defaced." The church celebrated its one hundredth anniversary on July 15, 1956, with the dedication of a new educational building. In 1991 the church moved to its present location on Embrey Mill Road (Virginia Route 733), off Winding Creek Road (Virginia Route 628).

Ramoth Baptist Church was organized in 1866 by a former chaplain in the 30th Virginia Infantry. (Jane M. Conner)

Located at the intersection of Ramoth Church Road (Virginia Route 628) and Accokeek Furnace Road (Virginia Route 651), Ramoth Baptist Church * was organized in October 1866 by Walter R. D. Moncure, formerly a chaplain in the 30th Virginia Infantry. Susan Musselman Black was one of the charter members. The current church (additions in 1953, 1957, and 1975) was built around the original church, which was erected on land donated from Woodbourne Farm by Rev. Walter Moncure. (Estheleen "Hutch" Blackburn)

Bethlehem Primitive Baptist Church * in White Oak was organized in 1870 by Rev. York Johnson, a former slave of the Dr. Hugh Morson family. At the time of its establishment, the church met in an old white Primitive Baptist church building. The current church building is off White Oak Road (Virginia 218) on Virginia Route 690, Chapel Green Road (becomes Virginia 602). (Fitzgerald)

Shiloh (Old-Site) Baptist Church was established in Ruby in 1870. (Jane M. Conner)

Shiloh (Old-Site) Baptist Church * was established in Ruby in 1870 (Virginia Route 610). The church split during the twentieth century, and in 1942 Shiloh (New Site) Baptist Church * was founded. It is located on U.S. Route 1 near Aquia.

Regester Chapel United Methodist Church (old) was once called Stafford Court House Church. (Jane M. Conner)

Oak Grove Baptist Church * in Widewater was founded in 1873. Originally called Saint Ross Baptist Church, the congregation met in a log cabin until formal structures could be built. Early families included Vaughan, Gaines, Miller, Strother, Jackson, Harris, and Speed. Oak Grove, the church home of artist Palmer Hayden, is located on Decatur Road (Virginia Route 635).

Oak Grove Baptist Church, founded in 1873, was the church home of artist Palmer Hayden. (Owen L. Conner)

Regester Chapel United Methodist Church * was conceived in 1877 with the formation of a building committee headed by Rev. Dr. Samuel Regester. Called "Stafford Court House Church," the name was later changed to honor Regester. The original building stood from 1880 to 1911, when it was replaced. That church was struck by a tornado on 1923, and another church was built (first used December 1924). Additional buildings were added in 1959 and 1984. (Ralph W. Rowley) The church was located diagonally across from the County Courthouse and Administrative Center. A new church facility is now located on Bells Hill Road.

Mount Hope Baptist Church * in Brooke began as a Sunday school of Silver Hill Baptist Church in Fauquier County. Rev. Natus or Nathan Washington moved his church to Brooke in 1877 and officially founded Mount Hope in October 1880. Originally meeting in the home of Jack Thornton and in the St. John schoolhouse near Brooke, the church was later established on a more formal basis. Early families included Rhones, Thorntons, Montagues, Jacksons, Richardsons, Tylers, and Mortons. Baptisms were initially conducted in Accokeek Creek. The church is on Brooke Road (Virginia Route 608). Rev. George Oscar A. Lowe has served as pastor since 1965.

Mount Hope Baptist Church
(Dorothy Jackson)

Also in the 1870s (precise date unknown), Ironside Baptist Church in Falmouth was established as a missionary church. Renamed Little Shiloh Baptist Church, it had fifteen members. Early members were baptized in the Rappahannock River. Organizing ministers were William F. Broaddus, George Dixon, and Peter Armstead. Rev. Cornelius S. Lucas led the church until his death in 1927. (Fitzgerald)

Mount Hope Church service, 1941
(Dorothy Jackson)

Hull's Memorial Baptist Church * was organized from Ramoth Baptist Church in 1888. Meeting originally in the Hull home, a new church building was constructed in 1897. According to Mrs. Lester L. Limerick, construction was accomplished by John Wiggington, a local lumberman, assisted by church members. The original church was remodeled in 1947, and a new church building was erected

Hull's Memorial Baptist Church, organized in 1888, held its meetings in the Hull home until a new building was constructed in 1897. (Jane M. Conner)

Stafford County, Virginia

Richlands Baptist Church celebrated its centennial in 1989. (Jane M. Conner)

Falmouth Baptist Church (current building shown) was established in 1891. (Jane M. Conner)

in 1959, with new additions to the church complex in 1985 and 1986. The church is located on Enon Road (Virginia Route 753). (*One Hundred Years of Christian Service: Hull's Memorial Baptist Church 1881–1988*)

In 1889, Richlands Baptist Church * was founded. It had derived from the Grove Baptist Church in Goldvein (Fauquier County), which in turn had derived from Hartwood Old-School Baptist in Stafford. The church celebrated its centennial in 1989. It is located off U.S. Route 17 Warrenton Road in Hartwood.

Located at the intersection of U.S. Route 1 and Forbes Street is the original site of the Falmouth Baptist Church *, established in 1891 and now located at the Colonial Avenue-Butler Road intersection. The original church derived from the Fredericksburg church, and after unsuccessful efforts in 1818, 1861, 1868, and 1888, finally separated. The Falmouth Baptist Church remained in that location from 1892 until 1955 when the church building on Colonial Avenue was completed. In 1955 the Highway Assembly of God

Golgotha Church, formerly site of Falmouth Baptist and Redeemer Lutheran Churches (Jane M. Conner)

Salem United Methodist Church
(Owen L. Conner)

purchased the church and remained in it until the mid-1970s, when it was purchased by the Redeemer Lutheran Church (now in Spotsylvania). In 1988 the building was purchased by the Golgotha Church * of Our Lord Jesus Christ. Fund-raising efforts have been made by the Historic Port of Falmouth Association.

Salem United Methodist Church * on Brent Point Road in Widewater began in 1895 when a group of Widewater citizens gathered under the arbor brush for services. Noble Decatur gave 1.47 acres, and John Mason Lee and his wife gave 1 acre of land on Brent Point Road. The church was built and opened in 1896 and continues in the Widewater area. (Kendall)

Twentieth-Century Churches

Four black churches were formed in the early twentieth century: Macedonia Baptist Church, led by Rev. J. T. Brown; Locust Grove Baptist Church, near the Courthouse; Richland Baptist Church (not to be confused with Richlands Baptist Church), which was known to exist in 1913; and Mount Zion Baptist Church. (Fitzgerald)

Little Forest Baptist Church * was organized in north Stafford in 1905. The first pastor was Rev. Uriah Johnson of Baltimore, Maryland. It is located off U.S. Route 1 (3600 section).

Mount Ararat Baptist Church *, founded in 1907, is located at 65 Toluca Road off Garrisonville Road (Virginia 610) in northern Stafford.

Howard Grove Baptist Church, per Fitzgerald, was established near Berea in June 1913, with Cornelius S. Lucas as moderator

In 1915 Moncure Memorial Chapel, in honor of Dr. John Moncure, was founded as an Episcopal church for Stafford blacks. Per Fitzgerald, the minister was "L. A. Morgan, who moved to Louisiana in 1919." Actually, his name was Rev. Sandy Alonzo Morgan, described in Sara Lawrence Lightfoot's biography of Margaret Morgan Lawrence, *Balm in Gilead* (*Widewater to Vicksburg*). It contains yet another newcomer's view of Stafford (including bad geography) and black church life in the early twentieth century:

Widewater was another small rural town, dreary and isolated, and Mary (Margaret's mother) dreaded the move. Reverend Morgan, in typical fashion, saw it as an opportunity and was ready to leave Newbern. "My father would stay a year or a year and a half at a place and then get a call to go someplace else. If the people didn't suit him, he shook the dust off his feet and moved on. It was fairly easy to get a call. You just had to let the bishops know that you were ready to move and somebody would call you." Sandy Morgan's optimism was mixed with impatience and some measure of ambition…

When the Morgans arrived in Widewater, Mary took to her bed. Each uprooting had disastrous effects on her energy and spirit…Margaret's memories of Widewater are vivid. "I can see a crossroads between Quantico and Washington (sic)," says Margaret, sketching the geography on a desk. "The church was on the main road and along a side road nearby. On a knoll is the two-story house where we lived. There was a big apple tree in the front. Somewhere between the church and the house was a two-story barn. There was a swinging bridge over the brook, and the pigs were on the other side of the bridge." The scene, which Margaret calls a "screen memory," is connected to more painful memories of family struggles in this remote, country town. "My father had no experience whatsoever with rural living and neither had my mother…"

The neighbors and parishioners were generous country folk who felt sorry for the minister. "They offered their help to Reverend Morgan whose wife was sick. They didn't think emotionally sick; she was just sick." Margaret remembers the neighbors filling their house, the warmth and comfort of their talk and laughter. "The neighbors were good people. They came over and helped shuck the corn and kill the hogs…."

Morgan, unusually an Episcopalian, had graduated from the Bishop Payne Divinity School in Petersburg about 1906. That school had been founded in 1871 as St. Stephen's Parish School and later became known as Bishop Payne Divinity School, the only one training black Episcopal ministers and founded by Rev. Giles Buckner Cooke, last survivor of Robert E. Lee's staff.

New Hope United Methodist Church *, on New Hope Church Road (Virginia Route 605), was built in 1915. Originally Hopewell Methodist Church, its congregation dates to 1790 and it was used as a hospital during the Civil War and burned.

Union Belle Baptist Church *, in the White Oak area near Wild Cat Corner on Virginia Route 601 (Hollywood Farm Road), was organized in October 1922. Original members were Lucy B. Carter, Maggie Griffin, Angie Ray, Mary White, Easter Washington, Grace Greer, Nannie Barnette, Silas Ray, John Taylor, and Joseph Boxley. Rev. William Tyler was the church's first pastor. (Ruth Coder Fitzgerald)

As was previously mentioned, Shiloh (New Site) Baptist Church * was established in 1942 on U.S. Route 1 (3000 section) near Aquia Harbor.

Jerrilynn Eby lists churches in northern Stafford lost to the 1942 Quantico expansion: Bellehaven Missionary Baptist Church, Church of the United Brethren in Christ, Massadonia Baptist Church, Mount Zion Baptist Church, Providence Church, and Stafford Store Baptist Church.

Modern Churches

History continues to be made as Stafford churches established in the later twentieth century and early twenty-first century develop while serving their congregations' and community's needs.

(This listing is based on available information; some of these churches may be older and/or are based on older churches.)

Modern churches include Abundant Life Assembly of God Church * on Onville Road; Agape Fellowship Ministries * on Garrisonville Road (Virginia 610) and meeting at Moncure Elementary School; Bethel Baptist Church *, Bethel Church Road off White Oak Road (Virginia 218); Calvary Baptist Church *, White Oak Road; Calvary Southern Methodist Church *, Bells Hill Road; Canaans Faith Church of Christ * on Forbes Street (Virginia 627); Church of God of Prophecy *, White Oak Road; Church of the Redeemed *, Jeff Davis Highway; Colonial Baptist Church *, Jeff Davis Highway; Community Baptist Church *, Hansford Lane (Virginia 673); Cornerstone Baptist Church *, McWhirt Loop; and Covenant Family Worship Center *.

Also included among the modern Stafford churches are Emanuel AME Church *, Mountain View Road; Ferry Farms Baptist Church *, Mercer Lane in Ferry Farms; Fredericksburg Assembly of God Church * on Leeland Road in Bel Air Heights; Friendship Baptist Church *, Deacon Road; Garrisonville Church of Christ *, Shelton Shop; Kings Highway Baptist Church*, Cool

Springs Road; Hollywood Church of the Brethren *, Deacon Road; Kingdom Hall of Jehovah's Witnesses *, Virginia 628; Kingsland Chapel (Church of God of Prophecy) *, Kingsland Drive; three wards of the Latter-Day Saints Church * off Eustace Road in Garrisonville; Living Waters Tabernacle *, Harpoon Drive; Midway Baptist Church * at the intersection of U.S. Route 1 and Telegraph Road at Boswell's Corner; Mount Peniel Church of God in Christ *, Courthouse Road; and Mount Zion Ministries *, Jeff Davis Highway.

Other modern Stafford churches include: New Covenant AME Zion Church *, Brighton Way; New Horizon Ministries *, Onville Road; New Life Community Church *, Courthouse Road; New Life Restoration Bible Church *, Whitestone Drive; North Stafford Baptist Church *, Meadowood Drive; Saint Matthias United Methodist Church *, Deacon Road in Grafton Village; Saint Peter's Lutheran Church *, Courthouse Road; Saint William of York Catholic Church *, Jeff Davis Highway near Aquia Creek; Shiloh Christian Church *, Shiloh Way; SOME Ministries * on Sunny Hill Court; Stafford Baptist Church *, Jeff Davis Highway at Stafford Wayside; Stafford Church of God *, Garrisonville Road; Stafford Church of the Nazarene *, Garrisonville Road; Stafford Community Baptist Church *, Hope Road; Stafford County Christian Church *, Mountain View Road; Stafford Emmanuel Korean Baptist Church *, Onville Road; Stafford Freewill Baptist Church *, Joshua Road; Summit Presbyterian Church *, Shelton Shop Road; Temple Baptist Church *, Alley and White Oak Roads in the Chatham area; The Apostolic Faith Assembly *, Little Forest Church Road; Touch Hearts Christian Center * on Newbury Drive; Victory Baptist Church *, Telegraph Road; Vineyard Christian Fellowship *; and Winding Creek Community Church *.

Stafford also has a Jewish synagogue, Beth Shalom Temple *, Plantation Drive.

Chapter Nine
Places of the Mind: Stafford's Schools

This chapter was primarily derived from information contained in The Stafford Schools Project, *which was headed by Shirley C. Heim, then assistant superintendent of schools for finance and public information, and which is now in the* Hall of Memories *in the Alvin York Bandy Administrative Complex.*

Education in Stafford has mirrored and paralleled the county's history. No other part of county history so well reflects how far Stafford, Virginia, and America have progressed.

In the seventeenth century, the earliest years of the county, education was available only to the wealthiest sons (and to a far lesser extent, daughters) of the English nobility and gentry. Education thus derived from the near-feudal society transplanted from England. Only the most privileged sons and daughters could hope for anything resembling a liberal education of that day.

In the eighteenth century, upward mobility in the Colony raised a larger class of merchants, planters, and farmers, and educational opportunities expanded accordingly. Most of this education was still the direct result of paid tutors (often indentured servants), concerned parents, and self-education—with an occasional sortie by a "young master" to the College of William and Mary or northern schools.

Beginning with the nineteenth century, larger numbers of Virginia public and private colleges flourished, but elementary and secondary education of Stafford's young men and women remained a matter of privilege and affluence. Like most things in the Colonial, Revolutionary, Federal, and Antebellum eras of Virginia history, the results of education were uneven and haphazard—and progress came at glacier speed.

In Stafford, as writer Virginia Bare describes:

One young man, Charles Tackett, opened a thriving school early in the 1800s and later opened a boarding school called (ca. 1816) Harwood Academy at Mill Farm, according to (Strother) Harding… In 1815, Daniel Bell taught a school that included girls as well as boys. Harding said this school "at the Courthouse" was well attended and "continued for many years, giving to Stafford some of her best and most useful citizens"… Some boarding schools were "classical," the superintendent immediately adds. "One at Mill Vale, the residence of Colonel John T. Brooke, was conducted by a graduate of Princeton from 1825 to 1830."

Bare, still quoting Superintendent Strother Harding, adds:

One school, "larger and of wider scope…was taught by Mr. William Brent of 'Richland'…until he was appointed charge d'affaires to South America."

Special schooling opportunities included education for girls, training in the classics, and studies in ancient languages. One enterprise Harding mentioned was run by John M. Conway, who organized women to teach girls… About 1820, John Conway…"employed refined and educated ladies" to teach his own and area girls.

Also mentioned was a boarding school specializing in ancient languages conducted by Rev. Milton Henry in the 1840s. Although some antebellum schooling for the indigent was obtained from a literary fund, Harding continues that schools generally closed in Stafford during the Civil War.

Like everything else in Stafford, wartime devastation caused postwar school problems. Harding estimated that soon after the war, fewer than fifty students attended county schools. Yet, ironically it was the post–Civil War era that brought those Virginians and Staffordians a "new birth of freedom" educationally. Defeat in the war ultimately brought the "New South," in which public education, industrialization, and legal equality would become increasingly important.

Writer Cheryl Bradley cites Dr. H. Stewart Jones' *A Historical Study of Public Education in Stafford County, Virginia, from 1865–1965*, showing that the county received its first aid from the Commonwealth—some $593—in 1871. This supported 2,372 boys and girls attending school at that time in twenty-one schoolhouses. By 1899 there were 42 one- or two-room schools.

1890s Rectory School group, Widewater, including young Anne E. Moncure, fifth from the left. (Felicia Parlier)

The first educational opportunities for African Americans began to surface at this time. Yet, at what has been described as "the nadir of American race relations, from 1890–1920," subjugation of blacks politically depended on blocking their educational access. In 1896 the U.S. Supreme Court's *Plessy v. Ferguson* decision upheld the concept of "separate but equal" schools for the races. Until set aside in the 1954 *Brown v. Topeka* decision, this virtually guaranteed substandard education and segregation. In Virginia, it would be nearly a full decade after *Brown* before equal access would begin to be a reality. None of this happened quickly, but it did happen.

Turn of the Century

High school education did not begin until 1918 in a small school constructed for that purpose; students in western Stafford participated in an experimental program run by the Fredericksburg State Teachers' College, now Mary Washington College.

Widewater's Bloomington school in Widewater, the oldest known photo of a Stafford school (Stafford School Board)

Representative of the 1890s era is this depiction of students—"scholars in the making"—of the Falmouth School, a white frame building on the edge of Union Church property on Falmouth's Carter Street. The entire school—needless to say, an all-white assembly of boys and girls drawn from Falmouth and surrounding areas—posed in front of the Union Church (still a complete building). Mr. Richard Moncure taught the upper form; Miss Maggie Maddox taught the lower form. The identified children's names were Snellings, Lightner, Young, Payne, Brooks, Ellis, Bryant, Berry, Ballard, Hart, Curtis, Sullivan, Cox, Boutchyard, Wheeler, Brickett, Fritter, Brown, Stephens, Mills, Roberson, Jefferson, Hewitt, Shelton, Armstrong, and Tyson.

(Stafford School Board)

George Milton Weedon, school superintendent in 1890, was a veteran of the 4th Virginia Cavalry. During the war, he had also been a courier and scout. (Stafford School Board)

Sallie V. French was a turn-of-the-century teacher at Concord School.
(Stafford School Board; Sally Lou Fitzhugh)

Concord School in 1914 (Stafford School Board; Sally Lou Fitzhugh)

Sherwood School group poses at Wild Cat Corner.
(Stafford School Board)

Concord School group, 1914
(Stafford School Board; Sally Lou Fitzhugh)

1920s

Stafford's Anne E. Moncure in her 1917 yearbook entry, Fredericksburg State Teacher's College or Normal School. Much beloved, "Miss Anne E." taught mostly at the elementary level and supervised county elementary education for forty-three years.
(Stafford School Board)

Old Stafford High School (left) and Elementary School, late 1920s or early '30s (Stafford School Board)

A History of Our Own

1930s

Falmouth High School under construction, 1930s (Stafford School Board)

Stage Road School, 1930s (Stafford School Board)

Falmouth High School May court, 1933 or 1934
(Stafford School Board)

Berea School, 1935 (Stafford School Board)

Stafford County, Virginia

Brooke Colored School, 1935
(Stafford School Board)

Falmouth High School, 1935
(Stafford School Board)

Leland School, 1935 (Stafford School Board)

Ramoth School, 1935 (Stafford School Board)

Stafford High School, now Bandy Building, 1935 (Stafford School Board)

May queen, Stafford High School, May 1939 (Stafford School Board)

1940s

School bus waits outside Stafford High School in 1940. (Stafford School Board)

Chappawamsic School, Shackletts, 1940. This was one of the schools in the Quantico-confiscated portions of Stafford in October 1942. (Stafford School Board)

Drama Club, Stafford High School, 1940: (row one) Muriel Grove, Carmen Grey, Wesley Freeman, Dorothy Blackburn; (row two) Mrs. Sacrey, Norvin Decker, Cecil Barlow, Lucille Lambert (Stafford School Board)

Falmouth High School group, 1940s (Stafford School Board)

Girls' basketball, Falmouth High School, 1940s
(Stafford School Board)

Boys' basketball, Falmouth High School, 1940s
(Stafford School Board)

Bill Bolton was a popular principal and coach at Falmouth and Stafford High Schools in the 1940s.
(Stafford School Board)

Stafford County, Virginia

May Day, Stafford High School, 1951 (Stafford School Board)

1950s and 1960s

More changes took place in Stafford in the 1950s–1960s than in the previous 200 years. Schools experienced growth combined with the social cataclysm of racial integration. The title of the 1956–1957 School Board "Progress Report" was still too optimistic. It related that the annual cost of educating a student had "risen rapidly since 1945"—from $68 to $175 per year. Teachers' salaries had similarly climbed from an average $1,725/year in 1948–1949 to $3,179.24/year in 1956–1957 (80 percent of the national average and 99 percent of the state average). County school enrollment in March 1956 was 2,816 in one high school (all-white), one black junior high school, six white elementary schools, and two black elementary schools. The school system disbursed $554,676 that year. Revenues consisted of $265,503 (47.9 percent) from the county; $260,072 (46.9 percent) from the state; and $29,100 (5.2 percent) from the federal government.

School buses, 1956. Pupil transportation of Stafford's 2,816 students was described as a "gigantic undertaking." (Stafford School Board)

Local school buildings associated with black education reflect a tortuous path. The Rowser Building (now a county property) began as a four-teacher building for black students, constructed in 1939 by the Works Progress Administration (WPA). Originally named the Stafford Training School, its students could attend through the eighth grade. Other rooms were added in the next decade. In 1954, an addition was constructed. Classrooms then served the ninth and tenth grades, and the school's name was changed to H. H. Poole Junior High School. In 1959, further improvements were made to the school, allowing it to accommodate the eleventh and twelfth grade. The name was then changed to H. H. Poole High School. Poole High School graduated the class of 1961 and the class of 1962. (White Jr.)

May pole dance, Little Falls Elementary School, 1958 (Stafford School Board)

Little Falls Elementary School, 1959 (Stafford School Board)

Mr. Smith and seventh grade, H. H. Poole Junior High School, 1953–1954
(Stafford School Board)

In August 1962, Poole's eleventh- and twelfth-grade classes were transferred to Stafford High School and the Poole school reverted back to being a junior high school. After integration in the mid-sixties, Poole school became a vocational annex, and its name was changed to the Rowser Building, honoring Mrs. Ella Rowser, a popular Poole teacher. After the vocational annex closed, the Rowser building was used for the Board of Supervisors chambers and other county offices. When the county opened its new administration building, the Rowser building was used to house the Stafford County School Board. (White Jr.)

On September 1, 1960, five seniors from all-black H. H. Poole High School—Steve Tyler, Lois Vines, Gary Mercer, Rudolph Beverly, and Gordon "Sherman" White—applied in person for admission to all-white Stafford High School. Admission was denied, and they were sent back to H. H. Poole. A front-page photograph in the Fredericksburg *Free Lance-Star* on September 5, 1960, depicts those five individuals standing outside Stafford High School after being denied admission. Mr. Edward Smith, principal of Stafford Training School/H. H. Poole High from 1948 to 1960, worked behind the scenes to orchestrate the desegregation movement. He was also the pastor of Mt. Hope Baptist Church in Brooke and a counselor and civic leader. On September 5, 1961, two black sisters, Doretha and Cynthia Montague (enrolling in the first and third grades, respectively), entered the previously all-white Stafford Elementary School, marking the first desegregation of schools in the immediate area.

Miss Giles and eighth and ninth grades, H. H. Poole Junior High School, 1953–1954
(Stafford School Board)

Third-grader Cynthia Montague claims her rights as an American.
(Free Lance-Star)

A History of Our Own

On August 26, 1962, under a plan approved by the Commonwealth of Virginia's Pupil Placement Board, the entire eleventh- and twelfth-grade classes at H. H. Poole High School, consisting of thirty-four students, were transferred to Stafford High School, followed by the ninth and tenth grades. This process continued downward until integration was completed throughout Stafford County in 1964. (White Jr.)

A revealing 1960s "snapshot" document on Stafford education is a March 1961 insurance inventory. The Poole School was valued at $220,000, while Stafford High School was valued at $997,000. Comparing the document with earlier insurance documents (especially 1935), we can see progress and modernization.

Poole Junior High School, February 1961. As Stafford's black school, Poole saw many changes. By arrangement with Fredericksburg, high school students of eleventh and twelfth grades were transported to Walker-Grant High School; Stafford paid tuition and transportation costs. Poole was briefly a high school before integration irrevocably changed Stafford's schools.
(Freeman-Washington Agency)

Oak Grove School, February 1961
(Freeman-Washington Agency)

Ferry Farms Elementary School, February 1961
(Freeman-Washington Agency)

Falmouth Elementary School, Butler Road, February 1961
(Freeman-Washington Agency)

White Oak School, February 1961. Five miles east of Fredericksburg on Virginia 218, the school was rated as "renovated" and "in good condition" and valued at $53,000. It is now the White Oak Civil War Museum and Research Center. One of the school's classrooms has been preserved, providing visitors with an insight into 1950s/1960s Stafford education, as well as a chance to view a collection of Civil War artifacts.
(Freeman-Washington Agency)

New Hope School, February 1961
(Freeman-Washington Agency)

Leland School, February 1961 (Freeman-Washington Agency)

Little Falls School, February 1961
(Freeman-Washington Agency)

Gari Melchers School, later T. Benton Gayle School, February 1961
(Freeman-Washington Agency)

Stafford Elementary School, currently Alvin Y. Bandy Building, February 1961
(Freeman-Washington Agency)

Stafford High School, February 1961
(Freeman-Washington Agency)

Another "snapshot" of that period is the 1964–1965 "Memory Book" for T. Benton Gayle Junior High School. The school was named for the division superintendent of schools who was retiring that year. The school's first faculty and staff are shown: six men, of whom one is black; and fourteen women, all white. The school clubs and activities photo still reveal a sea of white faces. Black faces appear in the pictures of the track team (three of twenty-nine students); seventh- and eighth-grade band students (four of thirty-eight students); and girls' glee club (three of twenty-nine students). No black students were pictured in the photos of the Student Cooperation Association; Panthers Den Staff; Basketball Team; Cheerleaders; Intramural Captains; Future Homemakers of America; 4-H Club; Drama Club; and Science Club. The photo of the eighth graders at lunch shows four black girls sitting together at an otherwise empty table; all other tables are filled with white students. Two of eleven students pictured in the library are black. None of the boys shown in industrial arts class is black; however, the teacher is black. Two of the twenty-four girl students shown taking physical education were black. (Rosie and Edgar Morris)

From such insights, it is clear that Stafford, like America, has come far in race relations and providing equal opportunity and access to its citizens. Yet it is equally clear in the growing body of available histories that during the same periods that Stafford and Virginia struggled with the issues of integration and civil rights, the rest of America was also slow to implement *Brown v. Topeka*. In the North, the concept of "neighborhood schools," especially in the highly compartmentalized northeastern cities with their ethnically and racially divided sections, had effectively the same results as "massive resistance" and segregation in the South. Confrontation, not justice, changed the old order.

Recent

Among the numbers associated with the 2000 census in Stafford, one causing most concern revealed that more than a third of the new county residents, totaling 11,026 people, were school-aged children—a decade's jump of 61 percent. At the start of the 2001 school year, 21,124 students (23 percent of the population) were registered in Stafford's 23 schools with an annual budget of $1.5 million.

Diversity also became a factor—in 1990, 91 percent of the county residents were white. The white population of Stafford dropped in 1990–2000 to 82 percent (72,807 people). Some 11,211 people or 12.1 percent of the county residents were black. Hispanics, which can be of any race, were not counted separately; but those claiming Hispanic heritage amounted to 3,342 or 4 percent of the county population. Some 1,512 residents (1.6 percent) were Asian; 417 (0.5 percent) were Native American; and 93 (0.1 percent) were Native Hawaiian/Pacific Islanders. Another 1,123 (1.2 percent) were listed as "Other race."

(See Chapter 11 for other recent developments.)

Colonial Forge High School, 2003. In June 2003, Stafford's four high schools graduated 1,578 seniors—slightly less than the entire county school population in 1930. This school has its own Virginia historical sign, showing its historic location. (Jane M. Conner)

Chapter Ten
Stafford's Industries and Businesses

Transportation systems, vital to Virginia's economic development, have had equally strong impacts on Stafford's history. Beginning with no transportation infrastructure, initial settlements on Virginia's eastern coastline and Eastern Shore were interdependent on ships and boats plying the oceans and the Chesapeake Bay and its tributaries. Indian paths to the interior were expanded and improved, creating Colonial villages and markets where marketable natural resources and nonperishable produce could be found and harvested.

Roads and Highways

Virginia's state highway system's history identifies four periods of development: 1607–1782, a period of settlement and growth; 1783–1815, a period of experimentation; 1816–1865, a period of expansion; and 1866–1906, a period of reconstruction. (Howard Nelson Jr. and Nathaniel Mason Pawlett—Nelson and Paulette, Eby)

The early history (1607–1782) speaks of two networks of Indian trails and inland waterways in the western and eastern parts of Virginia. The eastern route was called the "Potomac Path," extending from current Petersburg to the Potomac's fall line near Fairfax. In Stafford, Creekside Road (now Virginia 218) was one of the earliest roads. Such rudimentary roads were extended to join adjacent plantations and farms and to facilitate waterway travel. After Jamestown was settled, the eastern transportation network developed along Tidewater lines to move the main crop, tobacco. The first highway law in the New World (in 1632) provided that highways would be created in areas designated by the governor and his council and/or where agreed upon by the "parishioners of every parish" of the established church. (Nelson and Paulette, Eby)

Eventually, courts controlled establishment of "convenient wayes" between counties and to churches, courthouses, and forts. Philadelphia was ultimately the market destination for the eastern route until Virginia's and Maryland's ports developed. Soon, Virginia's road system turned its eyes westward to the source of raw materials and access to new settlements, beginning construction of east-west lines of communication. Even after the Revolution, courts still determined where, when, and how roads would be built, including bridge and ferry construction sites. Early experience revealed that private road construction would often try but fail and that county administration was uneven. It became

Traces of Accokeek Furnace, one of Stafford's oldest industries
(George Washington's Fredericksburg Foundation)

increasingly clear that the state would have to assume greater control of the highway construction movement. (Nelson and Paulette, Eby)

Travelers passing through Stafford in stagecoaches, wagons, and on horseback stayed at wayside taverns and "ordinaries." There they could consume meals, drink, game, and sleep in whatever level of luxury they (white males) could afford. After 1768 Stafford taverns included "Peyton's Ordinary" of Yelverton Peyton. Peyton married Elizabeth Heath; after his death (ca. 1794–1795), she operated the ordinary. George Washington was known to have stopped at Peyton's Ordinary, which is believed to have been located on the ridge east of present Aquia Towne Center, at least three times: twice in 1769 and once in 1772. (Nelson and Pawlett, Eby)

The experimentation period (1783–1815) saw Virginia capitalizing on western markets by developing systems of internal improvements—canals, portage roads, and riverine links. Merchants, fearing the dominance of the western "Great Waggon Road" trade route to Philadelphia and the new Ohio system to the Mississippi and New Orleans, clamored for transportation improvements. As Stafford suffered declines after 1790, it was bypassed by the first intrastate road projects. Presidents Washington and Jefferson became increasingly convinced that the upper Potomac River should be the principal trade route linking the Ohio Valley with the Chesapeake Bay and the wider world. Virginia areas around Washington, D.C. (especially Alexandria), Richmond-Petersburg, and later Norfolk then became mercantile and governmental centers. Virginia struggled, reluctant to exert control at the state level. Industrial development in the North pushed ahead of the South. (Nelson and Pawlett, Eby)

From 1816 to 1860, the Virginia "highway movement" took off in earnest, and the state created governance, bureaucracy, and funding to conquer enormous natural east-west transportation and commercial obstacles. The "turnpike era" saw establishment of turnpike companies operating under state guidance and supported by state funding. In 1816 there were eight turnpike companies.

By 1840 there were forty-seven turnpike companies. By 1860 some 190 existed. By 1851, via the James River, the canal from Richmond to Buchanan (Botetourt County) was completed. Road surfaces ("plank" and "macadamized") were improved, bridges and tunnels were designed and constructed, and weight and vehicle classification limits were introduced. (Nelson and Pawlett, Eby)

1820 map of Stafford County showing sparse road network (Library of Virginia)

Regulations For Hauling ...ON... Improved Roads in Stafford Co.

At a meeting of the Board of Supervisors of Stafford County held at Stafford Court House on September 1, 1913, all members of the Board being present, it was resolved that it shall not be permissible to haul on any of the permanently improved roads in Stafford County loads of lumber or ties heavier than the following:

On tires less than three inches wide not over eight hundred feet (800) of pine lumber or five hundred feet of oak or hardwood lumber or fifteen (15) ties.

On tires three inches wide and less than four inches wide not over fifteen hundred feet (1500) of pine lumber or one thousand feet (1000) of oak or hardwood lumber or twenty (20) ties.

On tires four inches wide and less than six inches wide not over two thousand feet (2,000) of pine lumber or fifteen hundred feet (1500) of oak or hardwood lumber or thirty (30) ties.

On tires six inches wide and over three thousand feet (3,000) of pine lumber or two thousand feet (2,000) of oak or hardwood lumber or forty (40) ties.

The hauling of lumber or ties is prohibited on wagons with tires less than three inches wide hereafter purchased.

Driving in the ditches on the sides of any of the improved roads in Stafford County is prohibited.

Drivers of all teams must be either on the wagons in control of the team or on one of the team hitched at the wheel and the violation of any of the provisions of this order shall be a misdemeanor punishable by fine of not less than five dollars ($5.00) nor more than fifty dollars ($50.00).

It is further ordered that this enactment shall go into effect September 15, 1913, and that the sheriff of this county shall post a copy of this order at each of the voting places in the said county and at the front door of the Court-house at least ten days before September 15, 1913.

A Copy Teste
G. W. Herring Clerk
B. S.

This 1913 notice of the Stafford Board of Supervisors reflects concerns about the county's ever fragile road network.
(Barbara Kirby)

As civil war loomed, the highway movement became a scramble for militarily significant roads. Wartime brought an end to construction and saw many of the usable roads such as those in Stafford damaged or destroyed. (Nelson and Pawlett, Eby)

Stafford's roads—more precisely, the lack of roads—played distinct roles in area Civil War engagements, none more powerfully than in Gen. Ambrose Burnside's January 1863 "Mud March." After the Federal defeat at Fredericksburg in December 1862, Burnside tried to restore army morale by crossing the Rappahannock River at Bank's Ford (part of Celebrate Virginia-Stafford) and attacking Robert E. Lee's army. The march began on January 19 (Lee's birthday), but that night a warm front thawed frozen roads "with 48 hours of pouring rain." To Burnside's humiliation, Confederates taunted the drenched Federals with signs: "This Way to Richmond" and "Burnside Stuck in Mud." The abortive movement ended on January 23, and two days later Lincoln replaced Burnside with Gen. Joseph Hooker.

After the war and well into the twentieth century, Stafford's road networks slowly came back but only to levels that could support local movement of produce and people in optimal weather. Railroads had eclipsed road expansion, and in Stafford, rail and steamboat networks combined to supplant the stage lines and turn roads into local remedies. All efforts were made to connect Virginia to the industrial and commercial North. Henry Ford's first commercially successful automobile was introduced in 1893; however, due to inadequate roads, it would be some time before Stafford saw any advantage from the automobile. Only the development of Virginia's highways and the federal interstate system would again bring commuting residents and travelers through and to Stafford.

Modifications to the county's transportation infrastructure influenced the county's slow development. In the 1920s, an all-weather road was finally

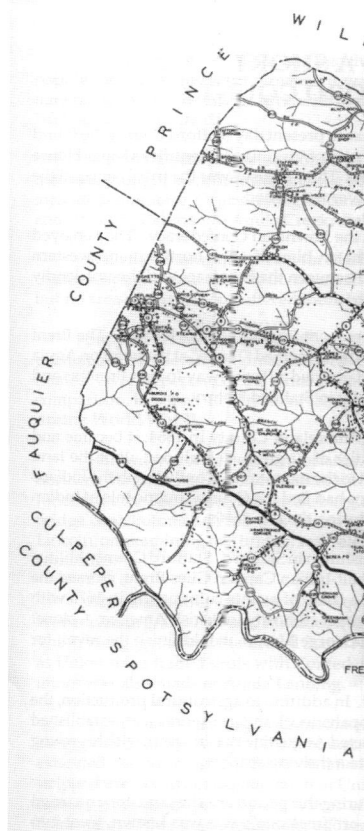

A History of Our Own

built through Chopawamsic Creek, reliably connecting Stafford to the north.

Antebellum Railroads and Steamboats

On February 25, 1834, in hopes of attracting business to Virginia, the General Assembly authorized construction of a Richmond-Aquia (planned to Washington) rail link. Four years later, track had been laid from Richmond to Fredericksburg. During construction, stagecoaches linked the rail terminus to a steamboat terminal at Stafford's Potomac Creek—hence, the Richmond, Fredericksburg, and Potomac (R,F&P) Railroad's designation. By November 1842, the line was extended to newly established Aquia Landing. Thereafter, Washington passengers could travel three and a half hours down the Potomac River by boat to Aquia Landing and transfer to a train to Richmond, another five-and-a-half-hour trip. These improvements opened new markets for Stafford's agricultural, fishing, and light industrial enterprises. Fishing especially prospered as huge Stafford shore nets yielded herring, shad, rockfish, and other varieties. (Musselman)

Fish were salted and shipped to Washington and Richmond. The largest net was located in Widewater, its seine four miles long, and the ropes linking it to the shore were another four miles in length. Boat traffic from Washington to Aquia Landing and the railroad to Richmond made Stafford an important north-south transportation hub before and during the Civil War. Stafford began an economic recovery, taking advantage of improved transportation and new techniques and discoveries in agriculture, fishing, and lumber production. Antebellum farms averaged 300 to 400 acres, primarily raising corn and "truck" produce, swine, and cattle. (Eby)

The R,F&P, the only American railroad that has existed for more than a century without a reorganization and operates with its original name, played a key role in Stafford's history. The need for railroads was apparent as freight

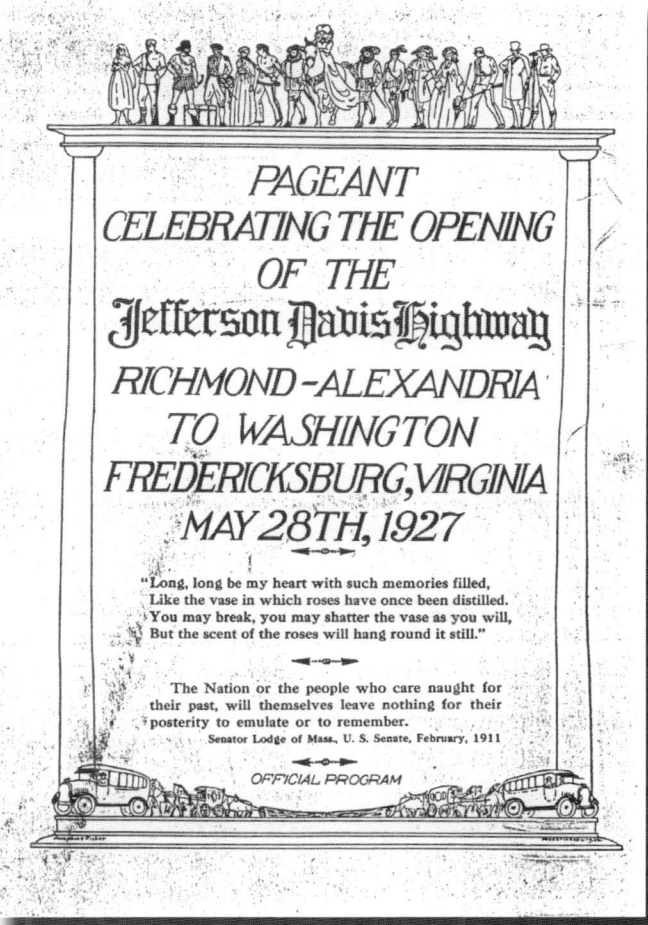

The May 28, 1927, opening of Jefferson Davis Highway was such an event that it called for celebration and a pageant. (Nancy Southworth)

The first state highway map of Stafford in 1932 revealed little change from an 1864 map, except for improvements of north-south U.S. Route 1 and the east-west Virginia Route 38 (Warrenton Road, now U.S. Route 17) and 37 (now Virginia Route 3 to the Northern Neck) roads. (Stafford County)

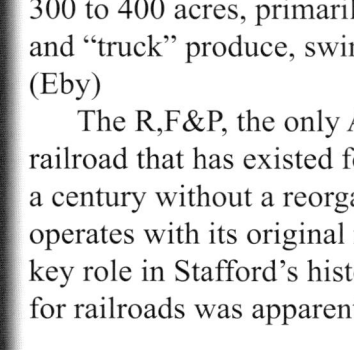

Stafford County, Virginia

moved to river landings on large animal-drawn wagons, and people traveled on jolting stagecoaches. Transportation of goods and passengers was slow on dirt roads that followed land contours and fell prey to the seasons. After heavy rains, wagons sank hub-deep in mud, and dry-weather roads were deeply rutted dust piles. Improved transportation modes became vital. Since 1784, Virginia had encouraged transportation projects by stock subscriptions to canal, turnpike, and toll bridge companies, and it licensed private companies to build roads and charge usage toll fees. Road surfaces gradually improved. East-west movement advanced, but north-south travel remained poor. A stagecoach trip from Richmond to Washington required some thirty-eight hours with stops at Hanover Courthouse, Bowling Green, Fredericksburg (an overnight stop), Falmouth, Stafford Courthouse, Dumfries, Colchester, and Alexandria. In 1815 steamboat service commenced from Stafford's Aquia and Potomac Creeks to Washington. Travel to and from Richmond was reduced to twenty-four hours. (William E. Griffin Jr.—Griffin)

In 1830, steam engine passenger rail service was initiated in South Carolina, and the nation caught "railroad fever." Virginia's first railroad project was the Chesterfield Railroad, from Richmond to mining operations. The project was surveyed by Claudius Crozet, while Moncure Robinson, a "brilliant young engineer," superintended construction. Robinson was then hired in 1833 to survey a railroad between Richmond and Washington. Surveys were speedily completed between October 1833 and January 1834, and Robinson proposed that the line go from Richmond to Fredericksburg, then to Stafford's Potomac Creek, connecting with the steamboat line. Thus, the R,F&P Railroad came into being in February 1834. (Griffin)

Officially, the RF&P was the sixth railroad chartered in Virginia, and only two predecessors had used steam-powered locomotives. The R,F&P was capitalized at $700,000 ($100 per share), and its president and directors were authorized to increase stock to $1,000,000. Stockholders, in an unusual move, were exempted from all taxes until 1912. The Commonwealth bought 2,752 of the 7,000 initial shares, and construction began. An arrangement was made to put trains into operation quickly (in 1836, to the South Anna River), and people and cargo transferred from end-of-track to Edwin Porter's stage line operating to Potomac Creek. For seven years this arrangement worked. Washington-to-Richmond travel, still a grueling twenty-four-hour journey, involved steamboat, stagecoach, and rail. Except for the *Roanoke*, purchased from the Petersburg Railroad, R,F&P's locomotives were initially purchased from England's Bury Company. These five- to six-ton locomotives, given proud names of *Richmond, Fredericksburg, Washington, Potomac, American,*

Jefferson, Virginia, and *Florida*, were later named for directors, other southern states, and R,F&P stations. (Griffin)

By January 1837, the R,F&P operated from Richmond to Fredericksburg. There passengers off-loaded onto stagecoaches, operated by Jordan Woolfolk and later Lucius W. Stockton, to the steamboat wharf at Potomac Creek. That year, chief engineer Moncure Robinson recommended using the steamboat wharf at Aquia Creek instead, as the channel had greater depth. Within a few years, the R,F&P formed a link in what was referred to as "the inland route" (distinguishing it from the Norfolk-Baltimore-Chesapeake steamboat route). After stockholder agreement, the Fredericksburg-Aquia Creek link was operative in November 1842. Stage lines were dispensed with, and the R,F&P purchased half the capital stock of the new Washington and Fredericksburg Steamship Company (in 1845 R,F&P leadership took over actual control). Thus effected, revenue-sharing and efficiencies were introduced, to the rail and steamship lines' mutual benefit. Moncure Robinson was the fourth president of the line (1840–1847).

By the mid-1850s, the Washington and Fredericksburg Steamboat Company became the Potomac Steamboat Company. *Powhatan, Mount Vernon, Baltimore*, and *Maryland* were the steamships engaged on the line in 1855. Sadly, efficiency and prosperity of the R,F&P peaked on the eve of civil war. (Griffin)

Civil War Railroading and Logistics in Stafford

After Virginia seceded (April 17, 1861), the Federals confiscated the four steamships of the Potomac Steamboat Company. Apparently, much like his Stafford-born namesake, R,F&P President Peter V. Daniel Jr. was enraged by the Yankees' actions. Virginia authorities quickly defended rail facilities and equipment from Union capture. In the early months of the war, the railroad was forced to employ its own guards, as Virginia forces were still organizing and training. The R,F&P used four-foot-eight-inch-gauge track (the Confederacy suffered from a lack of uniformly gauged railroads), thus allowing connection with the nearby Virginia Central (Hanover Junction [now Doswell] to Gordonsville), Orange & Alexandria (north and south from Gordonsville), Richmond & York River, and Richmond & Petersburg lines. Technology hindered the R,F&P, as by 1861 the most commonly used track was the wrought-iron "T" section. Its only advantage was that it could be re-rolled and returned to track use. Some eleven and three-quarter miles of R,F&P track used the "strap" rail, an even cruder version. As no antebellum need had existed for double-tracking, the R,F&P had only five miles of secondary track on its main stem of seventy-five miles. The railroad began constructing its own locomotives (three) before the war.

Gen. Herman Haupt (Library of Congress)

Andrew J. Russell photograph of Potomac Creek Bridge "beanpole and cornstalk bridge" (Library of Congress)

Andrew J. Russell photograph of improved bridge with "shad bellies" strongpoint, Potomac Creek (Library of Congress)

Gen. Herman Haupt's rail-to-barge transloading system moved 800 tons of supplies a day. (National Archives)

The R,F&P was one of the companies seeking Confederate government support—some $60,000 at one point—but it was one of the very few Southern lines to make more from passenger traffic than cargo. (Robert C. Black III, *The Railroads of the Confederacy*)

On the northern fringe of the Confederate rail system, the R,F&P was susceptible to the vagaries of warfare in its area. Union efforts in military railroading in Stafford were impressive:

(Union military railroads chief Gen. Herman) Haupt's pressing assignment in May of 1862 was to rebuild the railroad from Aquia Creek, on the Potomac, thirteen miles to Falmouth, across from Fredericksburg. Retreating Confederates had wrecked the line, reducing the railhead at Aquia Creek to ruins, tearing up miles of track and burning three bridges (Accokeek Creek, Potomac Creek, and the Rappahannock River). The roadbed itself had been churned by cavalry and turned into a quagmire by constant rain. Haupt put his newly formed Construction Corps to work around the clock. "I threw out a dragnet and raked in all the lanterns to be found," he wrote. "We unloaded iron by candlelight, put it on cars hauled by soldiers to the end of track, and kept on laying and spiking all night." The most daunting obstacle in the path of the construction Corps was a chasm 80 feet in depth at Potomac Creek. Haupt spanned it with a bridge constructed mostly of fresh-cut logs. It was perilous work. "We got three men at different times in the river, but fished them out," Haupt reported to the War Department. "A fourth is missing, supposed to be drowned." After only twenty-one days of labor, the railroad had been restored and Federal supply trains were chugging along it every hour...

The Potomac Creek bridge had been constructed in nine days, using 2 million feet of green lumber and inexperienced labor troops.

Haupt later replaced this "beanpole and cornstalk bridge" construction marvel (see Chapter 5) with one more architecturally sound, using prefabricated truss sections nicknamed "shad bellies." To secure the bridge, a strong point was constructed nearby (now in a planned residential subdivision). Haupt developed another innovative approach to transporting supplies to Stafford in the fall 1862 build-up for the Battle of Fredericksburg:

Stoneman's Switch or Station outside Falmouth was a Union logistics center and forward supply depot. (National Archives)

…Haupt received orders to transport unprecedented quantities of food, forage and munitions from depots near Washington to the Federal forces assembling near Fredericksburg. No rail line connected the two places, but Haupt set up a supply route down the Potomac River to Aquia Creek and from there by rail to the Fredericksburg area. He also devised a way to avoid the tedious unloading of freight at the transfer points between land and water. His trains ran to the river's edge at Alexandria. There the cars were pushed onto flat-bottomed barges. Two barges bolted together could hold eight freight cars. Four of them could ferry a typical sixteen-car train thirty-five miles to the landing at Aquia Creek in six hours and put it ashore, ready to roll.

Haupt struggled to make the system work, but his main enemies in Stafford were not Confederate raiders: Union commanders confiscated railcars to use as warehouses, and quartermasters failed to off-load supplies and return cars for additional trips. One paymaster commandeered a vitally needed car as his office and had to be forcibly ejected. Troops, always in search of wood and water for fires, bathing, and laundry, grabbed spare ties and purloined steam water for locomotive. Nevertheless, Haupt managed to move 800 tons of supplies a day to Burnside's army, poised before Fredericksburg in December 1862. A dimension of the Civil War as the first "modern" war, Union actions earned Stafford yet another arguable title: the "birthplace of modern military logistics." (William K. Goolrick)

Yuba Dam, showing the railroad wharf (left) and wagon wharf under construction (right)
(Mary Rust; Library of Congress)

Returning to the R,F&P in Civil War Stafford history, McDowell's Union army moved in following Confederate withdrawal in March–April 1862 as part of the projected Peninsula Campaign (May–July 1862). McDowell openly doubted Haupt's efforts, and stated no train would ever operate from Aquia Landing. On May 4, 1862, McDowell rode the first train to cross Accokeek

Evacuation of Aquia Landing, June 1863
(Mary Rust; Library of Congress)

Aquia Landing. Supplies are in-bound on the *New York*. (Mary Rust; Library of Congress)

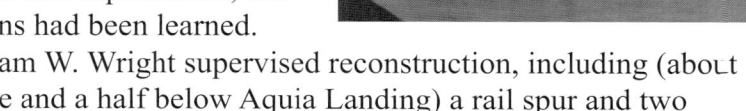

Ships at Aquia Landing
(Mary Rust; Library of Congress)

Creek's 150-foot-long, 30-foot-high bridge, erected in sixteen hours. After greater exertions at Potomac Creek, Haupt's trains rolled in one of the most extensive military transportation feats in world history. Even when it became possible (August–September 1862), the Confederacy never retook the R,F&P section in Stafford. However, when Ambrose Burnside believed the Southerners would try, he burned Aquia Landing's wharfs and destroyed Haupt's rail line. Ironically, Burnside would pay for this folly when he returned to Stafford to face Lee's army across the river. The railroad and wharves at Aquia Landing had to be reconstructed, and Haupt's Construction Corps had to rebuild the lost supply line. Fortunately, his corps was now 300 strong, better tooled and experienced, and lessons had been learned.

William W. Wright supervised reconstruction, including (about a mile and a half below Aquia Landing) a rail spur and two wharves. The railroad wharf, some 840 feet long connected to a wagon wharf about 380 feet long, was named "Burnside Wharf." The operating railroaders called it "YouBe Dam" or "Yuba Dam." It, and Aquia Landing resurgent, played key roles in the Battles of Fredericksburg and Chancellorsville, as logistical advantage accrued to Hooker's army during the winter of 1862–1863.

During the Pennsylvania Campaign, on June 22, 1863, a detachment of Confederate cavalry under Maj. Charles Read Collins (15th Virginia Cavalry) again burned the Aquia buildings and wharf. Five weeks later, the tracks between Aquia and Falmouth were removed and carried away, and the bridges were again destroyed. Collins, receiving conflicting guidance from Secretary of War Seddon, General Lee, and local commanders, committed a few of his own errors, losing valuable materiel. In May 1864, to resupply Grant's forces in the Overland Campaign (May–June 1864), the Union again rebuilt the Aquia-Fredericksburg rail line. This final time, it took but nine days to reopen the line to Falmouth. (Griffin, John Fortier)

Union wharves at Belle Plain in White Oak and King George were added to Federal capabilities to resupply and back-haul prisoners of war. After May 22, 1864, the Fredericksburg-Aquia line ceased operation. Union logistics operations, supporting the Richmond-Petersburg siege, shifted to City Point on the James River. (Griffin)

This October 1864 photograph of Aquia Landing shows a number of tall-masted vessels. (Mary Rust; Library of Congress)

Postwar Railroading

At war's end, the R,F&P was largely damaged or destroyed. By 1866, however, it had recovered sufficiently to establish operations between Richmond and Hamilton's Crossing (below Fredericksburg). Stage line service again connected Hamilton's Crossing to Potomac Creek while Aquia steamship facilities were under construction. By September 1866, the Aquia steamship wharf was rebuilt and Washington steamboat service resumed. The following year, tracks were opened to connecting lines south to Weldon, North Carolina. Passengers could then travel without changing cars. Adverse weather conditions, which closed Potomac River traffic during the winter of 1867–1868, recreated demand for a continuous rail line from Washington to Baltimore. A new line was decided upon in 1870 to run from Stafford's Brooke Station north to Alexandria. Stafford's Potomac Steamboat Company terminus, however, moved from Aquia to Quantico Creek.

Varied numbers and types of boats and ships were used at Aquia Landing. (Mary Rust; Library of Congress)

Andrew J. Russell photograph of Upper Wharf at Belle Plain (Library of Congress)

Andrew J. Russell photograph of Lower Wharf at Belle Plain. Ship activity is visible. (Library of Congress)

Stafford County, Virginia

Right, Maj. E. T. D. Myers built the first railroad bridge across Aquia Creek. It was a trestle bridge 1,065 feet long with a 29-foot draw span. Myers was later R,F&P general superintendent from 1870 to 1889 and president from 1889 to 1905. (Richmond, Fredericksburg and Potomac Railroad)

The October 12, 1894, train robbery took place on this isolated stretch of rail line north of the Aquia Creek Bridge in Stafford.
(Lawrence R. Duffee/Free Lance-Star)

$1000 REWARD!

WILL BE PAID BY THE

Richmond, Fredericksburg and Potomac

Railroad Company

For the Arrest of the Party or Parties concerned in the Robbery of the Northbound Night Mail Train, near Aquia Creek, Va., on the night of October 12, 1894.

E. T. D. MYERS, Prest.

IN ADDITION,

to the above Reward, the Governor of Virginia offers a reward of ONE THOUSAND DOLLARS for the arrest of the Robbers, or One Hundred and Fifty Dollars for the arrest of any one of them.

The R,F&P posted a $1,000 reward for the arrest of any of the robbers. The Commonwealth offered another $1,000 reward, but required the arrest of both robbers or $150 for any one of them.
(Richmond, Fredericksburg and Potomac Railroad)

In 1872, the Alexandria and Fredericksburg Railroad was completed to Quantico. Night trains ran all the way from Richmond to Washington; during the day, passengers changed to the Potomac Steamboat Line. All-rail service was soon preferred, and the steamboat contract (1872) was terminated. "Express freight" commenced as a regular service. (Griffin)

An 1894 Stafford train robbery demonstrated postwar changes. Valuables, such as gold, securities, cash, etc., were transported on passenger cars by special agents. These trains had to stop frequently, and criminal elements could readily board. Train robberies became a popular American pastime:

On the night of October 12, 1894, Engineer F. T. Gallagher and Conductor M. A. Birdsong took charge of R,F&P Train No. 78 at Byrd Street Station, departing on their run to Washington at 7:00 P.M. The train reached Fredericksburg on schedule and, after pausing to take on water, took up her run again. Just a few miles ahead the uneventful trip would come to an abrupt halt. As the train slowed to cross the draw span of the Aquia Creek bridge, two masked men climbed on top of the train and crawled toward the locomotive. Just after crossing the bridge, they jumped onto the tender and forced Engineer Gallagher at gunpoint to stop the train. In order to give the appearance of a large gang, the robbers ran back and forth along the train firing their weapons in the air. That settled any question as to resistance by the passengers. Satisfied that the passengers and train crew had been subdued, the robbers then forced Engineer Gallagher and Fireman Henry Washington to detach the locomotive from the rest of the train and move it forward. When this was accomplished, they made for the express car. By this time, express managers B. F. Crutchfield and Henry Murray were fully aware that a train robbery was in progress and they bolted the express car door from the inside. Not to be denied, the bandits promptly blew the door off the car with a stick of dynamite. Further persuasion was unnecessary—Crutchfield and Murray wisely surrendered. All the pouches containing money and other valuables were cut open, and one of the express men was forced at gunpoint to unlock the heavy safe. After rounding up all the money and valuables within their reach, the two robbers boarded the locomotive and ran it about a

The 1905 Aquia Creek Bridge and drawbridge
(Richmond, Fredericksburg and Potomac Railroad)

A History of Our Own

mile northward to a point near Arkendale (in Widewater) road crossing. There they unloaded their loot, threw the throttle open, and turned the locomotive loose. Fortunately, the R,F&P agent at Arkendale heard the rapid approach of the locomotive and when he went out to investigate, discovered it was a runaway. He promptly telegraphed that fact to the Quantico station. At Quantico, Mr. C. G. Leary, who retired in 1954 after sixty-two years service with R,F&P, threw a switch to divert the locomotive to a sidetrack. A few moments later, the locomotive roared into Quantico at a frightful rate of speed, diverged from the mainline, crashed into four empty coal cars on the sidetrack, and plunged from the end of the coal trestle. The locomotive was damaged but not destroyed. Luckily, no one had been injured.

The Stafford railroad robbery made news as far north as New York City, where the *Herald* reported:

The *George Wythe* crosses the 1946 Aquia Creek Bridge, still in use today. Built at a higher elevation, the 1,321-foot-long steel and concrete bridge stands witness to the 20th-century rise of railroads. (Richmond, Fredericksburg and Potomac Railroad)

The "hold-up" of a train at Aquia Creek, Va., forty-one miles from Washington, on the Richmond, Fredericksburg and Potomac Railroad, and the robbery of a sum estimated at one hundred and fifty thousand dollars from the Adams express car, is bringing train robbery a little too near home.

The robbers were quickly apprehended and identified as Charles J. Searcy and Charles Morgan (alias Charles Morganfield). Morgan was tried in February 1895. The *Richmond Times* wryly added:

…old Stafford was visited…by a larger delegation of strangers than at any time in her history, except, probably during the war.

Stafford courts, never quick to laugh off a felony, convicted and sentenced the miscreants expeditiously. Searcy was sentenced to eight years, and Morgan, apparently the leader, was sentenced to eighteen years in the state penitentiary. No mention is made of recovery of the money, however. (Griffin)

Between 1865 and 1890, national railroading freight volumes had increased from 10 billion to 79 billion ton miles. In 1870 the R,F&P, still operating to Aquia Creek, "transported 8,999 tons of through freight, had 31,200 miles run by freight trains and through freight revenues of $8,398." By 1880 "only eight years after the all-rail route was established, through-freight revenues exceeded local-freight revenues for the first time in company history." In the twentieth century, American railroading surged, as did the

R,F&P: from 1903 to 1907 the entire line was double-tracked, increasing volume and infrastructure, including a new wooden double-track trestle bridge across Aquia Creek (1905).

That wooden bridge was replaced in 1923 by a steel and concrete structure, but the 1923 bridge, limited in allowable speeds to thirty-five miles per hour, was replaced in 1946 with the modern bridge in service today.

Stafford County, Virginia

Pig-iron ingots found near the site of the Hunter's Iron Works (Blaisdell Collection)

Hunter's Gravesite at Union Cemetery in Falmouth (Myron E. and Mary Lyman)

A wistful thought:

> Downstream from the Aquia Creek bridge, nothing remains to mark the site of the R,F&P's old steamboat landing. Bypassed by the rerouted mainline, the wharf and more than forty years of rail and steamboat operations endure only as memories of a time when both the R,F&P and America were young. (Griffin)

Stafford area commuters—driving on modern highways and passing over Aquia Creek on today's Virginia Rail Express (VRE) from Brooke, Potomac Creek (Leeland), and Fredericksburg—may reflect on the rich history of steamboats, stagecoaches, and railroads, the Civil War U.S. Military Railroad, the 1894 robbery, and America's rise to international transportation and commercial prominence.

Early Industries: Accokeek Furnace and Hunter's Iron Works

Stafford had two important Colonial ironworks, each with its own interesting story.

Accokeek Furnace was one of the earliest iron blast furnaces in Virginia and America. In 1725 John England (coincidentally from Staffordshire), who managed the Principio Company's American interests in Maryland, discovered a high-quality iron deposit on 1,600 acres in Stafford—property owned by Augustine Washington. The subsequent agreement stipulated that Washington would be paid for all ore dug from his mines, and Principio initially intended to ship Accokeek ore to their furnace in Maryland. They soon determined, however, that the Accokeek site possessed all features required by a blast furnace and built one on Accokeek Run near the mines. Accokeek-produced "pigs" were sent to either Principio's Maryland forges for processing or to England as ballast on tobacco ships. The furnace, operative in 1728, thrived until the unfortunate 1734 death of John England. This likely catalyst induced Augustine Washington to move his family from "Wakefield" to "Mount Vernon," then to the Rappahannock River plantation or "Ferry Farm." When Augustine Washington died in 1743, his interests in the furnace went to his eldest son, Lawrence, who was actively involved with Accokeek and Principio and aided company expansion efforts. When Lawrence Washington died in 1752, his interests in Principio passed to his daughter. Principio took this opportunity to concentrate efforts in their four Maryland furnaces and forges. Accokeek was closed down, movable property sold, and the area lay abandoned until the mines were reopened in 1777 by James Hunter, another Stafford ironmaster.

(Eby) Ironically, another Maryland-based firm, the Michael T. Rose Companies, would deed 3.2 acres of the Accokeek Furnace site to Stafford County in 1989.

Stafford's Hunter's Iron Works, its relation to other Virginia iron industries, and its aid to the Revolution are all fascinating parts of Stafford history:

> Off the highways of America are scores of crumbling monuments that recall this country's stark beginning. These are the remains of venerable furnaces where iron ore was smelted to shape the destiny of America…

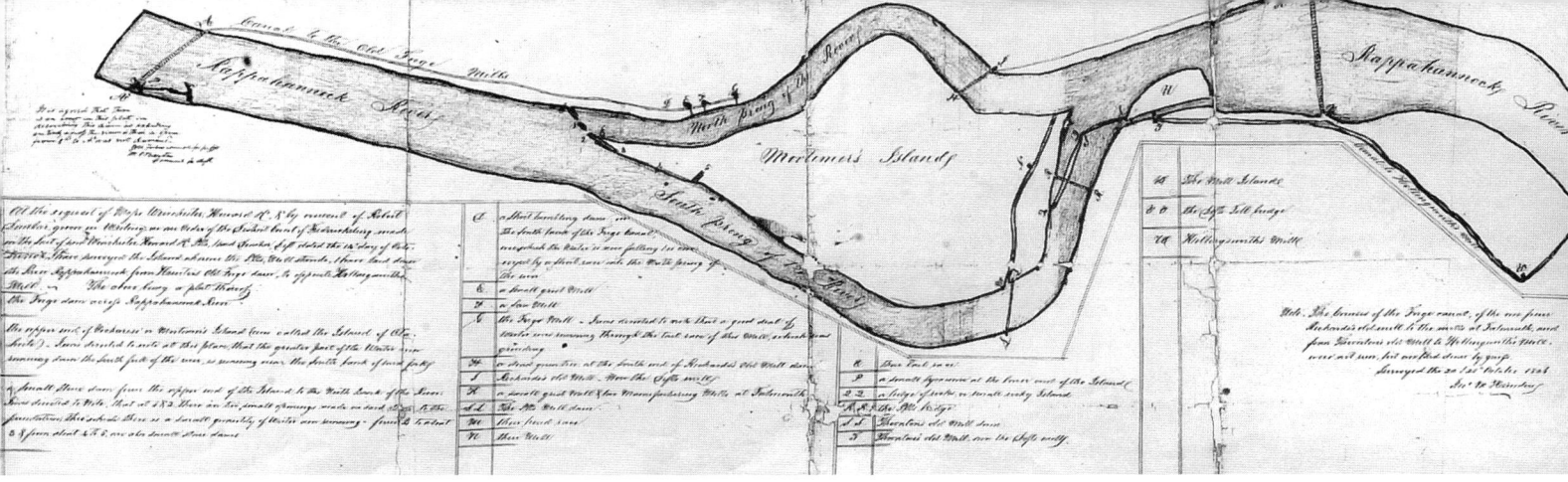

James Hunter, born in Scotland in 1721, settled permanently in the Falmouth area in 1746. There he became a leading ironmaster of his day as well as a wealthy merchant. In the mid-1750s Hunter set out to build a forge and mill complex on the north side of the Rappahannock River, and the facility was operating as early as 1759. This complex, capable of manufacturing a wide variety of consumer goods, was unique in North America. Its products ranged from wool and cotton combs to textiles to nails and wire. By 1776, efforts at Hunter's Iron Works shifted from domestic goods to war materiel. In June of that year, he demonstrated a production model musket with bayonet. Legislators approved the design and ordered as many muskets as Hunter's gunsmiths could manufacture during the next year. Hunter was to receive six pounds for each "stand" or completely finished weapon. (Eby)

In 1777 the legislature, backed by Gov. Patrick Henry, recognized Hunter's Iron Works, also known as Rappahannock Forge, by subsidizing plant expansion. By the end of the following year, the works included steel and brass furnaces, a new iron furnace, wire, plating, and splitting mills, grist mills, forges, and a saw mill. The manufacturing mills were described as "one for making iron for the army and navy, one for fashioning arms, entrenching tools, and anchors, one for splitting and plating iron, and another for producing wire." A British customs officer had already described Hunter's facility as "the greatest ironworks that is upon the Continent." Gov. Thomas Jefferson wrote Hunter in 1781 indicating his concern for the works' safety, asserting "its significance to the safety of the colonies." Virginia moved to secure the works. A state debt to Hunter for 180,000 pounds (the modern equivalent of $800,000) attests to production levels at the works and the value of Hunter's muskets, wall guns, swords, and equipment. Prior to 1781, state

Hunter's Raceway Dam, built in 1770, played a role in the operation of the Hunter's Iron Works during the Revolutionary War, as depicted on an 1806 map. (Davis Turner/Free Lance-Star)

Persistent stories that James Hunter had "died a pauper" and was unceremoniously buried in Union Cemetery, Falmouth, led a group of citizens during the 1976 U.S. Bicentennial Celebration to hold a memorial service for the Revolutionary War patriot and industrialist. Rev. Thomas G. Faulkner Jr. conducted the service, attended by Bicentennial Commission members and others. (Barbara Flack)

Stafford County, Virginia

officials paid substantial amounts to James Hunter, though it is unclear exactly how much he was owed. After 1781 the General Assembly, essentially broke and unable to pay its bills, failed to issue full payment on Hunter's outstanding warrants. Apocryphal stories abound that he died penniless and was buried at night to avoid creditors, but these appear incorrect. It is unlikely creditors would have dug up his body for retribution, and the wrought-iron fence wouldn't have kept out anyone. (Eby, George D. Taylor, Dr. H. Stewart Jones and Dr. Oscar H. Darter)

Far from being destitute at his death, Hunter actually held substantial assets including his plantation house, "Stanstead," some 6,000 acres of land in Stafford (and additional acreage in other places), and numerous slaves. Due to nonpayment of monies owed him by the state, his estate was burdened with substantial debts, but the exact balance is unknown. Regardless of Hunter's financial situation, his contributions to the Revolution were great and personified the 1776 Philadelphia pledge committing "our Lives, our Fortunes, and our sacred Honor." (Eby)

As removal of ninety-one-year-old Embrey Dam on the Rappahannock takes place in the near future, Hunter-related mysteries may be resolved, including Hunter's dam, built diagonally on the river ca. 1758 to power his ironworks, and an 1855 crib-dam.

The man behind the success of Hunter's Iron Works was John Strode, a Pennsylvania Quaker who managed the manufactory from ca. 1760 to ca. 1779, when he moved to Culpeper. Strode, a millwright and engineer, was responsible for much of the design and building carried on at Rappahannock Forge prior to the Revolution. James Hunter died in 1784, and the Revolution officially ended shortly afterward. Production continued at the works on a greatly reduced scale. Numerous attempts by the heirs to sell the property were unsuccessful. Not until the early nineteenth century did Falmouth businessman Joseph Ficklen purchase the property. It is not known whether iron smelting resumed, but the forge and merchant mill continued in operation, and Ficklen used parts of the works for his flour mills. Though heavily damaged by flooding, Union occupation, and time, many foundations remain on the forge site as does most of the three-quarter-mile-long canal that directed water from the river to the manufacturing mills. In 2001–2002, the Stafford County Historical Society purchased a Virginia Historical Marker to commemorate the "famous" Hunter's Iron Works, ironically so perilously close to oblivion. (Eby, Lymans, Pezzullo)

Silk Industry

Virginia's silk industry had an odd history, beginning in the seventeenth century by encouragement of royal governors Sir William Berkeley and Edward Digges. By 1666 the Virginia industry was able to send a royal gift of 300 pounds of silk from annual production, and experimentation and small-scale production continued into the eighteenth century as Virginia looked for product alternatives to tobacco. In Stafford, the law requiring mulberry trees to be planted was also in effect, and Thomas Ludwell Lee of "Bellview" (1730–1798) attempted to produce silk at "Berry Hill." Other Stafford planters attempting to produce silk included William Fitzhugh of "Chatham" as well as the Brents, Wallers, Witherses, Fowkes, and Carters. Their efforts ultimately failed because silkworms struggled to flourish in Virginia. "Berry Hill" was sold off by the Lees in 1806 and 1810. Later, another effort was made by the Potomac Silk and Agriculture Company of Fredericksburg to revive "Berry Hill." It, too, failed. (Eby)

Stone Quarries

(See Chapter 6.)

In addition to the Government Island quarry, there were other quarry sites in Widewater at Rock Ramore (also rendered "Rock Rimmon," "Rock Raymer," and "Rock Raymond"). The Rock Ramore quarry, known at least for a time as the "George Washington Quarry," operated from an unknown date into the 1920s and shipped blocks downstream on the adjoining creek to Aquia Creek and via the Potomac River north to Washington and Alexandria. The farm was later owned by the Harpers, who called it "Mount Pleasant." Only a cemetery remains. At the end of Quarry Road (Virginia 692), the property was associated with Conways (who operated several sandstone quarries along Aquia Creek) and Wallers. (Eby)

Another active quarry in the 1800's was the Robertson Quarry located [near] present day Austin Ridge.

[Light] Industries

[Th]e 1800s witnessed development of Stafford's light industries [in additi]on to its agriculture and fishing. Power saws, driven by water [wheels a]nd later steam engines, provided a means to harvest lumber for [incre]ased building demands. (Eby)

One vestige of Falmouth's industrial days is the visible section of the Falmouth Canal.
(John J. Johnson/ Historic Fredericksburg Foundation Inc.)

Flour Mills

Early flour mills were particularly interesting as nine mills were in operation in Virginia by 1649. The first grist mill was credited to Giles Brent (I) in 1668. Initially used to feed the Brents and their workers, slaves, and neighbors, it became a commercial enterprise that survived into the 1900s, supplying the neighborhood, back country and District of Columbia customers. Severe shortages in grain and flour in Europe, created by the Napoleonic Wars from 1793 to 1815, caused the European markets to turn to the New World. Falmouth emerged as a flour industry center, with five mills producing more than 60,000 barrels a year by 1813. By 1810, Brent's Mill had included a distillery. Identified as having 1600s Stafford origins were Lyle's Mill (like Brent's, a water mill), Waugh's Mill (Potomac Creek), and Fitzhugh's (of Bedford) Mill (in what is now King George County, called Gray's Mill on Civil War-era maps). From 1793 to 1859, two mills existed in Aquia (from 1807 by Robert Crutcher and Benjamin Ficklen). Tackett's Mill in the western part of Stafford existed by 1820. Tackett had owned one earlier mill at Aquia about 1816 and was known to own two mills (per Eby, one was a grist mill and the other a saw mill on the same property) by 1820. (Johnson, *Foundation Stones* and *Journal of Fredericksburg History*.)

Tackett's Mill in northern Stafford, 1930-'40s (Felicia Parlier)

Mining

In a sense, given Capt. John Smith's 1608 trip up Aquia C to find an Indian antimony mine, mining could facetiously s be Stafford's first industry. As with other parts of Virginia, in mining natural minerals came early. In the eighteenth iron ore was mined to supply previously described Acc Furnace and Hunter's Iron Works. A lone gold discove mentioned in Thomas Jefferson's 1787 *Notes on Vir* "found in Stafford about four miles below Frederic north side of the Rappahannock." Nineteenth-cer primarily centered on gold, and minerals were in Hartwood.

"Gold fever" struck the area about 1829 panned, crudely crushed, and sifted in stre gold mines date from 1836 to 1850. (Eby

Silk Industry

Virginia's silk industry had an odd history, beginning in the seventeenth century by encouragement of royal governors Sir William Berkeley and Edward Digges. By 1666 the Virginia industry was able to send a royal gift of 300 pounds of silk from annual production, and experimentation and small-scale production continued into the eighteenth century as Virginia looked for product alternatives to tobacco. In Stafford, the law requiring mulberry trees to be planted was also in effect, and Thomas Ludwell Lee of "Bellview" (1730–1798) attempted to produce silk at "Berry Hill." Other Stafford planters attempting to produce silk included William Fitzhugh of "Chatham" as well as the Brents, Wallers, Witherses, Fowkes, and Carters. Their efforts ultimately failed because silkworms struggled to flourish in Virginia. "Berry Hill" was sold off by the Lees in 1806 and 1810. Later, another effort was made by the Potomac Silk and Agriculture Company of Fredericksburg to revive "Berry Hill." It, too, failed. (Eby)

Stone Quarries

(See Chapter 6.)

In addition to the Government Island quarry, there were other quarry sites in Widewater at Rock Ramore (also rendered "Rock Rimmon," "Rock Raymer," and "Rock Raymond"). The Rock Ramore quarry, known at least for a time as the "George Washington Quarry," operated from an unknown date into the 1920s and shipped blocks downstream on the adjoining creek to Aquia Creek and via the Potomac River north to Washington and Alexandria. The farm was later owned by the Harpers, who called it "Mount Pleasant." Only a cemetery remains. At the end of Quarry Road (Virginia 692), the property was associated with Conways (who operated several sandstone quarries along Aquia Creek) and Wallers. (Eby)

Another active quarry in the 1800's was the Robertson Quarry located near present day Austin Ridge.

Light Industries

The 1800s witnessed development of Stafford's light industries in addition to its agriculture and fishing. Power saws, driven by water wheels and later steam engines, provided a means to harvest lumber for the increased building demands. (Eby)

One vestige of Falmouth's industrial days is the visible section of the Falmouth Canal.
(John J. Johnson/ Historic Fredericksburg Foundation Inc.)

Tackett's Mill in northern Stafford, 1930-'40s (Felicia Parlier)

Flour Mills

Early flour mills were particularly interesting as nine mills were in operation in Virginia by 1649. The first grist mill was credited to Giles Brent (I) in 1668. Initially used to feed the Brents and their workers, slaves, and neighbors, it became a commercial enterprise that survived into the 1900s, supplying the neighborhood, back country and District of Columbia customers. Severe shortages in grain and flour in Europe, created by the Napoleonic Wars from 1793 to 1815, caused the European markets to turn to the New World. Falmouth emerged as a flour industry center, with five mills producing more than 60,000 barrels a year by 1813. By 1810, Brent's Mill had included a distillery. Identified as having 1600s Stafford origins were Lyle's Mill (like Brent's, a water mill), Waugh's Mill (Potomac Creek), and Fitzhugh's (of Bedford) Mill (in what is now King George County, called Gray's Mill on Civil War-era maps). From 1793 to 1859, two mills existed in Aquia (from 1807 by Robert Crutcher and Benjamin Ficklen). Tackett's Mill in the western part of Stafford existed by 1820. Tackett had owned one earlier mill at Aquia about 1816 and was known to own two mills (per Eby, one was a grist mill and the other a saw mill on the same property) by 1820. (Johnson, *Foundation Stones* and *Journal of Fredericksburg History*.)

Mining

In a sense, given Capt. John Smith's 1608 trip up Aquia Creek to find an Indian antimony mine, mining could facetiously said to be Stafford's first industry. As with other parts of Virginia, interest in mining natural minerals came early. In the eighteenth century, iron ore was mined to supply previously described Accokeek Furnace and Hunter's Iron Works. A lone gold discovery, mentioned in Thomas Jefferson's 1787 *Notes on Virginia,* was "found in Stafford about four miles below Fredericksburg on the north side of the Rappahannock." Nineteenth-century activities primarily centered on gold, and minerals were again being mined in Hartwood.

"Gold fever" struck the area about 1829, when ore was mostly panned, crudely crushed, and sifted in stream beds. Hartwood area gold mines date from 1836 to 1850. (Eby)

Virginia Historical Marker E-77 (U.S. Route 17, one-half mile north of Hartwood Post Office) relates:

Gold Mining in Stafford County
Near here are located ten of the nineteenth-century gold mines of Stafford County. The best-known were the Eagle, Rattlesnake (Horse Pen), Lee, New Hope, and Monroe mines. The Eagle Gold Mining Company, Rappahannock Gold Mine Company of New York, Rapidan Mining and Milling Company of Pennsylvania, United States Mining Company, and Stafford Mining Company operated here between the 1830s and the early twentieth century. Mining activities gradually ceased because of declining profits.

In modern terms, some thirty-four minerals continued to be mined in this region. In 2001, Stafford mined some 1,239,832 tons of minerals. Sand and gravel, deposited some 70,000 years ago from ocean tides and storms, are the most heavily harvested minerals. They are primarily used locally and in Northern Virginia construction projects. Granite, as mined at the Vulcan Materials' northern Stafford plant, is dated to about 410 million years of age. Thin gold veins, created by ancient volcanic activity, still run through Stafford and neighboring jurisdictions. They are known as the Chopawamsic Formation. (Rusty Dennen)

Waller girls rowing on the Potomac with their family's employees.

Turn-of-the-Century Watermen

Significant commercial fishing emerged off Widewater's Potomac shores in the 1880s and 1890s. The fishing enterprise operated by Mrs. Anne E. Stribling Waller and her eight daughters was based on the antebellum shad and herring fishery business of her husband, Withers Waller, and his partner, Henry Moore of Maryland (which may have been the basis for Stafford's Civil War "secret line").

Anne E. Stribling Waller
(Stafford County)

The Wallers ran the "largest family-owned drag seine fishery of the Chesapeake Bay and estuaries." This Widewater business, at its height, employed some fifty black watermen. As later described:

Fishing for shad began in late March and generally lasted until early June. During these months, seine hauling was conducted at high slack water, twice daily, including Sundays. Nets were stretched by oar-powered shad drag-seine galleys for three miles across the Potomac between Widewater and Mallows Bay in Maryland, then hauled ashore with the aid of horse-powered capstans. Once ashore the fish were salted, smoked, canned, or packed in ice and shipped to Baltimore, Washington, New York, Philadelphia, and as far west as Chicago, via the Widewater freight station of the Richmond, Fredericksburg, and Potomac Railroad, only 200 feet from the beach…

Belle Plain, Potomac Creek, has seen generations of watermen harvesting the rivers and estuaries of Stafford. Shown here in the 1940s are members of the Newton family bringing in crabs.
(Newton Collection)

Buildings, especially those associated with county government, have suffered a variety of fates, ranging from fire to collapse. The demise of some, such as the Old Stafford County Jail, may have been a blessing. Although information exists that the jail was built in 1866, a Civil War description by a Union chaplain seems to fit: "the jail, which stands in the middle of the road, is a miserable two-story affair, built of rough stone. The lower story is occupied by hogs, and the upper is reached by stairs from the outside."
(Stafford County)

Other smaller fisheries existed in Widewater in the late nineteenth century. Exploiting the Potomac's vast resources, similar activities took place at Potomac Creek and, on a smaller scale, on the Rappahannock. Watermen's lives were difficult and dependent on the riverine ecology. Yet, the water's lure was great for those living along river shores and tributaries. By 1897, Potomac River commercial fisheries had become the largest on the U.S. East Coast with some 2,382 vessels and nearly 6,000 men participating. Off Stafford, primarily in the Brent's Point-Smith's Point sector, 139 men worked on 41 vessels. Markets in Alexandria, Washington, and Georgetown teemed with shad, herring, hickory jacks, diamondback terrapins, and sturgeon (the latter two becoming endangered species). Oysters, too, accounting for about half of the fishery profits, were a water crop harvested in great profusion. After the turn of the century, this volume trailed off due to over-fishing. Family-operated yards, building and repairing river craft, existed in virtually every Potomac estuary, including Widewater and Coal Landing in Stafford. (Frederick Tilp, *Chesapeake Bay* magazine, Eby)

The $200 Million Bonfire

In the 1920s, the U.S. government eliminated hundreds of unused World War I 3,500-ton wooden troopships. These 260- to 300-foot vessels, placed in a restricted James River anchorage, were purchased in 1923 by a salvage company and sent to Alexandria for dismantlement. Stripped of all useful machinery and parts, the dismantled hulls were taken off Widewater where they were burned in September 1925—hence, sardonically the great "$200 Million Bonfire." The charred hulks were then towed to shallower Mallows Bay, Maryland, and further stripped. During the Depression, they were further picked over and some materials were sold as scrap iron to prewar Japan.

A New Courthouse

Chronicled destruction of Stafford courthouses is legendary, especially in the Colonial era. In 1922, when it became necessary to demolish the courthouse used since 1840, Stafford built a new courthouse. The Board of Supervisors selected Philip N. Stern as the architect. Stern had been trained at the Karlsruhe Technical Institute and had been practicing in Fredericksburg since 1909. A founder of the Virginia Chapter of the American Institute of Architects (1914), he later served on the Advisory Committee for the Restoration of Colonial Williamsburg. The project's general contractor was Walter Snellings, who received $19,263.55 for the work. The completed courthouse, a temple-form building crowned by a belvedere and fronted by six columns, stands today. It was renovated and expanded in 1992.

Illicit Business

During Prohibition, the river trade also dabbled in the manufacture and transport of illicit liquor locally and to customers in Alexandria and Washington. Even the sunken hulls from the $200 Million Bonfire were used—some twenty-six stills operated there for a period of ten years. Local accounts tell of watermen rowing from White Oak to Maryland to purchase the illicit brew.

Stafford Courthouse as it appeared about 1923 (Stafford County)

Lumber and Firewood

During the Union occupation (April 1862–June 1863), Stafford lost most of its timber resources. However, by the late nineteenth century, the forests renewed sufficiently to become a viable cordwood source. Destined for residential and business stoves in Washington and Baltimore, thousands of cords of wood were shipped to Coal Landing and Belle Plain wharves. Cordwood proved to be one of the few profitable industries in postwar Stafford, and cutting and selling the cordwood, and railroad ties continued through the Depression era. Marlborough resurfaced as a cordwood source into the 1930s and played a continuing role in riverine activities. This brought to life a lumber industry that had once flourished in Stafford. Mountain View Road was once known as the "Wood Cutting Road," and the area around Ramoth Church was referred to as "the Woodcutting." That designation dates to the eighteenth century, when this road ran directly between Accokeek Iron Furnace to Hunter's Iron Works near Falmouth. Most of the charcoal needed for Hunter's furnaces came from there. (Eby)

A scene at Stafford Courthouse, probably in the 1930s
(Felicia Parlier)

Depression-Era Stafford

A convincing case has been made that the "Fredericksburg area" and Virginia did not suffer as greatly as other parts of the nation in the Great Depression. Staffordians also benefited from the addition of: a Sylvania plant in 1929, which produced a version of cellophane; G&H Manufacturing (established 1915), which did piecework in the garment industry, Morganstern and Company pants factory (1924); Virginia Shoe Company; Cassco (1929); Montgomery Ward and W. T. Grant (both 1929); Pender Grocery Company (1931); and the Stratford Hotel. Fredericksburg survived the Depression in relatively good shape. This naturally had spillover effects in the surrounding counties. The R,F&P Railroad remained important economically as well. Contributing to regional economic survival were Virginia Electric and Power Company, which had purchased earlier local firms; the Fredericksburg and Spotsylvania National Military Park (which provided a basis for a nascent tourism industry); a strong banking and insurance community; sound state government finances and policies; Federal assistance through the Civilian Works Administration/ Works Progress Administration (CWA/WPA), and Civilian Conservation Corps (CCC), and relief efforts by the Salvation Army, Red Cross and American Legion; and the growth of Mary Washington College. (Eric Powell)

Perhaps this paints too bright a picture for Stafford, which, after all, was still recovering from the Civil War and Reconstruction and lagged behind much of the rest of the country. Life in the county remained economically and socially backward, and the people, as had been their previous lot in life, struggled to survive by subsistence agriculture and hard work in often menial and thankless labor. But the Depression also brought new approaches from the national government as well. Many were experimental and cast a long shadow on the future of governing America, and many also brought hope to the working classes. The Berea CCC Camp is representative.

Established on August 7, 1935, it was designated CCC Company No. 2363, in Soil Conservation No. 11, District 3, Third Corps Area. The installation was called "Camp Stafford" and located off Warrenton Road (U.S. Route 17) across from Berea Baptist Church on a portion of McWhirt's farm on Greenbank Road (adjacent to the current Geico complex). (Dino A. Brugioni—Brugioni)

Fredericksburg area residents Conrad C. "Jiggs" Brennan, Thomas J. Jenkins, Virginia E. Myers (widow of Clyde N. Myers), and Walter M. Preston provided reflections on the CCC and Soil Conservation Service in Stafford. Young men arriving in the

area were met by army personnel (the U.S. Army was charged with administration of the CCC) and trucked to the camp. There they were placed in tents, as the barracks buildings weren't constructed until spring 1936. They lived in a World War I–style tent camp through the winter of 1935–1936. The youngsters were processed much like military recruits, and the camp commander, a captain, regulated their daily activities when not on assignment with the Soil Conservation Service. CCC men stood regular inspections but did not receive any military training (e.g., drills, weapons training, etc.). Soil conservation projects included planting trees, digging diversionary ditches, and cutting fire lanes and roads through forested sectors. Where farmers provided the materials, CCC men also constructed fences. The Berea Camp served Stafford, King George, Spotsylvania, and Fauquier Counties. (Brugioni)

The WPA, or Works Progress Administration, provided work that only government would or could support. This included an effort to document the social history of localities by describing people and places in detail and preserving the information for future generations. These WPA reports on Stafford, now residing in the Virginiana Room Collection of the Central Rappahannock Library, provide an unequaled window into the county's past.

Depression-era Stafford scenes depict a rural life little changed from the previous century. Life primarily consisted of subsistence farm work interspersed with church and occasional social activities. (Felicia Parlier)

Stafford County, Virginia

Businesses

Geico Regional Center (Stafford County)

One of Stafford County's more notable businesses—celebrating its one hundredth birthday in 2003—is representative. The Hilldrup Moving and Storage Company began in Fredericksburg in 1903 as a horse-and-carriage transportation service. R. G. Hilldrup was the firm's president; there were ten employees and numerous horses. When purchased in 1940 by Charles B. McDaniel, the company's focus shifted to household goods moving and storage services. In 1964 Hilldrup became a part of the United Van Lines agency family, shifting to a worldwide market. In 1976 Charles G. McDaniel became the company's third president. He led Hilldrup through its next twenty-seven years of substantial growth, operating in Stafford since the 1950s. The corporate center and offices were subsequently moved to Stafford. Achieving a century of operations in 2003, Hilldrup has grown into one of the largest and most successful domestic and international moving companies. With eight full-service centers throughout the southeastern United States, Hilldrup's 800 employees and 300 pieces of interstate and intrastate moving equipment serve major corporations with worldwide service. In 2002 it was the fifth largest and most honored agent for United Van Lines, and it received the coveted Customer Choice Award for an unprecedented tenth time. Further, Hilldrup was ranked first or second in all lines of business—national account, residential, international, and governmental.

Colonial Circuits (Stafford County)

In the past two decades, a number of companies have found Stafford a positive place for their businesses to operate. Major firms include Geico, Intuit, Colonial Circuits, and Garrett Construction. Staffordians also work for other Fredericksburg area firms, including the Silver Companies. Currently, Stafford hosts some 1,400 businesses, employing 25,000 people. Most have forty or fewer employees.

Improving the quality of the Stafford workforce has been facilitated by the James Monroe Center of Mary Washington College. The Stafford campus assists in graduate and adult education for improving the working capabilities and credentials of local residents.

James Monroe Center of Mary Washington College (Jane M. Conner)

Small Businesses

Local general stores once abounded in Stafford. Those in the countryside served surrounding farms and small communities. Despite the growth of chain groceries, some of these small businesses have survived; others, such as Nelson Berry's Store, have been converted to other uses.

Tourism: Stafford's Newest Old Industry

Tourism is one of Stafford's oldest industries. The Virginia Historical Marker recalls on sign E-79 on U.S. Route 1:

Peyton's Ordinary

In this vicinity stood Peyton's Ordinary. George Washington, going to Fredericksburg to visit his mother, dined here, March 6, 1769, and stayed here again on September 14, 1772. Rochambeau's army, marching north from Williamsburg in 1782, camped here.

As previously discussed, a good part of Stafford's earlier history centered on transportation. Part of the natural flow of this traffic were taverns and inns, strategically placed along routes at a one-day interval to accommodate travelers. Vital to Colonial and Federal era commerce, they served all classes of people and provided post offices and modest social interchange while contributing to the local economy. Innkeepers, who were respected members of the business community, often held public trusts and offices. "Peyton's Ordinary" in northern Stafford was apparently Stafford's primary contribution to the Fredericksburg-Washington trade. "Spotted Tavern" in Hartwood seems to have been the primary stopover place on the way to Warrenton, surviving until at least the Civil War, and "Temperance Hotel" or Tavern in Falmouth was once part of the same network (see Chapter 7).

Other taverns or ordinaries may have existed at briefer intervals. For instance, George Mason (IV)'s mother appears to have operated an ordinary, or planned to, at "Chopawamsic Farm." Hospitality in the existing inns and taverns (as well as private homes) may have been particularly strained during the Civil War, but many Stafford families survived and saved their places by accommodating and feeding Union troops. (Eby, HRS)

Discussion of local businesses and industries frequently focuses on Fredericksburg; however, Falmouth and Stafford also had roles in the evolving business of tourism. Once again, transportation was a significant factor as roads, waterways, and railroads were followed by better roads. Although such efforts were not always effectively planned or coordinated, America's twentieth-century love affair with the automobile definitely came into play.

Nelson Berry's Store as it appears in art painted by Gari Melchers about 1918 (top photo) and in photographs around the 1920s (middle) and 2003.
(Belmont/Mary Washington College) (Stafford County) (Jane M. Conner)

Stafford County, Virginia

For tourism, there needed to be something to visit or see. The 1922 creation of the Kenmore Association and the 1927 establishment of the Fredericksburg and Spotsylvania National Military Park provided a focus on historical tourism. History, it turned out, was at the heart of Virginia's tourism potential, yet better roads brought higher traffic volume. This promoted economic development, but threatened historic sites. One account shows regional interdependence and the need for regional planning:

> Accessibility by automobile drove the emerging tourism industry. An official from the State Highway Department claimed that their calculations and projections of travel spending, related to the Yorktown Sesquicentennial in 1931, showed that tourism would probably generate annual revenues in Virginia to rival the state's tobacco production. In 1946, state-sponsored construction crews completed U.S. Alternate No. 1 Highway (the current Jefferson Davis Bypass) around Fredericksburg. The bridge across the Rappahannock River was at Falmouth, where bridges had been constructed since the early nineteenth century. There had been several privately funded spans at Falmouth, but the one built for the highway department, at public expense, was better designed to withstand periodic river flooding. Falmouth had always sat astride the north/south overland route and such travel could now be accomplished on an excellent road, over a new bridge that ran parallel to the long-forgotten ford. The U.S. Route 1 Bypass, with its solidly built bridge, strengthened Falmouth's position in the region's economy. Unfortunately, the commercial attraction of this new infrastructure caused problems for Fredericksburg. The Route 1 Bypass certainly improved traffic flow, but it drew activity away from the downtown business district. To maintain its economic viability, Fredericksburg would need to annex portions of Spotsylvania County that included strategic sections of the improved roads. Fredericksburg's 1955 annexation, for instance, encompassed the intersection of the Route 1 Bypass and (Virginia) Route 3. After World War II, American automobile production exploded. The Federal Aid Highway Act of 1944 had anticipated a postwar need for more and better roads, but this initial effort appears ludicrously inadequate when compared with the federal funding eventually provided through the Interstate Highway Act of 1956. In the 1960s, road builders brought Interstate 95 across the Rappahannock River, upstream of both Fredericksburg and Falmouth. This road would cut into Fredericksburg's

Even into the 1940s and 1950s, Stafford was still viewed simply as a means to get to Fredericksburg and a place through which one could reach other places. A sampling of postal cards of the period recalls that all distances were measured from Fredericksburg.

(Barry Fitzgerald Collection)

Not all efforts to improve tourism have succeeded. One valiant effort that ended in failure was the Virginia Renaissance Faire, located in the Sherwood Forest Industrial Park in southern Stafford. Here Elizabethan-period members of the company cavort at the Stafford Courthouse with the Board of Supervisors. (Jane M. Conner)

share of the regional commercial economy, much as the Orange & Alexandria Railroad had cut into its agricultural base a century earlier. In 1980, a shopping mall opened where Interstate 95 intersects Plank Road (State Route 3). This development had a severe impact on downtown Fredericksburg as retail businesses moved to this new location where increased traffic held the promise of economic viability. National retailers, after all, build their stores where traffic volumes ensure a lucrative level of retail and commercial activity. Wal-Mart did not propose to construct a store near George Washington's boyhood home, for instance, until construction of a new road (the Route 3 Bypass) generated high traffic counts. In 1984 Fredericksburg annexed yet more land to gain a portion of the intersection of Interstate 95 and Route 3. This area has since become the economic power center called Central Park.

This account adds another stark comparison of Fredericksburg and Falmouth:

> Publicly funded roads reconnected Falmouth to the regional economy, but the interstate highway bypassed both communities. As an independent city, Fredericksburg had the option to annex its way back into regional prominence. Falmouth, which remains unincorporated, suffers the indignity of absorbing traffic bound elsewhere. (Nelson, *Tobacco to Tourism*)

Demonstrating that regional tourism issues remain unresolved, this cartoon in the Fredericksburg area's newspaper, the FreeLance-Star, points out the imbalance of emphasis received by the smaller jurisdiction in advertising. (Jones/Free Lance-Star)

The 2000 census revealed other surprising changes in Stafford's demography. The Stafford civilian work force was not the "work-at-home or commute to Washington" group many had long perceived. In order of magnitude, Staffordians worked in Stafford (26 percent), Prince William County (19 percent), Fairfax County (15 percent), "Elsewhere" (12 percent), Fredericksburg (9 percent), Washington, D.C. (7 percent), Spotsylvania County (7 percent), and Arlington (5 percent). Because these Staffordians now work closer to home, it can be expected that their interests, when stimulated, will also shift homeward.

Chapter Eleven
History Lives in Stafford

Stafford has fortunately been the home of many people and organizations committed to discovering, disseminating, and preserving its history. Cooperative efforts by individuals, public and private organizations, educational institutions and associations, family historians, foundations, and government have yielded positive results. It can truly be said that "History lives in Stafford."

This chapter highlights recent historical activities, organizations, and actions by individuals.

Works of Stafford History

"The Story of Stafford," a pamphlet by John Tackett Goolrick, was the first effort at a Stafford history. Written in 1939 while Goolrick was working at the Fredericksburg Battlefield Park, the pamphlet was reprinted by the county government in 1976, 1988, 1990, and 1992.

Since the mid-1980s, Stafford has enjoyed a historical renaissance. Numerous works listed in chronological order, highlight specific aspects of Stafford's history. A 1984 monograph, "Chatham: The Life of a House," was written by Ralph Happel. In 1987, Thomas M. Moncure Jr. and Molly A. Pynn wrote *The Story of Aquia Church*. *The Foundation Stones of Stafford County, Virginia*, a project of the Historical and Archaeological Committee of Citizens to Serve Stafford (CCSS), was published in 1991; a second volume was published in 1992. The committee consisted of Dr. H. Stewart

Ceremony at Catholic Monument
(Jane M. Conner)

Civil War reenactor with "recruit" at "Ferry Farm"
(George Washington's Fredericksburg Foundation)

Patawomeck tribal ceremony
(Stephen A. Gambaro)

Jones, Lisa B. Anderson, Estheleen "Hutch" Blackburn, and Ruth Carlone (also chairman of CCSS). Segments in *Foundation Stones* featured county authors' accounts of people, places, churches, folklore, and current government. The second volume expanded on people and events, scenes, homes, and reminiscences. Homer D. Musselman's unit histories of the 47th Virginia Infantry and the Stafford Artillery were written in 1991. In 1993 a Stafford oral history, *Conversations with Old Friends*, was produced by a Stafford County Historical Society committee including Anita Dodd, Barbara Flack, Barbara Kirby, and Suzanne Rowdon. Homer D. Musselman published *Stafford County, Virginia: Veterans and Cemeteries* in 1994, followed by *Stafford County in the Civil War* in 1995. Jerrilynn Eby's *They Called Stafford Home: The Development of Stafford County, Virginia from 1600 until 1865* was published in 1997. Eby's book described Stafford's historical homes from primary sources. These places were illustrated with original paintings, including artists' concepts of homes and buildings. This work also contained vignettes similar to *Foundation Stones*. William L. Deyo, tribal historian of the Patawomeck Indian Tribe, authored a number of genealogical booklets, several with Stafford content: *The Monteith Family and the Potomac Indians*; *Porch Family, the Forgotten Legacy of White Oak, Stafford County, Virginia*; *The Sullivan Family of Stafford, Virginia*; and *A Brief Outline of Recorded History of the Patawomeck Indian Tribe*. Jerrilynn Eby also published *Men of Mark in Stafford, Virginia, 1664–1991* in 2000, and in 2003 a

Civil War reenactors take part in a firing demonstration at White Oak Museum.
(Stephen A. Gambaro)

"Woodstock" Brent House archeological site
(Northern Virginia Chapter of the Archaeological Society of Virginia)

history of the Accokeek and Rappahannock Forges titled *Laying the Hoe: A Century of Iron Manufacturing in Stafford, Virginia.* Many genealogical works, historical journals, and newspaper and magazine articles have Stafford content; they can be found in the Virginiana Room, Central Rappahannock Regional Library.

Works of regional focus with Stafford content include Ruth Coder Fitzgerald's *A Different Story: A Black History of Fredericksburg, Stafford, and Spotsylvania, Virginia* (1979). In 1993, J. William Mann wrote *Bells and Belfries and Some of Neither*, a survey of regional churches. Many Civil War books mention Stafford activities (see bibliography). Most recently, they include the *Fredericksburg Campaign* by Frank A. O'Reilly (2002).

These works are valuable contributions to Stafford's historical knowledge base, and Staffordians are indebted to this dedicated band of researchers. Naturally, these works, those listed in progress below, and those in the bibliography were of immeasurable assistance in this pictorial history. Each of these Stafford historical works contains details and information beyond the scope of this work and should be consulted by those wishing to examine topics in greater depth.

Archeology: Recovering a Lost Past and Green Spaces

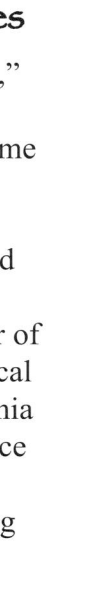

Archeologists led by David Muraca, formerly of Colonial Williamsburg, and including Anita Dodd (center) search for additional information at George Washington's boyhood home, "Ferry Farm." (Jane M. Conner)

"Woodstock," dating to about 1670 and the home of Brents until about 1725, has been investigated by the Northern Virginia Chapter of the Archaeological Society of Virginia (NVC/ASV) since 1997. That year archeologists dug everywhere at

"Woodstock" except the cemetery, resulting in finds of Indian and seventeenth-century artifacts. In 1998, ten larger test units were excavated in part of the cemetery. The last test unit revealed a shallow basement "filled with late seventeenth- and early eighteenth-century artifacts." In 1999, the original hearth and chimney base of George Brent's plantation house were discovered. (The house is referred to by NVC/ASV as the Brent Site 44ST130.) Archeology has yielded two remarkable artifacts from the shallow basement of the Woodstock house—a mariner's cross, shown in Chapter 2, and a King James II tuppence piece, shown in Chapter 3. Of special merit was the cooperative nature of the project featuring ASV volunteers, Fairfax County Park Authority (laboratory and storage space), and Maryland consultants Goodwin and Associates Inc. (conservation of artifacts); and financial support from Stafford's St. William of York Parish (field equipment and laboratory supplies). Maintenance, security, and surveillance support by the Knights of Columbus and local volunteer Rusty Lewis demonstrates how solid and unselfish cooperation can protect a historical archeological site.

Professional archeology has also been significant at George Washington's Boyhood Home, "Ferry Farm." Conducted by George Washington's Fredericksburg Foundation, archeology has yielded Colonial and Civil War artifacts and uncovered the foundation of the Washington homestead (which survived until the Civil War). Further, archeology and archival research worked together to solve the mystery of the Christmas Eve fire that took place on the "Ferry Farm" plantation (believed for years to have happened at

Archeological work at "Ferry Farm." Similar efforts in the 1990s found burned debris in a sixteen-by-sixteen-foot cellar hole and, from ceramic and mud dauber evidence, dated the fire to the second quarter of the eighteenth century. (Jane M. Conner)

Anita Dodd, a "Ferry Farm" archeologist, chairs the Stafford County Historical Commission. Her duties in both capacities require the will to "get in the dirt." (Jane M. Conner)

Hal Wiggins, U.S. Army Corps of Engineers, who is involved in virtually all Stafford's preservation projects, is shown at Daniel Cemetery.
(Stephen A. Gambaro)

either "Wakefield" or "Mount Vernon"). In October 1741, Richard Yates, a former tutor of Augustine Washington Jr., wrote to Augustine Washington commiserating about the "late calamity which you suffer'd by fire." Together with a letter to George Washington (Library of Congress) and archeology at the Stafford home site, the mystery has been solved. The letter, written to Washington by Robert Douglas in 1795, recalled that they had been playmates and Douglas had lived on the adjacent Strother plantation. He added, "I remember it well, that it gave me a very sore Heart that on Christmas Eve, his (Augustine's) great house was burned down & that he was Obliged with his good family to go live in the kitchen."

As Stafford has confronted growth, "Crow's Nest" became one of several highly visible places illustrating the struggle to preserve "green spaces," often equating to "historical spaces." March 2001 articles focused on preserving "Crow's Nest's" 3,800 acres as the largest county environmental preservation activity, and reported that the Board of Supervisors had endorsed its protection in 1999. The U.S. Fish and Wildlife Service identified the area's key supporting role for migratory bird populations—some fifty-seven species of neotropical migratory birds landed there in the spring of 1999 alone. "Crow's Nest;" Government Island (17.3 acres); Widewater Peninsula (1,100 acres), and Greenbank Farm site (Celebrate Virginia-Stafford—1,420 acres) are all areas of environmental and historical concern. (Ben Bagwell, *Stafford County Sun*) Its archeological potentials are untapped.

In June 2002, the Daniel Family Cemetery at "Crow's Nest" was refurbished and a 350-pound, six-by-three-foot granite marker was emplaced in the cemetery wall:

Daniel Family Cemetery refurbishment
(Stephen A. Gambaro)

A History of Our Own

"This stone tells the story of the people who lived here," said Travers Daniel, a descendant of Rawleigh Travers, the first owner of "Crow's Nest." Chiseled into the rock is a history of the land and its notable residents such as Hannah Ball, aunt of President George Washington, and Mildred Stone, whose father signed the Declaration of Independence.

The article also mentions other developments in the life of "Crow's Nest":

If its history weren't enough, Crow's Nest is also an ecological marvel. It boasts a variety of rare plant species and is home to a large blue heron rookery and bald eagle nests. But all this could change if the land's current owner, K&M Properties in McLean, develops the property. "Preserving this site is the best thing that could happen," Daniel said. The Crow's Nest Trust was established in January to do just that. The nonprofit group hopes to raise about $200,000 annually to maintain the property. If the trust members—made up of area residents and Stafford County officials—can raise the money, the U.S. Fish and Wildlife Service will try to get the money from Congress to buy the land and add it to the national refuge system. Then it would be opened to the public on a regular basis; now the private property is open only to private tours. Donations to the trust are steadily growing. "We've gotten a lot of public support," said John D. Mitchell, a local businessman and the chairman of the trust. In April, (the) Stafford County Board of Supervisors voted to give the trust $100,000 to save the land. It also hired Washington lobbyist Joann Payne to work with the landowner, Congress, and the Bush administration.
(Elizabeth Pezzullo/FLS)

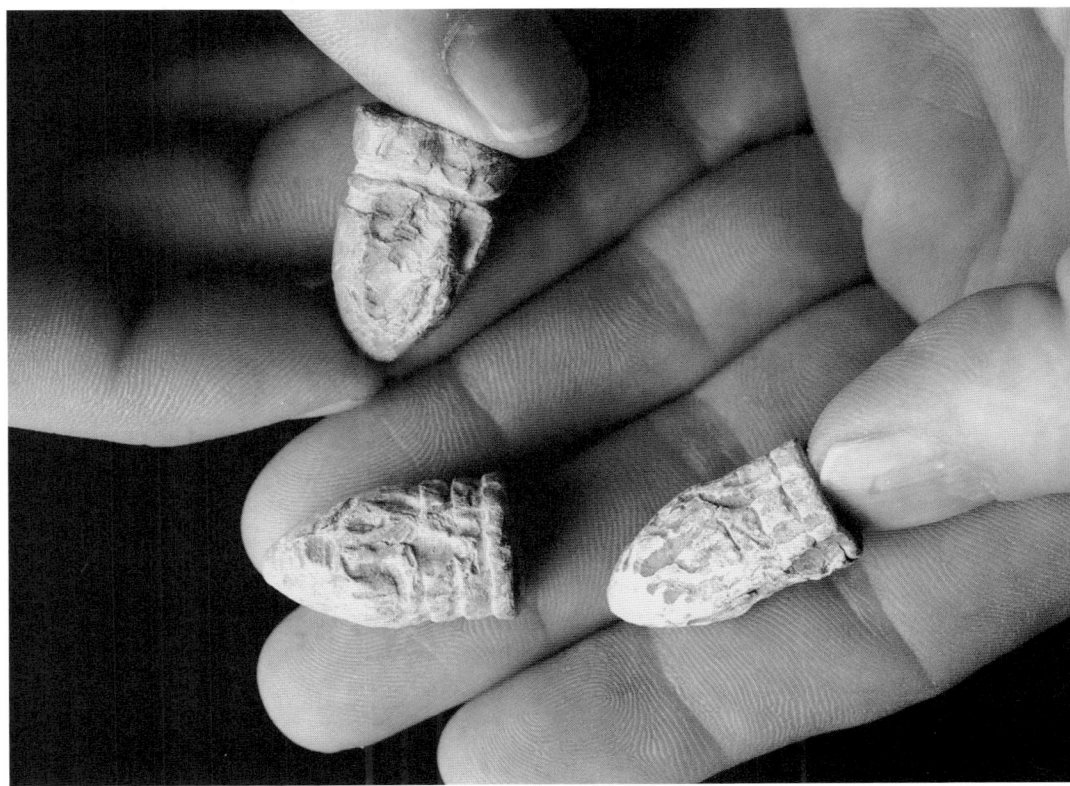

Mysterious Minie cartridges, White Oak Civil War Museum. Forensic work is under way to see if soldiers actually "bit the bullet" during surgery. (Free Lance-Star)

(Also see Chapter 7.)

Celebrate Virginia-Stafford, developed on Greenbank Farm by the Silver Companies, a locally based regional development firm, is an example of effective preservation while developing a large-scale recreational business campus (RBC). The professional services of CRI Inc. were employed to study and plan preservation of historical sites in the RBC. Known sites were identified during "walk-throughs" by local historical groups, including White Oak Museum, Stafford Cemetery Committee, Sons and Daughters of the American Revolution, War of 1812 Society, and the Stafford County Historical Society. (This information was also presented to the County Planning Commission.) CRI followed up with archeology and documentation of the project site. Silver Companies' coordinator, Chris Hornung, a Staffordian, and Dr. Matt Laird of CRI Inc. then briefed the Historical Society and public on the completed, first-phase archeological work in the planned area. The RBC has especially significant Civil War

State Sen. John Chichester (center) appears with his brothers, Commonwealth's Attorney Dan Chichester (left) and Richard Chichester, at celebrity roast benefit for a Stafford museum.
(Jane M. Conner)

contexts—two Federal army corps occupied it at the beginning and end of the Chancellorsville battle in May 1863. Evidence of prehistoric, Colonial, Federal, and Civil War-era activity and habitation also abound. Artifacts collected by shovel-testing (digging through the top soil to a level of sterile surface) were archived and stored by CRI and are available for future research. Using a combination of traditional archeological planning techniques and modern technological innovations (e.g., GPS precise location data and state-of-the-art metal detectors), an exceptionally large number (fifty-three) of interesting sites were identified and tested throughout the area. Of these, twenty-six required further study. It was determined that the development could be built around golf courses and not require extensive redistribution of earth. Thus, Celebrate Virginia-Stafford will not disturb historic sites. In fact, by careful study, the developers avoided construction around all historic remnants. The briefers noted that Civil War data from D. P. Newton, burial data from the Stafford Cemetery Committee's Charles Price, and Sons and Daughters of the American Revolution members Mike and Marty Lyman had been most helpful in their planning. The Silver Companies' careful planning and responsible development and stewardship resulted in preservation of Indian sites; Revolutionary-era gravesites; and Civil War artillery positions, cavalry videttes, and trench lines. In November 2002, Silver Companies donated more than 300 acres in the Stafford portion of the project as a conservation easement to the Northern Virginia Conservation Trust (which also owns a seventy-acre heron rookery site at "Crow's Nest").

The Historic Preservation Department of Mary Washington College has helped with archeological and preservation support for many local historical sites for more than fifty years. Through cooperative projects with public and private organizations and individuals, the department has furthered educational opportunities for its students by allowing them to "learn while doing" at local sites such as "Moncure Conway House." Faculty members have also acted as consultants and resources to local historical organizations.

Akin to historical archeology, responsible relic hunters produce meticulous sketch maps and notes. D. P. Newton's White Oak Civil War Museum has shed new light on local events by providing information to government and private historians, and has enhanced understanding of Union and Confederate occupation sites and emplacements. Such work can change history. For example, documentation of hundreds of firing ranges belie accounts of poor Union marksmanship training. On the lighter side, Civil War investigations can be both contentious and humorous while hopefully resolving long-standing controversies.

Historical Societies and Associations

The Stafford County Historical Society (SCHS) was formed in October 1965 as "Historic Falmouth Towne and Stafford County Inc." At their first official meeting (at Falmouth Fire House), officers and directors were selected. They were Robert Cadow, president; Agnes Wallace, vice president; Dr. H. Stewart Jones, secretary; and George L. Gordon, treasurer. Original directors were Norman C. Cambell, Kate Woods, J. Thomas Pribble, Willie Shelton, Ryland Heflin, Dr. H. Stewart Jones, Daniel Mitchell, Mrs. Randolph Brooks, Dr. Oscar H. Darter, Mrs. Lyn Franklin, Herbert Brooks, Mary Hinman, Kenneth Coe, Peggy Miller, George L. Gordon, Mrs. Dan Chichester, Robert Cadow, Agnes Harrison, and Dr. E. Boyd Graves.

In subsequent years, the Stafford County Historical Society grew in numbers and projects while retaining its original purposes to: bring together people interested in history, especially Stafford County history; discover and collect material on the history of the area; preserve sites and monuments of historic value; promote research and publish findings on local history; provide for a museum for the reception and preservation of photographs, paintings, artifacts, papers, genealogies, and other items typically found in museums; hold property coming into the possession of the society; disseminate historical information and arouse public interest through meetings, articles, etc.; and cooperate with similar organizations.

Drive Through Stafford County's History
with "driving tour map"
(Stafford County Historical Society)

Educational activities include monthly meetings featuring speakers discussing all aspects of Stafford's history and talks to local schools. Topics have included historical art; Colonial voting; Colonial mills; contemporary African-American history; Catholics in Colonial Stafford; Stafford's Civil War Confederate soldiers; Confederate Secret Service activities in Stafford; slavery in Stafford; Civil War uniforms; historic landscaping; current preservation activities; veterans salutes; Indian demonstrations and lectures; biographic talks and living-history reenactments; site and museum visits; and commemorations for historical signs. Meetings are held year-round and are open to the public.

Stafford Museum fund-raisers have included local celebrity roasts. Honorees have included Commissioner George Gordon; State Sen. John Chichester; Sheriff Ralph Williams; Delegate Bill Howell; Commonwealth's Attorney Dan Chichester; former Delegate and Court Clerk Tom Moncure; and former Supervisor Ferris Belman. Other fund-raising activities have included the sale of Stafford historical commemorative items, including coverlets featuring the county seal and historic sites; Christmas ornaments depicting the courthouse and George Washington's Boyhood Home; cookbooks; note cards; lapel pins; reproduced Civil War maps and belt plates; oral histories; and informational brochures.

Society members Jane Henderson Conner, Barbara Kirby, Vera Pastore, and Anita Dodd created the *Drive Through Stafford County's History* driving tour map, which combines an overview of county history with an opportunity for residents and visitors to drive to scenic places. Free copies are available at the County Administrative Center, "Belmont," Fredericksburg Visitors' Center, and Stafford's Porter Library.

The Society has sponsored home tours in Widewater, Hartwood, and Falmouth; members have given talks at local schools. In 2003, Society members disseminated historical information to more than 2,000 students at the Stafford Sheriff's Office's D.A.R.E. Day at Pratt Park.

Regional historical groups also have been involved in Stafford projects. The Historic Fredericksburg Foundation Inc. has been supportive of Stafford historical preservation activities, most notably "Ferry Farm," and has provided substantially to the body of knowledge of Stafford history through its annual journal. The Spotsylvania Preservation Foundation Inc. has also cooperated and collaborated on region historic preservation. The Fredericksburg Area Museum has developed and maintained collections of regional archives and artifacts. The Mary Washington Branch of the Association for Preservation of Virginia Antiquities is also involved in regional preservation activities.

Heritage Groups

Staffordians participate in local chapters of the Daughters of the American Revolution (DAR), Sons of the American Revolution (SAR), and the Society of Colonial Dames; the Society of the War of 1812 in Virginia; and the United Daughters of the Confederacy (UDC) and Sons of Confederate Veterans (SCV). In the region are the Overwharton Parish Chapter of the DAR, George Mason (I) Chapter of the National Society of Colonial Dames, James Monroe Chapter of the National Society of United States Daughters of 1812, the Matthew Fontaine Maury Camp 1722 of SCV, and Sons of Union Veterans (SUV), among others. All these groups support other historical activities and collect information on their ancestors. Most also support educational activities such as sign making, scholarships, and essay contests.

Other Historical Groups

Staffordians participate in two local Civil War Roundtables, the Fredericksburg and the Rappahannock Valley. The Fredericksburg Civil War Roundtable is one of the longest-standing groups in America and is distinguished by having been in continuous operation since 1957. In 1960 the group hosted the national Civil War Roundtables meeting. As of June 2003, it will have hosted 414 speakers on Civil War subjects. The Rappahannock Valley Civil War Roundtable, organized in 1989, is a force in Civil War historical discussion and battlefield preservation and has raised funds for the Central Virginia Battlefield Trust. Member Charles

Fredericksburg Civil War Roundtable officers (left to right) Al Conner and Kin Glover, and 1957 charter members Ed Thornton and Wally Mann at "Chatham" in Stafford
(Reza Marvashti/Free Lance-Star)

Rappahannock Valley Civil War Roundtable officers (from left) Gregory Mertz, Mac Wykoff, Melanie Jordan, Elsa Lohman, and Dane Hartgrove
(Robert A. Martin/Free Lance-Star)

Members and guests of the Rappahannock Valley Civil War Roundtable tour Redoubt No. 2, a preserved defensive post near Stafford's Aquia Creek. Shown (from left) are Joanne Huff, Dane Hartgrove, Sue Hartgrove, Mac Wykoff, and Marcus Lawrence.
(Robert A. Martin/Free Lance-Star)

Siegel researched and wrote the text for *A Driving Tour: The Army of the Potomac in Stafford County.* The Central Virginia Battlefield Trust, established in 1996, has no administrative overhead and uses all its income to purchase battlefield lands to be turned over to the National Park Service. It has Stafford members. Staffordians also participate in various "Battlefield Friends" organizations, which support specific battlefields and areas.

Staffordians also participate in a more recent creation, the Fredericksburg Revolutionary War Roundtable, which discusses all aspects of the American War for Independence. This group meets periodically and features guest speakers.

Veterans' Groups

The Veterans of Foreign Wars and the American Legion—particularly Bill Blasko and Glenn Hyatt—organizational color guards, and individual members participated in annual veterans' salutes by the Stafford County Historical Society and the "Celebrate Stafford Days" of the Committee of Citizens to Serve Stafford. These groups also supported ceremonies commemorating the 200th anniversary of the death of George Washington at the Stafford Courthouse and Union Church. The veterans' salutes honored those Staffordians who had fought in the First World War and subsequent conflicts through Vietnam.

Enos Richardson (left) and John Mitchell of the Central Virginia Battlefield Trust
(Robert A. Martin/Free Lance-Star)

Stafford County Historical Society and reenactor "Captain" Owen Conner salute World War II veterans, including John Scott.
(Stafford County Historical Society)

Living History Reenactors

A Revolutionary War reenactment company, Montjoy's Company of the 10th Virginia Regiment, brings Colonial-era drills and camp scenes to life. Members of the company, including Staffordians Thomas M. Moncure Jr. and Tom Mountz, have also added color and authenticity to Stafford historical commemorations and ceremonies, such as the courthouse commemoration of President George Washington's death, dedication of the historical sign celebrating Hunter's Iron Works, and Falmouth Day 2003. The 3rd Virginia Regiment of the Continental Line publishes an excellent newsletter, and the unit made its first public appearance at "Ferry Farm" on President's Day 2001.

The "Stafford Guards," a Civil War reenactment unit representing Company "I(3)," 47th Virginia Infantry Regiment, performs living-history presentations in Stafford and elsewhere. The company has performed at the White Oak Museum, "Ferry Farm," Fredericksburg, and in Stafford schools. Typically, unit members talk on the wartime lives of the individual soldiers, and the group demonstrates the tactics and weapons of the Civil War. Always "in character," such reenactments give spectators

Union Civil War reenactor Tom Mountz guides visitors to Redoubt No. 2 in Stafford.
(Davis Turner/Free Lance-Star)

View from rampart of Redoubt No. 2, a defensive post near Aquia Creek. A Union camp site has been constructed on this privately owned land.
(Robert A. Martin/Free Lance-Star)

the best possible insights into the soldiers' lives. Especially when placed in the setting of the Civil War Soldiers' Camp at the White Oak Museum or on the banks of the Rappahannock River, the Stafford Guards truly make the Civil War come to life. Stafford High School history teacher Eric Powell, leader of the high school history club and responsible for Stafford's first multicultural fair emphasizing historical contributions, is typical of the best efforts of this reenactment unit. Reenactment groups have supported all Stafford historical events, including Stafford Days celebrations, 1996 Falmouth Harvest Tour of Homes, and Falmouth's 275th Anniversary. Also in the area are Union reenactment units including Company "F," 2nd Rhode Island Volunteers, and Company "B," 28th Massachusetts Infantry.

James Madison, who bears a strong resemblance to Staffordian John Douglas Hall, speaks to the Stafford County Historical Society.
(Jane M. Conner)

On the individual level, living-history reenactors portray historical figures. Representative is Staffordian John Douglas Hall, who has portrayed President James Madison to perfection at "Montpelier;" a New York commemoration of a stamp honoring the "Father of the Constitution;" at Princeton University; and locally. Hall, a professional musician who performs Colonial music at Alexandria's Gadsby's Tavern, also entertained at Aquia Church in an unforgettable candle-lit Historical Society meeting and at Falmouth's 275th anniversary, leading the audience in numerous verses of "Yankee Doodle." Paul "Doc" Duvall of Stafford specializes in reenacting Civil War medicine. Local American Indian reenactors have portrayed their ancestors in camp sites at Committee of Citizens to Serve Stafford's Celebrate Stafford Day events. These reenactments demonstrate Indian crafts and put a human face on the image of the first Americans. Potomac Tribe members have given portrayals and talks at Stafford County Historical Society meetings, including a moving demonstration of Indian music and tribal history.

All "living history" is not the stuff of make-believe. A living reminder of Civil War days took place on the Quantico Marine Base in 2001 when unexploded artillery ordnance was discovered. *The Free Lance-Star*'s Lee Woolf, drawing on the *Quantico Sentry*, reported that some Quantico children had dug up a Schenkl round from a three-inch rifled gun in the base woods. The children gave the round to Capt. Milton Clausen, who contacted base fire and ordnance disposal units. They disabled the round. Woolf contacted D. P. Newton for comment; he related that there were still artillery rounds being found by relic hunters and accidental discoverers throughout Stafford. Individual rounds fired during skirmishes and engagements are uncovered, as well as abandoned ammunition stockpiles. One cache, near the former Potomac Creek railroad bridge, yielded seventy artillery rounds. Another Staffordian, Dan Poppen, contributed to a U.S. Navy manual on disarming Civil War ordnance.

Government and Private Activities

Stafford's Board of Supervisors and County Administrator's Office have been at the forefront of preservation efforts and recognition of groups and individuals. County government played a key role in the settlement of the dispute over "Ferry Farm" by the Wal-Mart Company and Kenmore Foundation (George Washington's Fredericksburg Foundation), permitting the preservation of that national treasure.

In the acquisition of Government Island, Board of Supervisors Ferris M. Belman Sr., Robert C. Gibbons, Linda V. Musselman, Kenneth T. Mitchell, David R. Beiler, Peter J. Fields, and Jack R. Cavalier, and County Administrator C. M. Williams took an even more direct and substantial part. They paid $200,000 and commissioned a study by a nationally renowned panel.

Volunteer Barbara Kirby records, stores, and flattens records in the Stafford Courthouse. Under Circuit Court Clerks Thomas M. Moncure Jr. and Barbara Decatur, an ongoing effort has been made to preserve existing records and to properly provide for their future retention. It is hoped future use can be made of a Stafford museum and archives. (Davis Turner/Free Lance-Star)

Dr. Jean Murray, superintendent of schools (top row, far left); Kim Austin, Principal (second row from top, far right); and the new faculty of the Dr. Kate Waller Barrett School were guests of Mary Cary Kendall (top row, center) at "Richland" as part of a historical orientation on the namesake of Stafford's newest school.

(Jane M. Conner)

In 2003 the county provided the land and initiated the work to develop a long-needed museum and archives. Further, the county uses resources from hotel taxes to encourage tourism. Such monies can assist preservation of "Ferry Farm" and Accokeek Furnace; "Belmont"; the White Oak Civil War Museum; and a future Stafford Museum. The current Board of Supervisors, consisting of Robert C. Gibbons, Jack R. Cavalier, Peter J. Fields, Mark Osborn, Kandy A. Hilliard, Gary F. Snellings, and Gary D. Pash, has formed a Museum Committee (Supervisors Mark Osborn and Kandy A. Hilliard, former County Administrator C. M. Williams, and Stafford County Historical Society representatives Jane Henderson Conner, Barbara Kirby, and Steve Gambaro) and allocated $100,000 in the current operating budget to begin work on a museum. The museum and archives will provide a centralized service to Staffordians and visitors that will interpret Stafford's history, direct visitors to county and regional historical tourism attractions, and provide an enduring Stafford center for receiving, preserving, and displaying artifacts, papers, and relics. The museum will also be an educational center and a repository for selected historic records.

Stafford's School Board, superintendent of schools, and the schools themselves have played important roles in preserving and disseminating Stafford's history. "The Stafford Schools Project," headed by Shirley C. Heim, made a concerted effort to assemble and display all available information on Stafford's schools. The collection, in a "Hall of Memories" in the Alvin York Bandy

Administrative Complex, contains numerous displays. In 2002, the School Board broke with previous precedent (naming schools for their locations or local educators) and named a new elementary school in honor of Staffordian Dr. Kate Waller Barrett. The Board's action has provided Stafford students with a lasting role model and inspiration from among the many worthy Staffordians deserving recognition.

Colonial Forge High School, near the site of Accokeek Furnace, complete with an accompanying state historical marker at its entrance, was the first school named for a specific historical site. Hopefully, future schools will bear the names of Staffordians Margaret Brent, George Mason (IV), Moncure Daniel Conway, George Washington, John Francis Mercer, and many others named in this book.

Individual schools have made concerted efforts to highlight Stafford history. For example, Rodney Thompson Middle School conducted a Stafford history competition among its students. Entries included dioramas, essays, and art work on historical themes and were grouped by students' ages. A history club at Stafford High School under Eric Powell assumed responsibility for the Green Family Cemetery on school grounds. A group from Colonial Forge High School assisted the "Keepers of the Knowledge" program. Students from Brooke Point High School helped clear space at the Indian Burial Ground. Jim Grayson, a sixth-grade teacher at Rodney Thompson Middle School, conducted a class exercise that personalized history by having students write letters from real or imagined Civil War characters—soldiers, abolitionists, slaves, doctors, nurses, or politicians.

The Stafford County Historical Commission, appointed by the Board of Supervisors to advise on historical preservation matters, is currently chaired by Anita Dodd. The commission includes Dr. H. Stewart Jones (Hartwood); Jane Henderson Conner (Rock Hill); Mary Cary Kendall (Griffiths-Widewater); Ted Jones (Falmouth); Cessie Howell (George Washington); and Stephen A. Gambaro (Aquia). The commission deals with a broad range of preservation and policy issues and has engaged historian Eugene C. Scheel to produce the highly detailed Stafford County Historical Map.

"Moncure Conway House," on River Road in Falmouth, is a private residence, but it is one of Stafford's most significant buildings. Constructed by merchant James Vass in the late 1700s–1807, the building was purchased from the William Cunningham Company of Glasgow, Scotland. A brick Federal-style building, it

"Moncure Conway House," Falmouth
(Stafford County)

has a central hall and is noteworthy as the boyhood home of Stafford abolitionist and author Moncure Daniel Conway. The Conways moved into the house in 1838 from a farm north of Falmouth, and it served as Civil War hospital and provost marshal outpost. "Moncure Conway House" has been subjected to flooding several times but has been lovingly restored by two families: Stephen and Leslie Crowther Fore, and Norman and Lenetta Schools. The Fores concentrated on internal restoration during their ownership, which included a devastating 1996 flood. The Schools have continued internal improvements and searched grounds, attic, and basement for household history clues. They improved the grounds, based on antebellum and Civil War-era descriptions and images, and assembled an artifact collection. Additionally, the Schools have made the house a living-history center, hosting Stafford County Historical Society meetings with speakers on Moncure Conway's life and works. At the August 2001 meeting, guests included Walter E. Beach of Dickinson College (Conway's 1849 alma mater) and Conway's great-niece, Katherine Conway Haymes. A new portrait of Conway, commissioned by the Schools, represents the image of him that saved the house from destruction by Union soldiers. Artifacts collected on the property have been assembled and displayed on these occasions, and a growing collection of images and papers is emerging. In June 2003, Ohio recognized Moncure Conway for transporting his family's slaves to freedom in Yellow Springs. Lenetta Schools and Frank White Jr. represented Stafford. These citizens' efforts are "textbook examples" of effective private ownership and stewardship.

Stafford Boy Scouts have aided in cutting trails and clearing areas on Government Island. Stafford Boy Scouts and Girl Scouts, as well as members of local Civil War Roundtables, participate in an annual luminaria display (a light by each of 15,000 graves in the National Cemetery in Fredericksburg). National Park Service historian Don Pfanz has coordinated this effort for a number of years.

Media Activities

The Free Lance-Star, published daily by Josiah P. Rowe III, has been constant in its coverage of Stafford and Fredericksburg history and provides steady focus on historical topics. Its weekend magazine, *Town and County*, edited by Gwen Woolf, continually features articles on Stafford and regional history, Civil War battles and ancestors, and historical preservation groups, as well as feature articles by local historians. The paper's Stafford Bureau, under Lee Woolf, provides detailed coverage of Stafford's historical activities and preservation efforts and features articles on historical topics. Lee Woolf himself has authored historical articles fully meriting the description of newspapers as "the first draft of history." Current and former staff members Judy Jones, Elizabeth Pezzullo, Jonathan Hunley, Laura Hutchison, Rusty Dennen, and Pamela Gould have enhanced local historical understanding. By taking a responsible, long-term view of preserving the unique historical treasures of the region, the *Free Lance-Star* has contributed immeasurably to conservation and preservation activities. Likewise, the weekly *Stafford County Sun*, a Media-General newspaper, provides coverage of historical preservation and educational activities. Former editor Ben Bagwell, current editor Garrett Ebling, and writers Virginia Bare and Carol Thomas Horton have ably reported on historical issues. Both newspapers have steadily supported responsible historical preservation and governmental and private stewardship through their editorials.

Preservation Activities

George Washington's Boyhood Home, now protected by George Washington's Fredericksburg Foundation, has been one of Stafford's most important preservation efforts. Parson Weems' tales of the cherry tree and coin/stone-throwing incidents made the Rappahannock River plantation famous; Chapman's 1833 painting portrayed the "domestic complex" and riverfront; and it again became famous—although not enough to preclude destruction and financial troubles—during the Civil War. Subdivided in the 1870s, the riverfront portion was sold in 1900 to James Colbert, who owned a large dairy farm. Preservation efforts began with the Citizens' Guild of George Washington's Boyhood Home, created in 1926 to acquire the site for public benefit. Later incorporated as the George Washington Foundation, this group acquired the property in the late 1920s, intending to reconstruct the house and open it for public visitation. Although this group attracted national attention, depressed economic times killed the plan's chances and the mortgage was forfeited. The land was reclaimed by the Colbert family. A new organization, the George Washington Farm Inc.,

"Surveyor's Building" at George Washington's Boyhood Home, "Ferry Farm," Stafford County.
(George Washington's Fredericksburg Foundation)

emerged in 1945. Together with George Washington Boyhood Home Restoration Inc., the site was again purchased, and plans were made to develop a memorial and chapel. After several years of public viewing in the 1950s and 1960s, this group dissipated, and Youth for Christ International attempted to create a boys' home (1962), constructing the present administration building. The farm, a museum, and a ferry operated on the site as tourist attractions until 1968. This effort also failed, and the site was purchased by Samuel and Irma Warren in 1969. Despite broad public and private support, all efforts failed to put the site on a firm financial footing. In the 1970s the site was nominated for the National Register of Historic Places (1972), and attempts were made at legislation. The Fredericksburg Bible Institute occupied the administration building in the 1970s, but little else was done. Because little remained from Washington's era, the National Park Service (NPS) resisted attempts to include it in its system. (NPS)

In 1990 the Warrens deeded the site to Stafford County, which initiated the Ferry Farm Project, yet another public attempt at a historical park. Ferry Farm Project also acquired part of Accokeek Furnace archeological site. The deed was in exchange for commercial (B-2) rezoning the portions of the site not containing Washington-association. A 2002 NPS Special Resource Study describes what happened:

In 1995, the retailer Wal-Mart optioned to buy the B-2 portion of the property from the Warrens with the intention of building a large store and parking lot. This set off a preservation battle led by the "Save the Farm" Committee of Historic Fredericksburg Foundation Inc. to protect the setting of the Washington domestic complex. Kenmore Association (now George Washington's Fredericksburg Foundation) joined the preservation initiative and negotiated a purchase of thirty-nine-plus acres from the Warrens in 1996.

Stafford County provided assistance to Wal-Mart in locating another site, and the Board of Supervisors later conveyed the remaining forty-six-plus acres by a deed of gift to the Kenmore Association. The association also enlisted Congressional support for the property, an effort that led to the authorizing legislation for this study; the appropriation of $2 million; and the NPS purchase of a conservation easement.

Stafford divisions surfaced over Wal-Mart's presence—viewed as both an economic bonus and historical disaster. The Wal-Mart legal team was required to inform the Stafford County Historical Society of its proffers and plans. After president Jane Henderson (later Conner) examined the plans, she alerted Society members and community elements. A grass-roots movement in Stafford, Fredericksburg and Spotsylvania confronted the issue.

The "Save the Farm" Committee meets to protest Wal-Mart's plan to build a store on "Ferry Farm." (Stafford County Historical Society)

The Stafford contingent allied with the Historic Fredericksburg Foundation Inc. (notably Bill Beck and Larry Tomayko). All were active in "Save the Farm" activities, which featured rallies, T-shirts, buttons, ribbons, signs, and even a theme song by Barry Fitzgerald. The fight united the region and resulted in the issue's national exposure, including a news interview of spokesperson Cessie Howell by the NBC "Today Show." A children's news show on the Nickelodeon cable network highlighted the arguments and filmed local children at "Ferry Farm." News articles were disseminated nationally via the wire services.

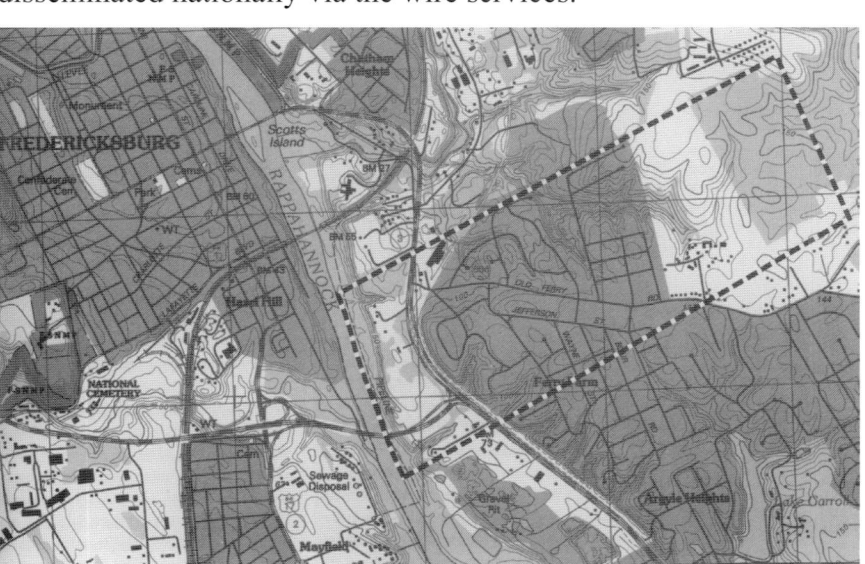

Approximate boundary of original Washington plantation superimposed on a modern map (National Park Service)

Stafford County, Virginia

The "Save the Farm" organization and many local citizens were delighted when the Kenmore Association, headed by W. Vernon Edenfield, stepped in and purchased the property. Wal-Mart relocated farther down Virginia Route 3, thus preserving its economic potentials for the county.

In February 2000, "Ferry Farm" was designated a National Historic Landmark. Although no structures remain from Washington's occupancy, the present 76.92-acre tract affords enormous historical archeological potential and eventual public visitation. Congress (Section 509, Public Law [P. L.] 105–355) mandated the site's protection and study, and it directed the NPS to enter into agreements with the property owner "and other entities" to develop programs, services, and facilities for public use of George Washington's Boyhood Home. George Washington's Fredericksburg Foundation now owns the Stafford property and manages its development, along with Stafford's Accokeek Furnace site, gifted to the county in the mid-1990s and conveyed to the Foundation by the Board of Supervisors. In fiscal year 2000, Congress also appropriated $2 million (P. L. 107–277) to enter into a cooperative agreement for managing the site. Once the agreement was signed, the Foundation received the nonexpended funds ($1,595,000 or $2,000,000 minus the $405,000 paid in June 2000 for a conservation easement) as a grant. The NPS Special Resource Study reviewed the range of site resources and associated themes from Washington's tenure through the Civil War period and examined alternatives and costs. The cooperative agreement cited P. L. 106–914, ordering funds transferred to the Foundation "for the conduct of archeological investigations at the site, research into the life of George Washington's family at 'Ferry Farm,' development of interactive educational programs, development of visitor programs, and other activities that complement the Service's programs and missions in the Fredericksburg area."

"Ferry Farm's" preservation effort is a tribute to the hard work and dedication of private citizens, groups, and public officials. After long economic struggles, the stewardship of George Washington's Fredericksburg Foundation provides this historically significant site its best opportunity to date to realize its potentials.

Of equal historical magnitude to preserving George Washington's Boyhood Home was acquiring and preserving Government Island, the Aquia Creek quarry site that provided the sandstone for the White House, Capitol, and other significant buildings. The island's significance emerged from a 1979 graduate

Rex W. Scouten, former curator of the White House, chaired the Government Island Committee of the Stafford Board of Supervisors. He is shown on the pathway to Government Island.
(Marcia Keener)

research paper by Jane Henderson (later Conner), a Stafford teacher. The island, then divided into potential home sites, was threatened. After reading the paper, a Richmond lawyer purchased the island for ten dollars and services rendered. Henderson felt she had saved the island at that time only to discover twelve years later that the lawyer wished to sell it for $400,000. She contacted interested organizations, but no funds were available. She next approached White House Curator Rex Scouten. This led to Scouten's commitment to preserving the island. He sponsored special visits to the quarries and invited county officials to the White House to discuss acquiring and preserving the site. Henderson met with County Administrator C. M. Williams in 1992, discussing the history of the island and sought his cooperation in helping Stafford purchase it. Williams adds:

> Through Scouten, Jane arranged for a tour of the White House for me and members of the Stafford County Board of Supervisors. At the time the exterior masonry was undergoing its first restoration since being burned by the British in 1814. The Aquia stone had been stripped of some forty or so coats of paint, revealing the intricate eighteenth century carving and the warm color of the Aquia sandstone that had originated at Government Island. I think it was at that point that I and the Board of Supervisors became fully committed to the preservation of Government Island.

White House Christmas ornament containing Aquia Stone (Jane M. Conner)

Negotiations continued, involving C. M. Williams, Ferris Belman, and Ken Mitchell, but the price remained high. Persistence paid off, however, and in 1998 Williams and the Board made a $200,000 offer, which was accepted. On August 19, 1998, Government Island was deeded to Stafford County and preserved for posterity.

The 1998 purchase of Government Island by Stafford's Board of Supervisors and County Administrator saved the island and recognized the need for future stewardship. The Government Island Committee was created by Board Resolution R99–285 on July 13, 1999, to "recommend appropriate measures for historic preservation; advise on interpretation of the resources; provide advice on access to the island; and to recommend appropriate visitation alternatives." This distinguished committee consisted of Rex W. Scouten, former curator of the White House (chair); Charles H. Atherton, secretary, U.S. Fine Arts Commission; Jane Henderson Conner, Stafford and Government Island historian; William L. Ensign, former acting architect of the Capitol; Dr. Robert J. Kapsch, senior scholar in the NPS and former chief of the national architectural and engineering documentation program; Marcia Keener, program analyst, NPS; William Seale, editor of *White House History*; Calder Loth, senior architectural historian, VDHR; C. M. Williams, Stafford County administrator; and Wendy Mallow, Committee administrative assistant.

The Government Island Committee Report recommended continued preservation and county nomination of Government Island for National Historic Landmark status; future retention; parking facilities and trail development (including boardwalk and bridge); development of a publicly accessible, low-cost, low-impact site; capital investment to accomplish recommendations and create appropriate historical signage; annual appropriation for recurring costs; and seeking technical assistance and forming a non-profit advocacy group. U.S. Representative JoAnn Davis; Ronald A. Sarasin, U.S. Capitol Historical Society; Neil W. Horstman, White House Historical Association; and J. Carter Brown, U.S. Commission of Fine Arts, supported the report.

In 2000, with cooperation of Stafford's government, small pieces of Aquia Stone were crushed and molded into hardened miniature replicas of the north and south facades and framed with a gold wreath as the official White House Historical Association Christmas ornament honoring the building's 200th anniversary. Stafford was thus fittingly represented.

AQUIA QUARRY ON GOVERNMENT ISLAND

Government Island Committee
Stafford County, Virginia
January 30, 2002

January 2002 Government Island Committee Report (Stafford County)

On February 17, 2003, an Aquia sandstone block was presented to the Nixon Presidential Library to be used as a cornerstone in a replica of the White House East Room. Pictured are (from left) County Administrator C. M. Williams; Falmouth Supervisor Mark Osborn; Assistant Administrator David Gayle; Staffordian Jane Henderson Conner; and Rock Hill Supervisor Robert Gibbons.
(Douglas Brown)

In May 2002, Congresswoman Davis succeeded in passing a House resolution declaring Government Island a historic site, setting the scene for National Landmark status application. Davis was one of approximately 300 members of Congress who participated in a rare special session held at Federal Hall, New York City, to honor the first anniversary of the September 11, 2001, terrorist attack on the World Trade Center buildings. The plaque they presented to Federal Hall that day was appropriately placed on Aquia Stone.

Saving Government Island is an excellent example of how one citizen can research a topic and influence historical preservation, working cooperatively with concerned public officials.

The establishment of White Oak Civil War Museum is another remarkable account of one citizen's vision and determination to preserve part of Stafford's past. After lifelong responsible relic hunting in the Stafford area, D. P. Newton of White Oak, working with family and friends, had amassed an enormous collection of Civil War relics and artifacts, which he desired

White Oak Civil War Museum and Research Center (Jane M. Conner)

to see effectively interpreted. Newton contacted several possible museum hosts but was unable to find one with the same vision—a dignified tribute to common soldiers of the war. He then set his own course, purchasing the former White Oak Elementary School building from Stafford County. Using his own cabinet-making skills, he fashioned museum displays, including a reconstructed, life-sized camp site commonly used by Union soldiers during the winter of 1862–1863 and one with thousands of spent and dropped bullets found in the camps and firing ranges. Complementing displays, Newton developed a growing research center with photographs, official reports, private accounts, and other historical records in thematic notebooks. Also available are meticulously drawn maps documenting the various sites at which relics were found. Union occupation is also presented on a hand-drawn picto-map of a fifteen-mile Stafford area.

Restoration of Widewater's Clifton Chapel is a shining example of historical preservation by a group of inspired volunteers. Like so many projects, this one began with good intentions and an idea. Unlike so many others, however, this group of concerned Staffordians doggedly pursued their goal. Lee Woolf sets the stage:

> Mary Cary Kendall, the soft-spoken matriarch of Widewater, maintains that there was never anything wrong with Clifton Chapel that couldn't be remedied with some loving attention. "And now," she said of the little country church that is nearly 150 years old, "it's being lovingly restored by a special group of people."

Clifton Chapel before restoration
(Milli Moncure)

The small chapel's history, linked to Widewater, relates that it was built by the 1850s on two acres of land donated by "Clifton's" Waller family. A "chapel of convenience" for those who couldn't regularly travel to worship at Aquia Church, in the Civil War it was part of "Camp Clifton" (1861–1862 base camp of the 47th Virginia Infantry). As a well-defined place yet remote from view, the chapel was ideal for a covert role in the Confederate communications and intelligence line running from Brooke Station-Evansport (Quantico)-Dumfries-Manassas. The Lees, occupying "Richland" after the war, had helped with earlier restoration efforts.

Dave Wirman and John Scott mix concrete for new footings for Clifton Chapel in the summer of 2000. (Milli Moncure)

Restored Clifton Chapel (Milli Moncure)

Despite this substantial history, Ms. Kendall's optimism about restoring the old chapel was challenged by reality. Forty years of vacancy and vandalism had left broken windows, cracked interior walls to bare lathing, and interiors and exteriors in poor condition. Nevertheless, her faith in "Old Stafford" remained firm as she enlisted support from Aquia Church vestry, Stafford County Historical Society, and Widewater residents. At a chapel community reception on a cold, wet day in 1999, guests sipped hot cider, ate cookies, and surveyed grim effects. Yet most saw possibilities in the intricate interior woodwork, and some even spoke of "God's hand" in renovating the chapel. A band of volunteers formed, promising to work every Saturday that it did not rain. The group included Dave Wirman, Milli Moncure, John Scott, John Weagraff, Chris Wanner, and Jon Boers. Divine inspiration was further suggested when it did not rain on a Saturday from January to May 1999.

A May 5, 2001, Eventide Service was conducted in the little chapel by Rev. Cuthbert Mandell of Aquia Episcopal Church. Clifton Chapel was so crowded that some attendees surrendered seats to old-time residents and stood watching through the windows. The restored chapel now stands in a tribute to community and neighborhood preservation, old-fashioned hard work by dedicated volunteers, and church stewardship.

"Chatham," certainly the most important standing historical residence in Stafford, is preserved through its connection with the NPS. In a similar manner, "Belmont"—which combines the historical antebellum home of the Ficklens with the twentieth-century story of artist Gari Melchers and his wife, Corinne—is protected by its connections with the Commonwealth of Virginia and Mary Washington College. These two remarkable complexes were not left to the whims or vagaries of time, and their preservation is a lasting tribute to John Lee Pratt and the Melchers, who worked to preserve them with vision, prudence, and wisdom (see Chapter 7).

Clifton Chapel at Eventide Service, May 5, 2001
(Rhonda Vanover/Free Lance-Star)

Interior view of restored Clifton Chapel, the older stained-glass window was reproduced by Milli Moncure from historic photographs. (Milli Moncure)

Stafford County, Virginia

Right, Kathy Bradford (left) escorts Leonora Bennett (center) and Polly Decatur, former parishioners of Clifton Chapel.
(Milli Moncure)

Robertson Home site, 1806, sketched by Benjamin Henry Latrobe
(Maryland Historical Society, Baltimore)

When Benjamin Henry Latrobe visited Stafford in 1806, he sketched the Robertson home site on Rocky Run (on the edge of the Austin Ridge subdivision; also see Chapter 5). The foundation of that Robertson House was connected to a stone house built by Thomas Towson between 1820 and 1840. Towson, a land speculator from Baltimore, moved to Stafford when the house was built. Now known as the "Robertson/Towson House" after the two families that lived there, it is unique for its use of Aquia Stone as a building material. In the 1700s and 1800s the stone was almost exclusively used for basements and trim in private homes. This house was constructed entirely of sandstone. The Robertson Quarry, along with the quarries on Government Island, contributed the stone for the U.S. Capitol. Initially, it was attached to the wooden structure built by Robertson. In 2002 it looked as if the house was headed for the same fate as so many other old Stafford buildings. However, preservation and stabilization of the building was effected by Rick Wolff, executive vice president and chief operating officer of the George H. Rucker Realty Corporation of McLean, Virginia, the developer of Austin Ridge. With the aid of Shelton Alley, president of Vincente Stone Inc. of Reston, Virginia, and by consulting with NPS and other experts, Wolff was able to ensure the building

Robertson/Towson House, 2002 (Jane M. Conner)

was cleared of brush, stabilized structurally, and fenced off. This project, which reportedly cost the developer some $100,000, is an excellent example of responsible building and preservation.

"Keepers of the Knowledge"

The Keepers of the Knowledge program was initiated by the Stafford County Historical Society to recognize individuals "whose dedication, special witness, and enduring contributions are a vital link in recording and understanding our local, regional and national history." Drawing on American Indian traditions and conceived by Stephen A. Gambaro, it honors community members who seek knowledge and preserve it by passing it on to successive generations.

While the title "Keeper of the Knowledge" recognizes past service, it is also a working definition: recipients continue to serve as consultants and advisers to the Stafford County Historical Society. As of 2003 "Keepers of the Knowledge" include:

George L. Gordon, lifetime Staffordian and former commissioner of the revenue, for providing institutional memory on all aspects of county history. He is noted for his detailed knowledge of county people, places, buildings, farms, roads, and government during the past three-quarters of a century. (Stephen A. Gambaro)

Dr. H. Stewart Jones, retired county educator, member of the county historical commission, and a major force in Stafford historical activities. She wrote her doctoral dissertation on public education in Stafford County from 1865 and was involved in preparations for the historic celebration of Hartwood Presbyterian Church on its 175th anniversary. She headed the Historical and Archaeological Committee of Citizens to Serve Stafford, which published *The Foundation Stones*. (Stephen A. Gambaro)

D. P. Newton, lifelong Stafford resident, for his single-minded efforts to create the White Oak Civil War Museum to honor the common Civil War soldiers who camped and fought in Stafford County, especially in the winters of 1861-1862 (Confederates) and 1862-1863 (Union Army of the Potomac). (Suzanne Carr)

Stafford County, Virginia

Mary Cary Kendall, who has made lifelong contributions to the documentation and preservation of Stafford history. Her home, "Richland," is one of Stafford's historic treasures, associated with the Lees, Fitzhughs, Whitings, and Wallers, and the former home of Gen. Fitzhugh Lee, later governor of Virginia. A veritable fountain of knowledge on all aspects of Stafford's people, lands, and businesses, Mary Cary is a living reminder of more genteel days and gentle Stafford people. Her efforts have contributed to the preservation of Clifton Chapel and have provided background on many projects. She actively participates in the Stafford County Historical Society and represents Widewater on the Historical Commission. (Suzanne Carr)

Barbara S. Kirby, who represents the best and highest standards of dedication to preserving Stafford's history, especially its historical documents. She is a source of knowledge on all aspects of county history and stands as a trusted sentinel on the County Planning Commission and Architectural Review Board to protect that history. Her knowledge of past Staffordians and county records (here and elsewhere) is unsurpassed. Whether the inquiries come from political figures, genealogical researchers, or casual tourists, all find help from Barbara's seemingly endless supply of historical information. A member of the board of the Stafford County Historical Society, she co-chairs the Museum Committee. (Stephen A. Gambaro)

Marion Brooks Robinson, a lifetime county resident, educator, lecturer, and expert on Falmouth, Colonial history, and Stafford's American Indians and Pocahontas, for her contributions to county historical knowledge. (Stephen A. Gambaro)

Homer D. Musselman for being one of the most prolific writers on Stafford's military history. He authored unit histories of the 47th Virginia Infantry and the Stafford Artillery (portions of a larger work) in 1991. *Stafford County in the Civil War* was written in 1995. Musselman had also published *Stafford County, Virginia: Veterans and Cemeteries in 1994*, the most detailed work on Staffordian veterans in all of America's wars and on Stafford cemeteries. He is an active participant in the Stafford County Historical Society and Civil War roundtables, and volunteers with the Fredericksburg and Spotsylvania National Military Park. (Suzanne Carr)

Frank White Jr., a longtime resident of White Oak, for being instrumental in developing, promoting, discussing, and disseminating Stafford's rich African-American history. After an Air Force career, he reestablished his Stafford roots and brought an insatiable curiosity for historical detail and recollections. Following in the footsteps of his father, Frank White Sr. (left), Mr. White has steadily amassed unequaled knowledge of Stafford's black history. An active lecturer and a regular participant in the Stafford County Historical Society, he has promoted knowledge and pride in telling the rich story of black Staffordians. (Stephen A. Gambaro)

Charles H. Price (center), Joyce Withers (left), and Richard Knight survey a possible slave cemetery on what was once the "Ellerslie" plantation, now part of England Run North subdivision.

(Reza Marvashti/Free Lance-Star)

Cemeteries

Stafford Cemetery Committee, with members Charles Price (chair), Richard Knight, and Joyce Withers, supports ongoing county needs to record and protect all burial places. The committee, an investigative body and information clearinghouse for new data, works closely with the County Planning Commission and Planning Department staff to provide information to builders and others involved in construction. Homer D. Musselman and Mike and Marty Lyman have been significant contributors.

Celebrate Stafford Days

The Committee of Citizens to Serve Stafford, chaired by Ruth Carlone, has sponsored and coordinated a number of Celebrate Stafford Days, the latest planned for September 2003. These celebrations have historical components including living-history

Amerindian Activities and the Continuing Saga of Stafford's Potomacs

Staffordians still live with an American Indian past. Paleo-Indian, Archaic, and Woodland Indians habitations have increasingly clashed with modern activities—particularly construction. Problems began by at least 1869, when artifact hunters and curiosity seekers searching for "aboriginal art objects" uncovered a large Indian burial ground at Stafford's Indian Point. One of the largest burial finds on the East Coast, the Smithsonian Institution (1930s) excavated many of the estimated 700 remains. Complicating matters, houses had already been constructed on some of the burial sites.

In 1990 Congress passed the Native American Graves Protection and Repatriation Act (NAGPRA), directing 5,000 government agencies and federally funded institutions to return skeletal remains, funerary, and sacred objects to American Indian tribes and Native Hawaiians. In 1993 Stephen A. Gambaro, Barbara Kirby, and other concerned citizens began searching for appropriate American Indian reburial sites in Stafford. One was found about two miles from the original Potomac village. Located at Brooke Road and Canterbury Drive, the Indian Memorial and Reburial Site at Aquia Landing was dedicated on July 1, 1995. Cooperation between county government, which leased out the site for one dollar a year for five years, renewable at ten-year intervals, and the American Indian Society, which cleared land and cut a trail, was essential. The Rappahannock Valley Civil War Roundtable established stewardship for nearby Aquia Landing historical sites, and the Stafford County Historical Society contributed to establishing the site. In 1995, Circuit Court Clerk and Historical Commission Chair Thomas M. Moncure Jr. coordinated land use and activities with the American Indian Society, Tri-County-City Soil and Water District (Gordon Linkous), and Stafford County Cooperative Extension Agent John A. Gray.

Robert Two Eagles Green, Stafford American Indian leader, poses at Marlborough Point in 1996.
(Lou Cordero/Free Lance-Star)

Today in Virginia, there are eight recognized Indian groupings. Two are the Pamunkey and Mattaponis, each with reservations in King William County. Six other groupings, although not on reservations, are recognized. Despite a well-documented early history and established archeological trail, Stafford's Potawomeck or Potomac Tribe has struggled to gain state and national recognition. An estimated 1,500 people living in Stafford in 1995 were believed to be descended from the Potomacs, according to tribal leader Robert Two Eagles Green. Attempts to reconstruct the lineage of the tribe among Staffordians were complicated by earlier reluctance to acknowledge Indian blood, particularly when it would mark them socially as "colored" and thus prevent them from attending white schools, while also subjecting them to other forms of discrimination. According to Lisa Gerrard, that attitude had substantially changed, and many of the Greens and the "close-knit Newton community in the Belle Plain area" now recognize their Indian lineage. Many also have earliest English settlers' surnames. Green related in October 2002 that there were 427 members of the Patawomeck Tribe in the Stafford area, and lack of recognition of the tribe by Virginia hindered requests to return 134 Indian Point bodies exhumed by the Smithsonian in the 1930s. (The 1995 NAGPRA inventory disclosed the Smithsonian alone held some 14,000 Indian remains, 2,000 of which had already been returned to tribes for reburial.) Anthropologists from the College of William and Mary, which has conducted detailed archeological work on Indian Point, have assisted tribal research efforts.

Archeological work at Indian Point. A 1996 study examined the Indian Point site, discovering more than 10,000 artifacts in one relatively small excavation. Progress has been impeded by the lack of tribal recognition by Virginia authorities and therefore by national authorities.
(Stephen A. Gambaro)

Homeowners—especially in the Marlborough Point and Indian Point sections, but also elsewhere in the county—have also played important roles in preserving Stafford's rich Indian history. *Washington Post* author Linda Wheeler states how local families, seeking peaceful home sites on the river, found themselves stewards for an unfamiliar past:

Chey and Robert DeBlasi learned (of "the conflict between the living and the dead") when the U.S. Army Corps of Engineers told them they couldn't excavate their steep shorefront hill and create a sweeping down into a new bulwark that would keep their property from disappearing. So the DeBlasis are getting used to the idea of building their seawall along the existing shoreline and adding fill dirt to the hill to stabilize it. "We are in compliance," Chey DeBlasi said. "We are preserving what is there. We won't move or touch a thing." Or, as U.S. Army Corps (of Engineers) scientist Hal Wiggins put it, "we are entombing the village." Entombment might work in some places to guard the buried history, but in other areas that are more open, no trespassing signs are posted, and relic hunting is not allowed.

Wheeler continues that erosion is the greatest danger to the Indian Point site. Linda and Jack Fellers of Indian Point are listed among the residents who, though concerned about erosion issues, admire the zeal of historical preservationists and are committed to complying with "history-friendly" actions. Mrs. Fellers adds that they have enjoyed working with Hal Wiggins. Wheeler relates another confrontation with Indian history:

Lesley "Buddy" Oden is among the Indian Point residents who has taken pains not to disturb the remains. Although the county gave him a permit to build a new septic drain field and a larger house on the four acres he bought in 1995, he delayed the project after Wiggins asked for time to arrange a dig. Where the drain field was to go, historians from the College of William and Mary discovered a cache of arrowheads and pottery pieces dating to the 1400s, Oden said. "When I bought the property, I didn't realize all that stuff was there," said Oden, who owns a heating and air-conditioning business. "It makes me feel a part of that Indian mystique, to walk where they walked. In the summer, when we see the fireflies, we talk about whether the Indians are there also." He hasn't built that new drain field or the house to go with it.

Indian Point's story affirms citizens' asserting stewardship, whether sought or unsought, for history that they have "inherited."

Stafford-Staffordshire Ties Remain Strong

Many American and European jurisdictions have formed friendship partnerships to establish "people-to-people" ties. Few of these relationships, however, have as strong a historical dimension as the 400-year-old connection between Stafford, Virginia, USA, and Stafford Borough and Staffordshire, UK—examples abound throughout this work.

Another British link occurred in November 1950, when Mayor A. V. Baker of Falmouth, England, visited a number of East Coast U.S. cities of the same name, including Falmouth in Stafford. In the 1970s additional contacts were made. (*Foundation Stones*)

The Stafford, Virginia-Stafford, England, Friendship Association Inc. (SVSEFA) conceptually began with attendance by Stan Weale, representing the Stafford, England, citizens and Rotary Club, at the dedication of the Stafford County Administration Center on November 16, 1991. Beginning with a trans-Atlantic telephone conversation, the communities grew closer.

2002 Welcoming Ceremony at Stafford's Augustine Country Club. Stafford Board of Supervisors Chairman Bob Gibbons (center) welcomes Ralph Cooke, the mayor of Stafford Borough, Staffordshire, UK. To the right are Sara Fartro, president of the Stafford, Virginia-Stafford, England, Friendship Association Inc., and UK counterpart Mary Austin.
(John and Josie Webber, UK)

Typically, the visiting group stays in homes of association members and conducts pre-arranged tours to historical and cultural sites in the visited country. Social engagements are included during the exchange to renew old friendships and establish new ones. Exchange visits have taken place in 1992, 1994, 1996, 1998, 2000, and 2002. The next exchange, in England, will be in 2004. Related exchanges have taken place including students and a veterans group (British Parachute Regiment) visiting Stafford under Association auspices. This highly successful relationship demonstrates the ability to effectively integrate modern social interaction with historical appreciation. It is a tribute to the openness, hospitality, and kindness of the British and American peoples and an affirmation of their mutual historic bonds, still alive in the twenty-first century.

Symbolic of the tie between the two communities (Stafford, Virginia, and Stafford, England) is the replication of the Staffordshire Knot, an ancient heraldic identifier of the jurisdiction, used in official seals and regimental cap-badges, in English boxwood at the Stafford Courthouse and Administrative Center. (Jane M. Conner)

Works in Progress

Several works by Stafford historians are currently in progress. These include *Birthstones of Freedom* by Jane Henderson Conner, which will expand knowledge of the use of Aquia Stone in the construction of the White House, Capitol and other public buildings; and *Not For Fame or Reward: Virginia Military Institute's (VMI's) Civil War Soldiers* by Albert Z. Conner, which includes biographies of a dozen Staffordians and others from this region among 2,108 men connected with antebellum and wartime VMI.

A 1991 newspaper article related that "…visions of a new 'downtown Stafford' around the courthouse" had been under discussion for several years and the renovation of the 1922 courthouse was under way. The $7 million expansion of court and administrative facilities in a campus-like setting represented Stafford's vision and hope to preserve the town square or courthouse square as a hub for future beautification and development. This was a part of the general vision to improve the appearance of Stafford's U.S. Route 1 corridor. Some improvements have resulted, but much remains to be accomplished to bring that component of the county landscape to life.

Stephen A. Gambaro, Stafford historian, photographer, and American Indian activist
(Jane M. Conner)

Jerrilynn Eby, Stafford historian and expert on Stafford places, speaks at Aquia Church.
(Rhonda Vanover/Free Lance-Star)

The Historic Port of Falmouth Association began in 1998 as a neighborhood association of historic district property owners. Although not a historical organization per se, it has been involved in many of the county's historical activities, including the 200th anniversary commemoration of George Washington's death, and is deeply concerned with the preservation of historical structures in Falmouth, including Golgotha Church. Celebrating the 275th anniversary of Falmouth in 2003, the association has developed civic and community interest and promoted preservation.

The Marine Corps Heritage Center is scheduled to open on November 10, 2005, the 230th U.S. Marine Corps anniversary. Built on a 135-acre tract between U.S. Route 1 and Interstate 95, immediately outside the front gate of the Quantico Marine Base, the Heritage Center will be in the Prince William County section adjoining the base, and exhibits from the current U.S. Marine Corps Air-Ground Museum, in the Stafford County portion of the base, will gradually be transitioned to a state-of-the-art facility.

In January 2003 the Trust for Public Land, a national nonprofit organization, negotiated purchase of 1,100 acres on Widewater Peninsula (including Brent's Point) from Dominion Lands Inc. The Trust purchased the land, assessed by the county at $7.1 million, for an undisclosed amount with the intention of turning the property over to Virginia for a state park. Dominion had changed its plans to build 720 homes, a marina, golf course, and hotel there and had been divesting itself of the property for two years. The Sierra Club expressed interest in its preservation in March 2001, and in December of that year the Commonwealth of Virginia expressed its desire for the property to become a state park. Stafford supervisor Jack Cavalier was identified as a strong backer of the park plan. Widewater State Park will require several years of planning and development to properly operate. Environmentally, this will ensure freedom from ecological intrusion into aquatic and plant life systems. Historically, this will preserve much of the original Brent lands and home sites of early Stafford history. "Crow's Nest," Stafford's other large environmental and historical at-risk site, is also expected to benefit from the same $119 million bond referendum that facilitated some aspects of this transaction.

Retha Walden Gambaro, Staffordian and Native American activist, is also a nationally renowned sculptor. (Jane M. Conner)

Historical Writers and Artists

In addition to many dedicated preservationists throughout the county, Stafford historical writers have contributed to a better understanding of our national history. Civil War historians Robert K. Krick and Robert E. L. Krick were Stafford residents. A cadre of other outstanding NPS historians work from the Fredericksburg and Spotsylvania National Military Park at "Chatham" in Stafford. They include John Hennessy, Donald C. Pfanz, Kelly O'Grady, Frank O'Reilly, Greg Mertz, and Mac Wyckoff—all of whom have contributed locally and nationally to better understanding Civil War military history. In addition to their larger works of history, they are frequent contributors to local journals and newspapers, and they lecture to historical groups and conduct excellent NPS outreach programs. Current Stafford historical writer-residents include Homer Musselman, Jerrilynn Eby, Thena S. Jones, and Dane Hartgrove. Dino A. Brugioni of Hartwood, who tracked down information on the CCC Camp in Berea, has also authored a number of books on Civil War Missouri, historical photo-fakery, and the Cuban Missile Crisis. Area writers Ruth Coder Fitzgerald and Paula S. Felder write on subjects with Stafford content.

Stafford historical artists include painter Donna Neary, specializing in military historical subjects, and sculptor Retha Walden Gambaro, a Native American who has produced works with strong spiritual, natural, and historical themes. She and husband, Stephen A. Gambaro, a photographic artist, have been active in a wide range of Native American, Civil War, and general historical preservation efforts. Other artists who have worked in historical themes are Lee Conlon, Norma Starkweather, and Marcia Chavez.

Ending where we began, the developing story of Stafford paleontologists, led by Jon Bachman and Robert Weems, continues to reveal new data on our most ancient life forms and geology.

Stafford resident Jon Bachman is an amateur paleontologist who, with colleague Robert Weems, has found numerous prehistoric sites in Stafford County. (Joe Amon/Free Lance-Star)

Still "Places of the Heart"

Many Stafford homes have been destroyed by fire, neglect, and war. Some have been preserved and restored to their original condition. But perhaps more symbolic of Stafford's long history are those houses which have "evolved." "Cedar Lodge," on Widewater's Brent's Point, Stafford's oldest point of English habitation, was purchased by Herb and Diane Harmon from the estate of Miss Ellen Brooks. The house was built in three parts, the oldest of which traces to the late 1700s or early 1800s and is linked to the Brents. The second part was added by Moncures before the Civil War. After the Civil War, the last section was added. In the 1870s, a twelve-foot fireplace was added and a Pennsylvania Dutch saying, "Welcome ever Smiles, and Farewell goes out sighing," was painted on the bricks by the Peyton family of Philadelphia, which used the place for duck hunting and raising carriage horses to sell at home. President McKinley visited to hunt. Mr. Peyton left the house to Jake Brooks Sr., who in turn left it to his wife, Mary. She left it to their oldest child, Miss Ellen Brooks. The Harmons chose the name "Cedar Lodge" because of its cedar tree-lined lane and its hunting lodge history.

"Cedar Lodge," located on Widewater's Brent's Point, is Stafford's oldest point of English habitation. (Diane and Herb Harmon)

Epilogue

What can we conclude from Stafford's heritage and legacy to those of us living in the twenty-first century? What gifts and lessons has Stafford left us?

Stafford has been a place of great ideas—individual rights and religious tolerance—so essential to our constitutional Americanism that they are easily ignored in daily life. Further, Stafford has given the nation the substance of our greatest symbols of freedom—the White House and Capitol. And it has given the nation and state remarkably independent thinkers and people of great conviction. Though not always popular or accepted by society at large, Staffordians Giles Brent (I), Margaret Brent, Ann Thomson Mason, George Mason (IV), Mary Ball Washington, George Washington, John Mercer, John Francis Mercer, Richard Brent, Peter Vivian Daniel, John Moncure Daniel, Anne E. Stribling Waller, Moncure Daniel Conway, and Dr. Kate Waller Barrett, to name but a few, are remarkable for holding strong views and "standing for something." They weren't always on the winning side of their struggles, and they weren't even always "right" in their beliefs, but they always held those views with integrity.

Stafford has developed a patriotic, hard-working, and determined people with resilience and a distinct lack of pretentiousness. Staffordians have long been committed to the primacy and decency of "the people" as a social, legal, and political standard. Politicians at any level who fail to grasp that are at-risk.

Stafford has demonstrated a steadily growing tolerance for change and diversity. We have learned to celebrate differences among us in religion, race, section, and politics.

What historic failures haunt us?

Stafford has, through misfortune, apathy, and neglect, lost irreplaceable historic treasures; these gifts are no longer here to enjoy or inform us. By failure to come together in defense of our community and its architectural, natural, and other historical resources, we have lost some "collective memory" through destruction of "familiar landmarks." Yet because of concerned citizens and researchers among and around us, we are not "historically illiterate." However, the fate of Stafford's remaining and future historical treasures is in our hands and the outcome is still undecided.

Stafford has not yet found an effective means to display, study, and discuss its history in a way that will give all of us a better sense of community and identity and introduce our history to residents and visitors.

Many of our historical attractions are not yet ready for prime time and marketed effectively.

What does the future promise for "Old Stafford"?

Though our future may not be easy or entirely without conflict, we need to remember how very far we've come in this small, rural place. The road ahead may be difficult, but many here have traveled far more difficult roads and we should be mindful of that. We can only hope that we may maintain and preserve Stafford County's extraordinary natural and historic resources in an environment that supports responsible growth and economic development while retaining quality of life.

In practical terms, this requires a county museum and visitors' center that features all of our history, with an archival records center and places for individuals and groups to meet and discuss local history and its modern implications.

This requires comprehensive and concerted plans; clear and unambiguous laws, rules and regulations; and positive public and private attitudes and actions centered on developing a sense of place, community, and identity in Stafford. Through stewardship and vigilant protection of our historic and natural resources, we can be worthy of our past and build a better place for our posterity.

At some level, we finally recognize that the past is truly prologue, and, unless we act, Stafford will be what it has long been—a place to get someplace else. As a minimum, it will require thorough planning to offset that reality and to cause those people who "pass through" Stafford—whether residents or visitors—to "stay awhile." The most frequently ignored dimension of Stafford tourism is the practical need for "internal tourism"—whereby the large number of people residing in Stafford, perhaps little aware of its interesting history, actually visit its historical sites. If Stafford's more than 100,000 people and 30,000 families would all visit county historical attractions and take their visiting relatives and friends there, it would boost tourism in ways not previously realized.

"Discover Stafford" should be more than a slogan for the approaching (2007) "Come Home to Virginia" and Jamestown 400th Anniversary campaigns. It should be our watchword and rallying cry.

Selected Bibliography
(roughly in order of their first appearance in this work)

Stafford County, Virginia. Courthouse Dedication, June 12, 1993.
Stafford County, Virginia. Adopted Budget, 1997.
Stafford County, Virginia. Adopted Budget, 1999.
Virginia Division of Mineral Resources. "Publication 12, Early Eocene Vertebrates and Plants from the Fisher/Sullivan Site" (Nanjemoy Formation) Stafford County, Virginia (Charlottesville, Va.: Commonwealth of Virginia, Department of Mines, Minerals and Energy, 1999).
Virginia Department of Historic Resources. *Window on the Past, Threshold to the Future,* Teacher's Guide, 1995.
Gwynn Litchfield, compiler, Virginia Historical Society. *The Story of Virginia: An American Experience,* Teachers' Guide and Resource Book (Richmond: n.d.).
John W. Swanton. *The Indian Tribes of North America* (originally "Bureau of American Ethnology Bulletin 145," published in 1952) (Washington and London: Smithsonian Institution Press, 1969).
Miriam Haymie. *The Stronghold: A Story of Historic Northern Neck of Virginia and Its People* (Richmond: Dietz Press, 1959).
Grace Steele Woodward. *Pocahontas* (Norman, Okla. and London: University of Oklahoma Press, 1969).
Marion Brooks Robinson. "Pocahontas: The Virginia Princess," monograph (lecture), Stafford County Historical Society, n.d.
John Tackett Goolrick. *The Story of Stafford* (Public Works Administration project, 1939); reprinted by the Stafford County government in 1976, 1988, 1990, and 1992.
Dr. H. Stewart Jones, editor, Lisa B. Anderson, Estheleen "Hutch" Blackburn, and Ruth Carlone. *Foundation Stones of Stafford County, Virginia* (project of the Historical and Archaeological Committee of Citizens to Serve Stafford [CCSS] 1991; 1992).
Jerrilynn Eby. *They Called Stafford Home: The Development of Stafford County, Virginia, from 1600 until 1865* (Bowie, Md.: Heritage Books, 1997).
_____ *Laying the Hoe: A Century of Iron Manufacturing in Stafford Virginia* (Westminster, Md.: Willow Bend Books, 2003).
David Hackett Fischer. *Albion's Seed: Four British Folkways to America* (New York and Oxford, U.K.: Oxford University Press, 1989).
Warren M. Billings, editor. *The Old Dominion in the Seventeenth Century: A Documentary History of Virginia, 1606–1689* (Chapel Hill, N.C.: University of North Carolina Press; published for the Institute of Early American History and Culture at Williamsburg, Virginia, 1975).
Thomas R. Morris and Larry J. Sabato. *Virginia Government and Politics* (Richmond: Virginia Chamber of Commerce and University of Virginia's Center for Public Service, 1990).
Rappahannock Patriot. "The Rappahannock Patriot, a Newsletter for and about the 3rd Virginia Regiment of the Continental Line, No. 8," April/May 2003.
Frederick Warren Alexander. *Stratford Hall and the Lees* (Oak Grove, Virginia, 1912).
Ruth Coder Fitzgerald. *A Different Story: A Black History of Fredericksburg, Stafford and Spotsylvania, Virginia* (U.S.A.: Unicorn, 1979).
Thomas Fleming. *Liberty: The American Revolution* (New York: Viking Press, 1997).
F. Stansbury Haydon. *Military Ballooning During the Early Civil War* (Baltimore, Md. and London: Johns Hopkins University Press, 1941).

Homer D. Musselman. *Stafford County in the Civil War* (Lynchburg, Va.: H. E. Howard Inc., 1995).

_____*47th Virginia Infantry* (Lynchburg, Va.: H. E. Howard Inc., 1994).

_____*Caroline, Parker and Stafford Artillery* (Lynchburg, Va.: H. E. Howard Inc., 1992).

Robert K. Krick. *9th Virginia Cavalry* (Lynchburg, Va.: H. E. Howard Inc., 1982).

_____*Fredericksburg Artillery* (Lynchburg, Va.: H. E. Howard Inc., 1986).

Robert J. Driver Jr. and H. E. Howard. *2nd Virginia Cavalry* (Lynchburg, Va.: H. E. Howard Inc., 1995).

James L. Nichols. *General Fitzhugh Lee: A Biography* (Lynchburg, Va.: H. E. Howard Inc., 1989).

John Bakeless. *Spies of the Confederacy* (Mineola, NY: Dover Publications, 1970).

William C. Allen. *History of the United States Capitol: A Chronicle of Design, Construction and Politics* (Washington, D.C.: U.S. Government Printing Office, 2001).

Jane Henderson Conner. "Government Island: Its Forgotten History and Interesting Stone," *Aquia Quarterly*, IV No. 2 (Spring 1980), 81–102.

I. T. Frary. *They Built the Capitol* (Richmond: Garrett and Massie, 1940).

Robert J. Kapsch. "The Labor History of the Construction and Reconstruction of the White House," 1793–1817, Ph.D. dissertation, University of Maryland, 1993.

Harley J. McKee. *Introduction to Early American Masonry, Stone, Brick, Mortar and Plaster* (Washington, D.C.: National Trust for Historic Preservation and Columbia University, 1973).

Lee H. Nelson. *White House Stone Carving: Builders and Restorers* (Washington, D.C.: U.S. Government Printing Office, 1992).

U.S. Government Printing Office. "Report of the Commission on the Renovation of the Executive Mansion" (Washington, D.C.: U.S. Government Printing Office, 1952).

William Seale. *The President's House: A History* (Washington, D.C.: White House Historical Association, 1986).

_____ *The White House: The History of an American Idea* (Washington, D.C.: American Institute of Architects, 1992).

Charles F. Withington. *Building Stones of Our Nation's Capitol* (Washington, D.C.: U.S. Government Printing Office, 1981).

Erik F. Nelson. *Tobacco to Tourism: The Varying Fortunes of Fredericksburg and Falmouth, Fredericksburg History and Biography* (2002*)*.

Ralph Happel. *Chatham: The Life of a House*, National Park Service, 1984.

Thomas M. Moncure Jr. and Molly A. Pynn. *The Story of Aquia Church* (Stafford, Va.: Aquia Church Association, 1987).

Paula S. Felder. *Fielding Lewis and the Washington Family* (Fredericksburg, Va.: The American History Company, 1998).

William E. Griffin Jr. *One Hundred Fifty Years of History along the Richmond, Fredericksburg and Potomac Railroad* (Richmond, Va.: R,F&P Inc., 1984).

William K. Goolrick. *Rebels Resurgent: Fredericksburg to Chancellorsville* (Alexandria, Va.: Time-Life Books, 1985).

Index

~A~

A Brief Outline of Recorded History of the Patawomeck Indian Tribe 221
"Accakeek Farm" 18
Accokeek Creek 9
Accokeek Creek rail bridge (Civil War) 201-202
Accokeek Furnace 21, 194p, 210, 213, 234, 235, 238, 240
Accokeek Run 206
Adies 152
Adie, Lt. Hugh, Jr., (Civil War) 88p, 89p, 88-89, 153
A Different Story: A Black History of Fredericksburg, Stafford, and Spotsylvania, Virginia (1979) 222
A Driving Tour: The Army of the Potomac in Stafford County 230
Agnes, Princess 107p, 107
"A Kiss to the President," [sic] 122, cast 123p
Albemarle Sound 13
"Albion" 69, 70, 132, 132p
Alexanders 43, 96, 135
Alexander, General 102
Alexander, John 33
Alexander, William 138, 156
Alexandria and Fredericksburg Railroad 204
Amblers 38
American Indian Society 257
American Legion 214, 230
American Red Cross 105, 214
"Anchorage, The" 65, 152
Anderson, Lisa B. 7, 221
Andrew Methodist Episcopal Church * 166, 166p
Andrews' 135
Andrews, George (1693) 136
Anglicans 37,
Anne, Queen 16
Anne Arundel County and "Cedar Park," Maryland, 52
Anne E. Moncure Elementary School 132, 153
Anacostins 14
Antioch College 49
Antioch United Methodist Church * 166, 166p
Anurans 10
Aquia 135
Aquia Creek 9, 78p, 79p, 104, 152, 210, 240
Aquia Creek railroad bridge (Civil War) 205, 205p
Aquia Episcopal Church * 54, 95, 108, (bicentennial) 122, 124p, 125p, 125, 132, 158p, 160p, 160-161, 166, 232
Aquia Harbour, Incorporated 129
Aquia Harbour Yacht Basin 124
Aquia "freestone" 124
Aquia Landing 76, 197, 202p, 203p, 257
Aquia Quarry 151
Aquia Stone 103, 104, 244p
Aquia Towne Center 37, 132, 195
Archaeoornithominus 11
Argall, Captain Samuel 15
"Arkendale" 65, 152
Arkendale 205
Arkendale train crossing 122
Armstead, Rev. Peter 169
Armstrong, Mr. and Mrs. James, Jr. 166
Ashbys 53
Atherton, Charles H. (Government Island Committee) 242
Austin, Kim 234p
Austin, Mary, SVSEFA 260p
Austin Ridge subdivision 248
Austin Run 152
Averell, General W.W. (Civil War) 61, 86

~B~

Bachman, Jon 10, 264, 264p
Bacon, Nathaniel 14
Bacon's Rebellion 14
Bagwell, Ben 7, 237
Baileys 134
Baker, Mayor A.V. of Falmouth, U.K. 260
Ball, Hannah 225
Ball, Colonel William 133
Ballards 135
Ballard, Thomas 23
Baltimore, Lord 26
"Baltimore" (steamboat) 199
Banks Ford 118, 196
Baptists 37
Baptizing Day (c. 1945-1946) 58, 59p
Bare, Virginia 176, 177, 237
Barnes, Harrison 132
"Barnes House" 132, 132p
Barnette, Nannie 173
Baroody, Tim and Kristin 7, 83
Barrett, Dr. Kate Waller (Katherine Harwood Waller) 56p, 57p, 57-58
Barrett, Robert South 57
Barry, Charles C. 47
Barton, Clara (Civil War) 9, 105, 105p, 106, 134
"Basil Gordon House" 84p, 140, 145
Batie (Patie) 26
Beachs 135
Beach, Walter E., Dickinson College 236
"beanpole and cornstalk bridge" (Civil War) 200
Beaverdam Run 96
Beck, Bill 239
Beiler, David R. 233
Bell, Alexander Graham 119
Bell, Daniel 176
"Bell-Aire" 86
Bellfair Mills 96
Bellehaven Missionary Baptist Church 96
Belle Plain, White Oak 110, 112, 203, 203p, 212p, 258
Belle Plain lumber activities 213
Bells and Belfries and Some of Neither (1993) 222
Belman, Ferris, Sr., 228, 233, 242
"Belmont" 122, 130p, 143, 143p, 144p, 234, 246
Belmont/Gari Melchers Foundation

(Belmont/MWC) 7
Belmont Hills 12
Benjamin, Judah P. (Civil War) 108
Bennett, Leonora 248p
Berea Baptist Church* 86, 88, 165, 165p, 214
Berea Civilian Conservation Corps (C.C.C.) Camp 214-215
Berea C.C.C. Camp and Stafford, King George, Spotsylvania and Fauquier Counties 215
Berea School 1935 181p
Berkeley, Sir William 33, 209
Berreth, David 7
"Berry Hill" 209
Bethlehem Primitive Baptist Church * 168
Beverly, Rudolph 188
Billings, Warren M. 17, 31,
Bill of Rights, U.S. (1791)
Birdsong, M. A. 204
Birthstones of Freedom 261
Bishop Payne Divinity School, Petersburg 173
Black, Susan Musselman 168
Blackburns 96
Blackburn, Estheleen "Hutch" 7, 168, 221
Blackburne, Thomas 138
Blackford, Lieutenant B. Lewis (Civil War) 108
Black Churches 50
Black History Month 256
Black Schools 51
Blaidells 11p, 206p
Blasko, Bill 230
Blight, David W. 50
"Bloomington" 95p, 96, 152
Bloomington School 1800s 178p
"Blysdale Farm" 71p
Blythedale 22
Boers, Jon 246
Bolton, Bill, 1940s teacher, 185p
Bon Food 153
Booth, John Wilkes (Civil War) 112, 112p
"Boscobel," Staffordshire, 34
Boscobel (subdivision) 105
Boswell's Corner 95
Boswell, Captain James Keith (Civil War) 116p
Bowling Green 111
Boxley, Joseph 173
Boyd, Belle (Civil War) 108, 108p
Boys' basketball, Falmouth High School 1940s 185p
Boy Scouts 236
Bradford, Kathy 248p
Bradley, Cheryl 177
Brawners 96
Breckinridge, Major Cary (Civil War) 88
Breen, T. H., 32
Brennan, Conrad C. "Jiggs" 214
Brents 25, 120, 135, 150, 151, 265
Brent, Anne Carroll Brent 27
Brent, Daniel Carroll of "Richland" 43, 74, 126, 126p, 138, 150, (1760-1815) 151, 159
Brent, Eleanor Carroll Brent 27, 37, 102, 150

-270- A History of Our Own

Brent, Elizabeth Greene of Bermuda 35
Brent, Elizabeth Jacquelin Ambler 102-103
Brent, George of "Woodstock" 26, 34, 36, 125, 138, 223
Brent, Giles (I) 25, 34, 150, 210
Brent, Giles (II) 26, 35-36, 135, 150
Brent, Jane 37
Brent, Margaret 8, 33-34, 32p, 151, Brent 235
"Brent, Mary" ([I] see Kittamaquad ---Brent, Mary (sister of Giles [I] and Margaret) 26, of "Peace" 150
Brent, Mary Sewell Chandler 35
Brent, Richard (son of Giles [I] and Kittamaquad) 26
Brent, Sir Richard (1573-1652) 32, Lord of Stoke and Admington (1573-1652) 150
Brent, U.S. Senator Richard 38, 42-43
Brent, Robert of "Woodstock" (1730-1780) 27, 138
Brent, Sarah
Brent, William (I) (b. 1677) 150
Brent, William (II) (born 1710) 150
Brent, William (III) of "Richland" 27, 150
Brent, William (IV) 151
Brent, William (1732- ca.1782) 37
Brent, Colonel William 102
Brent, William (1733-1782) 102
Brent, William 37
Brent, William, Jr., 74 159
Brenton or Brent Town 26
Brent Cemetery 29, 30p, 117, 138
Brent's Mill 150, 210
Brent's Point 26, 262
Brentsville 109
Brent Quarry 103
Brezina, Richard 10
Bridges, Ambassador Peter 54
Bridwell, Sergeant Robert, VRM 99
Briggs' 133
Briggs, David 72
Bristow, Robert 26
Bristow 109
British invasion 159
British Parachute Regiment veterans 261
Broaddus, Rev. William F. 169
Bronaugh, John W. 136
Brooke area 158, 169
Brooke, James Vass 55, 55p
Brooke, Jane Morrison 55
Brooke, John Taliaferro of "Mill Vale" 43, 56, 176
Brooke Colored School 1935 182p
Brooke, Louisa 56
Brooke, Samuel Selden, Sr., 56, 84
Brooke, Captain Samuel Selden, Jr., (Civil War) 55-56, 55p
Brooke, William 55,
Brooke, William, Jr. 145
Brooke Point High School 235
Brooke Station 111, 203, 245
Brooks' 142
Brooks, Mrs. B. 84
Brooks, Miss Ellen 265
Brooks, Herbert 227
Brooks, Jake, Sr., 265
Brooks, Mary 265
Brooks, Mrs. Randolph 227
Brooks Park 12
Brown, Dr. Gustavus of Maryland 73
Brown, J. Carter, (Chairman of the U.S.

Fine Arts Commission) 242
Brown, Norman B., VRM 98, 99
Brown, Mrs. R. T. 84
Brown, John (abolitionist) (Civil War) 48
Brown, John 145
Brown v. Topeka (1954) 51, 178
Brugioni, Dino A. 214, 263
Brunswick Parish Church in Falmouth 142
Bryant, Dr. James II, NPS and Shenandoah University 256
Buchanan, Andrew 144
Buckland [or Buckner], William 135
Burns, Anthony 46-47, 46p
Burnside, General Ambrose (Civil War) 85, 86, 114p
"Burnside Wharf" (Civil War) 202
Burroughs' 95
Burton, Robert 7, 101p
Butler, Stafford Unionist 116
Buxton, Mrs. William 84
Byrd, U.S. Senator Harry Flood 50

~C~

Cabel (Cabell) 26
Cadow, Robert 227
Calvert, Cecil, Lord Baltimore 32
Calvert, Governor Leonard 32
Cambell, Norman C. 227
Campbell, Captain Albert H. (Civil War) 109
"Camp Clifton" (Civil War) 111, 166, 245
"Camp Stafford" 214
Cannons 96
Cape Henry Lighthouse 129
Capitol, U.S. 8, 108, 124, 125p, 128p, 240, 248
Carlone, Ruth (also chairman of CCSS) 7, 221, 252
"Carlton" 85, 85p, 107, 144, 145p
Caroline County 9, 109
Carr, Suzanne 7
Carrington, Colonel Edward of Cumberland 103
Carrolls of Marlborough, Maryland 27
Carroll, Daniel of "Carrollton" 27
Carroll, Daniel (II) (known as "The Commissioner") 27
Carroll, Father (Archbishop) John, S.J. 27, 150
Carters 149, 152
Carter, Charles 131, 139
"Cedar Lodge" 119, 265, 265p
Celebrate Stafford Days, Committee of Citizens to Serve Stafford 230, 231, 252
Celebrate Virginia - Stafford 214, 225-226
Cellophane production 214
Central Park 219
Central Rappahannock Regional Library 222
Central Virginia Battlefield Trust 230, 230p
Centreville 109
"Chapel Green" 132, 133, 133p
Chapman, Lieutenant Colonel (Civil War) 111
Chapman, John Gadsby 237
Chappawamsic School 1940 184p
Charles I, King 33
Charles II, King 33, 125
Chase, Samuel 27
"Chatham" (also see "Lacy House") 48p, 68, 85, 104, 105, 122, 134, 134p, 246
Chatham: The Life of a House (1984) 220

Chavez, Marcia 264
Chopawamsic Baptist Church 162
Chopawamsic Creek 197
"Chopawamsic Farm" 19, 95, 217
Chopawamsic Formation 211
Chopawamsic Island 119
Charles I, King 25
"Chelsea" 96
Chichesters 149
Chichester, Captain Daniel M., VRM 98
Chichester, Daniel, Jr., Commonwealth's Attorney 226p, 228
Mrs. Dan Chichester 227
Chichester, Senator John H. 5, 226p, 228
Chichester, Richard 226p
Chilton, Samuel 55
Chiskiack 32
Chotank Parish 158
Christ Church, Alexandria 125, 126p
Church of the United Brethren in Christ 96
Churches in northern Stafford lost to the 1942 Quantico expansion: Bellehaven Missionary Baptist Church; Church of the United Brethren in Christ; Massadonia Baptist Church; Mount Zion Baptist Church; Providence Church; and Stafford Store Baptist Church. 174
Churchill, John, Duke of Marlborough [ancestor of Winston Churchill] Blenheim, 1704 135
Citizens' Guild of George Washington's Boyhood Home 237
City Point on the James River 203
Civilian Conservation Corps (C.C.C.) 214-215
C.C.C. Company No. 2363 214
Civil War [see individual entries marked (Civil War) and Chapters 4 and 10]
Civil War Roundtables 236
Civil Works Administration (C.W.A.) 214
Clark, Ben 164
Clausen, Captain Milton 233
"Clearview" 85, 144, 145p
"Clermont" 95, 96
Cleveland, President Grover 63, 118, 118p, 151
Cleverley, Staff Sergeant William, VRM 99
Clift, Albert 84
Cliftons, 27, 151
"Clifton" 27, 56p, 121, 151
Clifton Chapel 62, 245, 245p, 246p, 247p
"Clifton Lodge" 151
Clifton Primitive Evangelical Church * 166
Cloes 95
Cloe, John Haile 7, 91, 97
Cloe, Private William Weedon, USA, 91, 91p, 94, 95, 96, 99 (VRM)
Cloe, Peggy and Bill 7
Coal Landing lumber activities 213
Coalters 134
Coalter, Hannah of "Chatham" 47, 47p
Coe, Kenneth 227
Colberts 237
Colbert, James 237
Collins, Major Charles Read, 15th Virginia Cavalry (Civil War) 202
Colonial Circuits, Inc. 7, 216, 216p
Colonial Forge High School 21, 193p, 235
"Come Retribution" hypothesis (Civil War) 108
Committee of Citizens to Serve Stafford (CCSS) 162, 252-253

Committee of Citizens to Serve Stafford's
Celebrate Stafford Day 232
Commonwealth of Virginia 263
"Concord" 27, 131, 131p, 132
Concord School 155
Concord School 1914 179p, 180p
Confederate prisoners of war (Civil War) 110p
Confederate Secret Service (Civil War) 109
Conlon, Lee 264
Conner, Albert Z. 256, 261
Conner, Jane M. (also Jane Henderson and Jane Henderson Conner) (Government Island Committee) 7, 124-129, 228, (SCHC Commissioner Rock Hill) 235, 239, 239p, 242, 244p, 256, 261
Conner, Gavin C. 7
Conner, Marshall A. 7
Conner, Owen L. 7, (WWII reenactor) 230p
Constitution, U.S. (1787)
Continental Army and Navy 41
Continental Congress 38
Conversations with Old Friends 221
Conways 53, 209
Conway, Dr. G. I. (Civil War) 116
Conway, John M. 177
Conway, Moncure Daniel 45p, 45-46, 47, 84-85, 235, 236, 256
"Conway Slaves" (Civil War) 49, 256
Conway, Walker Peyton 84, 145
Cooke, Elizabeth 151
Cooke, George M. 75
Cooke, John 74, 126, 136, 138, 159
Cooke, John of "Marlborough"/"West Farm" 43
Cooke, Colonel John (1755-1819) 151
Cooke, Ralph, Mayor of Stafford Borough, U.K. 260p
Coolidge, President Calvin 122p, 122
"Cotton Warehouse" 142, 142p
"Counting House" 142
Crawford, Marshall 110
CRI, Inc. 225-226
Crookshanks, Barbara 108
"Crow, The" (vessel) 137
"Crow's Nest" 104, 137-138, 224, 226, 263
Crutcher, Rev. Horace 164
Crutcher, Robert 210
Crutchfield, B. F. 204
Cuba 63
Culley, John 68p
Culpeper County 9
Cunninghams 50
Curtis' 155

~D~

"Dabney" (slave spymaster) (Civil War) 49, 49p
Dahlgren Naval Surface Weapons Center 158
Dana, Richard Henry, Jr., 46
Daniel, Elizabeth Travers (died as an infant) 137
Daniel, Frances 72
Daniel, Lucy Randolph 44
Daniel, Hannah Ball (1737-1829) 137
Daniel, John Moncure (Civil War) 53-54, 53p
Daniel, Margaret Stone
Daniel, Mildred Stone
Daniel, Peter (1706-1777) 137
Daniel, Justice Peter Vivian 44, 44p, 53, 104, 138
Daniel, Peter V., Jr. 199

Daniel, Miss Sarah 165
Daniel, Travers, Sr., of "Crow's Nest" 43
Daniel, Travers, Jr. 43, 72, 138
Daniel, Travers (1741-1824) 137
Daniel family cemetery,
"Crow's Nest" 224-225, 224p
Danville area, the "Last Capital
of the Confederacy" 109
Darter, Dr. Oscar H. 137, 227
Daughters of the American Revolution 226
Davis, Jefferson 108
Davis, U.S. Representative JoAnn 242, 244
Day, Solomon 152
D.C. Boundary marker 128p
Deacon farm "Grafton" (not to be confused with the Waller home in northern Stafford). Union IIIrd Army
"Deep Run" 21
De Baptist, John 41, 41p, 72
DeBlasi, Chey and Robert 259
Deborah (slave) 40
De Broke, Lady Elizabeth Willoughby 32
Decatur, Barbara 233
Decatur, Noble 171
Decatur, Polly 248p
De la Warre, Governor Lord 15
De Polignac, Major General Camille Armand Jules Marie Prince (Civil War) 54
Depression-era Stafford 214-215, 215p
DeShazo, Mrs. John 84
DeShields, Annie 68p
Devores 134
Deyo, William L. 7, 221
Dickens, Charles 9, 104, 104p
Dickinsons 96
Dickinson, Carl B. 101p
Dickinson, Curtis 70p, 71p
Dickinson, Dorothy 101p
Dickinson, Nancy 7
Dickinson College (Pennsylvania) 45
Digges, Edward 209
"Dipple" 95
Diresubawn 26
Dishmans 50
Dixons 144
Dixon, Rev. George 169
"Doc Stone Commons" 53
Dodds 144
Dodd, Anita 7, 221, 222p, 223p, 228, 235
Doegs (Nanticokes, etc.) 14
Dogwood Air Park 149
Dominion Lands, Inc. 263
Doniphans 151
Donn, Edward 142
Douglas, Robert 224
Downmans 43, 96
"Downtown Stafford" (U.S. Route 1 corridor in Stafford County) 261
Doyle, Alexander and Eliza 152
Dragon 41
Drama club, Stafford High School 1940 184p
Dred Scott decision (1857) on the
Fugitive Slave Act. 45
Drew Middle School 149
Drive Through Stafford County's History 228

Dr. Kate Waller Barrett Elementary School 235
Dr. Kate Waller Barrett Elementary
School faculty 234p
Duck hunters, Widewater 120p-121p
Dumfries, Prince William County 52, 135, 245
Dunbar, Mrs. 107
Duncan, Annie (Barnes' slave) 132
Dunmore, Lord 38
Du Pont, E.I...de Nemours and Company 67
DuVall, Paul "Doc"
(Civil War medical reenactor) 232
Dye, Mrs. George 84

~E~

Eagle Tavern (also see "Temperance Inn") 131
"Eastwood" 86, 156p
Ebenezer United Methodist Church * 167, 167p
Eby, Jerrilynn 7, 26, 39, 44, 46, 96, 105, 118, 130-157, 156, 157, 161, 162, 221-222, 262p, 263
Economic Development Department, Stafford County 255
Edenfield, W. Vernon 7, 240
"Edge Hill" 152
Edlund, Jack and Gail 145
Edmonds, John 110
Edringtons 152
"Ellerslie" 73
Elmore, E.C. 54
Embrey Dam 208
Emerson, Ralph Waldo 47
England, John 206
English Cavaliers 32, 33p
English Counties 33-34, 33p
Ennivers 131
Ensign, William L.
(Government Island Committee) 242
Eolambia 11
Essex Journal (Connecticut) 19
Eustaces 153
Eustace, Hancock 74, 159
Eustace, Ruth 163
Evans, Larry 130
Evansport (Quantico) 111, 245
"Eventide" service at Clifton Chapel 246, 247p
"Express Freight" 204
Eyeball to Eyeball: The Inside Story of
the Cuban Missile Crisis 263

~F~

Fairfax County Park Authority 223
Falls Run 108
Falmouth (town) 9, 102p, 104, 106-107, 131, 134, 139, 140p, 147p, 148p, 149p, 218
Falmouth Baptist Church * 170, 170p
Falmouth Beach 39, 140
Falmouth Canal 210p
Falmouth Elementary School 149
Falmouth Elementary School,
Butler Road,
1961 190p
Falmouth Fire House 227
Falmouth School 1890s 178p

Falmouth Harvest Tour of Homes (1996) 232
Falmouth High School 1930s 181p
Falmouth High School 1935 182p
Falmouth High School students 1940s 185p
Falmouth High School 69, 98
Faneuil Hall, Boston, 46
Fartro, Sara SVSEFA 2 Farm" 132
"Ferry Farm" Christmas Eve fire 224
Ferry Farm Project 238
Ferry Farms subdivision 22
Ferry Farms Elementary School 1961 189p
Ferry Farms Shopping Center 22
Ficklens 43, 246
Ficklen, Ann Eliza Fitzhugh 143
Ficklen, Benjamin 210
Ficklen, Ellen McGhee (died 1845) 143
Ficklen, Joseph Burwell of "Belmont" 132, 143, 208
Ficklen, Nannie of "Belmont"
(Mrs. Daniel Murray Lee) 65
Fields, Supervisor Peter J. 233, 234
Finnalls 149
Fischer, David Hackett 34
Fisher, Justice of the Peace 98
Fitzgerald, Barry, 147p, 218p
Fitzgerald, Ruth Coder 7, 39, 40, 44, 49, 169, 171, 172, 173, 222, 256, 263
Fitzhughs 8, 43, 96, 104, 120
Fitzhugh, Mrs. Ann 23
Fitzhugh, Anna Maria Sarah Goldsborough, 48p, 48-49, 49p
Fitzhugh, Henry 139
Fitzhugh, John 138, 139
Fitzhugh, Sally Lou of "Poplar Grove" 130, 155
Fitzhugh, William 35, 36, 136
Fitzhugh, William of "Chatham" 40, 134, 134p, 209
Fitzhugh, William Henry 48, 95
Fitzhugh, Major William H. 151
Fitzhugh, Mrs. William H. 151
Fitzhugh's [of Bedford] Mill (in what is now King George County; called Gray's Mill on
Civil War era maps) 210
Flack, Barbara 7, 221
Fleming, Thomas 18, 40
Flomer, Michael 10
Fleurrys 132
"Fleurry's, The" (homesite) 132, 132p
Foote, Richard 26
Forbes' 133
Forbes, Edwin (Civil War) 114p
Forbes, Murray 133
Fords 96, 152
Ford, Henry 122
Ford, Margaret Waller 117
Fore, Stephen and Leslie Crowther 236
Fortier, John 117
"Fort Kent," Maryland, 33
Fortress Monroe 129
47th Virginia Infantry (1991) (Civil War) 221
Foundation Stones of Stafford County, Virginia, (1991, 1992) 13, 220, 253
"Four Gables" 99
Fowkes 8
Fowke (or Fowks), Colonel Gerard 34, 137
Fowle, Ellen ("Nellie") Bernard of Alexandria

(Mrs. Fitzhugh Lee) 62, 62p
Fox, Nathaniel 138
Franklin, Benjamin 27
Franklin, Mrs. Butler of "Fall Hill" 133
Mrs. Lyn Franklin 227
Frank's Hardware and Crafts 153
Fredericksburg 6, 9, 90
Fredericksburg (2002) 222
Fredericksburg Area Museum 228
Fredericksburg Bible Institute 238
Fredericksburg Chapter, United Daughters of the Confederacy 90
Fredericksburg Civil War Roundtable 229, 229p
Fredericksburg and Spotsylvania National Military Park. 7, 68, 214, 218, 263
Fredericksburg News 56
Fredericksburg Normal and Industrial
Institute in Mayfield 51
Fredericksburg Recorder 77
Fredericksburg-Stafford Parks and
Recreation staff 143
Fredericksburg Star 83
Fredericksburg State Normal (Teachers) College
(now Mary Washington) 178
Free Lance-Star,The 7, 233, 237, 256
Freeman, Dr. Douglas Southall 122, 122p
Freeman-Washington Agency of Fredericksburg 189-193
Frenchs 155
French, Sallie V. 179p
French, Union General (Civil War) 131
French Declaration of the Rights of Man and the Citizen (1789) 19
French Huguenots 26
French King Louis XIV 26
French King Henry IV 26
French troops 41, 102, 102p
Fristoe, William 162

~G~

Gaddy, David W. 109
Gadsby's Tavern, Alexandria 232
Gaines' 96, 168
"Gallatroin, Miss," rape and murder victim 116
Gambaro, Retha Walden 263p, 264
Gambaro, Stephen A. (also Steve Gambaro) 7,
(SCHC Commissioner Aquia) 235, 249, 257, 262p, 264
Gari Melchers School 1961 191p
Garner, Margaret 80
Garrard, James (1749-1822) 133, 162
Garrard, Col. William (c.1715-c.1786) 133
Garrett Construction 216
Garrisonville Road 153
Gayle, David 244p
Geico 216, 216p
Geico complex 214
General Motors Company 68
George, David Lloyd 122, 122p
George Mason (IV) Chapter of the National Society of
Colonial Dames 229
George Mason Road 95
Georgetown College (now University) 27, 150
George H. Rucker Realty Corporation of
McLean, Virginia, 248
George Washington's Boyhood Home, "Ferry Farm" 223, 223p,

228, 237-240
George Washington Boyhood Home
Restoration, Inc. 238
George Washington Farm, Inc. 237
George Washington Foundation 237
George Washington's Fredericksburg Foundation (GWFF
- formerly the Kenmore Association) 7, 223, 233, 240
Gerrard, Lisa 258
Gibbons, Supervisor Robert C. 233, 234, 244p, 260p
Gibson, John of Dumfries 126-127
Giles', Miss, class, H. H. Poole Junior High School 1953/54 188p
Gilmer, Maj. Gen. Jeremy, Chief of Engineers, (Civil War) 109
Gilmer Map (Civil War) 109p
Ginsburg, Justice Ruth Bader 33
Girls' basketball, Falmouth High School 1940s 185p
Girl Scouts 236
Glass, Carter 50-51
"Glencairne" 149, 149p
Goldsborough, Governor Charles of Maryland 48
Golgotha Church * of Our Lord Jesus Christ 170-171, 170p, 262
Goodman, 1st Sergeant Clem, VRM 98
Goodwin and Associates, Inc. 223
Goolrick, John 68
Goolrick, John Tackett 7, 34, 111, 220
Gordons 155
Gordon, Allan M., Ph.D. 58
Gordon, Basil (or Bazil) 42, 42p, 139, 142, 146
Gordon, Celestine 155
Gordon, George L. 7, 227, 228, 249p
Gordon, Samuel 42, 139, (1759-1843) 145
Gordon, Samuel of "Kenmore," Fredericksburg 145
Gordon, William Wallace (Civil War) 155, 156
"Gordon Green Terrace" 145
Gould, Pamela 237
Government Island (also Wiggington's Island or Brent's Island)
103, 124, 124p, 126, 127p, 224, 236, 240-242, 243p, 248
Government Island Committee 233, 242
Government Island Committee Report (January 2002) 242
Government Services Administration (GSA) 129
G&H Manufacturing 214
Gallagher, F. T. 204
"George Washington Quarry" 209
"Grafton" (north Stafford farm) 78, 153, 153p
Grafton Elementary School 105
Grafton Village 105
Grant, Cary 122, 123p
Grant, Jason 50
Graves, Dr. E. Boyd 143, 227
Graves, Dr. and Mrs. E. Boyd 144
Gray, John A., Stafford County Cooperative Extension Agent 257
Gray, John Bowie (Civil War) 64, 64p
Grayson, Jim, Rodney Thompson Middle School teacher 235
"Great Waggon Road" 195
Greens 132, 142, 145, 258
Green, Duff 107, 146
Green, John 139
Green Family Cemetery 235
Green, Robert Two Eagles 258, 258p
Greenbank Farm site [Celebrate Virginia-Stafford] 224, 225-226
Greenlaw, Hunter W. 69-70, 69p
Greenlaw, Mary Lou 69-70
Greer, Grace 173
Griffin, William B., 197-199, 203, 206
Griffin, Maggie 173

Grimes, Leonard A. 46
Grimsley, Gary 10
Grogan, Charles, Company D, Mosby's Rangers 110
Grove Baptist Church in Goldvein
(Fauquier County) 170
Guilford Courthouse, North Carolina, 52
Gwinn, Dunmore 256
Gwinn, Julia 256

~H~

Haleman, Corporal Leonard C., VRM 99
Hall, Charlie 110
Hall, James O. 109
Hall, John Douglas (living history) 232, 232p
"Hall of Memories," Alvin York Bandy
Administrative Complex 176, 234
Hamilton's Crossing (below Fredericksburg) 203
Hammersley, Francis 136
Hamn, Sylvester 101p
"Hampstead" 133
Hampton, General Wade 111
Hanover County 109
Happel, Ralph 68, 106, 121, 220
Harding, Strother 176, 177
Harmon, Diane and Herb 7, 265
Harney, Lieutenant Thomas, Torpedo Bureau
(CS Secret Service) (Civil War) 111
Harpers' Ferry 48
Harris' 168
Harris, Willie C. 101p
Harrison, Agnes 227
Harrison, Benjamin 118, 118p, 151
Hartgrove, Dane 263
Hartwood 13
"Hartwood" 154, 154p, 155, 164
Hartwood (Old-School) Baptist Church 162, 170
Hartwood gold mines: Eagle; Rattlesnake (Horse Pen); Lee; New
Hope; and Monroe. The Eagle Gold Mining Company 211
Hartwood Presbyterian Church * 86, 87p,
154, 155, 164, 164p,
Hartwood Church Cavalry Engagement (February 1863)
(Civil War) 60-61
Hartwood Yellow Chapel 154
Hartwood militia company (1851) of Captain George Wellford
Cropp; (Cropp, Alexander, Armstrong, Anderson, Benson, Bridges,
Bradshaw, Burton, Beach, Ballard, Brown, Bloxham, Bowling,
Brooks, Bettis, Butler, Curtis, Conyers, Courtney, Dunnington,
Dodd, Dye, Duerson, Ellignton, Ennis, French, Graves, Garner,
Groves, Grinnam, Harding, Humphrey, Harris, Heflin, Herndon,
Hickerson, Helm, Jackson, Jacobs, Jones, Johnson, Kellogg,
Limbrick, Latham, Lunsford, Lane, Littrell, Leach, Monroe, Mills,
Nash, Porch, Patton, Patterson, Powell, Rodgers, Rose, Roberson,
Smith, Swetnam, Scooler, Stephens, Timberlake, Timmons,
and Tompins) 75
Harvard Divinity School 45
Harwood Academy at Mill Farm 176
Hasbrough, William H. 84
Hassinungaes 13
Haupt, General Herman (Civil War) 104, 199p, 200-203
Hayden, Palmer C. (Hedgeman, Peyton Cole) 51,
58p, 59p, 58-59, 256
Hayes, Colonel Rutherford B. (Civil War)
(later President) 85, 107, 106p
Haymes, Katherine Conway 236
Haer plantation) 85, 206, 231, 233, 234, 238p, 240
Henry, Patrick 21, 29, 207
Herold, David (Civil War) 112, 112p
Hewitt, William 152
H.H. Poole Junior High School 187
H.H. Poole High School 187, 188
"Hickory Hill" 133
Higginson, Thomas Wentworth 46
"Highland Home" 65, 97, 152
Highway Assembly of God 170
Hills 38
Hill, Frank 96
Hill, Jim 164
Hilldrup Moving and Storage Company 216
Hilldrup, R. G. 216
Hilliard, Supervisor Kandy A. 234
Hinman, Mary 227
Historic Falmouth Towne, and Stafford
County, Inc. 227
Historic Fredericksburg Foundation, Inc. 228, 239
Historic Port of Falmouth Association 262
Historic Preservation Department, Mary
Washington College 227
Historical and Archeological Committee, Citizens to Serve
Stafford (CCSS) 7, 220, 253
Historic Resources Survey (HRS) 130-157
Hobby, John 142
Holly Corner 134
"Holly Farm" 133
"Hollywood" 110, 156, 157
Hollywood Cemetery 45, 64
Holms, James 167
Holmes, Captain Oliver Wendell, Jr., (Civil War) 107p
Holmes, General Theophilus H. (Civil War) 77, 116
Hooe, Gerald 72
Hooker, General Joseph (Civil War) 85, 105, 114p, 196
Hope Creek (Willow Landing) 152
"Hope Grant" or "Hope Land" or "Hope Line" or
"Hope Spring" 152
Hope Run 159
Hopewell Methodist Church 173
Hore, Elias 72
Hornung, Chris, Silver Companies 225
Horstman, Neil W., executive vice-president of the White House
Historical Association 242
Horton, Carol Thomas 237
"Houseboat" 122, cast 123p
Howards 134
Howard, Professor A.E. Dick 51
Howard Grove Baptist Church near Berea 90, 172
Howell, Cecelia "Cessie" 147,
(SCHC Commissioner George Washington) 235, 239
Howell, Delegate (Speaker) William J. 5, 228
Howell, Delegate and Mrs. William J. 147
"Howell Log House" 146-147, 146-147p
Hubbert Tract (1654) 152
Hudson, Charles 155
Hugo, Captain William H. 83
Hull's Memorial Baptist Church * 169, 169P
Humphreys 145
Hunley, Jonathan 237
Hunter, Adam 131
Hunter, James 8, 41, 41p, 72, 131, 206-208, 206p, 207p
Hunter's Iron Works or Rappahannock Forge 41, 41p, 206p, 207,
207p, 210, 213, 231

Hutchison, Laura 237
Hyatt, Glenn 230
Hypsilophodont 11

~I~

Iguanadont 11
Indian Memorial and Reburial Site at Aquia Landing 235, 257
Indian Point 14, 137, 258, 259p
Indian Point homeowners 259
Indian remains 258
"Ingleside" 85, 144
Innes, James, Robert Carter's agent 131
Interstate Highway Act of 1956 218
Intuit 216
Irenesauripus 11
Ironside Baptist Church 169
Irvines 154
Irvine, John and William 154
Irvine, John William, 9th Virginia Cavalry
(Civil War) 154
Irvine, William 164
Irwin, Emmet (Union soldier) (Civil War) 88

~J~

Jacksons 168, 169
Jackson, Andrew 45
Jackson, Dorothy 7
Jackson, Samuel 101p
Jackson's Branch 152
James, King 16
James II, King 26, 34-35p
James River 13
Jamestown 14
James, William (ca. 1814) 144
James Monroe Center, Mary Washington College 216, 216p
James Monroe Chapter of the National Society of United States
Daughters of 1812 229
Japan 59
Japazaws, King of the Patowmeke 14
Jefferson, President Thomas 195, 207, 210
Jenkins, Thomas J. 214
Jesuit missionaries 25
Jett, Cathy 11
Jett, Mrs.William A. 84
John Lee Pratt Park 68
Johnson, Clinton 101p
Johnson, Leonard 101p
Johnson, John Janney 96
Johnson, Rev. Uriah of Baltimore, Maryland 172
Johnson, Rev. York 168
Jones' 134, 145
Jones, Brevet Major Churchill 134, 134p
Jones, Dr. H. Stewart 7, 162, 177, 220-221, 227, (SCHC
Commissioner Hartwood) 235, 249p
Jones, Judith H. 46, 49, 237, 256
Ted Jones (SCHC Commissioner Falmouth) 235
Jones, Thena S. 7, 107, 263
Jones, William 134
Jordan, Jr., Ervin L. 45-46.

~K~

Kang, Michelle, Miss Virginia 71
Kapsch, Dr. Robert J.
(Government Island Committee) 242
K&M Properties in McLean 225
Keen, Hugh C. 111
Keener, Marcia (NPS and Government Island Committee) 242
Keepers-of-the Knowledge honorees 249-251
"Keepers of the Knowledge Program" 235, 249-251
Kendall, Mrs. Donald John
(the former Nita Pyke) 151
Kendall, Mary Cary of "Richland" 7, 103, 118, 121, 151, 171, 234p, (SCHC Commissioner Griffiths-Widewater) 235, 245, 250p
Kendall, Moses Kendall 43
Kenmore Association (now the George Washington's Fredericksburg Foundation) 218, 238
Kennedy property in southern Maryland 151
Kent Island, Maryland, 25
Kings 96
King, "Aunt" Puss 162
King George County 9, 109, 158
King William County 109
Kinsley, Ardyce 48, 62
Kirby, Barbara S. 7, 26, 44, 50, 53, 221, 228, 233p, 250p, 257
Kittamaquad (also "Mary Brent [I]") 8, 25
Knight, Captain J.W. 66, 66p
Knight, Captain Peter 35
Knight, Richard 252p
Knights of Columbus 220p, 223
Knox' 143
Knox, Annie Campbell 42
Krick, Robert E. L. 263
Krick, Robert K. 78-79, 111, 156, 263
Kurtz, Louise 100

~L~

Laird, Dr. Matt, CRI, Inc. 225
"Lacy House" (also see "Chatham") 85
Lacy, J. Horace of "Chatham" 47, 48p, 134
Lancaster, Luther 90
Langfits 149
Langley, Samuel Pierpont 119, 119p, 151
Langley Experiments 120p
Latham, Miss Piny 165
Latrobe, Benjamin Henry 103, 103p, 248
"Laurel Hill" 94
"Laurel Spring" 95
"Laurel View" 95p
Lawsons 144
Lawson, General Robert 52
Laying the Hoe:" A Century of Iron Manufacturing in Stafford, Virginia. (2003) 222
Leary, C. G. 205
Lebounie 26
Lees 38, 120, 152
Lee, Ann Carter 48
Lee, Anne Fenton (daughter of Thomas Ludwell Lee) 151
Lee, General Charles 52
Lee, Daniel Murray (brother of Fitzhugh Lee)
(Civil War) 65, 97, 152
Lee, Miss Edmo Corbin 97
Lee, General Fitzhugh of "Richland" (Civil War) 48, 59-64, 60p, 62p, 63p, 87, 151
Lee, General Henry "Lighthorse Harry" 48
Lee, Henry 138
Lee, Henry (brother of Fitzhugh Lee) 65, 152
Lee, Major John Mason (brother of Fitzhugh Lee) (Civil War) 65, 152, 171
Lee, Nannie Mason 152
Lee, Richard Bland 42
Lee, Robert Carter 48
Lee, General Robert E. (Civil War) 9, 108, 121p, 154, 203
Lee, Smith (brother of Fitzhugh Lee) 65, 152
Lee, Sydney Smith (Civil War) 48, 59, 59p, 151, 152
Lee, Thomas Ludwell 138, 209
Leland School 1935 182p
Leland School 1961 191p
L'Enfant, Pierre 103, 103p, 125
Lenzi, Olympic champion Mark 71, 71p
Leu, Colonel Richard 143
Lewis, Clifford M. 25
Lewis, Lieutenant Hunter H. Virginia Navy (Civil War) 76
Library of Congress 224
Lewis, Rusty 223
Lightners 146
Lightner, Mrs. George, Sr., 84
"Lightner's Store" 146, 146p
Limerick, Mrs. Lester L. 169
Lincoln, Abraham (Civil War) 85, 104, 104p, 105, 108, 121, 134, 196
Linkous, Gordon 257
Litchfield, Gwen (VHS) 31, 39
Little Falls Elementary School 1958-1959 187p
Little Falls School 1961 191p
Little Forest Baptist Church * 172
Little Shiloh Baptist Church 90, 169
Little, William A. 157
"Little Whim" 86, 157p
Lober, Georg J. 29
"Locust Grove" 95, 96
Loewen, James W., 32
Lohman, Elsa 263
Loomie, Albert 25
Loren, Sophia 122, 123p
"Lost Estates" to Quantico expansion ("Chopawamsic Farm," "Dipple," "Clermont," "Somerset," "Rectory," "Chelsea," "Providence," "Bloomington," and "Laurel View") 95
Loth, Calder (Government Island Committee) 242
Lowe, Rev. George Oscar A. 169
Lowe, Thad 117p
Lucas, Rev. Cornelius S. 90, 169, 172
Lucas, Daniel (Barnes' slave) 132
Luminaria, National Cemetery in Fredericksburg 236
Lunga Reservoir 95
Lyle's Mill 210
Lyman, Myron E. ("Mike") and Mary A. ("Marty") 7, 142, 226, 252
Lynn, Doctor 40
Lynn, William 145

~M~

MacGregors 131
MacGregor, Corporal Alaric R., VRM 99
Machodoc Creek 158
MacMurray, Fred 122, 123p
Maddox' 135
Madison, James 19
Mahaskohod 13
Mahocks 13
Mahone, William 50
Mallows Bay, Maryland, 212
Mallow, Wendy A. (Government Island Committee) 242
Manahoacs 12
Manassas 109, 111
Mandell, Rev. Cuthbert, Aquia Episcopal Church 246
Manly, Charles M. 120
Mann, J. William 7, 161, 222
"Marble Hill" 95, 96
Marine Corps Heritage Center (planned) 262
Marlborough (town) 9
"Marlborough" (plantation) 23, 135-137, 135, 151
Marlborough lumber activities 213
Marlborough Point 14, 135, 135p
Marlborough Point homeowners 259
Marlborough tobacco warehouse 138
Marshall, General of the Army,
George C. 121, 121p, 134
Marshall, Justice John 102-103, 102p
Martin, Luther 52
Martin, U.S. Senator Thomas Staples 50
"Maryland" (steamboat) 199
Maryland Constitutional Ratification Convention in 1788 52
Mary Washington Branch, Association for Preservation of Virginia Antiquities 277
Mason, George (II) 18, 95, Captain, "high sheriff of Stafford" 135
Mason, George (III) 18, 95
Mason, George (IV) of "Gunston Hall" 8, 18-20, 19p, 20p, 28p, 29, 95, 123, 127p, 235
Mason, Mary Thomson 151
Mason, Sarah Brent (1730-1806) 29
Mason, U.S. Senator Stevens Thomson 52-53
Massachusetts Historical Society (MHS) 47
Massadonia Baptist Church 96
Massie, Louis 101p
"Master Hobby's School" 142, 142p
Master's Mill 96
Matheny, Daniel 152
Mathews (Samuel) tract 159
Mattaponis 14
Matthew Fontaine Maury Camp 1722 of Sons of Confederate Veterans (SCV) 229
Mattox Bridge, Westmoreland County 159
May Court, Falmouth High School 1933/34 181p
May Day, Stafford High School 1951 186p
May queen, Stafford High School 1939 183p
Mays 134
McCarty, John Mason 53
McCoy, Ila and Don 7
McDaniel, Charles B. 216
McDaniel, Charles G. 216
McDaniel, David (North Carolina Slave Dealer) 47
McDowell, General Irwin (Civil War) 85, 104, 114p, 201

McHugh, Denise 20
McKee, Jean 256
McKinley, President William 119p
McWhirt's farm on Greenbank Road 214
Media-General 237
Melchers, Corinne Lawton of "Belmont" 67, 67p, 143, 246
Melchers, Gari of "Belmont" 51, 51p, 67, 67p, 143, (Stafford paintings) 148p, 246
Men of Mark in Stafford, Virginia, 1664-1991 (2000) 222
Mercers 151
Mercer, Elizabeth Mason 159
Mercer, Gary 188
Mercer, George (1733-1784) 24, 42,
Mercer, Dr. Hugh 22
Mercer, James (1735/1736-1793) 24, 38, 42, 42p, 136
Mercer, John Fenton (1735-1756) 24, 42,
Mercer, John Francis (1759-1821) 24, 52, 52p, 136, 235
Mercer, John of "Marlborough" 19, 23-24, 23p, 135, 159
Mertz, Greg 263
Meredith, Rev. Jaquelin Marshall 65, 96
Methodists 37
Mewborn, Horace 111
Michael T. Rose Companies 206
Middlesex County 36
Middleton, George 95-96
Millers 168
Miller, Mark 122
Miller, Peggy 227
Million, Robert and Keziah 162
Millsbrook 22
"Mill Vale" 56
Missouri Mills 96
Mitchell, Daniel 227
Mitchell, John D. 225, 230p
Mitchell, Supervisor Kenneth T. 233, 242
Mitchell, Margaret 130
Modern Churches: Abundant Life Assembly of God Church *; Agape Fellowship Ministries *; Bethel Baptist Church *; Calvary Baptist Church *; Calvary Southern Methodist Church *; Canaans Faith Church of Christ *; Church of God of Prophesy *; Church of the Redeemed *; Colonial Baptist Church *; Community Baptist Church *; Cornerstone Baptist Church *;Covenant Family Worship Center; Emanuel AME Church *; Ferry Farms Baptist Church *; Fredericksburg Assembly of God Church *; Friendship Baptist Church *; Garrisonville Church of Christ *; Kings Highway Baptist Church; Hollywood Church of the Brethren *; Kingdom Hall of Jehovah's Witnesses *; Kingsland Chapel (Church of God of Prophesy) *; Latter-Day-Saints Church *; Living Waters Tabernacle *; Midway Baptist Church *; Mount Peniel Church of God in Christ *; Mount Zion Ministries *; New Covenant AME Zion Church *; New Horizon Ministries *; New Life Community Church *; New Life Restoration Bible Church *; North Stafford Baptist Church *; Saint Matthias United Methodist Church *; Saint Peter's Lutheran Church *; Saint William of York Catholic Church *; Shiloh Christian Church *; SOME Ministries *; Stafford Baptist Church *; Stafford Church of God *; Stafford Church of the Nazarene *; Stafford Community Baptist Church *; Stafford County Christian Church *; Stafford Emmanuel Korean Baptist Church *; Stafford Freewill Baptist Church *; Summit Presbyterian Church *; Temple Baptist Church *; The Apostolic Faith Assembly*; Touch Hearts Christian Center *; Victory Baptist Church *; Vineyard Christian Fellowship *; and Winding Creek Community Church *. 174-175
Monacans 12

Moncures 8, 53, 96, 120, 132, 138, 149, 152, 153, 265
Moncure, Anne E. 177p, 180p
Moncure, Private (later Lt.) Eustace Conway, 9th Virginia Cavalry (Civil War) 111
Moncure, Frances 137
Moncure, Lieutenant Frank, VRM 98
Moncure, George V. 96
Moncure, John 74, 159, 163
Moncure, John of "Somerset" 43
Moncure, John Conway 54-55, 54p, 149
Moncure, Rev. John 95, Moncure, Rev. John of "Clermont" 137
Moncure, John II 95
Moncure, Dr. John 172
Moncure Memorial Chapel 172
Moncure, Milli 246, 247p
Moncure, Walter R.D. 168
Moncure, Rev. Walter 168
Moncure, R.C.L. 55, chief justice of the Virginia Supreme Court 149
Moncure, Thomas McCarty, Jr. 7, 19, 20, 83, 161, 220, 228, 233, 231, 257
Moncure, William E. 84
"Moncure Conway House," Falmouth 84-85, 84p, 235-236, 236p, 256
Monetons 12
Monroe, James 43
Montagues 155, 169
Montague, Cynthia 188, 188p
Montague, Doretha 188
Montague, Reginald 101p
Montague, Dr. Thadeus Claybrook (Civil War) 155
"Mont Anna" 54, 149
Monteith Family and the Potomac Indians,The 221
Montgomery Ward 214
Moore, Henry (Civil War) 211
Morgan, Charles (alias Charles Morganfield) 205
Morgan, Rev. Sandy Alonzo 172
Morgenstern and Company 214
Morris, Rosie and Edgar 7, 192
Morris, Professor Thomas 50
Morsons 110
Morson, Alexander, of "Hollywood" (1759-1822) 154, 156
Morson, Arthur 72, 139, (1734 or 1735-1798) 154
Morson, John and Hugh 154
Morson, Dr. Hugh 168
Mortons 43, 169
Morton, Annie 50
Mosby, Colonel John Singleton (Civil War) 9, 110, 110p
Mosby's Rangers (Civil War) 110
Mosby's Stafford raids, May 1864 (Civil War) 110
Mott, John and George 156
Mountain View Road 213
"Mount Airy," Richmond County 129
Mount Ararat Baptist Church * 172
Mount Hope Baptist Church * 169, 169p, 188
Mountjoys 43, 135
Mountjoy, Thomas 138
"Mount Olive" 95, 96
Mount Olive Baptist Church * 163, 163p
"Mount Vernon" 22,125, 224
"Mount Vernon" (steamboat) 199
Mountz, Tom (living history) 231, 231p
Mount Zion Baptist Church 96

Muddy Creek Church 159
"Mud March" 114p, 165, 196
"Mud March" 196
Mulberry trees 209
Munford, Colonel Thomas T. (Civil War) 87
Muraca, David 222p
Murray, Henry 204
Murray, Dr. Jean, schools superintendent 234p
Murray, John 138
Musselman, Homer D. 7, 60, 76, 77, 80, 105, 111, 167, 221, 251p, 252, 263
Musselman, Linda V. 233
Myers, E.T.D. 204p
Myers, Virginia E. (widow of Clyde N. Myers) 214
"Myrtle Grove" 152

~N~

NAACP programs 256
NAGPRA 258
Napoleon III 54
National Arboretum, 128p
National Florence Crittenden Mission 57
National Park Service, U.S. (NPS) 22, 230, 238, 246, 248
NPS Special Resource Study 238-239
Neary, Donna 264
Nelsons 53
"Nelson House" ("Thomas Nelson House,") Yorktown 129, 129p
Nelson, Erik F. 102, 218-219
Nelson, Peter 164
Nelson, Susan 164
New Hope United Methodist Church * 173
New Hope School 1961 190p
New Jersey, College of (now Princeton University) 44
Newlin, Joe T. 253
New Market (battle; May 15, 1864) 64
Newport Mercury (Rhode Island) 19
Newtons 212p, 258
Newton, D.P., White Oak Civil War Museum, 89, 226, 233, 244-245, 249p
New York Herald 205
New York Yacht Club station at Simms Point [west of Brent's Point] 121
Nichols, James L. 59-64
Nicholls, Captain, USA (Civil War) 111
N.N. Berry's Store 141, 217, 217p
Norfolk-Baltimore Chesapeake steamboat route 199
Normans 152
Norman, George 72
Norman, Thomas 72
North Ferry Farms 22
Northern Virginia Chapter of the Archaeological Society of Virginia (NVC/ASV) 222
Not For Fame Or Reward: Virginia Military Institute's (VMI's) Civil War Soldiers 261
NVC/ASV Brent Site (44ST130) 223
Northern Virginia Conservation Trust of Annandale, Virginia 226

~O~

Oak Grove Baptist Church * 168, 168p
Oak Grove School 1961 189p
O'Bannon, John 139, 144
Oberlin College 47
"Octagon, The" Washington 129
Oden, Lesley "Buddy" 260
Office of Price Administration 97
O'Grady, Kelly 75, 263
Old Capitol Prison 155, 156
Old Patent Office 129
Old Stafford High School 1920s/30s 180p
Old Stafford Jail 212p
Ontponies 13
Opechancanough 14
Orange & Alexandria Railroad 218
O'Reilly, Frank A. 222, 263
Orient, Megan 256
Ornithopod 10
Osborn, Supervisor Mark 234, 244p
Osborn, Mark and Wendy 146
Overland Campaign (May-June 1864) (Civil War) 203
Overwharton Parish 37, 158
Overwharton Parish Chapter of the DAR 229

~P~

"Palace Green" 152
Paleo-Indians 11
Palmer, Ben (Civil War) 110
Pamunkeys 14
Pash, Supervisor Gary D. 234
Pastore, Vera 228
Patawomeck Indian village excavations 137
Patomeke, Virginia 161
Patrick, General Marsena, provost marshal, Army of the Potomac (Civil War) 86, 110
"Patterson's Place" 153
Patton, William T. 84
Parlier, Felicia 7
Payne, Miss Edie (Edith) 141
Payne, Mrs. George 84
Payne, Janet, art coordinator of county schools 256
Payne, Terry 256
Payne, Joann 225
"Peace Point" of Giles Brent [I] 136
Peale, Malachi 135, 136
"Peale's Point" or "New Marlborough" 135
Pedigo, Mr. 50-51
Pender Grocery Company 214
Pennsylvania Evening Post 19
Perry, Commodore 59
Petersburg 63
"Petomek" 13
Peytons 8, 43, 138, 153
Peytons of Philadelphia 265
Peyton, John Lewis 37
Peyton, John Rowzee (1754-1799) of "Stony Hill" 37, 138
Peyton, Rowzee 74, 159
Peyton, Valentine 138
Peyton, Yelverton 195
"Peyton's Ordinary" 195, 217
Pezzullo, Elizabeth 225, 237
Pfanz, Donald C. 106, 236, 263
Philadelphia Navy Yard 59

"Phillips House" 84p, 85, 85p
Phillips, William 72
Pickett, Captain 45
"Pill Hill" 144
Piscataways 14, 25
Pitt, William, Earl of Chatham 134
Plessy v. Ferguson (1896) 51, 178
Pocahontas (Matoaka or Metoaka or "Rebecca") Rolfe) 9
Pohick Church, Fairfax County 49, 125
Poe, Edgar A. 53
Poindexter, Elnora 256
Pollard, E.A. (Civil War) 54
Pollocks 86
Pollock, Captain John Gray, Fredericksburg Artillery, (Civil War) 90
Pollock, Mrs. (Civil War) 85
Pollock, William (Civil War) 84
Poole, Addie 50
Poole, Henry Harrison 50
Poole Junior High School 1961 189p
"Poplar Grove" 155, 155p
Poppen, Dan 233
Porch Family, the Forgotten Legacy of White Oak, Stafford County, Virginia 221
Ports Act of 1691 136
Ports Act in 1710 136
Posey, Mary 38
Potomac Agricultural Club, The, 62
Potomac Anglican Church 73, 158, 159
Potomac Baptist Church 162
Potomac Creek 9, 104, 198, 203
Potomac Creek ferry 135
Potomac Creek railroad bridge (Civil War) 200, 200p
Potomac Parish 158
"Potomac Path" 194
Potomac River 9
Potomac Silk and Agriculture Company of Fredericksburg 209
Potomac Steamboat Company 199
Potomac Indian Tribe (Potawomecks or Patawomeks, etc.) 12, 135, 221, 232, 258
Potter, C. L. 166
Powell, Eric 214-215, 232, 235
Powhatan (Wahunsonacock or Wahunsenacawh) 13
Powhatans (Powhatan Empire) 12
"Powhatan" (steamboat) 199
Pratt, John Lee of "Chatham" 67, 67p, 121, 134, 246
Pratt, Dr. Frank 68
Presbyterians 37
Presbyterian Synod of Philadelphia 161
Pribble, J. Thomas 227
Price, Charles 226, 252, 252p
Prince William County 9
Principio Company 21, 206
Prohibition 212-213
Prosser, Gabriel 75
"Providence" 96
Provost marshal tent, Stafford, 113p
Preston, Walter M. 214
Purcell's Mill 96
Providence Church 96
Pyke, Alfred J. 151
Pyke, Edward, Esquire, of Southport, England 151
Pynn, Molly A. 7, 161, 220

~Q~

Quantico Creek 203
Quantico Marine Base 8, 91, 233, 262
Quantico expansion 1942 94
Quantico Sentry, The 233
Quiyough [Aquia Creek] 14

~R~

Raimey, Mabel of Wisconsin 46
Ralls' 153
Ramoth Baptist Church * 167-168, 167p, 169, 213
Ramoth School 1935 183p
Randolph, Edmund 44
Randolph-Macon College, Ashland, Virginia 67
Rapidan Mining and Milling Company of Pennsylvania 211
Rappahannock Gold Mine Company of New York 211
Rappahannock Patriot, The 24
Rappahannock River 9
Rappahannock River plantation (also see "Ferry Farm") 21, 21p, 22p
Rappahannock Valley Civil War Roundtable 229, 229p, 257
"Raspberry Plain," Loudoun County, Virginia 53
Ravensworth" (Fairfax County) 48
Ray, Albert 50
Ray, Angie 173
Ray, Silas 173
"Rectory" 96
Rectory School 1890s 177p
Reddishs 43
Redeemer Lutheran Church [now in Spotsylvania] 170
Redoubt No. 2 231p
Regester Chapel United Methodist Church * 168, 168p
Regester, Rev. Dr. Samuel 168
Reineau (Reno) 26
R. E. Lee Camp Confederate Veterans Home, Richmond, 63
Revere, Colonel Paul Joseph (Civil War) 114p
Rhones 169
Richards' 143
"Richard's Hill" 144
Richardsons 169
Richardson, Enos 230p
"Richland" 27, 102, 104, 121, 150, 150p
Richlands Baptist Church * 170, 170p
Richmond Examiner, The 53-54
Richmond, Fredericksburg, and Potomac Railroad (R, F& P) 97, 197-199, 204p, 205p, 214
R, F& P Train No. 78 204
Richmond Times 205
River Road 140
Roanoke (formerly Big Lick), Virginia 56
Roanoke Leader 56
Roberts, Walter V. "Pete" 7
Robertson home site on Rocky Run 248p, 248
"Robertson/Towson House" 248, 248p
Robertson Quarry" 209, 248
Robinson, Marion Brooks 15, 251p
Robinson, Moncure 198, 199
Rochambeau, General Count Donatien de 102, 102p
Rock Creek, DC 150
Rock Hill Baptist Church * 163, 163p
"Rock Ramore" ("Rock Rimmon," "Rock Raymer," or "Rock Raymond") 152, 209
Rodney Thompson Middle School 235
Roebuck, H.M.S. 38, 150

Rogers, John B. 253
Rolfe, John 14, 39
Rolfe, Thomas 16
Roosevelt, Theodore 118, 119p, 151
"Rosedale" 155
Roses 133
Rosner Motors, 153
Rountree, Helen C.13
Rouse, Olympic champion Jeff 71, 71p, 256
Rowdon, Suzanne 7, 221
Rowe, Josiah P. III 237
Rowser, Mrs. Ella 188
Rowser, "Uncle Jim" 50p, 188
Rowser Building 188
Roy, Wily 72
Ruby 168
Ruby, James S. 27
Ruggles, General Daniel 77
"Rumford" 85
Rust, Mary 7

~S~

Saint Catherines in Ontario, Canada. 47
Saint Clair Brooks Park 68
"Saint Gabriel," Maryland, 33
Saint.John schoolhouse near Brooke 169
Saint Mary's City, Maryland, 25
"Saint Mary's"(part of "Dipple" ?) 95
Saponis 13
Sarasin, Ronald A., president of the U.S. Capitol Historical Society 242
Sauroposeidon 10p, 11
"Save the Farm" Committee of Historic Fredericksburg Foundation, Inc. 238, 239p
Scheel, Eugene C. 235
Schenkl round 233
School Bus 1940 184p
School buses 1956 186p
Schools, Norman and Lenetta 114, 236
Scott, Rev. Alexander 19, 95, of "Dipple" 150, 158
Scott, John C. 144
John Scott 230p, 246, 246p,
Scouten, Rex W. (White House Curator and Government Island Committee) 241p, 242
Seale, William (Government Island Committee) 242
Searcy, Charles J. 205
Seddons 110, 149
Seddon, Confederate War Secretary James A. (Civil War) 64, 110, 157, 203
Seddon, Major John of "Snowden" (Civil War) 64,157
Seddon, John (duelist) 44
Seddon, Mrs. Mary of "Snowden" 43
Selden, Samuel 138
Setzler, Frank M. 137
Sewells 38
Shackakonies 13
Shackelford's Well Road, Hartwood
"shad bellies" 201
"Shelton Cottage" 143, 143p
Shelton, John C. 84
Shelton, Willien 227
Shelton Alley 248
Shepard, E. Lee 45
"Sherwood Forest" 70, 70p, 86
Sherwood School, Wild Cat Corner, 1900s 180p
Shiloh (New Site) Baptist Church * 168, 174
Shiloh (Old-Site) Baptist Church * 163, 168, 168p
Short, John 144

Siegel, Charles, Rappahannock Valley Civil War Roundtable 229-230
Sierra Club 263
Silver Companies 216, 225-226
Silver Hill Baptist Church, Fauquier County 169
Simpson, Samuel F. 166
Simpson and Associates Real Estate 142
Sisson, Allison Cover.p
"Sisters Freehold," Maryland, 33
Skinkers 133
Skinker, Thomas J. 84
Slaughter, John W. 145
Slaves at Government Island 126-127
Smith, Delia Forbes 133
Smith, Mr. Edward 188, 1953/54 188p
"Smith-Forbes House" 133
Smith, George 133
Smith, Captain John 9, 134, 135, 210
Smith, Nicholas 139
Smithsonian Institution 137, 257, 258
Snellings, Supervisor Gary F. 234
Snellings, Walter 213
"Snowden" 110, 156, 157
Society of the War of 1812 in Virginia 229
Soil Conservation No. 11, District 3, Third Corps Area 214
"Somerset" (once part of "Clermont") 96, 96p
Sons of the American Revolution 226, (SAR) 229
Sons of Union Veterans (SUV) 229
Southampton County 44
Southworth, Nancy 47, 48
Special Session of U.S. Congress, Federal Hall, New York City 244
Speeds 168
Spelman, Henry 16
Spelman, Sir Henry of Congham 16
Spence, Caroline 163
Spotsylvania County 9
Spotsylvania Preservation Foundation, Inc. 228
"Spotted Tavern," Hartwood 217
Sprigg, Sophia of Maryland 52
"Spring Dale" 95, 96
"Springfield" 95, 96
"Spring Hill" 152
Sproston, Lieutenant J.Glendy (Civil War) 77
Stafford African-American history pamphlet 256
...Stafford Artillery (1991) (Civil War) 221
Stafford camp of Pennsylvania infantry 113p
Stafford Catholics 25-27, 25p, 28-29, 29p
Stafford Cemetery Committee 226, 252
Stafford Committee of Safety 137
Stafford's contemporary black history 256
Stafford County Administrator's Office 233
Stafford County Board Resolution R99-285, 1999 242
Stafford County Board of Supervisors 94, 99, 129, 212, 224, 225, 233, 235, 239, 240, 241
Stafford County Branch, NAACP 256
Stafford County Colonial seal (King George II) 83
Stafford County courthouses 212, 213p
Stafford County Government 257
Stafford County Historical Commission (SCHC) 235
Stafford County Historical Map 235
Stafford County Historical Society (SCHS) 7, 142, 221, 226, 227, 230, 232, 236, 239, 249, 256, 257
Stafford County Historical Society Black History programs 256
SCHS-NAACP joint meeting 2003 256
Stafford County Museum (future)
Stafford County Museum Committee (Supervisors Mark Osborn and Kandy A. Hilliard; former County Administrator C.M.

Williams; and Stafford County Historical Society representatives Jane Henderson Conner, Barbara Kirby and Steve Gambaro) 234
Stafford County School Board 97, 188, 234
Stafford County Sun 7, 237
Stafford County Visitors' Center 143
Stafford County, Virginia: Veterans and Cemeteries (1994) 221
Stafford County in the Civil War (1995) (Civil War) 221
"Stafford Court House Church" 168
Stafford Elementary School 188
Stafford Elementary School 1961 192p
Stafford High School 1961 192p
Stafford High School 1935 183p
Stafford High School 188, 235, 253
Stafford Home and Garden 153
Stafford Mining Company 211
Stafford Parish 158
Stafford Quakers 155
Stafford Run 96
"Stafford Schools Project, The" 176, 234
Stafford School System 256
Staffordshire, UK 260
"Stafford Springs" 95, 96, 109
"Stafford Store" 96
Stafford Store Baptist Church 96
Stafford train robbery (1894) 204, 204p
Stafford Training School 187
Stafford Tricentennial Association 253
Stafford Veterans' Memorial 72p
Stafford, Virginia -Stafford, England, Friendship Association, Inc. (SVSEFA) 260-261, 260p, 261p
Stafford VRM "Minute Men" Company 97-98
Stage Road School 1930s 181p
Stamp Act of 1765 38, 137
"Stanstead" 131, 208
Stanton, Secretary Edwin McMasters (Civil War) 105, 105p
Starks or Starkes 95
Stark, William 72
Starkweather, Norma 264
Stegarakies 13
Sterns 43
Stern, Philip N. 212
Stevens' 133
Stevensburg, Culpeper County 88
Stewart, T.D. 137
Stockton, Lucius W. 199
Stone, Ernest 101p
Stone, Hannah 96
Stone, Dr. Hawkins 53, 72
Stone, Mildred 225
Stone, Thomas of Maryland
Stone, Governor William 26
Stone's Mill 96
Stoneman's Landing 135
Stoneman's Switch (Civil War) 201p
"Stony Hill" 138
Story of Aquia Church, The (1987) 220
Story of Stafford,The 220
Stratford Hotel 214
Stringfellow, Benjamin Franklin (Civil War) 108, 108p
Strode, John 208
Strothers 168
Strother, Anthony 21
Strother, Calvin 164
Strother, Mildred of "Albion" 104, 132
Strother plantation 224
"Structure B" (believed to be Mercer's plantation house) 137
Sullivans 134
Sullivan Family of Stafford,Virginia,The 221

Sumner, General E. V. (Civil War) 85
"Surveyor's House" or "Customs House" 141
Suttles 43, 132
Suttle, Charles F. 46
Swanton, John W. 13
Swift, Pina Brooks 140-141, 141p
Sylvania plant 214

~T~

Tackett, C. A. 84
Tackett, Charles 176
Tackett's Mill 210, 210p
Tauxitanians 13
Taylor, John 173
Tazewell County 63
T. Benton Gayle Junior High School 192
Tegniaties 13
"Temperance Hotel" or "Temperance Tavern" or "Falls Temperance House" or"Old Eagle Tavern,"
Falmouth, 145, 145p, 217
Theropod 10
They Called Stafford Home: The Development of Stafford County, Virginia from 1600 until 1865 (1997) 221
"This Land Was Ours" 253, 253p 254p, 255p
Thompson, Matthew S. 54
Thorntons 169
Thornton, Major Francis 156
Thornton, George 38
Thornton, Lieutenant Herbert L., VRM 98
Thornton, Jack 169
Thornton, Rowland 156
Thornton, William 139, 156
Threlkeld, Elijah 138
Tidwell, William A. 109
Todd, William 139
Tolsons 53, 96
Tolson, James 84
Tolson's Mills (2) 96
Tomayko, Larry 239
Tomlin, Fannie Dulany 54
Tourism Office 256
Town and County 237, 256
Towson, Thomas, of Baltimore 167, 248
Traquette (Tackett) 26
"Traveller's Rest" (southern Stafford) 64, 110
"Traveler's Rest" (north Stafford) 96
Travers 151
Travers, Rawleigh 137, of "Crow's Nest" 225
Travers, Sarah (1717-1788) of "Crow's Nest" 137
Treasury Building, U.S. 129
Tri-County-City Soil and Water District 257
"Trinity," Maryland, 33
Trust for Public Land 262
Turin, Kingdom of Sardinia 53
Turners 133
Turner, Nat 44, 75
"Tusculum" 153
Tutelos 12
Twentieth Century black churches: Macedonia Baptist Church; Locust Grove Baptist Church; Richland Baptist Church [not to be confused with Richlands Baptist Church]; and Mount Zion Baptist Church 171
$200 Million Bonfire 212
Tylers 169
Tyler, Steve 188
Tyler, Rev. William 173

~U~

Underground telegraph of the Confederacy ("Secret Line") 111
Union Belle Baptist Church * 173
Union Church, Falmouth, 142, 161, 161p
Union Church Cemetery 41, 142
Union generals headquartered at "Chatham" (McDowell, King, Burnside, Sumner, and Gibbon) (Civil War) 134
Union post office, Falmouth, (Civil War) 114p
Union soldier letters (Civil War) 115
United Daughters of the Confederacy (UDC) 229
United Methodist Church * 171, 171p
U.S. Alternate No.1 Highway (the current Jefferson Davis Bypass) 218
U.S. Army 73p, 76p, 86p, 214
U.S. Army Corps of Engineers 259
U.S. Congress, Native American Graves Protection and Joseph Saponis 13
Sarasin, Ronald A., president of the U.S. Capitol Historical Society 242
Sauroposeidon 10p, 11
"Save the Farm" Committee of Historic Fredericksburg Foundation, Inc. 238, 2. Fish and Wildlife Service 224
U.S. Marine Corps Air-Ground Museum 262
U.S. Military Academy at West Point 59, 60
United States Mining Company 211
U.S. Naval Academy 59
U.S.S. Anacostia (Civil War) 77
U.S.S. John S. Ide (Civil War) 112
U.S.S. Maine 90
U.S.S. Mississippi 59
U.S.S. Montauk (Civil War) 112
U.S.S. Mount Vernon (Civil War) 77
U.S.S. Pawnee (Civil War) 77
U.S.S. Reliance (Civil War) 77
U.S.S. Resolute (Civil War) 77
U.S.S. Thomas Freeborn (Civil War) 77

~V~

Van Buren, Martin 45, 103p, 104
Vass, James 55, 139, 139p, 235
Vass, Mrs. James (Elizabeth) 139p
"Vass House" (also see "Moncure Conway House") 140
Vaughans 168
Versailles Conference, France, 57
Vestavia Woods 152
Veterans of Foreign Wars 230
Vincente Stone, Inc., of Reston, Virginia 248
Vines, Lois 188
Virginia Constitutional Convention of 1901-1902 50-51
Virginia Declaration of Rights, June 12, 1776, 19, 123
Virginia Department of Historic Resources (VDHR). 11
Virginia Division of Mineral Resources 10
Virginia Eastern Shore 13
Virginia Electric and Power Company 214
Virginia Gazette 19
Virginia Herald 126
Virginia Historical Society (VHS) 11, 80,
Virginia Military Institute (VMI) 54, 55, 64, 65, 97, 261
Virginia Pupil Placement Board 189
Virginia Railway Express (VRE) 206
Virginia Readjuster Party 50
Virginia recognized Indian groupings: Pamunkeys; Mattaponis; Upper Mattaponi Tribal Association; Chickahominy Tribe; Chickahominy Tribe-Eastern Division; United Rappahannock Tribe; Nansemond Indian Association; and Monacan Tribe. 258
Virginia Renaissance Faire 219p
Virginia Reserve Militia (VRM) 97, 98p
VRM family names (some may be misspelled): Armstrong; Bayliss; Beagle; Beckham; Bolton; Brickert; Bridwell; Brooks; Brown; Catlett; Cleverley; DeShazo; DeShields; Flack; Goodman; Gordon; Green; Haleman; Harris; Heflin; Jett; Lunsford; MacGregor; Massie; McDaniel; Miller; Huntington; Monroe; Musante; Patton; Pearson; Snellings; Stone; Sullivan; Thomas; Tulloss; Walker; Wirman; Wyne; and Young 98-99
VRM Corporals (Jn W. Patton, H.A. Flack; William N. Cleverley; B.J. Musante, Jr.; Charles E. Walker; James E. DeShazo; E. Dallas Wyne; J.Lewis Monroe; Andrew Truslow; and J. Churchill Gordon, Jr.) 99
VRM new family names: Biglin; Bradshaw; Castle; Cox; Decatur; Dillon; Duncan; Homes; Karz/Kurz; Knight; Lockhart; Lowrey; Perkinson; Price; Solomon; Steward/Stewart; Timmons; Vaughn/Vaughan; Wine; and Woodwar. 99
Virginia Revolutionary Conventions 38
Virginia Shoe Company 214
Virginia Star (ca. 1881-1882) 56
Virginia State Highway Department 218
Virginia, University of 55
Virginiana Room, Central Rappahannock Regional Library 215, 222
Voss' 43, 143
Vowles, Henry (1725-c.1803) 134
Vowles Tavern 131, 134
Vulcan Materials' 211

~W~

Wallace, Agnes 227
Walker, Alexander (ca. 1822) 144
Walker, Lorraine 256
Walker-Grant High School in Fredericksburg 51
Wallaces 53, 73, 144
Wallace, G.W. 84
Wallace, John 72
Wallace, Michael 73
Wallace, Lt.Col. Gustavus Brown (1751-1802) 73, 73p
Wallers 8, 27, 43, 96, 131, 151, 152, 153, 209, 211, 245
Waller, Mrs. Anne Eliza Stribling 166, 211p, 211-212
Waller, Kate [later Dr. Kate Waller Barrett] 121, 151
Waller, Mary Cary of "Clifton" 151
Waller, Brigadier General S. Gardner, Virginia's Adjutant General 97
Waller, Sallie Medora Wickliffe 79, 79p
Waller, Colonel Thomas Conway, 9th Virginia Cavalry (Civil War) 78-80, 79p, 80p, 81p, 89
Waller, Sr., William 72
Waller, Withers of "Clifton" 151, 166, 211
Waller family cemetery 153
Wal-Mart 219, 233, 238-239
Chris Wanner 246
War of 1812 Society 226
War of 1812 veterans' graves (Charles Bussell, Berryman Cox, George Curtis, John C. Edrington, Jonathan Finnel, William C. Fitzhugh, Thomas Fristoe, Barnett Fritter, Joshua Kendall, William Kendall, Isaac Limberick, Edwin C. Moncure, John Moncure, Jr., John Moncure, Sr., Edward Norman, Matthew Norman, Thomas Norman, Alexander O'Bryhim, Thomas Roberson, William W. Robertson, Archibald Rollow, Lawrence Sanford, John Starke, Barnett Stewart, William Scandrett Stone, Jonas Sullivan, Benjamin T. Sullivan, and Thomas Wallace) 74
Ward, Commander James Harmon, Potomac Flotilla, (Civil War) 77

Warner, John 139
Warrens 239
Warren, Samuel and Irma 238
Warrenton, Virginia, 55
Warwick County 63
Washingtons 153
Washington, Augustine 21, 206, 224
Washington, Augustine, Jr. 224
Washington, Bailey of "Tusculum" 43, 138
Washington, Bailey, Jr., (1753-1814) 153
Washington, Charlie (cabin) 157p
Washington, Easter 173
Washington, President George 8, 18, 19, 21-22, 20p, 28p, 102, 104, 121, 125, 132, 134, 153, 195, 224, 230, 235
Washington, Henry 204
Washington, Lawrence 206
Washington, Mary Ball 21, 21p, 133
Washington, Rev. Natus or Nathan 169
Washington and Fredericksburg Steamship Company 199
Washington Street, Falmouth 132
Watkins, C. Malcolm 23, 40, 136-137
Watsons 134
Watson, Sergeant John William (Civil War) 80-83, 81p
Watson, Sully 46
Watson, William of Milwaukee 46
Waughs 135
Waugh, John 159
Waugh's Mill (Potomac Creek) 210
"Wayside" 152p, 153, 153p
Weagraff, John 246
Weale, Stan, of Stafford, England 260
Weedon, George Milton 179p
Weems, Parson 142, 237
Weems, Robert 10, 264
"West Cambridge Inn" or "The Eating House" or "Thompson House" or the "Ellis Apartment Building" 146, 146p
Westebbe, Richard and Barbara 133, 134
West River Bridge v. Dix (1849) 45
"West Farm" 151
Westmoreland County 158
"Westwood" 97, 152
(Dr.) Wheat's Mill 96
Wheelers 145
Wheeler, Linda 259-260
Whitaker, Rev. Alexander 16
White, Alda, Stafford County Attorney 256
White, Father Andrew 25
White, Mary 173
White, Frank, Sr., 251p
White, Frank, Jr. 51, 251p, 256
White, Gordon "Sherman" 188
White House 8, 108, 124, 125p, 129p, 240
White House Christmas Ornament (2000) 242, 242p
White House History, Journal of the White House Historical Association 242
White House visit, 241
White Oak Civil War Museum 225p, 226, 227, 232, 234, 244-245, 244p
White Oak Primitive Baptist * 162-163, 162p
White Oak School, 1961 190p, 245
Whitings 151
Whitman, Walt 9, 105, 105p, 134
Whonkenties 13
Widewater 9, 27, 151, 265
Widewater Peninsula 224, 262
Widewater State Park (projected) 263
Wiggenton's Mill, February 1863 111
Wiggington, John 169

Wiggins, Hal 224p, 259
Wilkinson, Thomas 159
William and Mary, College of, 52, 258, 260
William Cunningham Company of Glasgow, Scotland 235
Williams, Mr., CS spy in Widewater (Civil War) 111
Williams, County Administrator C.M. (Government Island Committee) 233, 241, 242, 244p
Williams, Sheriff Ralph 228
Williamson, Major Thomas Hoomes (Civil War) 76
Willis, Barbara Pratt 52
Wilson, George 94p
Wilson, President Woodrow 57, 141
Wilstach, Paul 104
Winchester Presbytery 164
"Windsor Forest" 46, 153
Wirman, Dave 246, 246p
Withers' 135
Withers, Joyce 252p
Woodbourne Farm 168
"Woodcutting, The" 213
Wood Cutting Road 213
"Woodford" 89, 153
Woods, Kate 227
Woodstock (town) 9, 138
"Woodstock" (plantation) 26, 132, 138, 222, 222p
Woolf, Gwen 237
Woolf, Lee 7, 47, 54, 233, 237, 245, 256
Woolf, Rick 248
Woolfolk, Jordan 199
Works Progress Administration (W.P.A.) 214
W.P.A. Reports on Stafford 215
W.T. Grant store 214
Wyckoff, Mac 263

~Y~

Yates, Richard 224
Yellow Springs, Ohio 49, 256
Yorktown Sesquicentennial, 1931 218
"You Be Dam" or "Yuba Dam" (Civil War) 201p, 202
Young, Gerry, Edwin and Wayne 71p
Young, E. M. 83
Youth for Christ International 238

Military Units:

Army of the Potomac (Union) (Civil War) 105, 105p
Balloon Corps, Union, (Civil War) 117-118
Company "A" (Stafford Rangers), 9th Virginia Cavalry (Civil War) 78, 88
Company "B," 28th Massachusetts Infantry (reenactors) 232
Company "C," 70th New York Volunteers (Civil War) 83
Companies "C," "E," "F," and "G," Mosby's Rangers, (Civil War) 111
Company "F," 2nd Rhode Island Volunteers (reenactors) 232
DeCesnola's Union troops (Civil War) 111
Wade Hampton's troops (Civil War) 155
Fitz Lee's Cavalry Brigade (Civil War) 87
Fitzhugh Lee's troops (Civil War) 155
Fredericksburg Artillery (Civil War) 90
Montjoy's Company of the 10th Virginia Regiment (reenactors) 231
. Fish and Wildlife Service 224
U.S. Marine Corps Air-Ground Museum 262
U.S. Military Academy at West Point 59, 60
United States Mining Company 211
U.S. Naval Academy 59
U.S.S. Anacostia ("Civid Guards" or Company "I (3)" 47th Virginia Infantry Regiment (reenactors) 231-232
Stafford Light Artillery (Civil War) 90
Stafford Rangers (Colonial Wars) 72
1st Virginia Regiment (Revolutionary War) 102
1st Virginia Infantry Regiment, Virginia National Guard (WWI) 91
1st, 2nd and 3rd Virginia Cavalry Regiments (Civil War) 87
2nd Tennessee Regiment (Civil War) 77
2nd Virginia Regiment (Revolutionary War) 102
2nd Virginia Cavalry (Civil War) 87
IIIrd Corps (Union) (Civil War) 105
3rd Pennsylvania Cavalry Regiment (Civil War) 154
3rd Virginia Cavalry Regiment (Civil War) 88
3rd Virginia Regiment of the Continental Line (reenactors) 231
4th New York Cavalry Regiment (Civil War) 88
8th Illinois Cavalry (Civil War) 89
9th Virginia Cavalry (Civil War) 90
12th New York Infantry, Stafford camp, (Civil War) 113p
15th Virginia Cavalry Regiment (Civil War) 117
16th Pennsylvania Cavalry Regiment (Civil War) 88
20th Massachusetts Infantry Regiment (Civil War) 107
23rd Ohio Infantry Regiment (Civil War) 107
30th Virginia Infantry 90, 168 (Civil War)
45th Virginia Militia Regiment, War of 1812, 73
47th Virginia Infantry (Civil War) 90, 166, 245
Other Stafford Confederate veterans' units (4th Virginia Cavalry, 6th Virginia Cavalry, 7th Virginia Infantry, 9th Virginia Infantry Battalion, 13th Virginia Infantry, 15th Virginia Cavalry, 17th Virginia Infantry, 23rd Virginia Cavalry, 24th Virginia Cavalry, 25th Virginia Militia, 43rd Virginia Cavalry Battalion (Mosby's Command), 55th Virginia Infantry, 62nd Virginia Mounted Infantry, VMI Cadet Battalion, 2nd Maryland Infantry, 5th Texas Infantry, 15th Louisiana Infantry, 16th Mississippi Infantry, Purcell Light Artillery (Va.), Staunton Light Artillery (Va.), Terry's Texas Rangers, and staffs, C.S. Navy and unknown units) 91
Other Stafford Union veterans' units (9th Pennsylvania Cavalry, 10th West Virginia Infantry, 16th New York Cavalry, 51st Pennsylvania Infantry, 56th Pennsylvania Volunteers, 98th Pennsylvania Infantry,118th Pennsylvania Volunteers) (Civil War) 91
61st New York Infantry, Drum corps, (Civil War) 113p
110th Pennsylvania Infantry, Falmouth (Civil War) 113p
116th U.S. Infantry, 29th Infantry Division (WWI) 92